This book is dedicated to Josh and Julie Hofstede
whose encouragement, enthusiasm, example, friendship,
godliness, love, sacrifice, and support have contributed
much to my life and ministry over the years.

Maranatha!!

D0061969

RON J. BIGALKE, JR.
GENERAL EDITOR

ONE WORLD

ECONOMY, GOVERNMENT
& RELIGION
IN THE LAST DAYS

21st CENTURY
PRESS
PUBLISHING WITH PURPOSE
WWW.21STCENTURYPRESS.COM

ONE WORLD:
ECONOMY, GOVERNMENT, AND RELIGION IN THE LAST DAYS

Copyright © 2005 by Ron J. Bigalke Jr., General Editor

Published by 21st Century Press
2131 W. Republic Rd.
PMB 41
Springfield, MO 65807

Unless otherwise indicated, Scripture quotations in chapter 18 are from the American Standard Version of the Holy Bible, 1901.

Unless otherwise indicated, Scripture quotations in chapters 4, 10, 12, 15-16 are from the King James Version of the Holy Bible.

Unless otherwise indicated, Scripture quotations in the preface, conclusion, appendix, and chapters 1, 3, 6-9, 11, 13-14, 17 are from the New American Standard Bible, © 1960, 1962, 1963, 1968, 1971, 1972, 1973, 1975, 1977, 1995 by The Lockman Foundation.

Unless otherwise indicated, Scripture quotations in chapters 2 and 5 are from The New International Version, ©1973, 1978, 1984 by the International Bible Society.

The views expressed in each chapter of this book are those of each individual author and may not reflect the views of every other author.

For more information about 21st Century Press visit our web site: www.21stcenturypress.com

ISBN 0-9749811-8-4

Cover Design: Keith Locke
Book Design: Terry White

21ST CENTURY PRESS
PUBLISHING WITH PURPOSE
WWW.21STCENTURYPRESS.COM

Acknowledgements

Thank you especially to Kristin who daily exceeds my desires and expectations of a godly wife and mother. *"Many daughters have done nobly, but you excel them all"* (Prov. 31:29). Thank you for the best of my years and those still to come. I also thank the support of my mom, Arlene, and sister, Mary, for enduring my sometimes ceaseless devotion to completing this project. I am grateful for your patience with my schedule and supporting me in every ministry that God has called me. Donnie and Patti (my new and treasured family), thank you for providing a place of refuge many times.

My greatest appreciation to Dr. Tim LaHaye for creating the Pre-Trib Study Group, and to Dr. Mal Couch for creating the Conservative Theological Society. The fellowship among fellow members at these meetings is directly responsible for allowing this work to be finished. I am deeply indebted to my fellow brothers who are members of those groups who have extended my understanding of Scripture and have allowed such rich fellowship in the love and wisdom of Jesus Christ our coming King. You brothers have greatly influenced my thinking and touched my life deeply through your faithful service and example to the Lord. Thank you specifically to the contributing authors for your kindness to participate in this project and the diligence you gave to your chapters.

I own a debt of gratitude to Dr. Lee Fredrickson, president in charge of 21st Century Press, who has been a continual encouragement through the editing and writing of this book. He enthusiastically agreed to give this project priority and has provided many helpful suggestions and criticisms. Thank you for your endless support of this work.

Terry James, always my consulting editor and dear Christian brother, without whom I would not have written one book. I am thankful beyond words for sharing your prayers and wisdom with me. Your friendship I do cherish.

Finally, an earnest thank you to all who have supported and continue to support Eternal Ministries through gifts and prayers. To all my students (who have persevered through my classes) over the years, you are an inspiration, and I pray this work will be a blessing to you as you have been a blessing to me. Thank you for the fullness and abundance of your friendship in the Lord over the years: Phil and Kathy Allman, Pastor Joe Hancock, Josh and Julie Hofstede, Todd and Valerie Johnson, Steve and Cheri Kowalski, Steven and Pam Mangold, and Joe and Kari Stokely. You are an encouragement of those who have not bowed the knee to the Baals of today (1 Kgs. 19:18). Many thanks to my Lord Jesus Christ for His grace in salvation, the privilege to serve Him, and the wisdom to complete this task. My prayer is that this work will bring glory and honor to You.

Contents

Part 3: The Coming One World Religion

PREFACE

The purpose of this writing is to provide a unique study of economy, government, and religion in the last days. It aims to fulfill this purpose as follows:

- give a brief historical overview of each of the subjects above
- reveal the strategies Satan is setting as a deadly snare for the end times
- reveal the biblical prophecies of each of the subjects above
- give a global and international perspective of the biblical prophecies
- provide a forewarning and encourage discernment
- clarify the characteristics of the millennium in relation to the subjects above

The theological perspective presented in each of the chapters is premillennial and pretribulational. It is the conviction of each of the authors that premillennialism and pretribulationism best explain God's prophetic decrees from eternity past to eternity future.

Much has been written on Bible prophecy in recent times—both positive and negative. One should not ignore the study or be ignorant concerning the subject of Bible prophecy. The issues in Bible prophecy are important because it is an aspect of the whole counsel of God's Word. Furthermore, knowledge of the future provides hope and perspective for the future. There are even several biblical admonitions pertaining to the study of Bible prophecy (cf. Mt. 16:1-3; 24:3). Hebrews 11:13-16 (cf. Lk. 21:34, 36) commends those who lived with an eternal perspective of God's future promises. Second Peter 3:11-14 emphasizes the urgency of being ready for the second coming, and First Thessalonians 5:1-11 commend the *you* (those who are able to understand the times in which they live) and condemn *they* (those who are unaware of God's prophetic decrees). Bible prophecy can be both dramatic and sobering as the Christian realizes the urgency to prioritize responsibilities to live a diligent life, in peace, spotless and blameless in Christ. The authors pray this study will help the reader understand the Scriptures better and, as a result, will grow in godliness, wisdom, and love for the Lord Jesus Christ and the Word of God.

PART 1

The Coming One World Economy

CHAPTER 1

ECONOMY IN HISTORICAL PERSPECTIVE

Ron J. Bigalke Jr.

General understanding of economics by the average population is often limited. However, one's life is affected directly and profoundly by the economy. It is imperative then for Christians to understand economics in the past, present, and future. Increasing one's understanding of economics will help to be more proactive in exercising a positive influence upon government. Understanding economics will also help to comprehend contemporary issues in the world.

It is important to understand the present time and to prepare for the future, but is equally important to examine past developments that have led to the present and will lead to the future. This chapter will provide an overview of economic thought in historical perspective. It is necessary to study the development of economic thought since this will help to understand current economic thinking and the thoughts of those who govern. To a large extent, current thoughts about man and the world have been influenced by the thoughts of those in the past. Although unbiblical in many of his theories, in *The General Theory of Employment, Interest, and Money* (1936), the British economist John Maynard Keynes rightly emphasized the need to understand past economic thinkers.

The ideas of economists and political philosophers, both when they are right and when they are wrong, are more

powerful than is commonly understood. Indeed, the world
is ruled by little else. Practical men, who believe themselves
to be quite exempt from any intellectual influences, are
usually the slaves of some defunct economist. Madmen in
authority, who hear voices in the air, are distilling their
frenzy from some academic scribbler of a few years back. I
am sure that the power of vested interests is vastly exaggerated compared with the gradual encroachment of
ideas.... But, soon or late, it is ideas, not vested interests,
which are dangerous for good or evil.[1]

This chapter will help explain "the gradual encroachment of
[economic] ideas" starting with the Middle Ages. Before considering the economic issues, it is first important to understand the
origins of economics from the Middle Ages, and consider the
backgrounds, key figures, and impacts of the Mercantilists and
the Physiocrats. It was these early views which set the stage for
Adam Smith and the birth of economics. Generally, economists
will agree that Smith was the "Father of Economics." However,
the question to be asked is what was taking place prior to 1776
that gave birth to economics, and why did it take until the 18th
century for economic theory to be systematized.[2]

The Beginning of Economic Thought

It is first beneficial to give several reasonably comprehensive
statements which will encapsulate several significant themes
(new ideas and religious changes) concerning the Middle Ages.
Since economic thought does not develop apart from the spread
of new ideas in Europe, but develops in harmony with such
thinking this will be an important historical survey. The new
ideas in Europe were the result of the expeditions of the
Crusades and Marco Polo (1254-1324). These events would prepare the world for the Renaissance and lead to the beginning of
economic thought.

The Crusades
The interest in trade and travel fostered by the Crusades

(1095-1272) radically altered medieval times. A result of the Crusades was the growth of cities and vast demand for goods in Europe. Western Europe was introduced to a new and more progressive culture because of the Crusades. New luxuries from the East were desired. The two Italian city-states of Genoa and Venice grew rich on trade from the East. Italian merchants satisfied the increasing demand of Europeans for new luxuries by acquiring the goods from the East at ports along the Mediterranean Sea and would sail back to European ports to sell the goods for a considerable profit.

During this time, Europe was in a condition of unrest. Due to the rise of cities and nation-states, medieval society was declining. As city populations grew, there was a greater demand for new goods and services, as a result, a new middle class and social disruption emerged. The serfs sought an escape from their economic and social oppression. The middle class and national governments desired greater wealth. The artisans and merchants moved to the newly developed cities and towns, which resulted in the importance of the populations. Towns now depended on trade, which, in turn, was reliant upon materials produced by the medieval manors. The bourgeoisie demanded that kings and nobles maintain armies and navies, fund public developments, and support general well-being of their people. Artisans and merchants demanded capital reserve for new economic endeavors. The clergy lost much of their financial support, and efforts of the clergy to exhaust money from any given area was resisted by both king and the new middle class.[3] At this time, individuals and groups are becoming specialized which results in the expansion of commerce.

The emergence of political national units during the 16th to 17th century is significant. Now, feudal loyalty to a local lord of a manor is being replaced with the idea of an enduring nation and identity with a group of people. Early economic thought is developed from the idea of individual actions that are beneficial to the national state, and how such actions make the nation powerful and wealthy. The embryonic growth of a national identity is an important factor in economics.

The continual development of the contemporary idea of

individuality is also important. In medieval society, an individual was to think of themselves as satisfying a definite task in the community. All thoughts about one's task in the world was to think in this manner. The medieval idea was that one should not try to change their destiny, but to commit their life to one's current degree or estate. The parson in Chaucer's *Canterbury Tales* encapsulates this idea: "God ordeyned that som folk sholde be moore heigh in estaat and in degree, and som folk moore lough, and that everich sholde be served in his estaat and in his degree" ("The Parson's Tale," 772-773). If a person is a lord of a manor, a member of the bourgeoisie, or even a serf, he should not attempt to change that occupational or social status.

In medieval society, avarice was regarded as the aspiration for any material possessions. The best example of the medieval attitude toward materialism is the view that the monks were the most holy since they renounced all worldly possessions. Christopher Marlowe's play, "The Tragical History of Doctor Faustus" (1590), encapsulates this idea. Covetousness is one of the seven deadly sins that speaks with Dr. Faustus: "I am Covetousness, begotten of an old churl in an old leathern bag; and might I have my wish I would desire that this house and all the people in it were turn'd to gold, that I might lock you up in my good chest: O, my sweet gold!" (VI.202).[4] Formerly, the aspiration of an individual was to discover his role in life and be committed to it. Near the end of the Middle Ages, there is the developing idea that some material possessions are acceptable.

Marco Polo

Marco Polo was the first European to travel the complete span of Asia (a 24 year journey). Rustichello of Pisa encouraged Polo to chronicle his expeditions, which were known in his time as *The Description of the World*, or *The Travels of Marco Polo*. His work gave a detailed account of the exotic luxuries of India and Africa, the strength of the Mongol Empire, and the wealth of Cathay (China), which made it one of the most infamous books in medieval Europe. Since a completely different world was introduced to the Europeans, an intense interest in trade and travel resulted from his accounts.

Formerly, education was reserved for the clergy and since the majority of books were written in Latin, the average person was quite uneducated. The average medieval person did little reading, but the interest in trade and travel created a "rebirth" in study. The emergent interest toward study caused a rediscovery of the art and literature of ancient Greece and Rome. Now, learning was not solely for the clergy. The Renaissance would begin in Italy and quickly influence Europe. Therefore, the impact of Polo's expeditions, ensuing in a new way of thinking, in Europe cannot be underestimated.

The changes in Europe helped foster the Age of Exploration, as Europeans wanted to find a direct sea route to the Far East. The Age of Exploration (13th to 18th centuries) is inseparable from advances in science. Copernicus (1473-1543), Galileo (1564-1642), Kepler (1572-1630), Brahe (1546-1601), and Newton (1642-1727) are searching for physical precedents in the world. Additionally, there are numerous inventions at this time.

If ships were to sail the seas, new instruments were needed. The compass was used to guide ships though uncharted seas. The astrolabe emerged in the Islamic world (c. 8th or 9th century) and was reintroduced to Europe by Islamic Spain in the 11th century. From the 16th to the 18th century (the time of the invention of the sextant) the astrolabe was the principal navigational instrument. Clocks and tables to calculate distance, speed, and time are common. Charts and maps are also greatly improved. Bookkeeping and contracts are established to maintain records of the booming trade. Gutenberg's movable type printing press (c. A.D. 1440) allowed explorers to chronicle their expeditions, which resulted in new discoveries and ideas spreading quickly. Society is becoming confident in their ability to find answers to the mysteries of the world. The rebirth of learning, characterized by the Renaissance, truly changed the world.

The Mercantilists

Generally, mercantilism is coupled to the new politics in the rise of the nation state. The increase of capital and considerable investments in trade gave impetus to the mercantilists. It is for this reason that mercantilism became the primary school of economic thought during the Middle Ages.

As already stated, the decline of medieval society was the result of the revival of learning and trade during the Renaissance. The medieval, feudal institutions were destabilized by the escalating use of money and greater dependence on trade within the economy. Whereas kings formerly relied upon the nobles, they were now becoming dependent upon the bourgeoisie and nation states to support them.[5] The kings now hired armies and navies to maintain peace and order, which led to greater prosperity, and the continual growth of nationalism.

Furthermore, the Protestant Reformation challenged the role and teaching of the Catholic Church which resulted in the civil role of the state expanding.[6] The decline of medieval society was greatly influenced by new developments in technology. The escalating use of money in the economy diminished the role of barter and reciprocity since people wanted to either sell goods or work for money. As a result, labor became more mobile as lords of feudal manors needed to employ laborers which inevitably resulted in the rise of free labor. If a lord could not employ laborers, then the land would be rented. Small farms with limited labor were compelled to change their attention to pasture and sheep as opposed to cultivating the soil. The popular nursery rhyme encapsulates the spirit of this time: "Baa, baa, black sheep, have you any wool? Yes sir, yes sir, three bags full. One for the master, one for the dame, and one for the little boy who lives down the lane."

The revival of travel led inevitably to more capital to finance commerce and trade. The ship captains had greater navigational skills due to new inventions and were safer due to improved design and structure. The surplus of goods transported across the Mediterranean Sea increased wealth and the production of even more goods, as commercial centers were developed. Mercantilist thought gave prominence to the construction of export centers, developing the power of national states, and increasing accumulation of gold and silver. A nation's wealth was determined by the amount of gold and silver in its treasury.

Export became much more import than export, since a steady supply of exported goods would result in more gold and silver.

Formerly, the view was accumulation of gold led to covetousness (one of the so-called "seven deadly sins"). Gold and silver were now regarded as wealth and the means of national power. One prominent economist wrote, "Foreign trade produces riches, riches power, power preserves our trade and religion."[7] If they were to acquire gold and silver, which would maintain national power and also allow safeguarding of one's religion, it was absolutely necessary for national states to trade.

Gold and silver was acquired through export and foreign trade to other countries. Kings were ardent supporters of mercantilist theory, and governments would support exploration of the New World as a means of further augmenting the mother country. Colonies were regarded as opportunities to supply gold or raw materials since they were suppliers of market and resources for finished goods. The goods would be transported by ships bearing the flag of the mother country (encouraging monopolization of colonial trade).

Accumulation of gold and silver through "favorable balance of trade" is witnessed in trade policies tending to import raw materials and export finished goods. Countries tried to avoid importing more than they exported, since they wanted to accumulate more gold in the treasury, as opposed to expending their gold for imported goods. There is obvious opposition among nations since some, of necessity, must accumulate more gold than others. The international policy is to accumulate as much good and silver in the treasury as possible. Strong central government and taxation is emerging.

Mercantilists wanted a sizeable number of low-wage laborers to manufacture exports in order to accumulate more gold for the nation. They thought low-wage laborers would allow greater means of export and amassing of gold. Many of the mercantilists supported child labor, since even the young needed to assist in the accumulation of gold and silver in the nation's treasury. The earlier those children began to work, the better it was for their country's prosperity. Even children as young as four years old were sent to the county workhouse where they were taught to read for a mere two hours, and the remainder of the day was exhausted by working in the productions of the workhouse, according to their ability, age, and strength.

Governments also wanted powerful entrepreneurs, or firms, travelling to foreign countries and exporting goods. In order to facilitate these entrepreneurial firms, the government would grant special favors since the firms would be collecting gold that would eventually be brought into the treasury of the country. Large companies were favored so export would increase, thereby accumulating more gold for the country. The firms were essential for acting upon existing opportunities, creating new opportunities, and being innovative to the market. Certain mercantilist theories are still implemented, such as a large trade surplus, low-wage workers, and government subsidization for large businesses.[8] The brilliant Austrian economist Ludwig von Mises wrote, "...economic history is a long record of government policies that failed because they were designed with a bold disregard for the laws of economics. It is impossible to understand the history of economic thought if one does not pay attention to the fact that economics as such is a challenge to the conceit of those in power."[9]

The amount of gold in the treasury meant a larger supply of credit and money. Accumulation of gold was the determining factor for financing future trade enterprises and allowing companies to borrow money. If there was a lack of credit, then companies would be forced to borrow money at high interest rates. However, gold and silver in the treasury increased a nation's wealth, thereby allowing companies to borrow money for investing in new business enterprises.

According to mercantile theory, an individual or colony existed solely for the benefit of the mother country. France and Spain discouraged colonization of the New World, but England encouraged it. England's goal was to develop a cooperative empire that would work together for her own benefit. Therefore, it was necessary for strict regulation of those colonies. Mercantilism viewed the existence of the colonies as the means for the mother country to increase her wealth. A favorable balance of trade was expected, wherein more goods were exported than imported so that other nations wanting to trade must pay in gold or silver. European countries enforced a strict mercantilist system of foreign trade. Mercantilism was strict government control of trade and dominated economic thinking from approximately A.D. 1500 to the end of the 17th century. Certain representative mercantilist thinkers will now be discussed, which will lead the reader to understand the advantages of free trade and the necessity of maintaining individual economic freedom, as exemplified by the ideas of free enterprise.

Mercantilist Thinkers

Josiah Child (1630-1699)

Josiah Child was an English merchant, mercantilist, and governor of the East India Company. As an English merchant, he sold supplies to the British navy (the modern equivalence of a defense contractor). He made a considerable fortune by investing in the British East India Company (a large trading company in his day), eventually becoming the largest single stock-holder in the East India Company.

His best known works are *Brief Observations concerning Trade and the Interest of Money* (1668) and *New Discourse of Trade* (1694). Since he was a defense contractor, and people would be naturally skeptical of someone with that occupation writing about what is good for national security, he published the latter work anonymously. It was not uncommon for business men who were mercantilists to write anonymously, nor was it uncommon for his time.

While he is working on early drafts of his *New Discourse of Trade*, the British economy is suffering considerably. Similar to modern concerns about Japan domination global markets, Dutch merchants are taking significant encroachments into the British markets. The British fear that the Dutch will accumulate all the gold. Furthermore, Britain suffered greatly when the Great Plague ("Black Death") spread to London in early spring of 1665. Then, on the night of 2 September 1666, the Great Fire of London destroyed 80 percent of the city. Child was appointed as a primary member of a royal commission to formulate a plan helping Britain from such great economic and physical calamity.

Since Holland offered a low rate of interest, Child's response was for Britain to offer the same. In order to create competition for the Dutch, he also suggested that the British East India Company should have a low rate of interest in order to borrow money and compete in the markets. Child wrote, "All trade is a kind of warfare."[10] Since the Dutch have the weapon of low interest rates, then the British also needed this weapon. His thinking is reminiscent of General Motors president Charles E. Wilson well-known statement during the 1950s: "What's good for General Motors is good for the country." Just as the country was suspicious of Wilson, the British government was reasonably hesitant about the recommendation. Child would have certainly benefited from low interest rates since he was a stock-holder in the East India Company. However, it was not clear how Britain would have benefited from low interest rates just because the Dutch government had low interest rates. There was no evidence that the Dutch maintained a policy of keeping low interest rates. Furthermore, Child did not recommend how the British government could finance the change in interest rates. He is a good example of mercantilist thinking in relation to public policy, since it was impossible for Child to examine it neutrally.

Jean-Baptiste Colbert (1619-1683)

Jean-Baptiste Colbert was a French Minister of Finance, a position he held from 1661 until his death, under King Louis XIV. He was born in Reims. Against the prodigious odds of the Sun King's extravagance, he managed to maintain some degree of solvency in state finances. Colbert believed strongly in fixed government control over the country's economy, and his efforts made France financially sound. He upheld mercantilist beliefs regarding the expansion of commerce and the safeguarding of a favorable balance of trade as the means for a wealthy nation. His policies, known as Colbertism, were all maintained according to mercantilist tenets and thoughts. As Minister of Finance, he possessed the power to enforce mercantilist thinking.

Colbert reasoned that a particular number of ships would be responsible for all foreign trade. Holland was one of the main competitors with France; therefore, both nations will compete regarding the ships responsible for foreign trade (which will result in greater accumulation of gold). Colbert wants to take action to ensure France will acquire the largest possible share of the trade. His plan of action is to declare war on Holland in 1672. Colbert burns their ships thus preventing any means to engage in foreign trade. Additionally, he offered subsidies to foreign trading companies and promotes copious favoritism to them so France would develop the most powerful companies to accumulate the gold.

During Colbert's ministry, the majority of imports were to gratify the fastidious needs of the court.[11] To ensure the courts' desires were gratified, Colbert regulated minute details in industry. For instance, he regulated the number of threads per square inch of cloth among cloth manufacturers. He organized government inspectors whose responsibility was to enforce his regulations for the fine clothing of the court.

Colbert does deserve some recognition though. He engaged himself with many tasks, from questions of finance to the naming of the King's illegitimate children. The King made him responsible for the intellectual and artistic life of France. He supported domestic developments (e.g. canals and roads), industries, trading, and even attempted to develop an independent system of weights and measures (which proved to be ineffective) to rival the Dutch. To build the roads, he used the corvée which was unpaid obligatory labor services required of the peasantry to his lord (usually they were threatened physically). As a mercantilist, he believed workers should be assiduous to enlarge the country's exporting and even approved laws mandating child labor. As Minister of Finance, he even reduced France's forty-one holy days to twenty-four.

Colbert was responsible for the creation of a powerful navy which made France a great power at sea. He created the Atlantic fleet which was organized as sailing ships and the Mediterranean fleet organized of galleys. To manage the Atlantic fleet, professional sailors were compelled to enlist for the king's service. To manage the galleys, Colbert convinced magistrates to sentence common criminals for the service; he also recruited political criminals, Protestants, and slaves detained from Africa and Canada to manpower the galleys. He was also responsible for sending explorers and colonists to America.

Colbert failed to maintain a balanced budget when his rival the Marquis de Louvois, the war minister, convinced Louis XIV to commence a costly progression of wars. Colbertism became synonymous with mercantilism, and his actions made it the most common European economic system of his day. He used unscrupulous means to accomplish his purposes and never once vacillated to use the power of state. Colbertism is still in existence in France as an extreme economic system of government control.

Bernard Mandeville (1670-1733)

Bernard Mandeville was born in Rotterdam, became a doctor at the University of Leiden, and travelled to England where he eventually settled and married. He had a respectable, professional reputation in London. His renown is as a prose writer and philosopher, not as an economist (but his work represents mercantilist thinking). He received distinction in Europe with his most important work, *The Fable of the Bees* (subtitled *Private Vices, Publick Benefits*).

The Fable of the Bees is a parable written of approximately twenty pages of verse. The 1714 edition contained a preface, the text of "The Grumbling Hive," an "Enquiry into the Origin of Moral Virtue," and "Remarks" on the poem. The "Remarks" are approximately two hundred pages of explanation lest the reader did not understand his social satire. *The Fable of the Bees* is about a dominant and strong hive of bees which attained their stature because of their avarice and sin. Later, the bees are transformed into generous and virtuous bees that become weak and are defeated by their enemies.

> Vast Numbers throng'd the fruitful Hive;
> Yet those vast Numbers made 'em thrive;
> Millions endeavouring to supply

Each other's Lust and Vanity
While other Millions were employ'd;
To see their Handy-works destroy'd;
They furnish'd half the Universe;
Yet had more Work than Laborers....

These were call'd Knaves, but bar the Name,
The grave Industrious were the same:
All Trades and Places knew some Cheat,
No calling was without Deceit....

Thus every Part was full of Vice,
Yet the whole Mass a Paradise;
Flatter'd in Peace, and fear'd in Wars,
They were th' Esteem of Foreigners,
And lavish of their Wealth and Lives,
The Balance of all other Hives.
Such were the Blessings of that State;
Their Crimes conspir'd to make them Great:
And Virtue, who from Politicks
Had learn'd a Thousand Cunning Tricks,
Was, by their happy Influence,
Made Friends with Vice: And ever since,
The worst of all the Multitude
Did something for the Common Good.[12]

Mandeville addressed many themes about "Virtue" making "Friends with Vice." He described the bees as assiduous, even the criminals "conspir'd to make them Great," and the dominance and strength of the hive is the result of everyone exercising great vigour. Later, when the bees are transformed into generous and virtuous bees, they cease stealing and cheating each other in the various trades. Mandeville continued,

Those, that remain'd grown temp'rate, strive,
Not how to spend, but how to live,
And, when they paid their Tavern Score,
Resolv'd to enter it no more....

As Pride and Luxury decrease,
So by degrees they leave the Seas.
Not merchants now, but Companies
Remove whole Manufactories.
All Arts and Crafts neglected lie;
Content, the Bane of Industry,
Makes 'em admire their homely Store,
And neither seek nor covet more.

So few in the vast Hive remain,
The hundredth Part they can't maintain
Against th' Insults of numerous Foes;
Whom yet they valiantly oppose:
'Till some well-fenc'd Retreat is found,
And here they die or stand their Ground.
No Hireling in their Army's known;
But bravely fighting for their own,
Their Courage and Integrity
At last were crown'd with Victory.

They triumph'd not without their Cost,
For many Thousand Bees were lost.
Hard'ned with Toils and Exercise,
They counted Ease it self a Vice;
Which so improv'd their Temperance;
That, to avoid Extravagance,
They flew into a hollow Tree,
Blest with Content and Honesty.[13]

As the bees are placated, they lose their dominance and strength. Writing as a social satirist, Mandeville communicates the necessity of people being assiduous in their work, and the favorable social outcome of personal actions of self-interest. The utility of "vices" is derived from Mandeville's description of all actions as uniformly merciless since all are motivated by self-interest. However, motives must be merciless since the outcome of those actions is frequently socially beneficial because personal comforts and wealth of society are produced. The acquisition of material goods is intricately related to importing and exporting across the seas which will produce profit. If such actions do not occur, and a nation does not increase trade, then it will experience the fate of the bees: being defeated by one's enemies. Mandeville's work addressed an issue that will be pivotal to understanding the policy of *laissez faire* (a French term meaning "let it be" or "hands off").

David Hume (1711-1776)[14]

David Hume was a Scottish philosopher, historian, economist, and essayist. He is one of the most significant individuals in the history of philosophical empiricism and skepticism. Geisler and Feinberg describe him as "a skeptic in an optimistic age, the eighteenth century. On the one hand, he questioned the knowledge claims of science, mathematics, and even logic. On the other hand, he allowed probabilistic standards for beliefs that go beyond our immediate experience."[15] In his day, Hume was known primarily as an historian; however, today he is known primarily as a philosopher. When he is writing, it is not uncommon for philosophers to address a number of various subjects. In the seventeenth and eighteenth centuries, the relationship between economics and morality was common and controversial topic at Scottish universities. Hume emerged as an economist with the writing of *Political Discourses* (1752). It is not certain the influence Hume had upon Adam Smith, a Scottish professor of philosophy considered the father of economic theory. Hume did not develop a complete system of economic thought as Smith did in his *Wealth of Nations*. However, he did introduce several new ideas which form the basis of classical economics which developed after him. Classical economists are generally considered the beginning of formal economic theory.[16]

Hume was an influential thinker who marked a turning point in the history of economics since he began to question mercantilist theory. Those economists who questioned mercantilism did not always have answers of their own, but they did have a sense of a problem which needed to be addressed. For example, as Hume writes essays in the 1740s and 1750s, he questions whether gold and money are equal to wealth. He stated,

Money is not, properly speaking, one of the subjects of commerce; but only the instrument which men have agreed upon to facilitate the exchange of one commodity for the other. It is none of the wheels of trade: it is the oil which renders the motion of the wheels more smooth and easy.[17] ["Of Money"]

Hume concludes gold is not the sole objective; rather, it just makes commerce work. "It was a shrewd observation of ANACHARSIS the SCYTHIAN, who had never seen money in his own country, that gold and silver seemed to him of no use to the GREEKS, but to assist them in numeration and arithmetic."[18] Hume's essay is a major challenge to current economic thought.

Hume recognizes the impossibility of an infinite accumulation of gold into a country and thinks about the results of having much gold in a country. According to Hume, the result would be a continual rise in prices making goods extremely expensive and difficult to export. Therefore, accumulating all gold into a single country may not be beneficial for the future since it will likely increase the difficulty of selling goods to other countries. Answering the question of what would happen if Great Britain accumulated the majority of the gold, he wrote,

Must not all labor and commodities rise to such an exorbitant height, that no neighbouring nations could afford to buy from us; while their commodities, on the other hand, became comparatively so cheap, that, in spite of all the laws which could be formed, they would be run in upon us, and our money flow out; till we fall to a level with foreigners, and lose that great superiority of riches, which had laid us under such disadvantages?[19] ["Of the Balance of Trade"]

According to Hume, a single country acquiring the majority of wealth will produce disadvantages. He proposes both exports and imports benefit a nation's economy.[20] Setting forth new thinking, Hume wrote,

The same method of reasoning will let us see the advantage of *foreign* commerce, in augmenting the power of the state, as well as the riches and happiness of the subject. It increases the stock of labor in the nation; and the sovereign may convert what share of it he finds necessary to the service of the public. Foreign trade, by its imports, furnishes materials for new manufactures; and by its exports, it produces labor in particular commodities, which could not be consumed at home. In short, a kingdom, that has a large import and export, must abound more with industry, and that employed upon delicacies and luxuries, than a kingdom which rests contented with its native commodities. It is, therefore, more powerful, as well as richer and happier. The individuals reap the benefit of these commodities, so far as they gratify the senses and appetites. And the public is also a gainer, while a greater stock of labor is, by this means, stored up against any public exigency; that is, a greater number of laborious men are maintained, who may be diverted to the public service, without robbing any one of the necessaries, or even the chief conveniences of life.[21] ["Of Commerce"]

Importing is also beneficial and will result in people being "richer and happier." Not only does he address the means for a nation to maintain its wealth, but also Hume is developing the idea of individualism (e.g. individuals may benefit for a nation's wealth). Another new idea from Hume is not to regard all trading states as enemies, but it is beneficial to trade with rich neighbors.

Having endeavoured to remove one species of ill-founded jealousy, which is so prevalent among commercial nations, it may not be amiss to mention another, which seems equally groundless. Nothing is more usual, among states which have made some advances in commerce, than to look on the progress of their neighbours with a suspicious eye, to consider all trading states as their rivals, and to suppose that it is impossible for any of them to flourish, but at their expense. In opposition to this narrow and malignant opinion, I will venture to assert, that the increase of riches and commerce in any one nation, instead of hurting, commonly promotes the riches and commerce of all its neighbours; and that a state can scarcely carry its trade and industry very far, where all the surrounding states are buried in ignorance, sloth, and barbarism.[22] ["Of the Jealousy of Trade"]

As Hume wrote, the ideas he articulated was a new way of thinking thereby introducing some of the new ideas which would form the foundation of classical economics in the late eighteenth century. His insights as an economist are as follows: "that wealth consists not of money but of commodities; that the amount of money in circulation should be kept related to the amount of goods in the market…; that a low rate of interest is a symptom not of superabundance of money but of booming trade; that no nation can go on exporting only for gold; that each nation has special advantages of raw materials, climate, and skill, so that a free interchange of products (with some exceptions) is mutually beneficial; and that poor nations impoverish the rest just because they do not produce enough to be able to take much part in that exchange."[23]

The Physiocrats

During the Age of Reason and Enlightenment (1650-1800), the French Physiocrats were the first systematic school of economics, and later, they would be the first group called economists. The actual title is économistes which was derived from a French term meaning "the rule of nature" or "managers of the household." They articulated new ideas about the economy and are responsible for bringing economic theory, "the rule of nature," into public discourse. According to the Physiocrats, value is created by nature, and harvested by man. All wealth commenced with the land, and agriculture alone could expand and multiply wealth.[24]

The simplest manner to understand the Physiocracy is that it develops contrary to the tradition of Colbert. They reject governmental control of all areas of life since this had led to numerous wars, distress by the corvée, heavy taxes to pay for foreign wars, the extravagance of court life and the competition for power and prestige among the courtiers. The Physiocrats are developing new ideas during great social volatility in France which will culminate in the French Revolution.

The Physiocrats believed economic power resulted from agriculture alone. They tried to convince the government of Louis XV to cease control and reduce taxes on French agriculture so poor France could imitate the more affluent Britain which developed a moderately *laissez-faire* policy.[25] The most important Physiocrat was François Quesnay (1694-1774)[26] (others would include Richard Cantillon[27] and Anne Robert Jacques Turgot[28]), who was a physician in Louis XV's court and also a doctor. Certainly, Quesnay was the individual who created the phrase "*laissez-faire, laissez-passer*" (*laissez faire* is the abbreviated form of the French phrase meaning to "let things alone, let them pass"). The Physiocrats adopted the term in opposition to government interference with trade (the phrase is now synonymous with firm free market economics). The idea of *laissez-faire* was quite a contrast to Colbertism which demanded absolute control of everything (e.g. the number of threads in the cloth). The new philosophy of "letting things be" was quite an appealing idea.

The Physiocrats believed a laissez faire policy would result in economic issues resolving themselves by the development of a natural pattern according to a natural law. Whenever the family and the individual form the basis of all societies by sustaining one and all through labor, such as increasing crops and manufacturing goods which inevitably encourage trade, then the natural pattern of structure within all societal groups is similar to the entire national supply of wealth. Although the emphasis upon natural laws may appear anomalous, the Physiocrats amalgamated Mandeville's idea of the materialists who attain their stature because of their avarice and sin with the idea of kings and lords as a component of the natural law. The idea is that different classes in society, such as landowners, farmers, merchants, create a natural pattern that is most effective when the government does not interfere with the function of supposed natural laws.

Quesnay's explanation of this natural pattern is the *Tableau Economique*, or the "economical table."[29] *Tableau* defined three different classes in society: (1) the proprietary classes, or landowners; (2) the productive classes, or farmers; and, (3) the sterile classes, which was manufacturers and merchant. It was believed the sterile classes were a burden to society since they consumed all their production leaving no surplus for the future. Quesnay believed only agriculture would create a surplus to be subsequently produced from year to year thereby stimulating economic growth. However, industry and manufacturing are thought to be sterile since the farmers were the productive classes because they are actually harvesting food. The sterile classes were preoccupied with the unproductive habit of trade. Quesnay mistakenly understood the sterility of manufacturing, but he was correct to attribute France's poverty to the mercantilist doctrines of Colbert. In modern times, however, there is the recognition of some value in trade.

The Physiocrats believed the mercantilists gave too much attention to sustaining industry and manufacturing rather than agriculture. Therefore, Quesnay desired the abolishing of many medieval regulations that governed agricultural production to allow the economy to develop its natural pattern. The natural pattern of the economy was understood as the balanced circular flow of income among economic component parts (i.e. sectors),[30] henceforth, different societal classes to capitalize the net manufactured goods.

When thinking of the *Tableau*, it is important to remember that Quesnay was a physician. Since he was familiar with new scientific theories about the circulation of human blood, he made comparisons to the circulation of blood and homeostasis in the body. As he pondered the different classes in society, Quesnay thought wealth should circulate through the economy in an analogous manner to the circulation of blood in the body. Supply and demand among the different groups would result in a "homeostatic" economy. For example, farmers would provide money for landowners which means food and manufactured goods are purchased from the sterile classes. Not only would farmers have food for themselves, but also they would sell food to both proprietary and sterile classes. The manufacturers and merchants would sell manufactured goods to the farmers helping them become more productive.

The reader should be able now to recognize the influence of the Physiocracy. For instance, the Frenchmen's Adam Smith, Anne Robert Jacques Turgot (c. 1727-1781), became French Minister of Finance under King Louis XVI from 1774-1776 (recall Colbert acquired the same position under Louis XIV in 1661). Within a mere two years as finance minister, Turgot abolished the government monopolies, required landowners to pay taxes, gave farmers more selling privileges, and reduced wasteful government spending. He argued for religious freedom, universal education, and a government-central bank. Turgot abolished the feudal guilds thereby allowing workers to be available to employers without restraint. Additionally, he ended the government's policy of forced labor (the corvée) and reinstated a more effective tax in money. Milton Friedman (1912-), one of the most influential living economists of free market and most important individual of the Chicago School against Keynesian economics, believes replacing certain types of taxes with taxes in money was one of the greatest expansions of human freedom. Louis XVI did not esteem such changes and dismissed Turgot in 1776. Thirteen years later, Louis XVI and Marie Antoinette found themselves in the centre of the French Revolution. Some historians have argued that the Physiocrats may have been the last opportunity for France to avert the Revolution.

The Physiocrats articulated early modern economic thought and should be understood as a major development in economic theory despite the imperfections. For example, economists today know to focus on the agriculture sector alone is disadvantageous. Furthermore, kings and lords are not components of natural law nor should monarchs control all spheres of life. Positively, the Physiocrats did propose an identifiable structure for analyzing different societal groups in relation to various sectors, and the relationship necessary among the different groups and sectors. The Physiocracy articulated theory that was not general knowledge. Moreover, Quesnay's work foreshadowed classical economics and Adam Smith specifically. The best manner to understand the significance of the Physiocrats is to quote from Smith. In fact, he is best understood as a response to mercantilist thinking who expanded Physiocratic ideas of free trade and the primary of the agricultural sector.

Adam Smith (1723-1790)

Adam Smith was a Scottish economist, philosopher, and professor moral philosophy in the department of logic at Glasgow University. He is regarded as the founder of modern economic theory. Classical economics, developed by Thomas Robert Malthus (1766-1834), David Ricardo (1772-1823) and John Stuart Mill (1806-1873) in the 19th century, is the legacy of Smith and considered the beginning of formal economic study. Even today, Smith's work inspires economists.

He frequently discussed issues with his personal friend, David Hume. Between 1757 and 1762, he also became friends with Benjamin Franklin (1706-1790) when the Pennsylvania Assembly sent Franklin to England to appeal the king for the permission to levy taxes on proprietary lands. It is believed that Smith wrote his most famous work, *An Inquiry into the Nature and Causes of the Wealth of Nations*, thinking purposely of the American colonies. In England, those who opposed strong monarchies were called patriots, or Whigs; the Loyalists, or Tories, were opposed to independence and remained loyal to the monarchy. The Whigs and Tories were also represented in the colonies. Adam Smith was a Whig (i.e. the Founding Fathers) who desired individual freedom in society. According to Smith, individual economic freedom would lead to the *summon bonum* not only for individual but also for society collectively.

Smith traveled to France in the 1760s where he met Quesnay and some of the Physiocrats; it was there that Smith began writing his masterpiece, *The Wealth of Nations*, a work published in 1776 about the Physiocrats, in the same year America declared independence from Britain. He quotes French political economist, Marquis de Mirabeau, favorably as follows:

"There have been, since the world began...three great inventions which have principally given stability to political societies, independent off many other inventions which have enriched and adorned them. The first, is the invention of writing, which alone gives human nature the power of transmitting, without alteration, its laws, its contracts, its annals, and its discoveries. The second is, the invention of money, which binds together all the relations between civilized societies. The third, is the Œconomical Table [*Tableau Economique*], the result of the other two, which completes them both by perfecting their object; the great discovery of our age, but of which our posterity will reap the benefit."[31]

The "three great inventions" are writing, money, and the *Tableau Economique*. There is great enthusiasm in response to these great inventions during this period of history since new manners of thinking about the world are rapidly developing. The desire for individual freedom is being considered as a means for society to cooperate together for the greatest good. Smith believed that materialism could benefit society collectively since it encourages competition in the free market. Additionally, people want to benefit their government, but also they are thinking that monarchies, monopolies, and strict government control are not the most effective manner to accomplish this purpose; rather, the policy of *laissez faire* ("letting things be") is a better approach.

The Physiocrats were responsible for dividing society into different classes and demonstrating how they can benefit each other. Each person benefits himself by his labor since he is able to earn income, but he also benefits society since valuable goods are produced so he can continue to earn income on the basis of his labor in a competitive market. The lasting influence of the Physiocracy, which Smith expanded, was to demonstrate that individual freedom produces the best structure of government. Furthermore, economic freedom and political freedom cannot be separated if man is to be completely free. Smith is one of the earliest adherents of capitalism, or the free market.

Adam Smith frequently used the metaphor of "an invisible hand" to mean every person uses his capital, talents, and time to create "industry of which the produce is likely to be of the greatest value."[32]

> He generally, indeed, neither intends to promote the public interest, nor knows how much he is promoting it. By preferring the support of domestic to that of foreign industry, he intends only his own security; and by directing that industry in such a manner as its produce may be of the greatest value, he intends only his own gain, and he is in this, as in many other cases, led by an invisible hand to promote an end which was no part of his intention.... I have never known much good done by those who affected to trade for the public good.[33]

Economics and Government

Socialism is the adversary of individual freedom. Consequently, the seminal essay, "Economic Calculation in the Socialist Commonwealth," originally published in 1920 by the Austrian economist, Ludwig von Mises, is just as relevant today. In 1922, he wrote *Socialism: An Economical and Sociological Analysis* which demonstrated that socialism is not a viable economic system since its goal is to abolish economics. Mises argued that private property is essential to the means of production since there is no other means to have economic calculation and price systems.

> Whenever Society is good or bad may be a matter of individual judgment; but whoever prefers life to death, happiness to suffering, well-being to misery, must accept society. And whoever desires that society should exist and develop must also accept, without limitation or reserve, private ownership in the means of production.[34]

The advocates of totalitarian control call the attitudes of their opponents negativism. They pretend that while they themselves are demanding the improvement of unsatisfactory conditions, the others are intent upon letting the evils endure. This is to judge all social questions from the viewpoint of narrow-minded bureaucrats. Only to bureaucrats can the idea occur that establishing new offices, promulgating new decrees, and increasing the number of government employees alone can be described as positive and beneficial measures, whereas everything else is passivity and quietism.

The program of economic freedom is not negativistic. It aims positively at the establishment and preservation of the system of market economy based on private ownership of the means of production and free enterprise. It aims at free competition and at the sovereignty of the consumers. As the logical outcome of these demands the true liberals are opposed to all endeavors to substitute government control for the operation of an unhampered market economy. Laissez faire, laissez passer does not mean: let the evils last. On the contrary, it means: do not interfere with the operation of the market because such interference must necessarily restrict output and make people poorer. It means furthermore: do not abolish or cripple the capitalist system which, in spite of all obstacles put in its way by governments and politicians, has raised the standard of living of the masses in an unprecedented way.

Liberty is not, as the German precursors of Nazism asserted, a negative ideal. Whether a concept is presented in an affirmative or in a negative form is merely a question of idiom. *Freedom from want* is tantamount to the expression *striving after a state of affairs under which people are better supplied with necessities. Freedom of speech* is tantamount to *a state of affairs under which everybody can say what he wants to say.*[35]

Mises is credited as greatly influencing the demise of communism in European and intellectually influencing modern economists, such as James M. Buchanan (1919-), Milton Friedman (1912-), Friedrich A. Hayek (1899-1992), and reviving interest in the works of Adam Smith. In his 1944 work, *Omnipotent Government*, Mises originated the term "statolatry" for the new Western irreligion which is idolatry of the state analogous to worship of idols. Statolatry is the glorification of the state or nation as the objective of all reasonable human ambition to the exclusion of anything else. American statolatry is the belief that the White House (or a local official) is a better provider than self, family, friends, or God. Virtually any political ideal could be statolatrous, but it is most prevalent under fascism or socialism (and less consistent with libertarian ethics). Mises correctly identified government as one of the foremost idolatries of the 20th century.

> People frequently call socialism a religion. It is indeed the religion of self-deification. The State and Government of which the planners speak, the People of the nationalists, the Society of the Marxians and the Humanity of the positivists are names for the God of the new religions. But all these idols are merely aliases for the individual reformer's own will. In ascribing to his idol all those attributes which the theologians ascribe to God, the inflated Ego glories itself. It is infinitely good, omnipotent, omnipresent, omniscient, eternal. It is the only perfect being in this imperfect world.[36]

Percy Bysshe Shelley's poem "Ozymandias"[37] aptly illustrates this religion of self-deification.

> 'My name is Ozymandias, king of kings:
> Look on my works, ye Mighty, and despair!'
> Nothing beside remains. Round the decay
> Of that colossal wreck, boundless and bare
> The lone and level sands stretch far away.[38]

Ozymandias believed he was omnipotent for even the mighty would despair when considering his power. However, the mighty did not despair because "nothing beside remains." The only thing that remains is the colossal wreckage of his monument, which only testifies to his egotism not his greatness. The uniqueness of Ozymandias was his monomaniacal inscription not his consequent lack of success to display his works. *And inasmuch as it is appointed for men to die once and after this comes judgment* (Heb. 9:27). Ozymandias, in addition to all men, will experience the judgment of God either to eternal life or eternal damnation. Shelley encapsulates the relative insignificance of mankind to the passage of time. Although Ozymandias is essentially a metaphor for the transient nature of political hegemony, it also gives a metaphorical characterization of the egotism and self-deification of all mankind regardless of a specific undertaking.

Ozymandias was ridiculed by his sculptor, his colossus fallen, and his command to "look on my works" is empty since the "lone and level sands" have buried them. His monument is fair judgment for he who sought greatness exceeding God. The finitude of all humanity is symbolized by Ozymandias. It is not the "frown, and wrinkled lip, and sneer of cold command"[39] enticing men and women to prosper and erect monuments but the aspiration for self-deification. Shelley understood this "edifice complex"—the aspiration to achieve immortality through fame and fortune—better than most today. Such ostentatious monuments enshrine the human spirit as opposed to the "cold command" of some sovereign whose finitude equals that of his subjects. Mises wrote, "The market economy needs no apologists and propagandists. It can apply to itself the words of Sir Christopher Wren's epitaph in St. Paul's: *Si monumentum requiris, circumspice.* (If you seek his monument, look around)."[40]

Death by Government

The growth of government should be a concern to all who cherish liberty. For example, the 20th century alone demonstrates death by government to an astonishing degree. R. J. Rummel, professor emeritus of political science at the University of Hawaii, documented these facts in his book *Death by Government* (1994).[41]

Death by government is a great wickedness of the 20th century, but history demonstrates it cannot be regarded as new phenomenon. For example, 1 Samuel 8 records republican Israel's growth of government and accurately describes the relationship which would develop between the people and governmental bureaucracy.

Then all the elders of Israel gathered together and came to Samuel at Ramah; and they said to him, "Behold, you have grown old, and your sons do not walk in your ways.

Now appoint a king for us to judge us like all the nations." But the thing was displeasing in the sight of Samuel when they said, "Give us a king to judge us." And Samuel prayed to the LORD. And the LORD said to Samuel, "Listen to the voice of the people in regard to all that they say to you, for they have not rejected you, but they have rejected Me from being king over them. "Like all the deeds which they have done since the day that I brought them up from Egypt even to this day—in that they have forsaken Me and served other gods—so they are doing to you also. "Now then, listen to their voice; however, you shall solemnly warn them and tell them of the procedure of the king who will reign over them."

So Samuel spoke all the words of the Lord to the people who had asked of him a king. And he said, "This will be the procedure of the king who will reign over you: he will take your sons and place *them* for himself in his chariots and among his horsemen and they will run before his chariots. "And he will appoint for himself commanders of thousands and of fifties, and *some* to do his plowing and to reap his harvest and to make his weapons of war and equipment for his chariots. "He will also take your daughters for perfumers and cooks and bakers. "And he will take the best of your fields and your vineyards and your olive groves, and give *them* to his servants. "And he will take a tenth of your seed and of your vineyards, and give to his officers and to his servants. "He will also take your male servants and your best young men and your donkeys, and use *them* for his work. "He will take a tenth of your flocks, and you yourselves will become his servants. "Then you will cry out in that day because your king whom you have chosen for yourselves, but the LORD will not answer you in that day." [1 Sam. 8:4-18]

First Samuel 8 is an accurate account of the great personal sacrifices when demand is made for the growth of government. Essentially, God warned the people that the government would seize their freedom, persons, and property. Although government was created by God to protect individual freedom, America has certainly experienced the growth of government in the 20th century. Unfortunately, most Americans do not understand the role of government and have tolerated its growth because of the growth of the American economy.

Growth of the American Economy

The United States has an exceptional history of astounding economic growth. During the entire 20th century, the American economy expanded at a real rate[42] (i.e., adjusted for inflation[43]) of 3-4% yearly. Since the inception of the 20th century, American families have experienced real incomes double approximately every 30 years. In each successive generation, parents have witnessed the standard of living (assessed by per capita[44] gross domestic product[45] [GDP]) for their children increase. Per capita income has increased in real terms from $3,000 in 1900 to $20,000 by the end of the 20th century. From 1900-1980, America created an average of 8,000,000 new jobs every decade. During the 80s, the United States created 18,000,000 new jobs. Not only was the standard of living in America the highest of any nation at the inception of the 20th century, but also at the end of the century. Even with rough measures of the average salary, the per capita GDP, or the extent of the economy divided by the population, is nearly five times better than at the inception of the 20th century.

> The US has the largest and most technologically powerful economy in the world, with a per capita GDP of $37,800. In this market-oriented economy, private individuals and business firms make most of the decisions, and the federal and state governments buy needed goods and services predominantly in the private marketplace. US business firms enjoy considerably greater flexibility than their counterparts in Western Europe and Japan in decisions to expand capital plant, to lay off surplus workers, and to develop new products. At the same time, they face higher barriers to entry in their rivals' home markets than the barriers to entry of foreign firms in US

markets. US firms are at or near the forefront in techno-logical advances, especially in computers and in medical, aerospace, and military equipment; their advantage has narrowed since the end of World War II. The onrush of technology largely explains the gradual development of a "two-tier labor market" in which those at the bottom lack the education and the professional/technical skills of those at the top and, more and more, fail to get compa-rable pay raises, health insurance coverage, and other benefits. Since 1975, practically all the gains in house-hold income have gone to the top 20% of households. The years 1994-2000 witnessed solid increases in real output, low inflation rates, and a drop in unemployment to below 5%. The year 2001 saw the end of boom psy-chology and performance, with output increasing only 0.3% and unemployment and business failures rising substantially. The response to the terrorist attacks of 11 September 2001 showed the remarkable resilience of the economy. Moderate recovery took place in 2002 with the GDP growth rate rising to 2.4%. A major short-term problem in first half 2002 was a sharp decline in the stock market, fueled in part by the exposure of dubious accounting practices in some major corporations. The war in March/April 2003 between a US-led coalition and Iraq shifted resources to the military. In 2003, growth in output and productivity and the recovery of the stock market to above 10,000 for the Dow Jones Industrial Average were promising signs. Unemployment stayed at the 6% level, however, and began to decline only at the end of the year. Long-term problems include inadequate investment in economic infrastructure, rapidly rising medical and pension costs of an aging population, siz-able trade and budget deficits, and stagnation of family income in the lower economic groups.[46]

The unprecedented growth of the economy in the United States has made many Americans forbearing of the growth of government as long as they are able to pay bills and enjoy a higher standard of living. The statistics from the *CIA World Factbook* have been provided to demonstrate the substantial growth of government in modern times. However, the statistics were not provided solely to demonstrate how government has grown, but for the reader to now exercise biblical discernment and understand the sinfulness of this growth of government.

Growth of Government

According to First Samuel 8, the sinfulness of the growth of government is how the development begins: idolatry is the foundation. *And the LORD said to Samuel, "Listen to the voice of the people in regard to all that they say to you, for they have not rejected you, but they have rejected Me from being king over them* (1 Sam. 8:7). The demand of the people was *now appoint a king for us to judge us like all the nations*. The same is true today. People want to be like *all the nations* and if there is something one nation possesses that another does not, then they demand the same. For instance, the argument frequently heard in America is the demand for a national health care system like all other industrialized nations. Just as Israel wanted a government *like all the nations*, Americans desire a government *like all the nations*. The problem with the demand for more government is it begins in idolatry and expresses itself in perversion and wickedness. According to 1 Samuel 8:3, even the judges *turned aside after dishonest gain and took bribes and perverted justice.*

Who is responsible for the cancerous growth of government? According to adherents of the "Social Gospel," a late 19th and early 20th century Christian movement emphasizing the application of Christian principles to the changing social and industrial conditions in the United States, the church is responsible for not doing all that she should. Charles Sheldon's *In His Steps* (1897) was one of the most popular and prominent books for the Social Gospel movement. According to Sheldon, the church should base her public and private actions as an answer to the question "What Would Jesus Do?", and then American society would experience a notable social revolution. In his book *Christianity and the Social Crisis* (1907), Walter Rauschenbusch excoriated the church for not taking more seriously the need to restore social order. Rauschenbusch's book was quite influential since it explained the nature and purpose of the Social Gospel. For instance, he praised *gemeinschaft*, a society which is not individualistic but extols the importance of community as opposed to self interest, and criticized the idea of *gesellschaft*, a social or civil society which is anonymous, atomistic, and individualistic wherein people are motivated by materialism and self interest.

The Social Gospel movement is wrong to excoriate the church for failure to meet the needs of the poor and unemployed, since this is not the responsibility of the church. Certainly private charity could help the poor and unemployed; however, the church is not commissioned to be a welfare organization but to make disciples and teach them (Mt. 28:18-20). Furthermore, Scripture is quite specific about who the church should or not help. For example, 1 Timothy 5:9-10 reads, *Let a widow be put on the list only if she is not less than sixty years old, having been the wife of one man, having a reputation for good works....* Private charities can be beneficial, but people must understand this is not the responsibility of the church. Without a saving relationship with Jesus Christ, the welfare state is a relatively empty achievement for those who are not *looking for the city which has foundations, whose architect and builder is God* (Heb. 11:10), and have become completely passive and reliant to the absolute planning of a more progressively structured society. The personal savings rate is a good example of the growth of government coupled with shameful self interest.

The personal savings rate in the United States is declining. Under the current tax system, a worker is taxed for money earned and if wages are deposited into a savings account there are taxes on the interest. In America, the double taxation system punishes those who save which have resulted in the personal savings rate steadily declining. However, the tax system is not the only reason for the decline in savings; shameful self interest is also a contributing factor. Planning for the future is a diminishing virtue among many Americans. In previous generations there was greater reverence for God's Word, and Americans planned sensibly not only for their lifetimes, but also for their childrens' lifetimes and even their grandchildrens' lifetimes.

Americans were thoughtful about providing for their families as Scripture instructs. *For children are not responsible to save up for **their** parents, but parents for **their** children* (1 Cor. 12:14c). Likewise, a *good man* plans for his grandchildren. *A good man leaves an inheritance to his children's children, and the wealth of the sinner is stored up for the righteous* (Prov. 13:22).

The 1980s became the "Me Generation" of status seekers. The national debt was $914,000,000,000 in 1980, but by 1986 it had reached $2,000,000,000,000. The prevailing attitude was "If you've got it, flaunt it," "I want satisfaction," and "You can have it all." Impulsive purchases and easy credit was normal behavior and "Shop 'Til you Drop" was the maxim. The "Me Generation" of the 20th century, and to the present time, was typically concerned with personal satisfaction and did not worry about accumulating massive credit card debts. Many Americans no longer thought in terms of their children (e.g. abortion) or their grandchildren; rather, they thought in terms on instant gratification. The high credit card debt (not student loans) of the average college student also reflects the present orientation as opposed to a future orientation (i.e. buy now, pay later). The large annual budget deficits are arguably the effects of the childless and essentially short-run philosophy of life of the Keynesian Revolution. The continual thinking of living for the present and inattentiveness about the future seriously weakens the stability of the American economy. Not only is the growth of government a contributing factor to the lack of personal savings, but also shameful self interest is responsible.

Irresponsibility and the desire of people to be like *all the nations* are contributing factors to the growth of government. However, there is a third factor which is the failure of the church to *preach the word; be ready in season **and** out of season; reprove, rebuke, exhort, with great patience and instruction* (2 Tim. 4:2). Beginning in the late 19th century the church was not teaching the Word of God faithfully; in fact, theological liberalism was rampant in the churches. Evolution, German rationalism, and general abandoning of the Gospel infiltrated the churches, and many church leaders were enticed by modernism which denied the fundamental truth of the Bible. As a response to the growing apostasy, brothers Lyman and Milton Stewart financed a series of articles with the general title, *The Fundamentals*, published in twelve volumes between 1910-1915. Nearly a century later, the church is encountering similar challenges to the fundamentals of the Christian faith from within and outside the church. Dr. Mal Couch, founder and president of Tyndale Theological Seminary, was responsible for organizing the "Issues 2000 Conference" in conjunction with the publication of *The Fundamentals for the Twenty-First Century*. The failure of the church to teach the fundamentals is also responsible for statolatry.

The Great Depression is another factor that contributed to the growth of government since more countries introduced insurance and social services as a response. President Roosevelt's "New Deal," the transformation of the Federal Security Agency into the Department of Health, Education, and Welfare by President Eisenhower, and the "Great Society" of President Johnson significantly expanded federal responsibility in all categories of social concern thereby cultivating the current unconstitutional welfare state. Roosevelt's "Second New Deal" created Social Security in the United States. Currently in America, federal welfare expenses surpass defense spending. It was the growing idolatry of the United States in the 19th and 20th centuries, just as it was in ancient Israel, which led to the growth of government. Commenting on charity and welfare, Dr. Archie P. Jones wrote,

> The basically Biblical view of the nature of man and of the proper, limited duties of civil government which underlay our constitutions and bills of rights meant that civil government was to promote the general welfare of the whole people, and not engage in schemes for the restructuring of society or in legalized theft in order to provide "welfare" for selected groups of people. The carefully limited role of civil government in general and of the central or national government in particular under the Constitution was intended to leave the American people free to do what the Bible tells men to do: provide

charity and help to the truly needy.[47]

The unrelenting growth of government broadening like gangrene is a symptom in American society of a more serious apostasy from the fundamentals of the Christian faith. Big government will continue to exert greater sovereignty over the people, which will lead to even more wrongdoing, until the more serious issue of statolatry is given response. According to 1 Samuel 8, the growth of government is not the remedy for criminality since it is the basis for even great corruption. Americans have been seduced into thinking the civil government is the solution to all problems. The rise of totalitarian civil government is reminiscent of the godless rulers over Israel. When civil government is restricted to its God-given purpose of punishing wrongdoing (Rom. 13), the free market system will provide benefit to all concerned.

If the American economy declines, *the voice of the people* will be in favor of more government control. When people favor that option they truly do not understand the influence of historic Christianity on early America and the subsequent freedom which followed. Growth of government only brings greater corruption, but most Americans do not understand that simple fact. People are happy if the economy is booming, but if it ever declines the majority always demands more government programs to remedy the situation. The Great Depression (1929-1940) should be an obvious example.

Although Republican President Herbert Hoover (1874-1964) strived to overcome the Great Depression, the American economy had become dreadful near the end of his term. Americans desired a new President to help them through the crisis, and believed that leader was Franklin Delano Roosevelt (1882-1945). Roosevelt enticed the nation with a "New Deal" which led to his election as President in 1932. Although he promised to restore the economy, his New Deal actually stimulated little prosperity and may have extended the Depression; however, it did expand the control of the federal government over agriculture, business, industry which established cancerous precedents for government intrusion in the nation's free market economy, especially by the Federal Reserve System. The New

Deal shifted America significantly from a constitutional republic toward a socialistic democracy. When the Great Depression finally ended, the growth of government had usurped many unconstitutional responsibilities and many Americans were reliant upon the government for life necessities.

From the 1960s to 1980s, the American government was quite liberal. When Ronald Reagan (1911-2004) won the Presidency in 1980, he restored conservative values and practices. However, for nearly two decades a liberal Congress severely damaged the nation even though Presidents Reagan and Bush strived to reverse the damage and the welfare dependence of the nation. When it was time for George H. W. Bush to candidate for reelection, the American people were convinced the economy was confronting a crisis. Americans desired new leadership and elected Bill Clinton as President in 1992. Conservative values, free market economy, and limited government characteristic of Reagan's Presidency were severely challenged. The current President George W. Bush has followed in the conservative direction of the Republican Party during the 1980s and early 90s. Each time the economy is affected negatively the people demand more government control.

The populace frequently makes demand for a more efficient government. People naively say, "We want all the government we pay for." BumperTalk.com has a funny (but truthful) bumper sticker stating, "Be grateful we don't get all the government we pay for." One of the wisest actions of the Framers of the American Constitution in 1789 was to make the government inefficient by having people sit in Congress debating issues. The American populace is aggravated by the actions of Congress, but they do not understand that the Framers of the Constitution purposed Congress to do exactly what they are doing, namely, talking issues to death.

Speaking to an overflow Wilson Hall audience at the James Madison Day Convocation in March 2001, United States Supreme Court Justice Clarence Thomas stated the Constitution may appear to be "an anachronistic hindrance,"[48] but that hindrance was purposely created. James Madison, for instance, designed the "separation of powers not because it would lead to strong government but because it would lead to inefficient government." The Framers cognitively purposed to make the government inefficient to protect society by maintaining individual liberty; they had the wisdom to prevent the assemblage of political power within a sole branch of the national government.

The Federalist Papers were a series of essays published between 1787 and 1788 in several New York state newspapers to convince New York voters to ratify the proposed constitution; it was signed by Alexander Hamilton, James Madison, and John Jay under the pseudonym "Publius." One of the principal figures to draft the Constitution and later to become fourth President of the United States, James Madison wrote, "The accumulation of all powers, legislative, executive, and judiciary, in the same hands, whether of one, a few, or many, and whether hereditary, self-appointed, or elective, may justly be pronounced the very definition of tyranny" (Federalist No. 47).[49] Madison continued to write, "the three great departments of power should be separate and distinct" because it is an "invaluable precept in the science of politics."[50] The separate and distinct powers of the Constitution are frequently inefficient, but it furnishes an essential defense against the latent exploitation of governmental power. Nevertheless, people demand action principally from the President contrary to a "do nothing Congress." The insistence for action from the President is actually a demand for totalitarianism. When the general populace continues to make such demands for efficiency of that type, America is in a grave situation. John W. Robbins, president of the Trinity foundation, wrote, "There is a direct connection between the Reformation cry of *sola scriptura* and the American idea of the Constitution—not any man or body of men—as the supreme law of the land."[51]

The Influence of the Reformation[52]

It was his study of Scripture that led Martin Luther (1483-1546) to argue for liberty as the very essence of the Christian faith. In his essay, "On the Freedom of a Christian" (1520), he argued that the conscience belongs to God alone and thereby defended Christian charity and freedom against the subjective control of either church or state. He also wrote,

> With great caution and humility, yet with decision and firmness, he entered upon his work. "By the word," said he, "must we overthrow and destroy what has been set up by violence. I will not make use of force against the superstitious and unbelieving.... No one must be constrained. Liberty is the very essence of faith."[53]
>
> No man has a right to compel his brother in matters that are left free.... The Word of God and moral suasion must be allowed to do the work. paul preached against the idols in Athens, without touching one of them; and yet they fell in consequence of his preaching. "*Summa summarum*," said Luther, "I will preach, speak, write, but I will force no one; for faith must be voluntary.... I stood up against the Pope, indulgences, and all papists, but without violence or uproar. I only urged, preached, and declared God's Word, nothing else.... I did nothing, the Word did every thing. Had I appealed to force, all Germany might have been deluded with blood.... But what would have been the result? Ruin and desolation of body and soul. I therefore kept quiet, and gave the Word free course through the world."[54]

Christian freedom is a belief that Luther deduced from biblical teaching concerning faith. Since faith is a gift of God (Eph. 2:8-9; cf. Acts 5:31; 11:18; 14:27; Phil. 1:29; 2 Tim. 2:25), man does not believe the Gospel because he exercises his free will. In fact, Luther argued for the absolute bondage of the will to sin. Depraved humanity will not believe the Gospel unless God draws the individual (Jn. 6:44). Luther contended that God's Word alone produces faith in contrast to any human compulsion. The Word of God must be preached faithfully, but the effects are *according to the kind intention of His [God] will...according to His purpose who works all things after the counsel of His will* (Eph. 1:5, 11).

By teaching biblically that faith is a gift of God, Luther weak-ened the effects of the Roman Inquisition and the Holy Office, and the "Index Librorum Prohibitorum" (an index of forbidden books published by Pope Paul IV in 1559), and articulated a the-ological foundation for religious liberty. Historian Philip Schaff demonstrates the principle of freedom, articulated by the Reformers, so clearly proclaimed in principle by Christ. He wrote,

> He [Luther] draws a sharp line between temporal power which is confined to the body and worldly goods, and the spiritual government which belongs to God.... While opposing the Pope's tyranny, Luther was far from advo-cating the opposite extreme of license. He was thor-oughly imbued with the spirit of the Epistle to the Galatians.... He means liberty according to the gospel; liberty *in* Christ, not *from* Christ; and offers this as a basis for reconciliation.[55]

> On the ground of Christ's word...he drew a sharp distinction between the secular and spiritual power.... It sounds almost like a prophetic anticipation of the American separation of church and state when he says:—"God has ordained two governments among the children of Adam,—the reign of God under Christ, and the reign of the world under the civil magistrate, each with its own laws and rights.... As no one can descend to hell or ascend to heaven for me, as little can any one believe or disbelieve for me; as he cannot open or shut heaven or hell for me, neither can he force me to faith or unbelief.... Faith is a voluntary thing which cannot be forced. Yea, it is a divine work in the spirit. Hence it is a common saying which is also found in Augustin: Faith cannot and should not be forced on anybody."[56]

The Reformation in Law and Economics[57]

In addition to constitutionalism, egalitarianism, and reli-gious liberty (often associated with the political theories of John Locke and the founders of the American Republic) as social con-sequences of the Protestant Reformation, there was also further explanation of individual independence because of the emphasis upon the doctrine of justification. Robbins wrote, "The individual, for the first time in human history, was widely recognized as the direct creation of God, as the image of God, and as the redeemed of God.... It was the individual person—the human soul—who was freed from pagan and medieval tyranny by the Christian Reformation, and from that freedom arose a free, humane, and civilized society."[58] Nearly 500 years later, the Protestant Reformation has produced a revival affecting all qualities of church and societal life. Harold Berman, professor of law at Emory University, has demonstrated the role of individual conscience according to the Protestant influence.[59]

> ...the key to the renewal of law in the West from the sixteenth century on was the Protestant concept of the power of the individual, by God's grace, to change nature and to create new social relations through the exercise of his will. The Protestant concept of the individual became central to the development of the modern law of property and contract. Economic relations became contract.... The property and contractual rights so created were held to be sacred and inviolable, so long as they did not contravene conscience....[60]

Luther preached that all work should be done to the glory of God (cf. 1 Cor. 10:31). Roman Catholicism taught only the labor of monks and nuns could be done to the glory of God, but Luther opposed such unbiblical teaching. He taught work was a sacred calling whether one was ministering the gospel, plowing the field, or scrubbing floors all honest work is pleasing to God. The Protestant work ethic developed from this conviction, and was eventually responsible for the development of capitalism. The doctrines of the Reformation contributed to the idea of freedom for the market and society as apposite economic and political expressions. Capitalism developed as the economic expression of the doctrine of justification.

Robbins wrote, "One of Luther's most brilliant followers, John Calvin [1509-1564], systematized the theology of the

Reformation. The seventeenth-century Calvinists laid the foundations for both English and American civil rights and liberties: freedom of speech, press, and religion, the privilege against self-incrimination, the independence of juries, and right of habeas corpus, the right not to be imprisoned without cause."[61]

> The great American historian George Bancroft stated, "He that will not honor the memory, and respect the influence of Calvin, knows but little of the origin of American liberty." The famous German historian, Leopold von Ranke, wrote, "John Calvin was the virtual founder of America." John Adams, the second president of the United States, wrote: "Let not Geneva be forgotten or despised. Religious liberty owes it most respect."[62]

German sociologist Max Weber (1864-1920) wrote *The Protestant Ethic and the Spirit of Capitalism* in 1905 which articulated the Protestant ethic as a moral standard emphasizing asceticism, hard work, and serving God as the logical organization of one's life. Weber demonstrated capitalism as an historical development "in Protestant countries because they inculcated those virtues that led to the development of capitalism: hard work, honesty, frugality, thrift, punctuality. These virtues, coupled with the idea of a calling [predestination], provided the impetus ending serfdom and establishing a free political and economic order."[63] The Protestant revival of biblical theology and virtues in the 16th century is the reason for the development and growth of western capitalism and civilization, even though it was not the intent of the Reformers who strived only to preach justification before God in Jesus Christ alone.

Benefits and Snare of Capitalism

Spiritual revival as a result of the Protestant Reformation furnished a new motivation, responsibility, and understanding regarding the dignity of labor. The development of capitalism was the natural result of the Protestant work ethic. Andrew

Carnegie (1835-1919), American steel industrialist and philanthropist, wrote *The Gospel of Wealth* (1889) as an expression of his principles of good stewardship. Carnegie's writing articulated the benefits of capitalism.

> The "good old times" were not good old times. Neither master nor servant was as well situated then as to-day. A relapse to old conditions would be disastrous to both—not the least so to him who serves—and would sweep away civilization with it. But whether the change bc for good or ill, it is upon us, beyond our power to alter, and, therefore, to be accepted and made the best of. It is a waste of time to criticize the inevitable.
>
> To-day the world obtains commodities of excellent quality at prices which even the preceding generation would have deemed incredible. In the commercial world similar causes have produced similar results, and the race is benefited thereby. The poor enjoy what the rich could not before afford. What were the luxuries have become the necessaries of life. The laborer has now more comforts than the farmer had a few generations ago. The farmer has more luxuries than the landlord had, and is more richly clad and better housed. The landlord has books and pictures rarer and appointments more artistic than the king could then obtain.[64]

Nevertheless, there is also a snare of capitalism. Alexis de Tocqueville, a Frenchman who came to America in the 1800s and wrote a book about democracy in America stated, "America is great because she is good and if America ever ceases to be good, America will cease to be great."[65] If men of any culture cease to be good (according to God's standard) they will also cease to be great, and the wealth and luxury of a capitalistic system will become morally debasing rather than providing commendable character. Money is neither good nor evil. However, when men love money more than God, they will find themselves embracing *all sorts of evil* (1 Tim. 6:10). *He who trusts in his riches will fall, but the righteous will flourish like the **green** leaf*

(Prov. 11:28). Scripture states, *Do not weary yourself to gain wealth, cease from your consideration of it. When you set your eyes on it, it is gone. For **wealth** certainly makes itself wings, like an eagle that flies **toward** the heavens* (23:4-5).

The Protestant work ethic is not to be confused with the self-centered modern consumer society. A truly biblical economic applies equal justice under law, free markets, personal responsibility, responsibility to society, right to private property, and stewardship of God's creation. The work ethic is not solely concerned with hard work, but serves God by being other-centered in its formation and function. The work ethic encourages working diligently which results in capital development, diligent saving which results in capital accumulation, and giving as much as possible which means capital sharing. One must recognize the blessing of yielding money and wealth to God, and to understand every possession as a gift of God to be used for His glory by giving through tithes, offerings, and charity. The blessings of the free market are great when individuals think biblically regarding wealth. Deuteronomy 8:10-11 communicates a wonderful principle: *"When you have eaten and are satisfied, you shall bless the LORD your God for the good land which He has given you. "Beware lest you forget the LORD your God by not keeping His commandments and His ordinances and His statutes....*

CHAPTER 2

SNARE OF WORLD ECONOMY

Wilfred J. Hahn

According to many global observers, the modern world is getting better and more prosperous every day. A benevolent, man-made, world economy is blooming and offers a globally-integrated safety net, material delights, and consumer freedoms for humanity. Such a view is entirely dependent upon a selective perspective. These global observers base their conclusions upon a single dimension—materialistic prosperity. According to this definition, human prosperity is being established on the coattails of new technology, financial innovation, and consumer free-doms. Moreover, in these terms, "prosperity" has boomed like never before in the past few centuries (especially during the past few decades).

However, this new world is not as safe or free as advertised. In fact, it masks a process leading to the exact opposite, that is, ensnarement and entanglement with a humanist agenda. Not only is the evidence supporting this conclusion clearly observ-able today, Bible prophecy states that the people of an endtime world will find themselves captive in a trap. For many, that day is already here.

A World Economic Boom: Brave New World or Snare?

The global materialists have no lack of statistics supporting their view. Mainly, they point to the rapid developments of the past century or so, in terms of wealth and technology. Total world financial wealth has multiplied by at least 40 times this past century to approximately $250 trillion,[1] using modern definitions. They take comfort from the fact that never before in the entire history of mankind has wealth accumulated so quickly and to such an enormous level. Of course, a contributing reason why growth in wealth has jumped so sharply is because of rapid population growth throughout much of the past century. One economist estimates that more wealth was created in the 20th century than during the entire history of mankind.[2] Viewed since the time of Christ, the monetary value of the average human's economic output in the world has risen to over $6,000 by the year 2001 from only $445 or so at the start of the first millennium AD (figures are in US dollars adjusted for inflation).[3] Employing this "financialized" definition, per capita output (the average annual income for each person in the world) has multiplied by at least 13 times over this period.

The global materialists proudly list other achievements. World-wide economic integration has also expanded sharply in recent centuries, having experienced its first major acceleration in the Gilded Age of the late 19th century of the British Empire. Today cross-border trade in goods, services, and capital flows are at new peaks. For all intents and purposes, a one-world economy exists today, spewing out goods and services of every whim. The same is true for the integration of global monetary systems.

While many predict the day that a single currency will soon rule the world, they have already missed the event. While not in name, as this would be too obvious in any case, a one-world currency effectively already exists. These days no economic player of any size deals in foreign currency transactions without the use of financial hedges. In this mostly unseen world of derivative instruments (which in itself has been the fastest booming financial phenomenon of all history) currency exchange rates can be fixed to each other. Through the use of these financial instruments, a one-world currency system already exists. Combining the various types of derivatives instruments, they today represent a notional monetary value equivalent to more than six times the annual size of the entire world economy.[4]

Another claimed advance has been in the forms of wealth. Much of what society regards as wealth today finds an expression in the form of stocks and bonds or other types of financial securities. Advances in this area have been exponential during the past century, especially in the past two decades. However, subject to violent ups and downs, securities markets wealth now amounts to more than two and a half times the value of all the annual income of every person on earth, increased by a factor of four over the past two decades alone according to this writer's estimates.

It may be hard to imagine that real wealth can be created this easily. This modern-day definition of wealth could be easily disputed. However, what is clear to see is that a boom in monetary and financial wealth is a phenomenon that is widely encouraged as the world lusts for wealth and gain. Certainly, a lot of this increase in monetarily-defined "securities wealth" is not real. Nevertheless, it is an apparition of wealth—real or false—that is highly alluring and visible. Its values are quoted every day, in fact, minute by minute.

Many more aspects of the economic and financial phenomena of the current time could be documented, not to mention the impact of the recent technological age. However, what do all these epochal trends really signify? The cheerleaders of these developments (mainly humanists) count them as evidence of human progress and enlightenment, offering mankind new freedoms and an elevated existence. Man and his worldly achievements are now worshipped. However, these trends all ignore a very important fact: man cannot live by bread alone (cf. Mt. 4:4).

Elements Behind an Endtime Economic Snare

It is beyond doubt that the material life standard and quality of life of a sizable segment of the world's population has indeed increased. Yet, as will be yet documented in this chapter, with the increased potential for physical comforts, come heightened vulnerabilities of both physical and spiritual proportions.

Why is it that after many millennia of human existence, world economic developments have exponentially boomed so suddenly? Documentation could be offered of all the contributing streams to the financial flood of recent history. Perhaps such examinations could include the impact of fractional reserve banking begun in Holland in the 15th century, the critical and necessary technological inventions at various times, the philosophical and religious groundswells that gave foment to capitalism, or Anglobalization.[5] Such historical research would find many contributing streams. Yet, the question remains mostly unanswered: why after thousands of years of glacial change, should such a materialistic phenomenon erupt upon the world stage in such a short space of time? Why did it not happen earlier or even later? Could it be part of the plan of the cosmos? Is it an endtime development?

Scripture provides some answers. In fact, the reader does not have to look very far into the Bible before beginning to uncover clues. The main constructs of the cosmos that begin to answer our question are already foreshadowed in the opening chapters of the Bible. The account of Adam and Eve in Eden (i.e. Gen. 1-3) forewarns how mankind could be deceived by three main temptations. It foreshadows how at the end of days, humanity could be duped into receiving a ruler that comes in the name of the world—a false Christ—settling for a cheapened heaven on earth and willingly opening themselves to economic ensnarement.

The majority of people would do exactly as the Apostle John counseled against. *Do not love the world or anything in the world. If anyone loves the world, the love of the Father is not in him. For everything in the world—the cravings of sinful man, the lust of his eyes and the boasting of what he has and does—comes not from the Father but from the world* [mammon] (1 Jn. 2:15-16). Mentioned by John are the three main temptations of the world: lust of the flesh (*cravings of sinful man*), lust of the eyes, and boasting of what man has and does. All three of these temptations were involved in mankind's Edenic fall into sin. The forbidden fruit was good for food (*the cravings of sinful man*); Adam and Eve wanted dominion over the tree (*the lust of his eyes*), which was the very thing they were not to covet; and they fell for "knowledge" or the key to self-determination (*boasting of what he has and does*). Prophetically, these three temptations can be seen to be at work in the world globally today as never before.

Preying on Three Human Weaknesses

Satan himself is working these human weaknesses to maximum advantage. Tactically, he targeted the same three innate vulnerabilities when tempting Christ in the wilderness. In Matthew 4 and Luke 4, there are the accounts of how Jesus was led out into the wilderness by the Holy Spirit where he fasted for 40 days. At the end of the fast, Satan, sensing an opportune moment, approached Christ with three proposals. As Christ was both man and God, sharing in all of the sufferings and temptations known to mankind, Satan targeted these three greatest vulnerabilities of Jesus' humanity.

Initially, preying on Christ's physical weakness and hunger, Satan appealed to the human flesh, enticing him to step outside the will of God to satiate himself by commanding a stone to become bread. Christ withstood him and replied, *"It is written: 'Man does not live on bread alone, but on every word that comes from the mouth of God'"* (Mt. 4:4). To the contrary today, it is readily apparent that much of the world of Christian heritage has already been seduced with this offer. Living in surroundings of consumptive largesse and apparent wealth, many are happy to settle for a world that promises no unsatisfied material cravings. They have put their stomachs ahead of God. The process of globalization has helped lubricate the slide.

Next, Satan tempted Christ with an appeal to the innate human lust for power and dominion. *Again, the devil took him to a very high mountain and showed him all the kingdoms of the world and their splendor. "All this I will give to you,"* he said, *"if you will bow down and worship me"* (4:8-9). Satan offered Jesus the intoxicating mix of power and dominion. As Satan does have the authority to dispense *all the kingdoms of the world and their splendor* over a Godless world, Christ countered this temptation saying, *"Away from me, Satan! For it is written: 'Worship the Lord your God, and serve him only.'"* (4:10). This statement confirms another: *You cannot serve both God and Money* [mammon, KJV] (Mt. 6:24). The world today is effectively ruled by elites that have accepted this offer. They are found in every country of the world. Even the poorest corners of earth have their despots and elites. These people—greater or lesser—have chosen to take the power, the money and the high-life, and work for the kingdom of mammon and its diabolical endgame.

Lastly, Satan lured Christ to self-determination. He asked Jesus to boast about his position, tempting him to arrogance and self-will, that is, to step outside the will and leading of His Father. Had Christ thrown himself down as requested, it would have been an act of *boasting*. He would have tested the will of his Father, taking an initiative on His own.

In a sense, Christ's trial was prophetic. While He resisted all three temptations, He would know that Satan would target these same three vulnerabilities in order to mislead an endtime, apostate world. Through these worldly affections, harbored in the hearts of every human, mankind would be ensnared into a diabolical endtime plan as complicitors, unwitting pawns, captives, or the suppressed.

Together, they lie at the root, providing the very impetus and energy, of an endtime globalization of mankind. Fitting the times, Satan's three temptations today are sophisticated. His proposals now operate under the aegis of globalism, financial monetarism, and technology. Each has its part in a developing endtime snare.

The Deceptions of Wealth

Measuring the state of the world from a materialistic perspective has its problems; it is a technique highly susceptible to deceit. The Bible explicitly warns of *the deceitfulness of wealth* (Mt. 13:22; Mk. 4:19). It is a one-dimensional measure that ignores spiritual, social, relational, emotional, and mental well-being thereby leading to a trap. Christ himself makes this point clear.

"Be careful, or your hearts will be weighed down with dissipation, drunkenness and the anxieties of life, and that day will close on you unexpectedly like a trap. For it will come upon all those who live on the face of the whole earth. Be always on the watch, and pray that you may be able to escape all that is about to happen, and that you may be able to stand before the Son of Man" (Lk. 21:34-36).

Here Christ clearly tells his listeners *that day will close on* [them] *unexpectedly like a trap*. The reader should be alerted to the fact that certain developments will emerge during that end-time that will ensnare many people and hold them hostage. Apparently, many people will be unable neither to understand the times nor to resist the trap very easily.

Jesus Christ reveals why much of humanity will fall into this trap. Conditions of *dissipation, drunkenness and the anxieties of life* are named as some of the contributing influences. All of these human attitudes can and do find expression in financial and economic terms today. In fact, a modern day economist would have no trouble finding equivalent words, such as, consumer society, leisure and entertainment boom, booming sin industries, a debt trap, employment insecurity, economic instabilities (and the list could continue). Indeed, the Christian needs to be discerning of an endtime trap.

The current group of key power-broking countries, which is hardly more than ten countries representing less than one-sixth of the earth's population, has already laid the groundwork for a worldwide snare. In fact, many of the citizens of this bloc of countries are themselves trapped. It is encroaching; manifold are all of a financial or commercial nature, and its process of invasion resulting in economic enslavement. These are not philosophical statements. They can be documented factually.

Impetuously Into a Spreading Money Snare

The world continues its impetuous run into financialization, a process that assigns a monetary value or transaction to an ever greater share of human activities. Human activity is being captured progressively in financial form. Probably as much as 60%-80% of human activity in the Western world is already counted or logged through a financial transaction.

Distinguished over the past two centuries, that represents at least a tripling of the role of money.

Indeed, the invasion of modern-day money has been rapid. In ages past, the state took control of money and credit and determined their value and operation by virtual fiat. Money has become a controlled (or more aptly, a manipulated) medium, not only nationally but also globally. Through means of central and fractional-reserve banking,[6] the medium of money has become the world's most controlling and invasive medium. Surely only a very abbreviated perspective on the devices and structures of world money systems is offered here. However, in the man-created order, there can be nothing else as powerful, as ubiquitous, as omnipresent, as manipulative and controlling, as the system of modern monetarism. It is not without reason that the Bible contrasts *God and Money*, as it the systematic idolatry of money (mammon) alone can approach the omnipresence and power of God on earth.

Maddening Modern-Day Money

Money has always existed in one type or another, yet it is only in recent centuries that it has taken a form both captivating and motivating broad human action; even transforming man's very thought lives into values that can be expressed monetarily. What is considered money today would be thought laughable in earlier times, that is, bits of cyber and biodegradable paper. The role of money, material progress, and prosperity has changed in such a way so that it intersects human life at almost every turn.

It seems unimaginable that an inanimate thing like money, which at one time served only as a medium of exchange, should become something so large and complex, requiring legions of people to manage the myriad arrangements of who owes it and who owns it. In the rich nations of the world, approximately 2 out of every 13 people are employed in some type of financial service industry.[7]

Even with today's powerful and inexpensive computing capacity, it requires a lot of people to administer the rights and privileges of owners and debtors. What it signifies is that there are many, many layers of financial relationships (obligations and enslavements in other words) that hang as millstones around the necks of humanity. Humanity today now lives in a cage where everything is defined by costs, prices, monetary gains and losses, which are all expressed in numerical form. At the same time, people know less about truth and values, either human or spiritual, than ever before.

At the Behest of Greed and Crises

The world's financial web continues to spread quickly giving life to new rulers and powers. Both greed and financial crises speed the encroachment. In recent years, worries of global financial instabilities are providing speedy impetus. Consider some of the ideas being proposed to address world financial instabilities:

- The creation of a World Financial Authority, an institution that would set policies for all financial institutions in the world.
- An establishment of an International Credit Insurance Corporation.
- Exchange rate system reform. The most radical form of this idea is to adopt a single world currency, issued by a World Monetary Authority.
- Reforms in the way international debt problems are resolved, allowing countries to declare bankruptcy protection in the same way as corporations. This solution would lead to an international bankruptcy court.[8]

While not a complete list by any means, it is obvious that most, if not all, initiatives point in the same direction, which is towards an increasingly centralized, global financial system. All of these above-mentioned proposals have their logic. Some are more practical than others. Which of these proposals will move forward? It is difficult to predict since it will likely take another big crisis to push the consensus to a conclusion. It is without a doubt that the risk of a major world financial crisis is extremely

high *and rising*. Financial markets are experiencing great instabilities and deceptions. As busts follow booms, and spectacular
bankruptcies follow high-flying business ventures closely, an
uncontrolled bust will inevitably occur again. In fact, one is
overdue. It would not be speculative to believe that the next one
could be the biggest, most globally-interlinked economic down-
turn of all time. If this is the economic collapse of the
Tribulation,[9] then time is indeed short.

The Rapid Annex of the Kingdom of Mammon

It is undoubtedly true that the worship of mammon today is
more unified across the world than ever before. This belief system has a common expression and language even more so than
at any other time since the rise of the Tower of Babel. The worship of the god of Gross Domestic Product (GDP) and the goal
of its annual and continuous growth has swept the world.
Monetary economics and numerical quantities have become the
new common language of this religion; the computers and
telecommunication systems are its megaphones and rapid conduits. The knowledge of how to stimulate economic growth and
to boost financial market values in money terms is considered
the new sacred wisdom. Financial markets, investment
exchanges, and central banks are the new temple sites.

This whole materialistic belief system, embracing a greater
portion of humanity more now than at any other time in history, is a process that has accelerated noticeably to blinding swiftness since the 1970s. It is only in this last shard of time, since
the prophetic pronouncement of Apostle Paul quoted earlier,
which amounts to less than 2% of the time span since his day,
has this monetary materialism taken such deep root.

Today, materialistic doctrines of money and economics are
finding a foothold in virtually every society in the world. Many
former communistic countries (e.g., the nations that were part of
the economic union under the United Soviet States of Russia, the
USSR) are now worshipping at this altar. The Chinese, as well,
in the quest for greater prosperity and world significance have
changed their communist beliefs to embrace some of the "free

market" principles of modern-day capitalism. They are proving to be very adept students of market-based economics. The Chinese, in addition to other major Asian nations, may yet eclipse the economic might of the United States and Europe. Even Islamic and Hindu nations, religions that have been slow to embrace materialistic values, are coming progressively to its schema. In recent years, gradual changes have taken place in their religious interpretations and financial systems that serve to bring them into line with the new global materialistic order ever increasingly. The pursuit of GDP growth, liberal trade policies, market economics, and monetarism are all policies finding a bigger global following. In many ways, this convergent path to materialism can be seen as a parallel, or handmaiden, to the ecumenical movement in world religions.

An Endtime Economic Snare: A Prophetic View

According to this writer's understanding of Scripture, God reveals much information about the monetary and economic condition of the world in the endtimes. Certainly, Scripture does not use the financial jargon that is familiar to society today. Yet, the foreshadowing of such endtime conditions is clear.

There are numerous biblical indicators that the people of the last days will be smitten with enormous, unsatiated greed, that is, rampant materialism. The most direct prophecy comes from Apostle Paul. In 2 Timothy 3:2, he clearly states that in the last days, *people would be...lovers of money*. There are other indicators in the Bible that this will take place.

A prominent financial characteristic of the last days is clearly revealed in the Book of James. *You have hoarded wealth in the last days*, he charges in his prophecy to rich people (Jas. 5:3). James continues his rebuke: *You have lived on the earth in luxury and self-indulgence. You have fattened yourselves in the day of slaughter* (5:5). It is a development that is already well in progress today. As already documented briefly, financial wealth has virtually exploded throughout this past century.

It is instructive to note that the last of the seven churches addressed by Apostle John in the Book of Revelation is one that has become fat, wealthy, and contented (i.e., one that has fallen asleep). The attitude of this Laodicean church is complacent and smug. This church says, *"I am rich; I have acquired wealth and do not need a thing"* (Rev. 3:17). If this church is intended to be an allegory of the church in the endtime, the last church, it certainly parallels the explosion of wealth foretold of the last days.

The account of Babylon the Great in Revelation 17 particularly indicates just how pervasive will be an endtime fixation with trade, wealth, and luxury throughout the world. The attitude of this Babylon is very similar to the church. While the Laodicean church had *acquired wealth and do*[es] *not need a thing*, Babylon the Great, Mother of Prostitutes, also regards herself complacently. She boasts, *"I sit as queen; I am not a widow, and I will never mourn"* (18:7).

It is evident from Revelation 18 that Babylon the Great is an endtime regime that will be global in nature. Its reign over the entire earth parallels the global reach of the fourth future kingdom that Daniel the Prophet foresaw in his four separate visions. The three previous kingdoms or kings that Daniel saw were indeed the leading powers of the known world in their day, yet they were not global as known today. Only the last kingdom is stated to have a world-wide scope spanning the earth. *All the nations* (14:8; 18:3, 23), *the kings of the earth* (18:3, 9), *the merchants of the earth* (18:3, 11), and the *world's great men* (18:23) are constituents of it.

Represented in this case is the nucleus of a coordinated international trading system that serves as part of a reigning world kingdom that *will devour the whole earth, trampling it down and crushing it* (Dan. 7:23). Here the Bible prophecies of the all-controlling aspect of this commercial regime operating under the sweet guise of prosperity. In order for a system such as described to overcome and devour the whole earth, global interconnection and worldwide mechanisms of coordination and influence are required. This is happening in many ways, along numerous conduits, rapidly converging towards the point where one man will take power at its apex and *shall destroy many in their prosperity* (8:25, NKJV).

Emergence of Centralized Economic Titans

Today, there are many systematic, endtime developments that function together to speed the world to the point of a centralized domination. For illustration, just two of these will be briefly reviewed before returning to an analysis of additional Scriptural evidence.

The first example is multi-national corporations (MNCs). The rise of the MNC within the past 50 years has been truly astounding. Whereas only a very small number existed at the turn of the century, indeed even as late as the early 1950s, today they control a significant portion of the entire world economy. In the space of five decades, this commercial fraternity has increased its share of world economic output by more than 10 times since the early 1950s.[10] These companies are headed by executives that have been schooled in similar ideologies. Their global activities represent the very seedbed of the rapid, economic globalization that has swept the world in recent decades. Seen through this prism, globalization is really nothing more that a world-wide convergence to a system where human behavior is driven by the incentive of material gain and the love of money. It is not incidental that a global securities boom documented earlier has played a key facilitating role in the rise of these global titans.

Global titans are a recent phenomenon, having moved into the power vacuum left by the weakened sovereignty of nations as the world has become rapidly globalized and marshaled by global capital. Global organizations such as the World Trade Organization (WTO), the United Nations (UN), and the Organization of Economic Cooperation and Development (OECD) have sponsored a virtual landslide of global regulatory reform in recent years that has opened the door to the free reign of global capital and the global business activities of MNCs. Over 90% of all rule changes in the past decade and a half, which is literally thousands of initiatives by over 100 countries, have been in the direction of giving more influence and reign to global money flows and direct foreign investing (the latter being mostly the domain of MNCs). Understood in the context of economic and financial history, these changes are both sudden and monumental. All indicators seem as if there is a big hurry to redistribute economic power in the world. Yet, what is the urgency behind all this frenzied corporate activity? The title of a recent management book, *Race for the World*, sums it up well.[11]

Convergent Global Financial Power

As most people already know, the world has a very powerful banking system. This modern network has also only come truly into a position of great power within the past 100 years or so. It is true that there have been international banking houses for many hundreds of years. However, the modern fractional-reserve system has only come into its own as a strong global influence in the past century. There were only 17 central banks in the world in the year 1900. Today there are approximately 10 times as many. Every major country now has a bank system based upon the fractional-reserve system.

As world trade and investment began to boom after World War II, the Bank of International Settlements (BIS) emerged as a coordinator of world banking activities. Based in Basle, Switzerland, it had originally been established to oversee the post World War I reparation payments of Germany and others. Today, virtually all central banks in the world are members of the BIS or act in accordance with its ordinances. In recent years the BIS has been attempting to revamp a universal set of rules and standards for all banks; it is a monumental project, called Basle II. It is so great and important that it is taking much longer than expected. What was originally planned to be completed by 2000 has now been delayed to at least 2006.

Why so long? Because this set of rules will be effectively apportioning world financial power. It is a battle for supremacy. Some global banking conglomerates are already very large in some financial sectors. For example, the seven largest banks active in derivatives markets and currency trading account for over 95% world share. It is sufficient to state that the new conventions being proposed by Basle II will be the key determinants in establishing future world financial power. Multi-national corporations and central-banking are but two examples of fast-emerging bastions of economic and financial power that play an integral part in setting an endtime economic snare.

A Trap Unfolds: A World Full of Slaves Emerges in the Endtimes

Large divisions of society in the rich nations of the world are already trapped. Many have been ensnared by debt, financial obligations to a high lifestyle, and long work days due to covetousness, lust, and the love of money. There is no shortage of individuals or companies that seek to take advantage of these vulnerabilities, *even to promote them*. Marketing agencies and psychologists are hired to study ways of ensnaring people by their lusts which often involves deception. The same perversions were noted during the idolatrous, Old Testament times of Israel and Judah. The false seers prophesied smooth things, that is, prosperity and peace as far as the eye could see.

God's prophets spoke otherwise. A few of God's many admonishments through Jeremiah the Prophet follow. *"You have not obeyed me; you have not proclaimed freedom for your fellow countrymen."* (Jer. 34:17). *"Among my people are wicked men who lie in wait like men who snare birds and like those who set traps to catch men. Like cages full of birds, their houses are full of deceit; they have become rich and powerful and have grown fat and sleek. Their evil deeds have no limit; they do not plead the case of the fatherless to win it, they do not defend the rights of the poor."* (5:26-28).

It is obvious that many people today became enslaved by the economic systems in the times of the Old Testament. The ultimate result? God eventually punished Judah and Israel severely.

Commenting on modern times, even as the apparitions of wealth and its financial imitations are amassing in unprecedented manners, economic slavery is enveloping the world. Paradoxically, even while "consumer choice" is expanding and many societies are at the seeming historical apex of prosperity, more people are trapped than at any time in history. Personal debt levels are at all-time highs around the world and continue to rise. A greater portion of household wealth is captive to globally-interlinked financial developments. Many retirement systems are destined for default as populations age, yet another unprecedented endtime phenomenon. A long list of factors could be documented here. Meanwhile, most citizens uncritically accept the mantras of "choice" and "freedom." Yet, these concepts are so misused that their very claim raises suspicions of deliberate deception. Sociologists now speak of the "paradox of choice." When the amount of choice becomes overwhelming, it can lead to anxiety and unhappiness. Even choice is a form of a trap.

Given to Perversions

God's longsuffering nature is balanced by the fact that He is also not mocked. At some point, refusal to heed His Word's warnings will lead to total perversion. In fact, a state of permanence can be reached where God himself will promote mankind's slide into idolatry and to give them over to perversions willfully. There are accounts in the Old Testament of a similar occurrence in God's dealing with Israel and Judah through the prophets. The Jewish people reached a point where their actions could not be reversed. After this point, it was God himself who put the lying spirits into the mouths of the false prophets. These lies met a willing reception: the itching ears of a society that pined for ease, wealth, and the fulfillment of fleshly desires.

Though only God knows, this writer is persuaded to believe that the entire world is already at this point where human actions will not be reversed. Globalism, market-based economics, massive global economic imbalances, increasing indebtedness, extreme stratification of wealth, society-wide endorsement of greed, *and much more* are setting the stage for the fulfillment of the impending Apocalypse. God or mammon? The world has chosen mammon. It is for this reason that great troubles lie ahead for unredeemed mankind.

A Challenge to Endtime Saints

Not only does an endtime, global regime as partly reflected

by Babylon the Great entrap great many people, but also it is inherently inhospitable to believers. *"Rejoice, saints and apostles and prophets! God has judged her for the way she treated you"* (Rev. 18:20). *"In her was found the blood of prophets and of the saints and of all who have been killed on the earth."* (18:24). The idolatries, humanism, and love of money underlying the advance of this global commercial/financial system are potentially deadly to Christians today.

How well is this emerging world system treating Christians? Are believers today comfortable living in it? Revelation 18:4 implores saints during the tribulation not to have any complicity with her: *"Come out of her, my people, so that you will not share in her sins, so that you will not receive any of her plagues."* The same admonition needs to be heeded today by Christians during this current time of endtimes stage-setting.[12]

Nevertheless, despite all that has been written, there is hope. Although conditions may seem difficult and falsehood and traps leave hardships in all directions, the Bible (as expected) provides the answer. In spite of all his heart-wrenching words, Jeremiah, provides a comforting promise: *"But blessed is the man who trusts in the LORD, whose confidence is in him. He will be like a tree planted by the water that sends out its roots by the stream. It does not fear when heat comes; its leaves are always green. It has no worries in a year of drought and never fails to bear fruit."* (Jer. 17:7-8). Living this life in the "Age of Global Capital," Christians can strive to stay mindful of David's exhortation: *though your riches increase, do not set your heart on them* (Ps. 62:10).

CHAPTER 3

ECONOMY OF THE FUTURE

Ron J. Bigalke Jr. and Thomas D. Ice

And he cried out with a mighty voice, saying, "Fallen, fallen is Babylon the great! And she has become a dwelling place of demons and a prison of every unclean spirit, and a prison of every unclean and hateful bird. "For all the nations have drunk of the wine of the passion of her immorality, and the kings of the earth have committed *acts of* immorality with her, and the merchants of the earth have become rich by the wealth of her sensuality"(Rev. 18:2-3).

"He who has the gold, makes the rules" is a popular slogan. At no time in all of history will the truth of this slogan be more evident than during the second half of the tribulation.

Babylon: A Biblical Wall Street

Throughout the Bible, Babylon is portrayed as a major commercial entity with enormous prophetic significance. Nebuchadnezzar and his empire, Babylon, are depicted as the head of gold on the figure in Daniel 2, implying great wealth. From Genesis to Revelation, the Bible associates Babylon with economic prosperity. Babylon has vast wealth. It is *the beauty of kingdoms* (Isa. 13:19), *the golden city* (14:4), *a golden cup* from which *all the nations have drunk* (Jer. 51:7); it is *abundant in treasures* (51:13).[1] Even extra-biblical tradition recognizes the second millennium B.C. ruler Hammurabi as the father of fractional reserve banking and inflation. Thus, it is not surprising to find a biblical association in Revelation 18 between Babylon, the

Antichrist, and commerce.

Revelation 17 and 18 articulate a relationship understood throughout the pages of Scripture. Religion, politics, and economics are consistently intertwined and associated with Babylon, a synonym for the kingdom of man. Economics and politics have always been utilized by those who would usurp devotion reserved only for God. Such a mixture will reach its zenith under Antichrist's tyranny during the tribulation. The focus of his coercive economic policies will revolve around the well-known mark of the beast: 666.

The Tribulation Trademark: 666

Either the right to rule of God or Satan is the core issue of the tribulation period God will demonstrate unequivocally that He alone has the right to rule. For the only time in history, people will have a deadline for declaring their allegiance to the gospel. Throughout the past 2000 years, people have been at different stages in believing or rejecting the gospel. People believe or reject this message at various points in their lives: some in childhood, some as young adults, and some at middle age or as seniors. During the time of the tribulation, the process will be accelerated (or forced) because of the mark of the beast, which means all humanity will be consciously divided into two segments: believers and unbelievers in the gospel of Jesus Christ. The polarizing issue is the mark of the beast (Rev. 13:11-18).

The mark of the beast has been the focal point of more rhetoric, ridicule, argumentation, and speculation than possibly any other single item in the Bible. The Bible teaches that it will be the false prophet, the spokesman for false religion, who will lead the campaign for the mark of the beast. Revelation 13:15 is clear that the key issue is worship of *the image of the beast*. The mark of the beast is simply a vehicle to force people to demonstrate their allegiance to either Jesus Christ or the Antichrist. All people will be polarized into two groups. It will be impossible to take a position of neutrality or indecision on this matter. Scripture is clear that those who do not receive the mark will be killed.

All classes of humanity will be forced to take sides: the small and the great, and the rich and the poor, and the free men and the slaves" (13:16). Dr. Robert L. Thomas notes the language "extends to all people of every civic rank...all classes ranked according to wealth...covers every cultural category.... The three expressions are a formula for universality."[2] Scripture is specific: the false prophet will require a *mark* of loyalty and devotion to the beast, and it will be *on their right hand, or on their forehead* (13:16).

There are several uses of the word "mark" in Scripture. It is used many times in Leviticus as a distinguishing characteristic, usually related to leprosy, rendering an individual ceremonially unclean. Interestingly, Ezekiel 9:4 uses *mark* similar to John's usage in Revelation. And the LORD said to him, *"Go through the midst of the city, even through the midst of Jerusalem, and put a mark on the foreheads of the men who sigh and groan over all the abominations which are being committed in its midst."* Here the mark was one of preservation, similar to the manner that blood on the doorposts spared those in the Passover from the death angel. In Ezekiel, the mark is placed on the forehead, which anticipates use of the term in Revelation. All seven instances of the Greek word *charagma* ("mark" or "sign") in the Greek New Testament appear in Revelation, and all refer to *the mark of the beast* (Rev. 13:16-17; 14:9, 11; 16:2; 19:20; 20:4). Dr. Thomas explained how the word was used in ancient times.

> The mark must be some sort of branding similar to that given soldiers, slaves, and temple devotees in John's day. In Asia Minor, devotees of pagan religions delighted in the display of such a tatoo [sic] as an emblem of ownership by a certain god.... In Egypt, Ptolemy Philopator I branded Jews, who submitted to registration, with an ivy leaf in recognition of their Dionysian worship (cf. *3 Macc.* 2:29). This meaning resembles the long-time practice of carrying signs to advertise religious loyalties (cf. Isa. 44:5)...and follows the habit of branding slaves with the name or special mark of their owners (cf. Gal. 6:17). *Charagma* ("Mark") was a term for the images or names of emperors on Roman coins, so it fittingly could apply

to the beast's emblem put on people.[3]

Some wonder why an exclusive term, as *mark*, is used to designate identification with Antichrist. Antichrist's mark appears to be a parody of the plan of God, especially God's *sealing* of the 144,000 witnesses (Rev. 7). God's seal of His witnesses is most likely invisible and for the purpose of protection from the Antichrist. On the other hand, Antichrist offers protection from the wrath of God—a promise he cannot deliver—and his mark is visible and external. Since unbelievers receive the mark of the beast willingly, it must be a point of pride to have Satan, in essence, as one's owner. Dr. Thomas wrote, "It could just as well denote loyalty, ownership, and protection, just as the seal given the slaves of God. The verb χαράσσω (*charassō*, "I engrave") is the source of *charagma* (cf. Acts 17:29). It will be visible and the point of recognition for all in subjugation to the beast" (cf. 13:7; 14:9; 16:2; 19:20; 20:4).[4]

The Treacherous Ticket

In addition to serving as a visible indicator of devotion to the Antichrist, the *mark* will be the required medium for commercial transactions during the last half of the tribulation. Revelation 13:17 states, *and he provides that no one should be able to buy or to sell, except the one who has the mark, either the name of the beast or the number of his name*. This has been the dream of every tyrant throughout history: to control his subjects completely so he alone determines who can buy or sell. Historian Sir William Ramsay noted, in the days when the book of Revelation was given to the apostle John, Roman emperor Domitian "carried the theory of imperial divinity and the encouragement of 'delation' to the most extravagant point...that in one way or another every Asian must stamp himself overtly and visibly as loyal, or be forthwith disqualified from participation in ordinary social life and trading."[5] History still remains for the yet future leader of the revived Roman Empire to perfect such a practice with the aid of the coming cashless society and modern computer technology.[6]

Throughout history many have appointed certain groups of people to death. Yet, there have always been means for a certain number to hide or escape oppression. As technology becomes more advanced, it seems that greater potential will exist to eliminate virtually every means of escape. In fact, such a scenario is corroborated by the Greek word *dunétai* ("provides") in Revelation 13:17, which conveys the notion of what "can" or "cannot" be done. The Antichrist will not allow anyone to buy or sell without the mark, and the coming cashless society will be the means he will use to enact his tyrannical policy. Control of the economy at the individual level on the basis of a *mark* corresponds perfectly with the biblical account of the future control of global commerce by the Antichrist, as outlined in Revelation 17-18.

The second half of Revelation 13:17 describes the mark as *either the name of the beast or the number of his name*. Precisely, this means the "number of the beast's name is one and the same with the name…. The equivalence means that as a name, it is written in letters, but as a number, the name's equivalent is in numbers."[7] The Antichrist's name will be expressed numerically as *six hundred and sixty-six* (666).

Calculating the Number

Here is wisdom. Let him who has understanding calculate the number of the beast, for the number is that of a man; and his number is six hundred and sixty-six (Rev. 13:18).

At this point, the apostle John changes his prophecy from one recording what he sees to one who now gives interpretative direction to his readers concerning what has been reported.

A reading of Revelation reveals that the wicked will not understand the tribulational events because of their moral rejection of Jesus Christ as Lord and Savior. In contrast, wisdom and understanding will be given to the elect of God during the tribulation to discern the identity of the Antichrist so that they will not take his mark. The Bible makes it abundantly clear that anyone taking the mark of the beast cannot be saved (Rev. 14:9, 11;

16:2; 19:20; 20:4). Those who take the mark will spend eternity in the lake of fire (commonly known as hell). The fact that wisdom and understanding is given to believers at this crucial point, relating to a matter of eternal importance, demonstrates that God will provide the knowledge His people need to follow Him faithfully.[8]

What does this wisdom and understanding allow the believer to do? The passage states he will be able to *calculate*. *Calculate* what? He will be able to *calculate the number of the beast*. *Understanding* is the primary purpose for warning believers about the mark; they will understand when it is in the form of numbers, *the name of the beast* will be *six hundred and sixty-six* (666). Instead of predicting his name, John received revelation of a shortened version of *the name of the beast* in the form of the number 666. Thus, believers who are experiencing the sequence of events in the tribulation, when offered the number 666 for their *forehead* or *right hand*, are to reject it even with the certainty of imminent death. This also means that anything prior to this future time-period is not *the mark of the beast* that Scripture warns.

Consequently, Christians in the present time do not need to act superstitiously about the number. If an address, phone number, or zip code includes the number, there is no reason to be afraid that some satanic or mystical power will then have influence. On the other hand, Christians must recognize that many occultists and satanists are attracted to the number because of its relation to a future evil time. The number has been used by occultists, and in the past ten or so years many rock bands have even used the number. However, the number itself does not contain mystical powers. To believe it does means a believer has fallen prey to superstition or to an occult interpretation of the number. The Bible teaches that there is no basis for attaching any superstitious powers to the number 666, or to any other number.

Jumping the Gun

Unfortunately, it is not uncommon for believers to make calculations and predictions of closeness to the coming of Christ by identifying the Antichrist through numerical calculations. Such approaches will always fail and should not be attempted. Phone books are full of names that might total 666. The wisdom of *calculating the number of the beast* is not to be applied in the present time since that would be "jumping the gun." Instead, the wisdom is to be applied by believers during the tribulation. As Daniel wrote, *these words are concealed and sealed up until the end time* (12:9); *these words*, of course, refer to the tribulation period.

In 2 Thessalonians 2, Paul taught that during the current church age the Antichrist is being restrained (2:6). Antichrist will not be *revealed* until *his time*. The Holy Spirit's selection of the word *revealed* indicates the identity of the Antichrist will be concealed until the time of his revelation, which will be a period of time after the rapture. Thus, it is not possible to know or to decipher the identity of the Antichrist before *his time*. What Paul has written explicitly is implied throughout Revelation. Revelation is clear, when the time takes place, the identity of the Antichrist will be understandable to believers. However, until that time, people must resist what has been a popular prophetic pastime: naming the number.

As previously noted, Revelation is clear that every believer during the tribulation will know that receiving the mark of the beast means rejecting Jesus Christ. At the time during the tribulation this will be understood universally by Christians. None of the suggestions of the past or any until the tribulation have merit. Revelation 13:17-18 clearly communicates that the number 666 will be the *mark* proposed for the *right hand* or *forehead*. No one in history has even proposed such a number similar to the conditions of the tribulation, therefore, past guesses as to his identity can also be nullified on this basis.

> The better part of wisdom is to be content that the identification is not yet available, but will be when the future false Christ ascends to his throne. The person to whom 666 applies must have been future to John's time, because John clearly meant the number to be recognizable to someone. If it was not discernible to his

generation and those immediately following him—and it was not—the generation to whom it will be discernible must have lain (and still lies) in the future. Past generations have provided many illustrations of this future personage, but all past candidates have proven inadequate as fulfillments.[9]

It is human nature to desire more knowledge than God has revealed, but Christians must not start the race until the gun is actually fired.

Technology and the Mark

How does all of this relate to the coming cashless society? Perhaps the best way to show how it *does* relate is by first showing how it *does not* relate. The mark of the beast, 666, is not cashless technology or biometrics. Some people have suggested that the mark of the beast will be a universal product code, a chip implanted under the skin, or an invisible mark that requires scanning technology to be recognized. Such applications do not align with the biblical teaching. The Bible gives clear information about what the *mark* will be.

- The Antichrist's mark; identified with his person
- The actual number 666; not a representation
- A mark, like a tattoo
- Visible to the naked eye
- On a person, not in them
- Recognized, not questioned
- Voluntary, not involuntary; thus, not given apart from the person's knowledge
- Used after the rapture, not before
- Used in the second half of the tribulation
- Needed to buy and sell
- Universally received by non-Christians, but universally rejected by Christians
- A mark of worship and allegiance to the Antichrist
- Promoted by the false prophet

- A definite sign that a person will receive eternal punishment in the lake of fire

Perhaps no other number in history, or in biblical studies, has captivated the minds of both Christians and non-Christians as 666. Even those who know nothing of the future plan of God, as revealed in the Bible, know there is significance to this number. Secular and religious writers, film makers, artists, and cultural critics allude, portray, and expound upon the number. It has been used and abused by evangelicals, as well as by others, and it has been the subject of much fruitless speculation. Too often, sincere students of prophecy have coupled the number to the potential of contemporary technology in an effort to demonstrate the relevance of their interpretation. Yet, such zealous intentions are putting the "cart before the horse," since prophecy and the Bible do not gain authority or legitimacy because of culture or technology.

In summary, the technology of the coming cashless society will be used by the Antichrist, but it will not be used as the identifying mark of 666. Whatever technology is available at the time of the Antichrist's ascent will be used for evil purposes. It will be used by the Antichrist, in conjunction with the mark, to control buying and selling (as mentioned in Revelation 13:17); it is likely that chip implants, scan technology, and biometrics will be used as tools to enforce the policy that one cannot buy or sell without the mark. As with other developments in the present day, there are many observable trends setting the stage that will facilitate the future career of the Antichrist.

The Good, the Bad, and the Ugly

Is it possible that someday the dollar bill will be reduced to a museum piece or that a generation of children will mature without knowing the pleasure of change jingling in their pockets? In the future that looms for humanity that is not unthinkable. Interest in the cashless society is growing. Bankers, computer engineers, economists, philosophers, private citizens, sociologists, and theologians, are watching its development but with mixed emotions. Each of these professional and vocational fields has advocates and detractors for a cashless society. The concerns are not only technological and philosophical, but also theological. There is much that needs to be discussed and evaluated: issues of freedom, privacy, and security. The public and private consequences will now be considered.

"Promised Land" or "No Man's Land"?

Are current technological developments causes for unrestricted celebration, or are there ramifications that should elicit pause? In *Technopoly*, a stinging critique of technology's effect upon contemporary culture, Neil Postman recounts the history of the development of the clock, which had its origin in the Benedictine monasteries of the 12th-13th centuries. Originally designed to assist the monks in synchronizing times of prayer, those outside the monastery walls soon found other uses for the clock, and it entered the larger society. Unfortunately, these other uses created some unintended negative consequences. Postman wrote,

> The paradox, the surprise, and the wonder are that the clock was invented by men who wished to devote themselves more rigorously to God; it ended as the technology of greatest use to men who wished to devote themselves to the accumulation of money. In the eternal struggle between God and Mammon, the clock quite unpredictably favored the latter.[10]

As the reader considers the coming cashless society, what parallels might be made with Postman's words? He warned, "Unforeseen consequences stand in the way of all those who think they see clearly the direction in which a new technology will take us. Not even those who invent a technology can be assumed to be reliable prophets."[11]

Most observers perceive significant changes for society in the future. Futurist Edward Cornish wrote,

When steam engines first appeared in eighteenth-century

Britain, no one dreamed that the curious contraptions were part of a sweeping historical transformation, now known as the Industrial Revolution. But we today have little doubt that computers and telecommunications have brought a new revolution and that this new transformation will affect human life even more profoundly than its predecessor.[12]

Nevertheless, all the experts do not agree with Cornish. Clifford Stoll, an astronomer, computer whiz, and best-selling author on computer technology, believes the cashless society is overhyped. Stoll argues that most people are as attached to real cash as he. "I want money to go to the coffee shop to pay for a cup of coffee. I want money to pay my child an allowance. I want money in my pocket, real money—not credit-card money."[13] Consequently, Stoll doesn't see much change on the horizon. "I feel the year 2025 won't be much different from the way it is today, just the way 1965 isn't much different from today."[14]

Better Safe than Sorry

One reason observers such as Stoll are critical of technology and the cashless society is because of the many technical problems that would challenge those who would implement it. Security and reliability are the two main concerns of those hesitant about the implementation of the cashless society. With funds being transferred from one account to another by the click of a button, how safe are they from manipulation and error? What safeguards would stop someone a computer savvy user from initiating an illegal transfer of funds for personal gain?

Computer technology has created a new class of criminals, known as hackers, who pose a significant threat for the cashless society. Vast amounts of research and time are expended to reduce the threat of computer criminals in the electronic-money marketplace. Companies, such as GTE, IBM, Visa, and MasterCard, work together closely to develop standard software for assuring security of electronic payments over the Internet. Following a recent agreement between two credit-card giants, Edmund Jensen, CEO of Visa International, stated, "A single standard eliminates unnecessary costs and builds the case for doing business on the Internet." Eugene Lockhart, CEO for MasterCard, lauded the agreement, proclaiming the new standard as a "critical catalyst for electronic commerce."[15]

Other attempts at reducing theft have already occurred. ISED Corporation of New Jersey developed the device which gives security to transactions over both the telephone and the Internet. Known as an SED (secure encryption device), this inexpensive instrument attaches either to a telephone or personal computer and is activated by "swiping" an ATM or credit card through it. Account information encrypted on the magnetic stripe of the card is electronically transferred through the hardware. Regarding the SED, CNN correspondent Marsha Walton wrote,

> As buying by computer catches on, the device could eventually be used to pay for everything from a pizza delivery to bailing a friend out of jail, and would be as much a part of the home computer as a floppy disk or hard drive. And just as consumers have grown accustomed to computers and ATM cards, the combination of the two could be another step toward a "cashless society."[16]

In addition to the issue of security, there is also the concern for the reliability of the cashless system and its supporting hardware. The electronic systems must not only be secure from threats of internal tampering and theft, but also they must be resistant to external threats such as natural catastrophes, terrorism, or sabotage. Every possibility of the system "crashing" or being destroyed must be reduced as much as possible.

Precautions, against such catastrophes, have been considered and implemented by at least one corporation, Visa International. In their headquarters in McLean, Virginia, the building that accommodates Visa's main computers has reportedly been constructed to withstand an earthquake equal to the magnitude of the 1906 San Francisco earthquake. The building has three power sources: the electric company, three diesel-powered back-up generators, and two banks of lead-acid batteries similar to an automobile battery.[17]

Advantages: The Good

What is it that makes electronic money, or e-money, so attractive? *First,* it may eventually become more convenient than traditional coins and currency. Today, almost half of homes in America have personal computers and businesses are dependent upon computers for almost every aspect of daily affairs.[18] In 1994, *Time* magazine reported almost one-fourth of all American homes had personal computers, and more than 900,000 subscribers had signed up with banking services via on-line information systems.[19] Currently, more than one-half of Americans are now accessing the Internet[20] and 95 percent of public libraries in the United States offer access to the Internet.[21]

Second, banks and other institutions using e-money would find it considerably cheaper to process than checks and other records. Regarding the high cost of processing checks, *Time* reported:

> Checks are too expensive to handle. About 55 billion checks are written every year (more than 37% of all consumer payments), and the processing costs the nation's financial institutions about $1.30 each. Banks end up losing money on about half of all checking accounts, since the handling costs often exceed the interest earned on lending out the deposits. An electronic transfer, on the other hand, costs only 15 cents per blip.[22]

Cash is even harder and more costly to handle. Donald Gleason, president of the Smart Card Enterprise unit of Electronic Payment Services Inc., stated:

> Cash is a nightmare. It costs money handlers in the U.S. alone approximately $60 billion a year to move the stuff, a line item ripe from drastic pruning. The solution is to cram our currency in burn bags and strike some matches. This won't happen all at once, and paper money will

probably never go away (hey, they couldn't even get rid of the penny), but bills and coinage will increasingly be replaced by some sort of electronic equivalent.[23]

Dollars deteriorate much easier than electronic images. A cashless society would alleviate some of the headaches associated with keeping fresh currency in the marketplace. *Times writer*, Thomas McCarroll, communicated,

> The push for a cashless society is gaining momentum, however, if only because making money disappear is also a way of saving money. There are about 12 billion pieces of U.S. paper currency, worth $150 billion, circulating worldwide, which works out to about $30 for every person on earth. Keeping all that paper in use is a costly chore for the government. Most $1 bills wear out after about 18 months. To retire, destroy and replace all aging currency costs the government an estimated $200 million a year. Currency is cumbersome for businesses as well. People have to count it, armored cars have to carry it, bank vaults have to store it and security guards have to protect it.[24]

A *third* advantage of electronic money is privacy. People using the Internet for personal and business commercial transactions may find that some forms of electronic money offer greater privacy than current credit cards. Nevertheless, the potential certainly exists for privacy to be compromised in the sphere of cyberspace. A major advantage argued by proponents of the cashless society is decreased crime. It has been estimated that in the United States alone illegal transactions form an "underground economy" that totals between 10 percent and 28 percent of the gross national product, and more than 50 percent of these are done in cash.[25] A cashless society might be a significant deterrent to such activity.

> The immediate benefits would be profound and fundamental. Theft of cash would become impossible. Bank robberies and cash-register robberies would simply cease

to occur. Attacks on shopkeepers, taxi drivers, and cashiers would all end. Purse snatchings would become a thing of the past. Urban streets would become safer. Retail shops in once-dangerous areas could operate in safety. Security costs and insurance rates would fall. Property values would rise. Neighborhoods would improve.

Drug traffickers and their clients, burglars and receivers of stolen property, arsonists for hire, and bribe-takers would no longer have the advantage of using traceable currency.... Sales of illegal drugs, along with the concomitant violent crime, should diminish. Hospital emergency rooms would become less crowded. Burglary statistics would fall.[26]

Perhaps this scenario is overly optimistic, but many experts do believe that a cashless society is an important means of significantly decreasing certain types of crime. The possibility, of course, remains that these sorts of crimes would simply become high tech. Placing too much hope in a cashless society significantly reducing crime seems unrealistic.

Disadvantages: The Bad

Decidedly, there are some advantages to not carrying or using cash, but what is the disadvantage here? The possibility of an electronic system "crashing" has already been mentioned. If this event occurred, the ramifications could send economic shock waves around the world. Both institutions and individuals could be seriously affected. The worst scenario would result in the loss of life savings and fortunes. Minimally, there would be significant anxiety and cessation of transactions until the systems could recover or backups restored. Since there would be no "paper trail," restoration or duplication of records could be an accountant's worst nightmare.

One vulnerable network of computers is Fedwire, which is run by the Federal Reserve and is the official network for clearing domestically issued checks. Also used by the Federal Reserve and

Treasury Department, this system processes $1 trillion dollars on an average day.

> Breakdowns are not unthinkable.... On November 21, 1985, a faulty software package kept the Bank of New York from receiving payments from customers. The bank paid its outstanding bills, but no money came in. By the time the error was detected late in the evening, the Bank of New York owed other banks on the Fedwire system 23 billion dollars.[27]

The breakdown at Fedwire was just a "quick slip" of one part of the system, yet it had enormous consequences. Joel Kurtzman wrote,

> The Bank of New York had to raise a lot of money in a hurry. It had just one place to turn: the Fed. It was forced to borrow $23 billion overnight from the Fed until the problem was corrected the following morning. That money was lent to the Bank of New York at an overnight rate of about 5 percent—a little over $3.1 million in interest payments for the night.
>
> The problem affected just one bank on the network, but the imbalance was still huge. What would have happened if the bank's software problem had spread? Or if the problem had been caused deliberately by a virus inserted in the nation's bank-clearing system by a computer hacker or "financial terrorist"?[28]

A glitch, like the one experienced by the Bank of New York, could have unbelievable ripple effects. While safeguards are being developed, the risk is still an ever-present danger. Kurtzman added:

> The fact that Fedwire was not secure poses no small problem. With $1 trillion traveling through the system each day, a malfunction (accidental or otherwise) could paralyze the country....

In all there are twenty-one major electronic networks around the world designed to move money. These systems move about $3 trillion a day. None of these systems is more secure or safer than Fedwire. Such are the perils of the information age.[29]

Disruption of these systems would create personal and international chaos. If this can happen on a macroeconomic level, how difficult would it be to interfere with one individual, or one family, or one group of people? The Fedwire fiasco was a software problem, but what happens when a typographical error enters the system? Just a simply typo can also create chaos. At Chemical Bank in 1994, automated teller machines deducted $16 million dollars by mistake from the accounts of 10,000 customers because of a typographical error in a single line of computer code. The result? The bank bounced 430 checks before the error could be fixed.[30]

The persistence of demarcation between the economic haves and have-nots is another serious concern about the cashless society. A cashless society assumes a certain level of economic and technological sophistication. Those with the sophistication and access would benefit, and those without it would not.

Potential: The Ugly

In addition to possible problems, there are some aspects of the cashless society that are blatantly ugly. Electronic footprints can be traced. When a credit-card purchase is made, the information becomes part of a much larger personal profile. Harvard legal scholar Anne Wells Branscomb wrote,

Far more pernicious than being submerged beneath a sea of catalogs, solicitations, and notices that you may have already won a million dollars is the compilation of data gathered from many sources, then correlated by computerized analysis to formulate profiles of our tastes, interests, and activities. This capability recalls the horror of George Orwell's novel *1984* in which Big Brother knows all about everyone and uses the exhaustive and reliable knowledge to manipulate their lives.[31]

On a macroeconomic level, there is the question of who is going to control the growth of electronic money systems. Will it be the government, the private sector, or the public sector? Wide-ranging fraud is one of the greatest concerns challenging the cashless society. Even with current technology, the Internal Revenue Service has reported the number of fraudulent electronic filings as doubling in the last few years. *Time* magazine reported:

> Such incidents have led critics to warn that the rush to automated payment systems is proceeding too fast even for computer experts. "The demands on software are far outpacing the development of software," says Dain Gary, a manager at the Software Engineering Institute at Carnegie-Mellon University.[32]

These concerns are real and the answers are not yet apparent. The cashless society will not transform the greed and the wayward desires of the human heart. Counterfeiting, money laundering, tax evasion, and theft will continue and could proliferate in a cashless society unless proper safeguards are developed. There are sizable regulatory gaps that currently "permit" electronic money laundering. These eventually need to be addressed. Stanley E. Morris, director of the Treasury Department's Financial Crimes Enforcement Network, reported that there are no laws presently to limit the balance of electronic currency that can be loaded on an electronic cash card. This allows for great potential criminal activity; hitherto, there is no way to define whose tax laws apply to transactions in cyberspace.[33] Similarly, Steven Levy warned of the darker side of the cashless society.

> Exactly what goes on inside smart cards, wallets, and computers won't be apparent. But the protocols chosen by the lords of e-money are all-important. Depending on

how they work, the various systems of electronic money will prove to be boons or disasters, bastions of individual privacy or violators of individual freedom. At the worst, a faulty or crackable system of electronic money could lead to an economic Chernobyl. Imagine the dark side: cryptocash hackers who figure out how to spoof an e-money system. A desktop mint! The resulting flood of bad digits would make the hyper inflationary Weimer Republic—where people carted wheelbarrows full of marks to pay for groceries—look like a stable monetary system.[34]

A greater concern than the issues of fraud are those of control and privacy. Kawika Daguio, Washington, D.C., representative for the American Bankers Association, poses the following questions:

- "Who is going to create the monetary value?"
- "What security features will be included?"
- "Will they work so the value will be restored if they're lost?"
- "Who's going to regulate electronic money?"
- "Who's going to pay for it?"[35]

For each of these questions, several different answers are being given and more than enough heated discussions have erupted. How these questions are answered is greatly important to all. However, the greatest concern is controlling the system which constructs the cashless society. Not everyone agrees there will be centralized control or that such a thing is even possible. Many desire that it not be centralized. Therefore, the pendulum of fear swings between a cashless society with too much governmental control and a cashless society with too little governmental control. Kurtzman expressed some of these concerns.

And what about governments in this networked world? They have been downgraded when it comes to running the economy. The trend that has been going on for more than a decade is for governments in every country to sell off their holdings and at the same time borrow more in the capital markets.... The power of government is decreasing at a rapid rate relative to the private sector.... Government, business, commerce, and trade are all being redefined as globalization proceeds with dispatch.

The convergence of those two trends, a future more difficult to predict and government less able to act, is alarming. It may signal a future where there is too little central authority to stop a calamity before it occurs. The world may lack sufficient control mechanisms to curb chaos when it begins.[36]

Terrorism on the Internet is also a growing concern being addressed by the government. Jim Settle, retired director of the FBI's computer crime squad is very concerned: "You bring me a select group of hackers and within 90 days I'll bring this country to its knees."[37] Cyberterrorism is a law enforcement, national security, and personal issue for all. According to *Newsweek*, the U.S. Airforce is so concerned about cyberterrorism that, in the past, they "designated a 20-person squadron in South Carolina as an information-warfare unit. Maj. Clem Gaines says both defensive and offensive strategies will be studied."[38]

Speedbumps on the Information Highway

The trip to the mailbox these days is usually followed by an elaborate ritual of sorting bills and correspondence from the proliferating array of advertisements, catalogs, pre-approved credit-card applications, sweepstakes, and other forms of junk mail. Merchants have found mass mailing to consumers to be a cost-effective method of reaching potential buyers. However, many consumers are frustrated by the growing volume of unwanted mailings. Removing one's address from the mailing lists of junk mail solicitors is not an easy task. How do many people have access to individual names and addresses, and how did they obtain this information? How many unsolicited calls for sales or contributions are received each week? Where do these companies obtain all the phone numbers? These questions pose significant concerns about personal privacy and how easy it is for someone to "get the goods" on an individual in order to market their goods.

So Much Information, So Many Decisions

Surfing the Internet can be overwhelming to the first-time user. It is exciting, and there is so much information available at the stroke of a key or the click of a mouse! Nevertheless, what happens to all this information? The information highway is here to stay and it is growing, but like the physical highways that many use daily, it has the potential for disaster as well as convenience.

The amount of information available is phenomenal. With the option of "burning" many publications on a single CD-ROM, or visiting Internet sites around the world with the click of a button, the possibilities for accessing information are almost endless. Ultimately, the ethical questions surrounding this new technology concern how the information is used. Information has little value unless it is applied. Clifford Stoll is correct when he wrote, "Networks bring a flood of both useful and useless information to our desktops. They help me work more efficiently yet still are counterproductive—they're equally great for working and goofing off."[39]

Highs and Lows on the Information Highway

Following the beginning of a new millennium, computer technology has thrust mankind into a brave new world. In one critique of technology, Professor Albert Borgmann wrote,

> Throughout modern history there has been the hope that happiness would burst forth from within technology, that science and ingenuity would design a device that would guarantee everyone's liberty and prosperity. The construction of the information highway has once more

kindled that hope.[40]

Computer software magnate Bill Gates is one having unbridled confidence in what the future has to offer mankind. "I'm optimistic about the impact of the new technology,"[41] he wrote.

> We are watching something historic happen, and it will affect the world seismically, rocking us the same way the discovery of the scientific method, the invention of printing, and the arrival of the Industrial Age did. If the information highway is able to increase the understanding citizens of one country have about their neighboring countries, and thereby reduce international tensions, that, in and of itself, could be sufficient to justify the cost of implementation. If it was used only by scientists, permitting them to collaborate more effectively to find cures for the still-incurable diseases, that alone would be invaluable. If the system was only for kids, so that they could pursue their interests in and out of the classroom, that by itself would transform the human condition. The information highway won't solve every problem, but it will be a positive force in many areas.[42]

Understanding new technologies, especially those that increase access to information, makes man keenly aware that the power can be harnessed, and sometimes privacy will be compromised as a result. It is because of the facts of biblical prophecy that Christians need to maintain both an optimistic, yet cautious posture. An uninhibited enthusiasm for the future makes society vulnerable to corruption and gross abuse.

The Perpetual Problem of Privacy

Privacy is one of the intersections of the information highway where computers and society merge. It is a place of potential collision, and many people, frustrated by the threat or the delay in moving from one goal to the next, shout their views at one another. Nevertheless, everyone acknowledges the need to be concerned about privacy in the cybernetic world. The difficulty is that present laws and regulations in countries throughout the world are inadequate for the issues mankind is now forced to confront. Security does not always mean privacy, especially in the electronic world. Observing the legal difficulties in Asia, one article stated:

> The legal systems still have to catch up with technology. Though laws prescribe punishment for theft of money, the theft of information remains fuzzily defined, at least in Asia. The Malaysian Penal Code was drafted in 1936. "When our laws talk about theft, they refer to movable properties, not information," says law professor Khaw Lake Tee of the University of Malaya. "So how do you prosecute?"[43]

While the Information Age has alleviated some problems, it has also created others, one being the inadequacy of national laws. Everette E. Dennis, executive director of The Freedom Forum Media Studies Center at Columbia University, wrote,

> What was once the stuff of graduate seminars in information theory or communications policy is now truly in the public arena, where it is beginning to dawn on people that the information revolution may affect them in helpful or harmful ways. In part, the message here is that what you don't know or don't protect can make your life quite perilous.[44]

Who owns their telephone number? What about personal email? How private are an individual's medical records? What about the public availability of financial transactions, and who should be able to access those records? Moreover, where does the government (at any level or location) fit into the privacy equation? All of these are standard legal questions that are compounded in complexity by computer technology and telecommunications.

There is a major speed bump in the information highway in

regard to privacy. Observing some of the new legal dilemmas, Anne Wells Branscomb wrote,

> No information society will reach its potential without addressing the legal foundation upon which information is exchanged. That foundation is as necessary a component of the information infrastructure or "infostructure" as the electronic global highways that we are rapidly constructing. The boundaries between what is considered to be public information and what is considered to be private have been moving targets for several generations now. Unless we are able to reach a consensus on the fair uses and prohibited abuses of information, we will never achieve the promise of living in an information society.[45]

Between a Rock and a Hard Place

The issues of privacy are positioned on a large philosophical pendulum. At one end of the arc, there are the advocates of complete anonymity in cashless society transactions. Yet, this opens the door to possibilities of abuse that may be unknown currently. No matter what laws are enacted, the unscrupulous will always seek an advantage. At the other end of the arc, there is the extreme position of complete identification and traceability. Few people in our society would advocate this position.

Steven Levy wrote of the dilemma of privacy:

> If anonymity becomes a standard in cyberspace cash systems, we have to accept its potential abuse—as in copyright violations, fraud, and money laundering. Innovative new crypto schemes have the potential for mitigating these abuses, but the fact of anonymity guarantees that some skullduggery will be easier to pull off. On the other hand, the lack of anonymity means that every move you make, and every file you take, will be traceable. That opens the door to surveillance like we've never seen.[46]

These are the concerns being voiced. Society cannot have complete anonymity and lack of anonymity. "In one direction lies unprecedented scrutiny and control of people's lives; in the other, secure parity between individuals and organizations. The shape of society in the next century may depend on which approach predominates."[47]

Convenience or Control?

The ability to gather vast amounts of information leads to the question of what information should become open or public and what should remain closed or private. How much should other people, institutions or governments be allowed to know about individuals and their activities? What are the boundaries and safeguards, and who will decide?

The amount of information someone obtains concerning individuals is certainly a factor in determining how much control the person exerts over them. Information, like technology, can be used for either good or evil. Privacy is the door that power must pass to access information about individual lives. Once the door to privacy is opened completely, individuals become vulnerable to control and manipulation. Futurist author Alvin Toffler believes the control of knowledge "is the crux of tomorrow's worldwide struggle for power in every human institution."[48] Russell Chandler, former religion editor for *The Los Angeles Times*, discerned an ominous potential for power, privacy, and technology.

> While we consider these technological wonders beckoning us to cross the threshold of 2001, it's essential that we grasp both the limitations and the potential for subversion inherent in technology. Information-hungry technology in a high-surveillance society can erode our freedoms and compromise our privacy...If worshipped, technology in the end proves to be a false god, corroding human values and desensitizing the spirit.... The siren song of "liberation technology" conceals the negative consequences of technical progress in contemporary society.[49]

While some cultural critics and political observers have expressed an unbridled optimism that democratic ideals will soon influence society globally, others are more constrained in their evaluations. In his book, *Has Democracy Had Its Day?*, theologian Carl F. H. Henry expressed some of the concerns about the survival of democracy that has been growing in the minds of conservatives and evangelicals in recent years. He offered words of hope, but also words of caution.

> Nothing has threatened the survival of modern political democracy more than Marxist communism. One might expect that the collapse of communism in our time would evoke for democratic political processes a torrent of international tribute, yet we are seeing instead a rising tide of doubt precisely at this time.
>
> The questioning of democracy occurs for different reasons in Latin America, in Asia, and even in Russia and Eastern Europe. But most astonishing, it appears more and more frequently in the United States, in the aftermath of the cultural loss of moral transcendence and of the privatization of religion.[50]

Although a cashless society offers welcomed convenience for all, concern is necessary because of its potential for unprecedented control of individuals and society collectively. So where does this leave the reader of this chapter in relation to the information highway? Should he refuse to use it because there may be hurdles to overcome? Certainly not. There is much to be gained from its use, and this author encourages the reader to become as familiar as possible with it. Nevertheless, like the automobiles driven today, there needs to be alertness to what is taking place since the individual is continuously affected. Not all roads lead to the same place, and there are some places that need to be avoided.

It is because this author believes resolutely in the Bible and its prophetic teachings, he discerns cause for concern about the potential uses of technology. An understanding of the Bible, and the worldview it expounds, certainly does not forbid the use of technology. However, Christians must be aware of its potential. The technology that is seen and used today may be used for evil in the near future. At some point, all which is intended for good is always in danger of being abused and corrupted by the human heart.

Hindrance, Hope, and Hype

The author of this chapter was reared in Texas and the general editor of this book was reared in Florida where the summer sun is merciless. Certainly, conditions in those two states cause one to appreciate air conditioning more than others. This marvelous technology, which allows the moderation of indoor temperatures when the thermometer outside soars near 100 degrees, makes life much more comfortable. However, are the authors "better" in an ethical and moral sense because of the technology? Probably not, except they are not quite so cranky in the summer. Are they "better" in a theological sense because of air conditioning? Absolutely not. The authors still have a sin nature, which climate control cannot alter. In fact, because of man's sinful nature, the multiplication of new technologies is often used by people as a diversion from addressing more important questions of morality and spirituality. Too frequently mankind would rather be amused with new technological toys than consider the timeless issues relating to the human condition.[51]

Technology by itself is not evil. The crucial question is how technology is used. An automobile in the hands of a drunk driver can kill many people, but an ambulance in the hands of a skillful driver can save many lives. The syringe, designed to be used by nurses and physicians to inject medicine to heal, can also be used by drug addicts to destroy their own lives. It is the application of an individual technology, not its presence or development that is often wrong.

Sometimes, You Cannot Win for Losing

Many of the advances propelling mankind toward the cashless society are good in themselves. Nevertheless, what may begin as good may be corrupted and used for evil purposes. The legitimate concerns regarding privacy, theft, and the difficulty of coping with the information explosion have been examined, in addition to the biblical teaching concerning future events. Mankind is being drawn closer to earth's final days daily, and even now, the world is being conditioned to facilitate the ascent of the Antichrist.

It is because man is sinful and self-serving, anything he creates and develops, whether it is art or architecture, electronics or eugenics, machines or music, can be and eventually will be distorted and misapplied. Theologian Carl F. H. Henry made the keen analysis of contemporary society:

> Much of the West, although technocratically preoccupied with the *what* of things may seem to have lost interest in the *why*. But the *why* is what continually confronts us, even Christians, not only through the human dilemmas of pain and evil but also and especially through the Bible where the living God of revelation searches the thoughts and intents of hearts.

The problem of evil is not an issue of technology but theology. Man is not to be afraid of technology or avoid it. Rather, he must be aware of how it might be used and wisely evaluate such uses and the ethical and moral boundaries of any participation with the technology. Man has the ability to do many awe-inspiring things, but it does not mean he should do it.

It is inherent in creation that people want to avoid their responsibility to God and shift the blame. This was the original response to sin in the Garden by Adam and Eve, and its popularity has not abated. In modern times, people often misassign evil to things that are not responsible. Crime, guns, hectic lifestyles, industrialization, poverty, and technology (to name only a few) are often blamed for evil actions instead of people whose actions are the true source of environmental and social realities. Yet, if everyone were capable of candid thought, it would be readily admitted that machines cannot make ethical decisions. Even the most advanced computer can only function according to its programs. It must be clear that men and women through their actions and decisions are the only agents who can put a moral imprint on anything. It is humanity that will lead to Armageddon, not armor.

Technology is carrying mankind to new frontiers in many areas of life, and therefore, man needs to critique continually the culture and society from a biblical perspective. Not all "progress" is ethically and morally desirable. There may be some technologies that Christians, individually, decide not to use because such use would violate biblical principles. For example, a person's view on theological issues relating to the beginning and ending of life may limit use of medical technology. Christians must know what they believe, why they believe it, and what the ramifications of those beliefs are to be in individual actions.

A Preview of Coming Attractions

The *sine qua non* of the cashless society is not that it is evil or immoral, but it is a sign of the end times. Before the feature film is shown in a cinema, there are frequently several previews of upcoming films shown to entice the viewer to return and watch them. Similarly, the cashless society is a preview or glimpse of life in the future. Unfortunately, the feature production will exceed any horror film known today. It will be a seven-year tribulation following the rapture of the church and the major "star" will be the Antichrist. The cashless society is only one aspect of his overall plan and today's technology.

It would, however, be wrong to think that because something may or will be used for evil in the future, it should therefore be avoided or resolutely rejected for use in the present. The cashless society is coming and the tribulation is coming. Nevertheless, the Lord Jesus Christ is also coming for His own before the terrors of the tribulation come to fruition. This author encourages the reader to consider first and foremost the consequences of living with a Christless soul rather than the consequences of living in a cashless society. *"For what will a man be profited, if he gains the whole world, and forfeits his soul? Or what will a man give in exchange for his soul?"* (Mt. 16:26).

CHAPTER 4

NATIONS' ROLE IN WORLD ECONOMY

Arno Froese

With the fall of Soviet communism, the world opened itself to receive a new form of economic globalism. The Bible reveals this successful model is not based on traditional, sound economics; rather, it is built upon a delusion identified in Scripture as being *drunk of the wine of the wrath of her fornication. For all nations have drunk of the wine of the wrath of her fornication, and the kings of the earth have committed fornication with her, and the merchants of the earth are waxed rich through the abundance of her delicacies* (Rev. 18:3).

Revelation 18:3 is the epitome of success for world economy. The reader must note the verse reads *all nations*. What did these nations do? They became drunk. This means they are unaware of their actions. An intoxicated person thinks more of himself than he should. Consider the devastating effects of drunk driving. Why do some people drive drunk? It is because they believe themselves to drive as well, or better, drunk than sober. They believe in a delusion.

The *wine of the wrath* has caused the nations to think or act irrationally. Who is involved? Scripture mentions *all nations* and *the kings of the earth*. This is the political power structure of the world. The world no longer has kings, at least not of any measurable significance, as far as the economy is concerned. These kings, no doubt, are the political leaders of the world who have committed fornication with *her*. Who is *her*? She is identified in Revelation 17:5 as *MYSTERY, BABYLON THE GREAT, THE MOTHER OF HARLOTS AND ABOMINATIONS OF THE EARTH.* In spite of these extremely negative connotations, this system is amazingly successful: *the merchants of the earth are waxed rich through the abundance of her delicacies.*

Scripture is stating *all nations* are involved, which includes their economists, financial experts, and leaders, in addition to their institutions and the global corporations. They have become drunk and committed fornication.

Fornication

The word *fornication*, appearing twice in Revelation 18:3, means an act committed with a harlot. *The New Unger's Bible Dictionary* defines "harlot" as a figurative term for an idolatress (Isa. 1:21; Jer. 2:20; 3:2; Ezek. 16:13-63; Rev. 17:1, 5, 15; 19:2).[1] Unger indicates the word "fornication" is derived from a Greek word, *porneia*, which "is used of illicit sexual intercourse in general (Acts 15:20, 29; 21:25; cf. 1 Cor. 5:1; 6:13, 18; 7:2; etc.)."[2] Additionally, the word is distinguished from "adultery."

Therefore, there is a distinction between adultery and fornication among nations where polygamy exists. "If a married man has criminal intercourse with a married woman, or with one promised in marriage, or with a widow expecting to be married with a brother-in-law, it is accounted *adultery*. If he is guilty of such intercourse with a woman who is unmarried it is considered *fornication*."[3]

Presently, "adultery" refers to an act when the person is married; fornication refers to an act when the person is not. Fornication may be defined as lewdness of an unmarried person of either sex. Its prohibition is based upon the fact that it discourages marriage, leaves the education and care of children insecure, depraves and defiles the mind more than any other vice, and thus is unfit for the kingdom of God (1 Cor. 6:9; etc.). The Lord forbids even the thoughts leading to it (Mt. 5:28).

In a figurative sense, the close relationship between Jehovah and Israel is referenced under the figure of marriage; Israel is represented as the unfaithful wife of the Lord, who is now rejected but who is yet to be restored. The church of the New Testament represents a pure virgin espoused to Christ (2 Cor. 11:2), and thus is differentiated from the nation Israel (1 Cor.

10:32). The worship of idols is naturally mentioned as fornication (Rev. 14:8; 17:2, 4; 18:3; 19:2), as is the defilement of idolatry, as incurred by eating the sacrifices offered to idols (2:21).

Progressive Fornication

Important to realize is fornication does not name other people or a future event, but it touches mankind individually and personally today. According to Matthew 5:28, the Lord declares guilty each and every person who even has an evil thought. *But I say unto you, That whosoever looketh on a woman to lust after her hath committed adultery with her already in his heart.* From that perspective, it is impossible to think anyone can claim to be innocent of this type of fornication.

The words "idolatry" and "idols" can be used in this connection. It should remind the reader of a substitution, or something not authentic. Prostitution, which relates to harlots and fornication, means "[offering] oneself or another as a paid sexual partner."[4] When one thinks on these matters, he realizes the discussion has to do with a substitution for the real thing. Mystery Babylon, the mother of harlots, is the epitome of substitution. She offers all of life's pleasures to those who will become one with her.

Marriage is a union between a single man and woman ordained by God. Scripture describes the union as two *shall be one flesh* (Gen. 2:24). Paul wrote to the Corinthians, *What? know ye not that he which is joined to an harlot is one body? for two, saith he, shall be one flesh* (1 Cor. 6:16). The goal of the mother of harlots is to have the entire world practice economic, financial, political, and religious fornication to become one flesh with her.

It must be stated this type of fornication is not a physical act between a man and a woman. On the contrary, it is a figurative way of communicating the reality of the union between this woman/city/system and the world *with whom the kings of the earth have committed fornication, and the inhabitants of the earth have been made drunk with the wine of her fornication* (Rev. 17:2).

Wine of Fornication

The cause of this apparent success is the drinking of *the wine of her fornication*. Again, this is a figure of speech. Thus, an additional question is necessary. How did the nation become intoxicated with *the wine of her fornication*? It is because they all desired to be healthy and prosperous. This woman/city/system is the originator of global prosperity: *And the woman was arrayed in purple and scarlet colour, and decked with gold and precious stones and pearls, having a golden cup in her hand full of abominations and filthiness of her fornication* (Rev. 17:4). Does that not sound like stocks and bonds, cash, and valuables? Is the world becoming intoxicated by these commodities today? Revelation 18:3 states ...the *merchants of the earth are waxed rich through the abundance of her delicacies*. Yes, she is extremely rich; *she hath glorified herself, and lived deliciously* (18:7). What about the politicians? *And the kings of the earth...have committed fornication and lived deliciously with her* (18:9).

This should lead the reader to ask another question. What is wrong with being rich and prosperous? Nothing. According to the Bible, Abraham—the father of all believers—was very wealthy. Joseph experienced great prosperity in Egypt and David possessed great wealth living in Jerusalem. These men trusted God, believed His Word, and acted in accordance with His will. However, this writer thinks it is possible to state with reasonable assurance that they possessed great riches rather than allowing the riches to possess them. Therein lays a big difference.

Financial Fornication

The Bible does not say money is the root of all evil; it states evil results from *the love of money* (1 Tim. 6:10). Here the reader enters into a territory exposing the success of the industrialized world in the present days: deception. Occasionally, a modern-day deception is exposed. Most recently, it was Enron in the United States, Parmalat in Europe, and the great Russian oil deal which was spoiled. Suddenly, investors awaken to a nightmare, that is, their capital has vanished into thin air and their riches are gone overnight. In the February 2004 issue of *Eternal Value*

Review, financial expert Wilfred Hahn wrote the following:

> ...Wall Street and those who have the means, motives and aspirations to play the "game." By its very nature, it is a game that not all can win though wealth management companies (the major brokerage firms, mutual fund companies, etc.) purposely deny this fact. They prey on gullible investors and savers, knowing full well that the lure of gains and easy retirement end up in the transfer of wealth to insiders, elite investors and the money mavens in this "rigged" game that still rules. The ways and means are no longer important in this respect. The bottom line is to make financial markets soar. The dangers of corruption, falsification, "fairy tales" and destruction of a country's backbone are ignored.
>
> The core of this rotten ideology is found in high places. Here, it is important to recognize that a very dangerous and deceptive change has occurred on the part of leaders and authorities. The lure of financial wealth – more, exactly, the perception of wealth—has become a deliberate policy tool. Wealth goes before all. Make most people think that they are becoming wealthier, that more wealth gains are probable, and national prosperity and economic growth will follow. It used to be the other way around. Honest vocation and industry led to higher living standards and wealth. Prosperity was an outcome, not a fabricated lure.
>
> This new demagoguery clearly emerged in the early 1990s in intellectual circles. A quote reflecting this thinking in a foreign policy magazine article in 1996 states that *"the new approach requires that a state find ways to increase the market value of its productive assets."* Such an economic policy that *"aims to achieve growth by wealth creation therefore does not attempt to increase the production of goods and services, except as a secondary objective."*[5]

One can almost sense how wealth is being created out of

nothing. Such a system is like a soap bubble ready to burst any moment. These words are reminiscent of Revelation 18:15-16 (*The merchants of these things, which were made rich by her, shall stand afar off for the fear of her torment, weeping and wailing, And saying, Alas, alas, that great city, that was clothed in fine linen, and purple, and scarlet, and decked with gold, and precious stones, and pearls!*). The people will realize they have been deceived, but it will be too late.

Perhaps even the youngest reader has some degree of familiarity with the Great Depression of 1929. Even to this day no one is quite certain about the cause. Some have speculated the system collapsed or the investors lost faith, but one thing is able to be known which is one thing led to another until there was utter chaos.

Certainly, life has improved greatly since the late 20s. Another Wall Street collapse like the one of 1929 is unlikely because the economies and financial systems are globally interconnected. Nevertheless, it stands to reason when something does go wrong, and it will, it will be global in scope.

Holy Revenge

What kind of fornication does the financial world commit with this woman/city/system? *Rejoice over her, **thou** heaven, and ye holy apostles and prophets; for God hath avenged you on her* (Rev. 18:20). Why does *heaven*, the *holy apostles and the prophets* rejoice concerning her destruction? Here one must read Revelation 18:24. *And in her was found the blood of prophets, and of saints, and of all that were slain upon the earth.* Pleasure, riches, and success caused the destruction of those who spoke the truth. There is no occasion for truth in the New World Order, but there is plenty of opportunity for success.

Furthermore, the Text states, *And they cast dust on their heads, and cried, weeping and wailing, saying, Alas, alas, that great city, wherein were made rich all that had ships in the sea by reason of her costliness! for in one hour is she made desolate* (18:19). In contrast to the *weeping and wailing* on earth, there is rejoicing in heaven because there is judgment upon the rich, the great and the powerful of this world, who have violated the basic human rights of the saints and Jesus Christ, who said "I am the truth" (cf. Jn. 14:6).

The Rich

When James wrote about the last days, he specifically mentioned the wealthy. *Go to now, ye rich men, weep and howl for your miseries that shall come upon you. Your riches are corrupted, and your garments are motheaten. Your gold and silver is cankered; and the rust of them shall be a witness against you, and shall eat your flesh as it were fire. Ye have heaped treasure together for the last days. Behold, the hire of the laborers who have reaped down your fields, which is of you kept back by fraud, crieth: and the cries of them which have reaped are entered into the ears of the Lord of Sabaoth. Ye have lived in pleasure on the earth, and been wanton; ye have nourished your hearts, as in a day of slaughter* (Jas. 5:1-5).

Be mindful of the fact that all the riches are generated by those who labor with dedication and faithful service to the rich. In the United States, for instance, the rich are idolized. Although many forget, in most instances, this wealth is not earned by the wealthy people themselves. On the contrary, it is earned by those who work for those who are prosperous. Many employers take advantage of their employees, who are often forced to make the company the only priority in their lives. Consider the following article, entitled "'Vintage-year' Divorces Swell in Japan," published in the May 2004 issue of *Midnight Call*.

- He averages 12-hour work days, followed by an obligatory round of drinks with co-workers and a long commute home.
- She dutifully waits up for him to return and prepares breakfast in the mornings.
- Then retirement rolls around, and he discovers that he is a stranger to his own family.
- The result is a phenomenon that Japanese are calling "vintage-year divorce," the fastest-growing component

of a marital breakup rate that has doubled since 1975.

- Reflecting larger changes in society, the divorces are more likely initiated by women, often after 20 years or more together.
- "Expectations are definitely changing. Many people are putting their happiness first, and if they think they won't find that in their marriage, they get out," said Atsuko Okano, 49, a divorcee and founder of a nationwide divorce counseling service, Caratclub.
- A record 289,838 couples divorced in 2002, the most recent year available, up 1.4 percent from 2001, the Health, Labor and Welfare Ministry announced in September. The divorce rate also hit a new record of 2.3 divorces for every 1,000 people—more than double the rate of 1.07 in 1975.
- A decade ago, divorce could mean a serious loss of face —or even a loss of career. Although the Japanese legal system makes it a relatively straightforward procedure and provides for alimony and child support, many couples long were deterred by the shame associated with divorce.
- But as the stigma rapidly fades, couples across the demographic spectrum are parting ways.
- In 1975, such divorces comprised less than 6 percent of the total. By the late 1990s, they were 17 percent.
- The country's low divorce rate, much like its crime rate, has long been cited as an example of Japanese social stability and group harmony. It is still lower than that of many industrialized countries. Its 2002 rate of 2.3 divorces for every 1,000 people compares to 2.82 in England or 4.0 in the United States.[6]

The beginning of the end of marriage is impending, in part, because of this mindset: "total dedication to the boss for the sake of money." Better yet, "the love of money!"

Economic Fornication

Today's economy differs considerably from the economy of

200 years ago. Production and sales no longer determine economic growth and stability; numerous circumstances associated with economies, finances, and politics determine failure or success. Global interdependency is a major contributing factor to the health of the international economy.

When the stock market plummeted in Hong Kong in the '80s, it affected the entire Asian market virtually overnight—and the rest of the world a little later. Economies are driven by circumstantial information that becomes available first to the insiders, then to the investors, and later to the public.

Often overlooked is that the average person is in the midst of this development. The nations are drunk with the wine of the wrath of Babylon's fornication. The world's political leaders have become an integral part of the religious power structure; thus, they have become one. Hence, fornication.

For example, it is unthinkable in the United States to elect an atheist to office. Politics and religion are so closely connected that they have become virtually inseparable. The same can also be said for much of the Asian and European countries, thus a religiously motivated philosophy is producing an unprecedented political economic power structure.

Christians must not try to move the fulfillment of Bible prophecy solely to some future time, but rather recognize that the stage for prophetic fulfillment is being set right now. These things do not happen suddenly. They were occurring long ago and are being implemented to a greater degree as each year progresses. In addition, the reader must keep in mind that deception can only be achieved by success. One simply cannot deceive someone by using force. A person may surrender to the use of force but he will not allow himself to be deceived.

Geographic Center of Fornication

The Bible identifies three continents: 1) Europe, 2) Asia, and 3) Africa. America and Australia were added later. At the center of those first three continents is where the Garden of Eden was located, according to the description of the rivers mentioned in the book of Genesis. Babylon, the first Gentile superpower, was established in that part of the world. Later, it was replaced by Medo-Persia, the second Gentile superpower, followed by Greece, which stretched across the empire from southern Europe to Ethiopia in the south and from India in the east to Libya in the west. Rome is the fourth and final Gentile superpower. While Rome did take possession of all the previous empires, the Roman forces moved north and conquered virtually all of Europe. Although the Roman Empire ceased to exist as a political and military giant, the Roman culture, civilization, and especially the laws, continue to extend across the globe today.

Global Europe

It is now important to consider the European power structure under the spirit of Rome. To the east lies Asia, a continent that has been subject to European rules and laws through colonialism. Even today, most Asian countries practice Roman laws and use European languages to communicate.

Africa is located south of Europe and was dominated by European colonial powers for centuries. Although virtually all countries are independent today, the education, history, infrastructure, and laws have been adapted by the newly independent countries. North and South America are products of European colonization. Moreover, in the far southeast is Australia, a completely European continent.

This is the fourth and final Gentile superpower responsible for the dominion of the entire world. One must be mindful that no other nation, groups of nations, or continents have ever dominated the world to such an extent as did the Europeans (Romans). However, there is still a problem because Europe does not rule the nations of the world. More than 200 independent sovereign nations are on planet Earth. How will they unite to form such an incredible block in order to fulfill Scriptures such as Revelation 18:3? The progress toward that goal began when printed paper money was introduced. Although even before then, one could identify the beginning of global economy as reported in Luke 2:1 (*And it came to pass in those days, that there went out a decree from Caesar Augustus, that all the world should be taxed*). Taxes were the first steps toward a world economy. Paper money is the next and current stage, and that will be followed by individual total control.

Antichrist and World Economy

And he causeth all, both small and great, rich and poor, free and bond, to receive a mark in their right hand, or in their fore-heads: And that no man might buy or sell, save he that had the mark, or the name of the beast, or the number of his name (Rev. 13:16-17). This verse describes ultimate control of the world economy. Again, the caution to the reader is not to place this prophetic Scripture into the distant future so it has no relationship to man at this time in history. While it is true that the mark of the beast has not yet been implemented (according to the author's understanding of Bible prophecy, it will not be offered before the Church has been raptured), the preparation for the mark of the beast is occurring.

The author does not mean the actual physical mark, as far as how it will be applied and what will be its composition. Such views are open to speculation, and they always do more danger than good. Believers do, however, know *all* the people in the world will be involved for the purpose of total control of buying and selling.

Imagine the tremendous advantage people would possess if business and finance were handled above the table. Governments would flood their coffers with tax money and businesses would flourish because customers would be controlled. Retailers would sell only products that were controlled. In some countries, the underground economy is larger than the official economy. The estimates for the extent of illegal commercial activity in the United States range between 5 and 15 percent. Total control would also mean no more crime, no more drug trade, and no more tax evasion, which would all result in the benefit of humanity. One can only imagine people standing in line for days to receive this coveted mark *in their right hand, or in their foreheads.*

Uncertainty is the greatest headache for any commercial

endeavor. Business owners wonder how their customers will react and what their profit margin will be. That will all be a thing of the past when total control has been implemented; everything will be in perfect order. No longer will businesses have to employ expensive consulting firms to determine how to operate their businesses most profitably because everything will be instantly available. All customers will be registered; all products will be accounted since all will be controlled by the mark of the beast!

The Final Deception

Some may think people will not be willing to surrender their privacy and become part of this global system by receiving the mark. The response to that is found in the following two verses: *And deceiveth them that dwell on the earth by **the means of** those miracles which he had power to do in the sight of the beast; saying to them that dwell on the earth, that they should make an image to the beast, which had the wound by a sword, and did live. And he had power to give life unto the image of the beast, that the image of the beast should both speak, and cause that as many as would not worship the image of the beast should be killed* (13:14-15). People will be deceived by the false prophet who will visibly demonstrate paranormal powers so people will believe a lie.

Notice the false prophet commands the people on earth (perhaps, the scientists or computer geniuses) to *make an image to the beast*. Whatever the image, it will certainly be man-made. This is only natural because man always worships self; the image of the beast will be a product, or better yet, an idol created by himself.

Revelation 9:20-21 explains how deceived people react. *And the rest of the men which were not killed by these plagues yet repented not of the works of their hands, that they should not worship devils, and idols of gold, and silver, and brass, and stone, and of wood: which neither can see, nor hear, nor walk: Neither repented they of their murders, nor of their sorceries, nor of their fornication, nor of their thefts.* The image of the beast will have the power to distinguish between those who truly worship and those who do not. As a result, the image will *cause that as many as would not worship the image of the beast should be killed.* Finally, all opposition will be eliminated. Peace and prosperity will prevail around the globe.

The Glory of the Antichrist

The Antichrist will not need to do much more than speak words of blasphemy against the God of heaven and the world will admire him. It is significant that the Antichrist will not be powerful or prestigious because of his own achievements; everything he has will be given to him.

- *and the dragon gave him his power* (13:2)
- *the dragon which gave power unto the beast* (13:4)
- *and there was given unto him* (13:5)
- *and it was given unto him* (13:7)

Although he will be a man of fierce countenance and a great deceiver, he will be the most benevolent leader the world will have ever witnessed, as indicated by the people's reaction. *And all the world wondered after the beast. And they worshipped the dragon which gave power unto the beast: and they worshipped the beast, saying, Who is like unto the beast? Who is able to make war with him?* (13:3-4).

The title of this chapter could easily have been reversed to "How World Economies Will Rule the Nations." No one in authority will have the power to withstand the global economy. No longer will any nation afford to be independent, for all nations today are interdependent. Nevertheless, this interdependence must be governed by some type of authority which is yet to come.

Global Rule

Although international jurisdictions are globally recognized, enforcement is still questionable. International rule already dominates the wealthy nations. For example, large corporations in the United States wishing to merge with others need special permission from the European Union, and vice versa. The World Trade Organization is growing stronger each year and will become a reckoning force in the not-too-distant future.

As each year progresses, one will notice a greater level of acceptance of global enforcement, interpretation, and law. The reader should be mindful there is a world court already in The Hague, Holland. Furthermore, Switzerland, an extremely prosperous and independent country, serves as host to many of the important global issues. Rome is another important location for globalization. It is the location of today's European Union which was created in 1957 based on the Treaty of Rome. Also in Rome is the United Nations' recognized Vatican, headquarters of the world's largest religion. The pope, leader of the Vatican, is now recognized as the leading moral authority for the civilized world. The players are all in place.

However, there is a problem: Europe still lacks a united voice, even though it represents the world's largest economy. In contrast to the United States, which speaks with one voice, Europe has 25 varying voices. Nevertheless, it is significant that the European Union recently adopted the slogan "United in Diversity" as its motto.

The United Nations

Another important global organization is the United Nations, headquartered in New York, which is somewhat isolated from the remainder of the nations. Much can be said—both positive and negative—about the United Nations. Quite frequently, one will hear statements such as "it is just a paper tiger" or "it is all talk and no action" describing the organization. Those may be accurate analysis at this point, but why is the United Nations powerless? One finds the answer in its members, particularly the United States, which is not too keen on being told what other nations desire, think, or actions they take. However, the United Nations is greatly respected by both developing and underdeveloped nations. The United Nations offers a platform where grievances can be voiced against the rich nations, which virtually monopolize global economy. The future of the United Nations and its location are left to speculation, but Scripture prophecies of a spirit of unprecedented global unity to prevail. The monopolizing activity will be in Europe.

The Fourth Beast

The Bible describes this final kingdom as global: *Thus he said, The fourth beast shall be the fourth kingdom upon earth, which shall be diverse from all kingdoms, and shall devour the whole earth, and shall tread it down, and break it in pieces* (Dan. 7:23). Notice the words *diverse* and *whole earth*. The fourth beast is the fourth global kingdom, eventually ruled by an individual whose activity Daniel described. *And in the latter time of their kingdom, when the transgressors are come to the full, a king of fierce countenance, and understanding dark sentences, shall stand up. And his power shall be mighty, but not by his own power: and he shall destroy wonderfully, and shall prosper, and practice, and shall destroy the mighty and the holy people. And through his policy also he shall cause craft to prosper in his hand; and he shall magnify* **himself** *in his heart, and by peace shall destroy many: he shall also stand up against the Prince of princes; but he shall be broken without hand* (8:23-25).

According to these, and many other biblical facts cited in this chapter, Revelation 18:3 will be fulfilled. *For all nations have drunk of the wine of the wrath of her fornication, and the kings of the earth have committed fornication with her, and the merchants of the earth are waxed rich through the abundance of her delicacies.*

Why Europe?

Revelation 18:3 was quoted at the beginning of this chapter. Now it will be prudent to highlight one more issue, that is, *the merchants of the earth are waxed rich through the abundance of her delicacies.* The statement by itself is not strange because merchants generally are rich. Merchants buy and sell products. Buying costs money, and between the purchase and the sale lays the profit. If a merchant can convert a purchase into a sale quickly, he will make his profit sooner.

Hahn's quote demonstrated how profits are being generated by different methods today. No longer is profitability based solely on products and productivity. Riches are based on this woman/city/system called "Mystery Babylon." *The merchants of these things, which were made rich by her* (Rev.18:15). Revelation 18:9 references, *the kings of the earth, who have committed fornication and lived deliciously with her*. Revelation 18:23 states, *for thy merchants were the great men of the earth; for by thy sorceries were all nations deceived*.

Nevertheless, not all nations are rich; therefore, one needs to seek a system that will virtually eliminate poverty. The author's wife, Ruth, does not always accompany him on various travels, but when returning home, there is always a standard question: "Was that a rich country?" The standard answer is: "All countries are rich; the question is, 'How many poor people do they have?'"

Poverty Problem

In the United States, one of the most successful countries in the world, poverty is the gaping weakness that most Americans do not want to acknowledge or discuss. *The World Fact Book* (published by the Central Intelligence Agency) lists 12% of America's population below poverty line.[7] Whenever this fact is mentioned publicly, the reaction is usually much protest: "America is the land of plenty! Americans discard more food than anyone else in the world." Such statements may very well be true, but it does not change the clear fact that food pantries are operated by churches across the United States. Millions of meals are offered to the poor during the Thanksgiving and Christmas holidays, testifying to the fact that millions of Americans do not have enough food.

Recently, Midnight Call Ministries received a postcard from the United States Postal Service which read, "Help the national association of letter carriers stamp out hunger." The solicitation also stated, "The National Association of Letter Carriers in conjunction with the United States Postal Service® will be collecting non-perishable food items like canned soup, juice, vegetables, cereal and rice on Saturday, May 8 to help families in need in our community." Hunger and poverty are obviously a reality in the United States.

One thing should now be clear. If the world, particularly the developing and underdeveloped nations, is to accept or adapt an economic model, it has to be one that is unquestionably successful. It must benefit everyone. Where does one find an example where poverty is virtually eliminated? The answer is the progressive European nations.

The fulfillment of Revelation 18:3 (*the merchants of the earth are waxed rich through the abundance of her delicacies*) requires the general public to become rich or minimally to enjoy a high quality of life. The following statistics about quality of life are quoted from the *Encyclopedia Britannica Almanac 2003*.[8]

Region/Bloc	Life Expectancy Male	Female	Infant Mortality	Water	Doctors/Patient
Africa	51.1	53.2	86.9	57	2,560
Americas	68.8	75.2	25.4	83	520
Canada	76.0	83.0	5.1	100	540
United States	74.2	79.9	6.8	90	360
Asia	65.8	69.0	50.9	75	970
Europe	70.0	77.9	10.8	99	125
European Union	74.9	81.5	5.1	100	134
France	74.9	82.9	4.5	100	141
Germany	74.3	80.8	4.8	100	128
Italy	75.9	82.4	5.9	100	143
Spain	75.3	82.5	5.0	99	136
United Kingdom	75.0	80.5	5.6	100	129
Oceania	73.2	78.8	24.0	86	117
Australia	76.9	82.7	5.0	95	120

The statistics on the previous page are quite transparent. People living in poor countries have a low life expectancy, high infant mortality, and scarce water supplies. In those countries, a large number of citizens depend upon the care of few doctors. Interestingly, the World Health Organization lists the United States in 24th position for life expectancy. According to the *2000 World Health Report*, the United States ranked 37th in health-related services.[9]

When comparing statistics it should be clear that Europeans, as individuals, have achieved a quality of life unsurpassed in the world. As a result, Europe has become the favorite destination for immigrants. Furthermore, the quality of life for Europeans is enhanced by the shortest work week and the longest vacation time. By contrast, the United States provides significantly low vacation time. The average vacation days per year for employees with one year of service is listed.[10]

Mexico – 6
U.S. – 10
Japan – 10
Canada – 10
Britain – 20
Australia – 20
Brazil – 22
Germany – 24
France – 25
Finland - 30

European Global Economy

Regardless of the previous statistics, one must be mindful that the prophetic Word teaches the last Gentile superpower must be diverse. No other power structure can compare with Europe in action, appearance, implementation, and power. The reader is reminded of the European Union's motto: "United in diversity." The door is open not only for additional European nations, but also because the Mediterranean countries desire to become "united in diversity." However, the door (or better yet, doors) is open to the rest of the world all because of diversity.

Today, the overwhelming amount of foreign aid is supplied by Europe, thereby opening the door for developing nations to follow in the footsteps of the European Union. In contrast, the United States supplies less than 10% of the world's foreign aid budget. Slowly, but surely, a multitude of diverse nations are establishing the wealthiest and most secure society in the world.

Rome dominated when Jesus came and Rome will dominate when He returns! These few examples should clearly demonstrate that mankind today is living in a global economy. That, in turn, indicates the time on Earth is limited. The trumpet will soon be heard and those believing *that Jesus Christ died and rose again* will be translated into the presence of their Lord *and so shall* [they] *ever be with the Lord* (1 Thess. 4:14, 17).

CHAPTER 5

THE CHURCH AND WORLD ECONOMY

Wilfred J. Hahn

A striking transformation has occurred over the past two millenniums. The start of the first millennium began when a man appeared, claiming to be the Son of God. Physical lusts, riches, world power, nor abilities of self-determination conquered this Man. He was neither destitute nor materially rich. *"Foxes have holes and birds of the air have nests, but the Son of Man has no place to lay his head"*, He said (Lk. 9:58). Truly, His kingdom was not of this world.

Nevertheless, during the course of 2,000 years, many that claimed to be his representatives have entertained delusions of empire, appropriated earthly riches, and accumulated a host of other regal entitlements. Hobnobbing with kings, paragons of political power, captains of commerce, and other high-profile personalities of worldliness, they claimed these liaisons and relationships as amongst equals: the evidences of God's promises and kingdom on earth. From the beginning an impulse that intertwined God and mammon was evident. Yes, the Gospel was preached. Nevertheless, more often than not, the gospel followed the gold trail. It may not always have been the explicit choice of the missionaries, but rather its wealthy sponsors, whether colonialists or kings seeking new domains. Though Christ came to proclaim the Gospel to the poor and disenfranchised, missionaries seeking to convert the heathens of faraway worlds, whether Catholic or Protestant, tended to go to those parts of the world first which promised earthly riches and prosperity. So it remains today in various forms.

Few serve God alone; many unapologetically serve mammon; most try to serve them both. This last approach is the most heinous behavioral system of all, giving birth to the greatest and most harmful deceptions of which the Bible most pointedly warns. In fact, mammonism—money and earthly kingdom worship—has become the world's greatest religion over the past several centuries, institutionalized at the highest levels of state and religion. In no way has it any association with the God of the Bible. Nevertheless, its founding ideologies have taken fertile root cloaked in claimed "Christian principals." How could "sanctified" mammonism have evolved from the gospel? What happened?

Choose Whom Ye Will Serve

You cannot serve both God and Money (Mt. 6:24). From the time of its very utterance from Jesus' lips, this statement plunged mankind into turbulent struggle and perplexity. It struck entirely to the heart of the cosmology of opposites, that is, good and evil, sin and righteousness.

Christ made this comment to His disciples just after telling the rich young ruler, *"Go, sell everything you have and give to the poor, and you will have treasure in heaven. Then come, follow me"* (Mk. 10:21). Christ's statement created an immediate debate among the disciples (10:24-31). They were clearly daunted by the challenges of property and the requirements of the kingdom of God. Conversely, wealth was considered a blessing of the godly since after all, Abraham was quite wealthy. In spite of this, Christ admonished, *"it is easier for a camel to go through the eye of a needle than for a rich man to enter the kingdom of God"* (Mt. 19:24). *"Who can then be saved?"* (19:25), they asked. Christ replied, *"With man this is impossible, but with God all things are possible"* (19:26).

Both the author and the reader are dealing with an "impossible" subject here. Understood in that light, both can only hope to examine the subject of the church and the world economy (i.e. money) in a spirit of humility.

A Marriage Made in Hell: Mammon and the Church

What could Christ have meant with the statement asserting

that God and mammon are mutually exclusive? First, the two opposites could neither be reconciled nor bridged. In this sense, it can be seen to be a prophetic statement indicating that mankind cannot ever overcome mammon in and of his own efforts and intellect. A sense of perpetual strife exists. Not only would the struggles of the heart in choosing its master be unending, but also economic injustice would be a permanent condition of the world. *"The poor you will always have with you,"* Jesus said (Mt. 26:11). By implication, mankind would never gain victory over mammon and its destructive works. The spiritual forces enervating mammon will maim mankind, and according to prophecy, will completely teem the world as the end of days approach. Indeed, this has already happened for the most part. As this chapter will briefly document, many voices claiming to speak on behalf of the church have made a deal with mammon. They have wedded the two.

This chapter will not offer any systematic formula to solve the struggle between God and mammon. To attempt to do so even trivializes the mountain of thought that has been given to this struggle between God and mammon by gifted and respected scholars over the centuries. The author does not wish to insult them, nor does he hardly think himself their equal. Nevertheless, as already mentioned, the author and reader are dealing with an "impossible" subject in purely human terms.

The proposal of this chapter is to provide only a brief history of the church's slide down the slippery slope towards endorsing the forces of mammon to achieve peace and prosperity upon earth. Many of those that do this see the task of earthly restoration by human institutions and systems as their commission. In reviewing this trend, it is important to avoid getting hindered in dialectical arguments that have trapped intellectual debate over past centuries. Instead, the intent here is to examine only the symptoms and conditions of the world today. After all, it is not theories or systems that are sanctified. Nor are they the ultimate expression of what is good or evil. It is by the results of one's actions he is known.

Therefore, no matter how eloquent and logical the conceptions of God's laws may be, according to Scripture, the way to distinguish the good tree from the bad is by the outcome. *"By their fruit you will recognize them"* (7:16). Therefore, it is reasonable to examine and draw inferences from the evident "fruit" in the world today. What is discovered as hanging evidence is clearly not what the God of the Bible would condone. These symptoms betray a chronic and despotic condition of last days significance, both for the world and the church.

The Slippery Slope

Examining the several hundred years of history one can clearly document a progression to rampant materialism (idolatry) within Christian religious streams. At first, devotion to serving God and practicing biblical stewardship resulted in rewards. These were not the object of faith, just the attendant blessings God gave in grace. However, as these rewards accumulated (mostly in forms of comforts, technology, and wealth), the pursuit of godliness for the sake of wealth itself become the focus. Idolatry began to acquire a lasting foundation. Next, the focus shifted to the processes of creating wealth and comforts which meant any kind, for that matter. Then, the "pursuit" of wealth and possessions itself became the idol. Lastly, wealth itself became the false god.

In this process, one can witness the five-stage progression of sin. First, man sins. Then man finds ways to justify it. Next, he boasts about the sin. Finally, goodness and truth are ruined. However, that is not the end. The last stage is judgment.

Applying the economic language of the current day, what once was honest vocation led to capitalism, then to the "spirit of capitalism," and in the recent decades, the outright idolatry of "greed is good." The incredible acceleration of this trend in recent times from piety to rampant greed causes believers to take urgent notice.

Man-made Prosperity as the Solution

How did this modern perspective of "greed is good" come into such wide acceptance? It is a relatively recent phenomenon in world history. This author can only attempt a brief review.

Throughout the centuries, Christians tried vigorously to find themselves on the right side of the divide between God and mammon. Generally, the pursuit of material gain had been scowled since it was viewed to be incompatible with a virtuous life. In fact, for a long time the church, and even the Roman Catholic Church, saw it as its duty to regulate economics and commerce. These fields were not necessarily under the rule of kings and sovereigns. Whether Christian or not, the Church sought to enforce moral conduct upon society in general. Greed, materialism, and usury were definitely the emblems of mammon. These were to be eradicated.

Responses ranged from monasticism (sc. hiding away in monasteries and taking vows of poverty) to the rigid enforcement of feudal life believing that as that not all men are made equal or the same, they should remain in their station, whether peasant, priest or lords of estates. However, perspectives began to change noticeably as of the late-1600s and early 1700s with Christianity at the very center of this shift. A transition was influenced by new philosophies, technologies and discoveries and most importantly religious shifts, the greatest of these being the Reformation which indirectly encouraged a strong work ethic and capitalism. Max Weber's *The Protestant Ethic and the Spirit of Capitalism*[1] is an illuminating analysis of these complex influences. R. H. Tawney's classic, *Religion and the Rise of Capitalism*,[2] provides a more critical analysis of these same transitions.

All of these forces working together—sometimes both in opposition and parallel—gave rise to a cauldron of change. Eventually, societies surrendered to the "spirit of capitalism" (as opposed to capitalism) and more recently, to the full-fledged, society-wide endorsed "love of money" (what can be termed "The Age of Global Capital"). Today, the "love of money" is invoked both as the solution to the world's troubles and the hope for future progress.

What at first was a gradual development eventually yielded to an inundation of materialism and the celebration of monetary wealth that mankind witnesses presently. Modern money which is based upon monetarism and fractional-reserve banking has become the most powerful force on earth (i.e. a figurative tyrant). Mostly, as the reader will understand, this tyrant is held in high esteem by much of modern Christianity.

Idolatry of Gold Left Rampant

Anyone who has eyes to see knows the world today is governed by materialism. More than any other time in history, people, nations, and virtually the entire world are almost totally preoccupied with the human pursuit of happiness, material prosperity, and peace. God does indeed want His people to be joyful, peaceful, and prosperous. However, this is not to be without Him, the true Source, and not without reverence and His glorification. Instead, what can be witnessed today is the accepted perversion that happiness, peace, and virtue are directly linked to prosperity. There is no need for God. The notion is to provide people with prosperity and there will be happiness and peace (a materialist utopia). Many so-called Christian organizations have adopted this mindset.

For example, this very view is directing much of the efforts today to tame the radical Muslim world. The working theory is as follows: all that is needed to solve the problem of an apparently untamable society, such as Iraq and other hotbeds of radical Islam, are some western creature comforts. Give them a chicken in every cooking pot, free-market capitalism, internet, libertine entertainment, and they will be content. Peace will follow.

To illustrate this institutional view, consider the policies of the World Economic Forum, which is hardly an altruistic entity, as its membership is comprised of approximately 1,000 multinational corporations.[3] Typically, their thinking is that a free-market and capitalistic revolution will solve all the problems of political and religious unrest. Close the large gap between the economical and financial wealth of the West and the low-income nations and the problem will be fixed. The high-income countries of the world[4] have an average income more than 27 times of the average Muslim nation, and 15 times the average of all 22 members of the Arab League of Nations.[5] In their eyes, this disparity must be the main source of the problems.

This same presumption is behind many efforts to establish peace and eradicate poverty from the world. Governments and various global agencies are generally united in this view,[6] supremely confident that the Western model of free markets, consumer hedonism and financial booms will bring contentment and peace (the notion being even an unruly nation such as Iraq can be completely transformed in a very short time through democracy and full stomachs). This is hardly likely for a number of reasons. To orthodox Islam, the complete idea of Western materialism and libertine living is seen as the very repudiation of their religion. While the West tends to view the schism as a material issue, Islam views it as a religious one.

In this respect, it does not matter that Islam is a false faith. The Islamic view of the Western world is a condemnation not only of materialism, but more explicitly, what they see to be Christendom. Islamic thinkers clearly see that idolatry has clouded the perspective of the so-called Christian high-income countries of the world, especially America and its sister nations.

Inside the Church: False Prophets of Mammon

So-called Christian organizations exist to validate the ideas of "free markets" and the "spirit of capitalism" as Scripturally-endorsed forces for good. These very ideas poise on the positive forces of self interest and the love of money. Yes, Scripture endorses good works as the natural effect of saving faith. Nevertheless, good works for Christians are the result of the work of the Holy Spirit in their lives; sometimes good works for believers and unbelievers come from inspired individual hearts, as opposed to systems or machines. True capitalism, like democracy, is only good if the majority of people have the One that is Good living in their hearts.

Apparently, not enough people realize the enormous temptations of gain and money. Surely, not every one is called to be wealthy as few are capable of being unstained by it (so says the Bible). God does choose to bless some individuals in this way; still others choose this blessing for themselves without God. In their unbridled wants, they then fall into a trap. *People who want to get rich fall into temptation and a trap and into many foolish and harmful desires that plunge men into ruin and destruction* (1 Tim. 6:9). There is no reason not to believe that the same principal applies to nations. Countries who vaunt prosperity as their chief aim eventually will plunge *into ruin and destruction*. The Bible repeatedly warns about the deceitfulness of riches. Satan is keenly aware of this beguiling nature of wealth and has used the human disposition towards the "love of money" to great advantage in the last days.

Nevertheless, Christian leaders are to be found among the proponents calling forth the benefits of "tamed" greed for the good of the world. The saddest aspect of America's fall into abject slavery to materialism is that some Christian theologians have used Scripture to whitewash a "culture of affluence." It evidences a diabolical agenda by dressing it in the array of godliness. Addressing a similarly false facade, Christ excoriated the Pharisees, saying, *"You are like whitewashed tombs, which look beautiful on the outside but on the inside are full of dead men's bones and everything unclean. In the same way, on the outside you appear to people as righteous but on the inside you are full of hypocrisy and wickedness"* (Mt. 23:27-28).

Underestimating the dangers and temptations of mammon, which the Bible clearly warns, such undiscerning leaders guide mankind astray. In effect, they have joined hands with mammon to bring about God's kingdom to earth. It would be difficult to bring a balanced and complete documentation to this topic in one chapter, but a few quotes from notable "Christian" thinkers will set the tone.

Whitewashed "Christian" Economic Ideals

Renowned Christian social theologian, Michael Novak wrote, "The church could lead the way in setting forth a religious and moral vision worthy of a global world, in which all live under a universally recognizable rule of law, an every individual's gifts are nourished for the good of all."[7] Novak's statement is underpinned by noble objectives. While that may be true, the methods proposed are worldly works of man. This scholar takes great lengths to claim that Christianity (mostly Catholicism, in his view) invented capitalism.

Others make sweeping statements that seem to imply the Bible needs major revision in regards to wealth in order to be relevant for this day and age. One such author wrote, "I have come to believe (in the light of fresh theory) that capitalism (for all its problems) is not just the greatest liberating power in human history, but also that its cultural workings provide an unusually good opportunity for the expressive of true Christian faith and virtue."[8] He also wrote, "that both these common perspectives—the cultural and the biblical—on faith and wealth have to be renovated in the light of fresh evidence and theory."[9] That is a broad statement. Elsewhere he argued, the complete moral situation of affluence is as different today as it could possible compared to previous times. Apparently, the ancient and modern moral traditions do not possess adequate resources to understand them, so there is need for a new theological response.[10]

Nevertheless, just where is this evidence and theory to be found? In the Bible? No. Much of the evidence cited is from secular research that appeals to "cultural" and quantitative techniques.

From this writer's perspective of the inner workings of the global financial circles and a theoretical understanding of capitalistic and monetary systems, he really does not understand much to have changed under the sun. Man's tools and systems today may be bigger, more powerful, and capable of global reach, but the underlying character of man and his chief enemy remains the same. In this sense, nothing needs to be revised in the Bible, nor does one need to distort God's word to please the panting lust for materialism today.

Secular economists have long harnessed the "animal spirits" of free-market capitalism for supposed good works. They see no conflict and only a little danger. For example, Lawrence Lindsay, the former economic advisor and director of the National Economic Council at the White House, proudly stated, "two aspects of the ethos of capitalism—materialism and individualism [greed and self-interest]—are what make humanitarianism possible."[11] Mr.

Lindsay makes the point here that two sins, if performed judiciously, can lead to a right. Could this really be true? While he does not speak with any claimed authority on behalf of Christianity, his views are little different than those that do.

Big Money behind God

A movement to join mammon to the worldly agendas of the church is at work under many guises. Some, recognizing that big money has big power in the present Age of Global Capital, even adopt the tactics of pillaging portfolio managers. They provoke their agents for change towards a Christian worldview (atop large church pension funds) actively prodding companies to adopt their views at the bayonet-point of transferring their investments. One recently founded organization, the Interfaith International Investment Group (3iG),[12] boldly proclaims its power for change by declaring that its 11 founding denominations wield over $7 trillion in wealth.

The formation of the 3iG seems rather ironic. Protesting the deplorable conditions of world poverty and supposedly representing He who often commanded His followers to give to the poor,[13] they amass $7 trillion in wealth. As will be further documented, it is sufficient to say that Christendom and some of its organizations are rich today.

Soaring to new heights of insight, Michael Novak even postulates, "But increasingly, in the West, it's going to be affluence that leads people to God."[14] Even secular economists who make no pretense of belonging to any religion know that this is not true. There are well-documented studies clearly demonstrating that as societies become more affluent, they become less interested in a faith in God.

Numerous quotes from many more sources could be given from this movement seeking to wed the good of mammon to the agenda of the physical establishment of the kingdom of God on earth. This is a serious indictment. Mammon, after all, is the entity opposing God. There are only two realms: God and mammon. How then can any good come by joining together two mutually exclusive realms?

Borrowing from Balaam

It is as if the church has decided to borrow the volatile fuel from mammon for its agenda to reform the world into its earthly conception of Christ's kingdom on earth. The perspectives developed in this regard are much more sophisticated than the well-known prosperity gospel which preaches it is every true Christian's divine right to be prosperous and have great supply. Apparently, it is only the "force" of faith that is in shortage. While the latter group caters to individual self-interest and self-esteem, the ideology this writer is examining here has much greater ambitions. It seeks to reform the world. However, its proponents ally themselves with fallen forces. By employing the two innate human proclivities of "self interest" and the "love of money" they have harnessed these "animal spirits" for the sake of winning world peace and abolishing poverty. Yes, even winning people for Christ.

The two human compulsions mentioned are dangerous material, like atomic fuel (e.g. plutonium). Yes, man can gather it into the controlled core of a nuclear reactor and produce energy to power an agenda. Nevertheless, man must carefully keep these plutonium fuel rods cooled lest they react uncontrollably and cause great damage. Unrestrained, this fuel can "meltdown" the entire reactor and wreak great destruction and emit widespread devastation. Even if all proceeds as planned, the toxic byproduct remains for centuries. Mankind must still bury the depleted fuel in lead containers. Undeniably, toxic byproducts of this philosophy can be seen accumulating all around the world.

It is one thing for lost humanity to live by the rules and powers of mammon. Quite another issue is to see the church enjoying mammon for a "heaven on earth" mission. At least two apostles expressly warned about this type of error.

This is especially true of those who follow the corrupt desire of the sinful nature and despise authority...these men blaspheme in matters they do not understand...with eyes full of adultery, they never stop sinning; they seduce the unstable; they are experts in greed—an accursed brood! They have left the straight way and wandered off to follow the way of Balaam son of Beor, who loved the wages of wickedness...for they mouth empty, boastful words and, by appealing to the lustful desires of sinful human nature, they entice people who are just escaping from those who live in error. They promise them freedom, while they themselves are slaves of depravity—for a man is a slave to whatever has mastered him (2 Pet. 2:10-19).

These are serious allegations. The result? Not freedom, but slavery. It is even worse as the above Scriptures also describe what is occurring today in the church. Here, the dangers intensify. *It would have been better for them not to have known the way of righteousness, than to have known it and then to turn their backs on the sacred command that was passed on to them* (2:21). Jude felt urged to write about the same error.

Dear friends, although I was very eager to write to you about the salvation we share, I felt I had to write and urge you to contend for the faith that was once for all entrusted to the saints. For certain men whose condemnation was written about long ago have secretly slipped in among you. They are godless men, who change the grace of our God into a license for immorality and deny Jesus Christ our only Sovereign and Lord.

Yet these men speak abusively against whatever they do not understand; and what things they do understand by instinct, like unreasoning animals—these are the very things that destroy them. Woe to them! They have taken the way of Cain; they have rushed for profit into Balaam's error; they have been destroyed in Korah's rebellion (Jude 3-4, 10-11).

Both Peter and Jude cite Balaam's error. What was it? While Balaam did not pronounce curses upon Israel as King Balak had requested, he did supply him with an even more powerful plan to ruin Israel. It was the strategy of infiltrating Israel with idolatrous beliefs and practices. It worked. The motive? Profit and self-interest. Balak wanted to preserve his kingdom and Balaam was being paid handsomely for his advice as an economic theologian and sociologist.

Today, similar perversions have led to an even greater, forlorn state. It is now a global problem. From a number of perspectives, there can be no doubt that the world's troubles today have deep religious dimensions. It is just as depicted in Zechariah's vision of the measuring basket found (Zech. 5). The contents of this basket (providing a depiction of greed), commercial and religious corruption, were covered with a lid made of the very same metal that can shield nuclear radiation (viz. lead).

A Pandering New Religion

Samuel Brittan, a noted columnist and economic historian questions rhetorically, "Is economics a form of religion? Alas, it depends on what you mean by religion. According to the 1990 edition of *The Dictionary of Christianity in America*: 'If belief in a god is necessary to define a religion, secular humanism does not qualify. If on the other hand religion, or a god, is defined as one's ultimate value, then secular humanism is a religion.'"[15] Economics belongs to humanism. Therefore, the field of economics is a faith system. Few secular practitioners of this field of humanism would disagree with this statement. However, many economic theologians who declare they are Christians do not see any contradictions. They almost exult in their friendliness with the world, secure in their "new" understandings (even revisionism) of Scripture. Such individuals seek to change the world in the name of good ethics.

Mammon is the worship of earthy power and prosperity for its own desired end. It has nothing to offer the eternal kingdom of God. Let the devices of mammon into the church, even by a shadow, and the road to destruction begins. Diversion of the believer's attention and worship from God for even a moment, or bemoaning unsatisfied physical wants, can result in being stung with poisons. As happened to Israel in the desert when they were dissatisfied to their physical circumstances, they were beset by poisonous snakes (Numb. 21). Only when they focused upon the bronze snake (figuring Christ) that Moses had set upon a pole, did they find relief.

Adam Smith, in his famous book, *The Wealth of Nations* (1776),[16] expressed the view that he thought the church (in his day, referring to the Church of England) was doomed. He reasoned since independent clergy relied upon the voluntary donations of their congregation for their income, they had little incentive to give them what they need, but rather what they want. The "men of learning and elegance" in the state church would eventually lose "market share" to those "popular and bold, though perhaps stupid and ignorant" independents. While believers today may not lament the demise of a state church as Smith did, he articulated a cardinal truth. Eventually, the "love of money" would lead to apostasy and false teaching, particularly as related to materialism and lusts of the flesh. Actually, Smith was not the first to observe this problem. Every movement of false teaching mentioned in the New Testament epistles reveals an improper infatuation with money and gain.

Priests, Prophets, and Teachers Alike

A similar self-interest works its distortion in religious academia. Theologians studying economics are also held hostage by "market forces." They are subtly forced to conform to accepted assumption and norms. After all, their well-being and long-term career is dependent upon tenure and perceived legitimacy. Any hint of a "personal relationship with Christ" and their career potential is impaired. Marketable theology sells because it is what the world demands. The most rewarded theological product is the type that marries mammon with Scriptural legitimacy. It meets a ready market in a materialist world having immersed itself in a "culture of affluence." Not only does it meet friends in high places, but it also appeals to the masses who still believe in the "American Dream." One incisive wrote,

> There two types of economic theologians. The first is an economist who functions as a theologian of the religion of progress by helping to provide and ethical foundation

for society. If economic progress is the route to salvation, these "priests" will be the experts on how to achieve that progress. Because society looks to economists for this knowledge, they logically become the leading priesthood of the age. The second way to be an economic theologian is to study economics from a theological perspective.[17]

The first-mentioned group is the main prophets of mammon, that is, economic "theologians" who have fallen for the "error of Balaam." They have sold their prescriptions and prophecies for a price, seeking to feather their own positions. They have elevated "progress" and "prosperity" as the solution to mankind's troubles. In doing so, whether professing to be Christian theologians or not, they prescribe ethics. The most perverted among them will whitewash this new human and global prerogative with twisted appeals to Scripture. Boasting their "Christian" credentials and claimed objectives of bringing good and new insight to the world, they sprinkle holy water on the volcanic forces that power mammon. Their water baptisms will prove sorely ineffective in cooling the burning furnaces of mammon. What will be the ultimate outcome of this continuing slide into idolatry for the church?

The Last Days Church

The Bible provides a number of revealing pictures concerning the church in the last days. It is not a pretty prospect.

Now listen, you rich people, weep and wail because of the misery that is coming upon you. Your wealth has rotted, and moths have eaten your clothes. Your gold and silver are corroded. Their corrosion will testify against you and eat your flesh like fire. You have hoarded wealth in the last days. Look! The wages you failed to pay the workmen who mowed your fields are crying out against you. The cries of the harvesters have reached the ears of the Lord Almighty. You have lived on earth in luxury and self-indulgence. You have fattened yourselves in the day of slaughter. You have condemned and murdered innocent men, who were not opposing you (Jas. 5:1-6).

Chillingly, James issues a horrible warning: *weep, and wail because of the misery that is coming upon you.* Without taking the time to provide solid evidence, he is also speaking to Christendom of the last days—the current generation.

It can be stated that the gap between the world's poor and the wealthy continues to widen. In fact, the "relative" wealth gap is now probably the largest in history. Certainly, this is true since third century Rome. Not only is this trend evident between countries, but also within countries (e.g. even in the wealthy ones such as the United States, Canada, and Britain). A large body of studies and statistics is available on this subject from various transnational organizations, particularly the World Bank, the International Monetary Fund (IMF), and the Organization for Economic Cooperation and Development (OECD). Indeed, the amount of erudite working papers and policy briefs these organizations produce on these phenomena cannot be dismissed.

What makes the situation of global wealth more astounding in the present day is that the world has experienced the biggest wealth boom in history this past century (the word "wealth" is used in its popular financial sense). According to researchers,[18] in this definition (as mentioned in Chapter 2), more wealth was created this past century than in the entire preceding history of mankind. More recently, this trend has even accelerated as the world has witnessed the largest financial boom in the entirety of the human record. One would think by now either poverty would have been eradicated or a less skewed distribution of wealth would have occurred. Nonetheless and quite to the contrary, the pattern of wealth distribution has continued to worsen.

Wealth Division by Religion

Just who would qualify as the rich of today? Let the reader consider some facts from the World Bank, headquartered in

Washington DC. It collects the most complete data on world development trends. The statistics provided by the World Development Indicators 2001 report offers further illuminating perspectives (at the time of this survey it covered 183 member countries and produced statistics from 203 nations). The 52 high-income countries of the world which the World Bank identifies accounted for 79.1% of total world income in 2000. In other words, less than one-sixth of the world's population garnered four-fifths of all income. In contrast, approximately five-sixths of the world's people earned only one-fifth of all income.

A revealing picture emerges when the rich countries are categorized by religious persuasion. One will discover that only 4 countries of all 52 high-income nations are Muslim (viz. Brunei, Kuwait, Qatar, and United Arab Emirates). These are all small, oil-rich countries accounting for less than 90 million in population which have become wealthy due to the boom of Western oil consumption. Three others are predominantly Buddhist (Japan, Hong Kong which is now part of China, and Singapore; these latter two are considered city-states). Exclusive of the Buddhist and Muslim countries, there remains a list of 45 other rich countries. Remarkably, this group of rich countries in the world (accounting for little more than a tenth of all people on earth) is of Judeo-Christian heritage (or conversion of some degree or time). Briefly, what is evident is that the 45 Christian-heritage nations (in the widest sense of this definition) account for greater than 60% of the world's annual income. Viewed another way, the rich Christian nations have an average income per person of $29,500 versus only $2,250 for the rest of the world. That is a factor difference of 13 times.

What can the reader conclude from these world income statistics? As any respected economist knows, income is the most reliable and valid proxy for real wealth. Various wealth surveys are available; however, they are incomplete and intermittent. It only follows that those with the highest incomes will also be the richest. Therefore, income surveys are valid measures of wealth differences. On that basis, what become evident today is that the wealthy countries, that is, the extremely rich people of the world, are the historically Christian nations.

A Rich Last Days Church?

A Martian would surely find it curious that the world is roughly divided into two parts: prosperous historical Christendom of the West and the relatively poor remainder of the world (materialistically, at least). The Bible can be interpreted to prophesy this situation.

> I know your deeds, that you are neither cold nor hot. I wish you were either one or the other! So, because you are luke-warm—neither hot nor cold—I am about to spit you out of my mouth. You say, 'I am rich; I have acquired wealth and do not need a thing.' But you do not realize that you are wretched, pitiful, poor, blind and naked. I counsel you to buy from me gold refined in the fire, so you can become rich; and white clothes to wear, so you can cover your shameful nakedness; and salve to put on your eyes, so you can see (Rev. 3:15-18).

Though Christ is speaking in a spirit of correction to the Laodicean church in the above passage, the allegations He makes against this congregation are very chilling. The church in Laodicea was *wretched, pitiful, poor, blind and naked.* The message was addressed to this first-century church. However, does it apply only to the time that Apostle John uttered these words? Alternatively, does it have a wider application, perhaps applying to the present day? A number of respected scholars would agree. Christ addressed the last of the five New Testament churches, therefore, possibly symbolizing the last days church. The admonishments are, of course, meant to be heeded by all past, present, and future churches. It is beyond doubt that many Christians in North America and the Western world would find the admonishment to the Laodicean church an affront were it directed to them. Nevertheless, does the message apply (i.e. *He who has an ear, let him hear what the Spirit says to the churches*)?

Without a doubt, were this message to the Laodiceans also intended to prefigure the last days church, there assuredly are some wide similarities to the present time not to be ignored. The symptoms are inescapable. It can be proved that what the world understands to be the church (Christendom in all it forms and guises, true or apostate; i.e. the West) is rich. Even though Europe no longer makes any pretense of being Christian (despite the many eponymous political parties), ask any Muslim and he will certainly identify it as Christian. It does not need mentioning this is equally true for America. The Laodicean church was rich and self-satisfied in its prosperity and displayed "nakedness" of faith. It is sufficient to state that God has become very small in the eyes of modern, technologically advanced humanity.

Christianity as a Means to Wealth

On a relative global scale, never before has Christendom been as wealthy as today. During various eras since the time of Christ, other cultures and religions (e.g., China, the Ottoman Empire, etc.) were considered among the most culturally advanced and magnificent. As already briefly reviewed, it was only with the beginning of the industrial age and modern-day monetarism that Judeo-Christian nations began to rise to the pinnacles of sustainable world power and wealth. In contrast, the early Christian church was identified very differently. Some of the early Christians were even called Ebionites (meaning "the poor ones"). Whether they were poor for the right reasons or not, at that time, it would be an understatement to state today's church does not identify with this reputation. Christ warned those who would follow Him for mere physical rewards: *But store up for yourselves treasures in heaven, where moth and rust do not destroy, and where thieves do not break in and steal* (Mt. 6:20) and *the Son of Man has no place to lay his head* (8:20). Unfortunately, a large component of the church today is more inclined to view God as little more than a means to attain prosperity and material blessings.

To the secular economic sciences community, Christianity, in whatever form, is only of interest in its connections to the material state upon Earth. In this thinking, the value of Christianity is simply reduced to a question of economic input and output. It is a force for good in the world if it can be proven that Christian beliefs contribute to the greater prosperity and productivity of the world. In other words, if the output of the "Christian sector" or the "religious sector" is greater than the labor and factor input, religion is to be encouraged (at the very least, left alone). Reflecting this thinking, it is material prosperity erected as the final arbiter of what is good and fine. Concludes one study that discerns positive connections between economic growth and religion: "These results accord with a perspective in which religious beliefs influence individual traits that enhance economic performance. We find that economic growth responds positively to the extent of religious beliefs."[19]

It is good, in this respect, that most social economists think that "Christian beliefs" are a positive force. The concepts of honesty, an industrious work ethic, personal calling, property rights, trust, and vocation are helpful to a smoothly functioning capitalism. Actually, these academics could not care less if Christians rested claim on these concepts. What matters here is not the means nor the religious ideology, but the result (improved productivity and prosperity). As already mentioned, these are the gods of the current age and theologians are competitively stamping their "Christian imprimatur" all over the Age of Global Capitalism.

A Church Poisoned in the Last Days

Imagine the day where the secular world begins to see Christians as an economic obstruction, that is, a hindrance to the vaunted goal of consumption, greater prosperity, and output for all. In every other realm, the veracity of Scripture and the views of the church have been debunked and disenfranchised. On issues of morality? Irrelevant. What about sociology and the family? Irrelevant to today's culture. Money? Here one discovers one of the few areas where there is comfortable agreement. By definition, this is an incriminating sign for the church.

For many, capitalism, democratic liberalism, and materialism (at least, whatever parody of these currently exist) are to be defended as biblically-based doctrines. Lofty maxims professing good "ethics," "governance," and "works" in the name of God, or some institution of Christian religious heritage, provides an external veneer to hide the true affections and motives of the heart. What people and organizations claim and expend great energy to legitimize with references to "Christian ideals" is not necessarily what they do or even plan to do. It is become an exercise in "spin" similar to Israel during Ezekiel's day. *With their mouths they express devotion, but their hearts are greedy for unjust gain. Indeed, to them you are nothing more than one who sings love songs with a beautiful voice and plays an instrument well, for they hear your words but do not put them into practice* (Ezek. 33:31-32). In like manner today, one hears and reads countless love songs about ethics and good works from churches, governments, and industries. Meanwhile, the world is witnessing apostasy, corruption, deepening sin, and economic injustices as perhaps never before.

The world and the church that has found a home with mammon will surely face a harsh judgment. Ezekiel's prophecy to Israel quoted prior also revealed a punishment: *I will make the land a desolate waste, and her proud strength will come to an end* (33:28). Likewise, when Christ addressed the Pharisees, he said they would not escape judgment for their duplicities and sins.

It must be clear to the reader that the church's understanding of economy is a serious topic of great significance for the last days. Not only does it embrace an issue that is "impossible" to develop perfectly by man, but also it is the place of a stronghold both camouflaged and fortified by deep deception and endemic enslavement. Satan, the very epitome of deception and lies, has laid the foundation for his stronghold there. In the process, the world and much of the church has been captured by rampant idolatry. Only for the latter has it involved a change of position. Even worse, the reader can find it is with help of religion that this process has been accelerated.

Original capitalism itself—a human system—and wealth is not evil, nor is the person evil because he is rich. Not at all. God has created material things for the blessing of His people. The issue concerns the heart of that which is possessed. If wealth and riches own the heart, then a man has come to be possessed by it. God must possess the heart, not possessions, though some

Christians may be billionaires. Money is an instrument of service, not the other way around. That is clear in theory. However, the Bible teaches riches are deceitful.

Mammon possesses alluring powers. Therefore, the reader can understand what began from good motives has long ago given way to the "doctrines of demons." It has become a system with little more than the worship of self-interest and greed as the common givers of good and prosperity for mankind. It is this "doctrine of greed" today playing the role of a new secular religion, one that is unifying much of the world. Free-trading financial markets are all-knowing and all-wise. False and deceiving forms of wealth are as acceptable as real wealth. Economic growth, for its own sake, is good. Consumption must be maximized as an inalienable proof of progress. Shockingly, Christian theologians are anointing these occultic aspects as tools, which they believe can be used judiciously to reform the world to Christ.

It is the achievement of a type of ecumenicism. Mammon is being merged with the kingdom of God. It truly betrays the image and character of the last days harlot depicted in Revelation 17-18: *BABYLON THE GREAT.*

CHAPTER 6

THE MILLENNIAL ECONOMY

Ron J. Bigalke Jr.

Then God said, "Let Us make man in Our image, according to Our likeness; and let them rule over the fish of the sea and over the birds of the sky and over the cattle and over all the earth, and over every creeping thing that creeps on the earth" (Gen. 1:26). From the beginning of human history, God mandated mankind to work and be accountable for their work. An entirely biblical economy was present at creation and will be restored in the millennium. The present reality of sin in this world means the work is often less than the initial aims and objectives. Nevertheless, Christians are reminded to be *abounding in the work of the Lord, knowing that your toil is not in vain in the Lord* (1 Cor. 15:58). This chapter will examine the nature of work, money, and wealth. The analysis here will reflect the conditions of the millennial economy.

Work is often the basis for obedience to the great commandment. It demonstrates love of God and loving service to one's neighbor (cf. Mt. 22:36-40). God leads individuals to a variety of callings, including businesses, ministries, schools, and services in society. The believer's work is given for faithful responsibility in accordance with the gifts that God bestows. The calling upon the believer is always to serve God and others. Through the gift of work, man can better explore and subdue God's creation for His eternal glory. God calls His people to be good stewards with His creation and to be responsible with energy, resources, talents, and time. Being a good steward creates the opportunity for greater service to God and others. In the present time, it should be the goal of each believer to seek appropriate work in response to God's Word.

"*But seek first His kingdom and His righteousness; and all these things shall be added to you* (Mt. 6:33; cf. Ps. 23:1). When Jesus spoke these words, He was demanding thought regarding the proper motivation in relation to *His kingdom and His righteousness*. Motivation is the reason for one's actions. There are certain actions which are necessary for biological survival, but Jesus was urging His listeners to give priority to the things in life which relate to the coming kingdom. Jesus did not want His listeners to neglect food, drink, clothing, or shelter; rather, His point was not to make those things the main motivation of life. One should not work solely for biological survival, but to earn a livelihood for the purpose of serving God.

Jeremiah wrote, "*The heart is more deceitful than all else and is desperately sick; who can understand it? "I, the LORD, search the heart, I test the mind, even to give to each man according to his ways, according to the results of his deeds* (Jer. 17:9-10). Self-centeredness and self-deception are the natural inclinations of mankind oftentimes affecting proper motivation. God has given His Word so Christians can understand the self and are without excuse for not allowing the mind to be transformed by the wisdom of God. Understanding one's motivation toward work is important for understanding how one desires to serve God.

The Issue of Money

The ability to witness positive results of one's labor is important to all and should not be considered an evil desire. Truly, *the worker is worthy of his support* (Mt. 10:10; cf. Rom. 4:4-5; 2 Thess. 3:8-12; 1 Tim. 5:18; Rev. 22:12). *He who tends the fig tree will eat its fruit; and he who cares for his master will be honored* (Prov. 27:18). It is good for the worker to receive worthwhile benefits and wages. Receiving remuneration from one's labor is the result of diligence in one's occupation. This principle is repeated in the New Testament. *Who at any times serves as a soldier at his own expense? Who plants a vineyard, and does not eat the fruit of it? Or who tends a flock and does not use the milk of the flock?* (1 Cor. 9:7).

Even the animals should enjoy remuneration from their work. *"You shall not muzzle the ox while he is threshing* (Deut. 25:4; 1 Cor. 9:9). Contrary to being an evil inclination, the desire to enjoy benefits and wages from one's work is a godly characteristic (Isa. 65:21-23; Phil. 1:22). The principle of sowing and reaping is a recurrent teaching of Scripture. According to John 4:36, both the sower and the reaper *may rejoice together.* Not only would the disciples of Jesus receive wages in the temporal life, but also they would gather *fruit for eternal life.* Serving God brings rewards in the present and the eternal. It is a blessing to receive remuneration from one's labor, but some of the faithful will even receive a blessing from another's laborer (i.e. a double blessing). Joshua 24:13 reads, *'And I gave you a land on which you had not labored, and cities which you had not built, and you have lived in them; you are eating of vineyards and olive groves which you did not plant.'* God works all things according to His eternal decree.

Since it is a godly characteristic to receive remuneration from one's labor, an evil characteristic is to reduce or withhold one's wages. Genesis 31:7 condemns Laban for cheating Jacob and changing his wages numerous times. Likewise, Jeremiah 22:13 reads, *"Woe to him who builds his house without righteousness and his upper rooms without justice, who uses his neighbor's services without pay and does not give him his wages.*

Not all work is good. Jesus warned, *"Do not work for the food which perishes, but for the food which endures to eternal life, which the Son of Man shall give to you, for on Him the Father, even God, has set His seal"* (Jn. 6:27). The one who engages in sinful deeds will experience *death* (Rom. 6:23). Believers are admonished *do not participate in the unfruitful deeds of darkness* (Eph. 5:11).

It is not ungodly to desire remuneration for one's labor, but it is sinful to make one's wages the sole focus of life. *For the love of money is a root of all sorts of evil, and some by longing for it have wandered away from the faith, and pierced themselves with many a pang* (1 Tim. 6:10). Furthermore, it is wicked to change or withhold one's wages. The one who desires money for power is sinning, in the same manner as the one who makes the acquiring of wealth the main purpose of life. Kaiser wrote,

> The sad fact is that few have ventured into those portions of Scripture that call for a balanced approach to the questions of wealth, health, and success. Instead, success, and the determined quest for it alone, is spoiling America's "worldly evangelicals...." The prosperity gospel does not appear to belong to any particular denominational group or brand of theology; in fact, it is so broadly spread over the American scene that it defies any easy categorization theologically. At times it has the emphasis of the possibility or positive thinking of a Robert Schuller and a Norman Vincent Peale. At other times it appears to be private preserve of faith-healing groups. But more than all of these it rests on our culture's heavy involvement with an affluent suburban Christianity.[1]

There is a biblical basis of authority in serving God, spreading the Gospel, and shepherding God's people. However, acquiring money as a means of power to exert authority over others is clearly wrong. Money can be a blessing from God, but its acquisition quickly becomes sinful when it is sought to satisfy one's own agenda among the church. When wealth becomes sinful it is an attitude of the heart. The best illustration is the Laodicean church who said, *"I am rich, and have become wealthy, and have need of nothing,"* and you do not know that you are wretched and miserable and poor and blind and naked* (Rev. 3:17).

Right to Private Property

Then to Adam He said, "Because you have listened to the voice of your wife, and have eaten from the tree about which I commanded you, saying, 'You shall not eat from it'; cursed is the ground because of you; in toil you shall eat of it all the days of your life. "Both thorns and thistles it shall grow for you; and you shall eat the plants of the field; by the sweat of your face you shall eat bread, till you return to the ground, because from it you were taken; for you are dust, and to dust you shall return" (Gen. 3:17-19).

Before God expelled Adam and Eve from the Garden of Eden for their rebellion against Him, He purposed that mankind would work *in toil.* However, the work would not be without purpose. *Poor is he who works with a negligent hand, but the hand of the diligent makes rich* (Prov. 10:4). God, who is merciful, will reward the diligent worker with private property. Proverbs 14:23 reads, *In all labor there is profit, but mere talk leads only to poverty.* God has created a world where private property is palpable to those who are conscientious toward God's plan. Therefore, man's right to property encourages mankind to be productive. Not only has God given the responsibility to work diligently, but also He has given the privilege to work for private property. As a reward for his work, man is able to rest and enjoy the right to property which is protected by God's Law.

According to God's Law, *"'You shall not steal"* (Exod. 20:15; Deut. 5:19). God clearly forbids stealing private property which means if something can be stolen there must be a right to property. The Eighth Commandment defends an individual's right to obtain and own property, and condemns its opposite, that is, stealing. The ethics of private property are based upon justice. *'You shall do no injustice in judgment; you shall not be partial to the poor nor defer to the great, but you are to judge your neighbor fairly* (Lev. 19:15). God does not exercise favoritism to the poor or the rich (cf. Mal. 2:9; 1 Tim. 5:21; Jas. 3:17). Any economic system, which favors poor or rich, is disobedient to biblical justice. Justice requires equality before the law, in contrast to those who would assent to views of certain different classes of individuals possessing special rights because of abilities or incomes that others do not. Commenting on the Eighth Commandment, John Calvin wrote,

The purport is, that injustice being an abomination to

God, we must render to every man his due. In substance, then, the commandment forbids us to long after other men's goods, and, accordingly, requires every man to exert himself honestly in preserving his own. For we must consider, that what every individual possesses has not fallen to him by chance, but by the distribution of the sovereign Lord of all, that no one can pervert his means to bad purposes without committing a fraud on a divine dispensation [*Institutes* II.8.45].[2]

Each man has the responsibility and the privilege to work honestly. The following is an excerpt from an essay on free enterprise delivered at the 2002 Texas Farm Bureau Citizenship Seminar. It expresses clearly the vision of America's founding fathers against a controlled economy as capitalism has been a defense against the establishment of a religious state.

Our forefathers were greatly influenced by the Judeo-Christian ideals of philosopher John Locke, and the Bible. Locke had the idea that all men are equal and independent by nature. The state was a "mutual contract" among men guided by their desire to safeguard their natural rights of life, liberty and property. Locke had a great influence on the early leaders of America such as Thomas Jefferson and James Madison, and that influence is evident in the Declaration of Independence, the Constitution, and other documents pertaining to the molding of America's future government.

Greatly influenced by the Bible, John Locke presents his view on laws made by man: "Laws human must be made according to the general laws of nature, and without contradiction to any positive law of scripture, otherwise they are ill made."[3]

The thinking of the day, "Thou shalt not steal...thou shalt not covet," applied to governments as well as individuals.

Our founders believed that by nature man is greedy, and they wanted to limit government so people would not suffer from totalitarianism, such as occurred with European dictatorships.

They embraced democratic capitalism for a number of reasons. The Bible not only grants the right to private property but also calls for men to be good stewards of their property. Biblical stewardship sees God as the owner of all things and man must account for the use of whatever he has and must work to increase the Owner's investment.

Locke stated, "God who hath given the world to men in common, hath also given them reason to make use of it to the best advantage of life, and convenience.[4] Thus the grass my horse has bit; the turfs my servant has cut; and the ore I have [digged] in any place, where I have a right to them in common with others, become my property, without the consent of any body. The labor that was mine hath fixed my property in them."[5]

Competition in a free market also works according to comparative advantage, which allows everyone to be the best producer of some service or good, and this validates the worth of each individual.

Capitalism is more socially just, encouraging the wealthy to create more wealth, thereby aiding all of society. The wealthy use the free market effectively to multiply the goods and services available, which in turn creates more opportunity for rich and poor alike.

Our founding fathers had those views in mind when they established our government, and they believed that justice was important to the economic system. Biblical justice is impartial in the protection of human rights, whereas the humanists' and Marxists' views of justice enforce strict equality.[6]

Since *the awesome God...does not show partiality...*[and] *executes justice* (Deut. 10:17-18), His people should not be characterized by economic injustice (Lev. 19:13; Jer. 22:13-17; Mal. 3:5; Jas. 5:4). Christians are obliged to demonstrate justice on both personal and societal levels since the Bible condemns the abuse of economic power. However, some Christians distort biblical teaching on justice by attempting to make it justify economic or political views which are not found in Scripture. One example is liberation theology which gives a modern meaning to the word "justice" and ignores the fundamental Old Testament concept of justice as righteousness.[7] Furthermore, liberation theology endeavors to regard modern ideas of distributive justice in the same manner as biblical assertions regarding justice. President of CAM International, J. Ronald Blue wrote,

> The liberationists' concern for the injustices in society is admirable, but to contend that society can be transformed solely through naturalistic forces is at best misguided if not naive. Social sin is, after all, simply a conglomerate of personal sin. Society does not commit acts of torture, murder, and rape. People do. Therefore society can only be changed when people are changed....
>
> The good news of the Lord Jesus Christ, who came to suffer the ultimate injustice of death on the cross to pay the penalty for man's sin and to thereby offer new life, eternal life, is still the best news of all. Though supernaturally redeemed individuals perhaps society can be relieved from so much injustice.[8]

Clearly, some Christians are misunderstanding biblical teaching concerning justice. As already stated, the fundamental Old Testament concept of justice is righteousness. To interpret justice according to modern ideas of distributive justice is clearly misguided. One should not understand Jesus' earthly ministry as providing salvation wholly for the economic and politically impoverished. Jesus did not come to earth for the sake of liberating the poor in a monetary sense; He came *to seek and to save that which was lost* (Lk. 19:10), namely, the *poor in spirit* (Mt. 5:3). It is because man is totally depraved, hence he is poor spiritually, that *the Son of Man has come.* Jesus' earthly ministry was to provide salvation for those who were without the righteousness of God—a righteousness only possible by grace through faith for the totally depraved—and liberate the spiritually impoverished.

Doctrine of Stewardship

The doctrine of Christian stewardship is consistent with the responsibility of man to work and the subsequent privilege to acquire private property. Private ownership (not collective or state ownership) and stewardship of property is the biblical norm (Exod. 22:1-3; 23:4; Deut. 8; Ruth 2; Ps. 112; Isa. 65:21-22; Jer. 32:42-44; Mic. 4:1-4; Lk. 12:13-15, 33; Acts 5:1-4; 2 Cor. 9:9; Eph. 4:28, etc.). Acts 2:41-47 does not support a socialist economy, but voluntary allotment among those in Jerusalem. Scripture does not support any compulsion of individuals to allocate their private income and wealth among others. Biblical teaching supports the freedom of private property. However, believers are directed to use their income and wealth for the benefit of individuals and society.

Acts 2:41-47 is one instance of the early church sharing material property for the general good of the community of believers, but this somewhat socialist practice was ephemeral. The "communal living and sharing" of the church in Jerusalem was the likely result of certain circumstances of "economic and social sanctions...undoubtedly imposed on the early believers." Therefore, the "communal living and sharing" would have been "a response to these pressures."9 Throughout history generally, the right of private property has not been condemned, rather it has been viewed positively.

Wealth (riches) is a major theme of both Old and New Testaments (Deut. 6:10-12; 8:10-18; Deut. 31:20; 32:15; 1 Sam. 2:7; Ps. 37:16; Prov. 10:2, 22; 11:4, 28; 13:7-8; 14:24; 15:6, 16-17; 16:8; 19:4; 21:6; 23:4; 27:23-24; 28:8, 20, 22; 30:8-9; Eccl. 5:9-20; 6:1-2; 7:112; 10:19; Isa. 5:8; Jer. 48:36; Hos. 12:8; Mt. 6:19-21; 13:22; 19:16-29; Mk. 4:19; 10:17-25; Lk. 12:15; 18:18-25; 1 Tim. 6:4-19; Jas. 2:6-7; 5:1-5; 1 Jn. 3:17). The Old Testament gives great attention to the godly and ungodly use of riches. Wealth itself was initially created as a component of God's creation over which mankind was given dominion (Gen. 1:26). Although the dominion mandate remained after the Fall, sin greatly tainted the process (9:1-3). Since wealth is a component of God's creation it should also be considered *good* (cf. 1:4, 10, 12, 18, 21, 25, 31). It is men who pervert the creation for evil purposes.

Although there are many condemnations of the rich and wealth in the Old Testament, there are also examples of righteous individuals who were wealthy. However, each Old Testament example of the wealth of the righteous demonstrates the riches to be the blessing of God. Abraham, for example, was promised a great nation, the nation of Israel, from his offspring which would experience prosperity in the land of Canaan; he was also promised a seed and that he would be a blessing to all nations (12:1-3, 7; 13:14-17; 15:1-21; 17:1-21; 22:15-18). Abraham's wealth was the result of forsaking earthly securities to trust and obey God (12:1) and his refusal to accept earthly resources for riches (14:23). The patriarchs also received great wealth from God as an initial token of this blessing (24:35; 26:13; 30:43). As a testimony before the Egyptians of His greatness, God also blessed the Israelites in Goshen (47:27). Solomon's wealth foreshadowed the kingdom of another "Son of David" who is yet to establish His earthly reign.[10]

Scripture communicates a responsibility for the use of income and wealth. The message of the parable of the talents (Mt. 25:14-30) teaches believers to be *good and faithful* with the talents the Master has entrusted to them. The *wicked, lazy slave* is rebuked because he *went away and hid* [his] *talent in the ground* (25:25). The *Master* responded that the slave should have done something: "*'Then you ought to have put my money in the bank, and on my arrival I would have received my money back with interest* (25:27). Although the parable is limited to a specific dispensational time, it does assume the validity of legitimate enterprising business. The *good and faithful slave* is rewarded by his Master and *shall more be given, and he shall have an abundance* (25:29). Similarly, the message of the parable of the unrighteous steward (Lk. 16:1-13) is to urge believers to be good stewards. The parable teaches a proper use of money that is faithful to God yet not bound by avarice and materialism. Wise stewardship of wealth is the result of one's character. *"He who is faithful in a very little thing is faithful also in much; and he who is unrighteous in a very little thing is unrighteous also in much*

(16:10). Faithfulness *in a very little thing* demonstrates the ability to be *faithful also in much*. Economic stewardship prepares a believer for greater responsibility, and with the blessing that God gives on the basis of His sovereignty is the privilege to use the wealth beneficially.

Christians should not be antagonistic toward a free market, money, or private property. All Christians recognize the need to have money to provide for basis necessities, such as clothing, food, and shelter. However, many are confused about the utility of money and the teachings of Jesus regarding wealth. Those who usually are antagonistic believe that wealth is incompatible with the teachings of Jesus and believe He was entirely empathic with the cause of the poor. Such mutually exclusive views are evident when one considers the plethora of prosperity preachers today and the words of Jesus regarding the chronic poor, *"For the poor you have with you always* (Mt. 26:11). On the other hand, Psalm 112:2-3 reads,

> Praise the Lord! How blessed is the man who fears the LORD, who greatly delights in His commandments. His descendants will be mighty on earth; the generation of the upright will be blessed. Wealth and riches are in his house, and his righteousness endures forever.

How should Christians reconcile the Psalmist's statement concerning the prosperity of *the man who fears the LORD* and Jesus' words in the Sermon on the Mount, *"No one can serve two masters; for either he will hate the one and love the other, or he will hold to one and despise the other. You cannot serve God and mammon [riches]* (6:24)? It is possible to ignore the tension these Scriptures provide and allow a godless culture to create even greater tension through feelings of culpability for misbehavior with money and wealth. Unfortunately, many Christians succumb to such tensions (instead of seeking balance in their lives) because they do not understand biblical teaching concerning money and wealth. In order to overcome this tension, the reader needs to understand what is represented by money and how does it differ from every other possession.

Webster's Third New International Dictionary defined money as "something generally accepted as a medium of exchange, a measure of value, or a means of payment." Money is described as "assets or compensation in the form of or readily convertible to cash."[11] Therefore, to utilize money well, it should not be exhausted in consumption *per se* but consumption should be reduced (sc. budget and convenience in daily life is the main motivator for poor consumption). A mature attitude toward wealth is to sacrifice daily consumption for the benefit of future income, that is, thrift. Quite contrary to the definitional understanding of money, mammon is "material wealth or possessions esp. having an evil power or debasing influence." Mammonism is "devotion to the pursuit of wealth; the service of mammon."[12] Literally, God is replaced in one's life by idolizing mammon. Wealth is "abundance of things that are objects of human desire; abundance of worldly estate" and "all material objects that have economic utility; *esp* : the stock of useful goods having economic value in existence at any one time."[13] Wealth is the "abundance of things" which has "economic value." There is both manufacturer wealth (wherein individual desires are satisfied indirectly by means of technological advances) and consumer wealth (wherein individual desires are satisfied directly).[14]

Jesus surely condemned neurotic "devotion to the pursuit of wealth," but never did He condemn wealth *per se*. He did not teach that money and wealth are evil. *For the love of money is a root of all sorts of evil, and some by longing for it have wandered away from the faith, and pierced themselves with many a pang* (1 Tim. 6:10). It is mammonism which the *man of God* must avoid and instead seek *righteousness, godliness, faith, love, perseverance **and** gentleness* (6:11). The proper use of money is emphasized in Scripture (cf. 2 Cor. 8:2-5; 1 Tim. 6:18-19). Jesus did not condemn private property or economic goods. Material riches are the blessing of God and to be used for His glory. The acquisition of riches as the purpose of life is the snare that Scripture warns.

Those rich who are condemned by Jesus misused their wealth. For example, the rich man was condemned because he made friends for himself *by means of the mammon of unright-eousness* (Lk. 16:9). Jesus warned His disciples of the deceitfulness of seeking riches in life since *"no servant can serve two masters...[one] cannot serve God and mammon"* (16:13). The unrighteous steward allowed his riches to become his sole desire of life which created enmity between him and God. He was attempting to serve *God and mammon* which is the reason for his condemnation. The passage communicates the truth that nothing is intrinsically wrong with a wealthy existence or anything virtuous concerning a poor existence. David wrote, *The earth is the LORD's, and all it contains, the world, and those who dwell in it* (Ps. 24:1). The passion of one's life is to use the gifts and talents that God gives for His glory alone. The earth, and everything in it, belongs to God since He alone has *founded* the world (24:2). Believers are given the wonderful privilege of stewardship of divine ownership.

The *King of glory* is the reason why anything exists. He brought the waters of the earth together and created the dry land; it is God who *established* the rivers on the exterior and subterranean surface of the earth (24:1-2; cf. Gen. 1-2). God alone is the Creator and rightful Owner of all creation (Job 38:1-40:2; 40:6-41:34). Believers are stewards of God's possessions. Whatever private property, money, or wealth that man possesses is temporary. As a steward of God's wealth, the believer has great responsibility to use the gifts of God properly. Man is responsible not only to be a good trustee, but also He is responsible for the method of acquisition. Christian stewardship must understand that God is the reason for blessing; consequently, it is God's resources which are to be used for His glory alone.

God asked His people, *And what does the LORD require of you but to do justice, to love kindness, and to walk humbly with your God?* (Mic. 6:8). Just and fair wages (Col. 4:1) must be given promptly for work (Deut. 24:14) which is the same as *just balances* (Lev. 19:36; Prov. 11:1; 16:11; 20:23; Ezek. 45:10). The Christian, who possesses great wealth, sins who uses God's blessing solely for self aggrandizement. The good steward is not commanded to surrender private property to be held in common, but he is commanded to share the blessing of God. *"Give, and it will be given to you; good measure, pressed down, shaken together, running over, they will pour into your lap. For by your standard of measure it will be measured to you in return"* (Lk. 6:38). Divine privilege results in responsibility. *And to whom they entrusted much, of him they will ask all the more* (12:48).

The doctrine of Christian stewardship is often distorted by liberal Christians (the religious left) who attempt to substantiate the enhancement of the state as an essential action in the realization of their political ideas. The liberal view requires the aggrandizement of social justice to follow the transfer of increasing degrees of money and sovereignty to the government. Such a view believes the government to be more compassionate and able to meet the needs of the poor. If this view is accepted and practiced, then the doctrine of stewardship will be distorted since Christians will be required to sacrifice their decision making, will, and resources to the state authority which will be viewed as God's proxy on earth.[15]

Christianity and economic theory have enjoyed a rich history together. For example, the Protestant work ethic (commendable character and will to work diligently) is generally attributed to the great Reformer, John Calvin. Of course, some historians view the connection negatively and others positively. Regardless of one's personal feelings, historians do recognize the influence of medieval and reformation theology upon economic theory.[16] Not only was the Christian influence felt in Western Europe, but also in the New World colonies. The Protestant work ethic was deeply ingrained in the minds of Americans during the great age of free enterprise capitalism in America (i.e. the latter half of the 19th century). Most Americans viewed work as a blessing from God; they believed their labor had great dignity since it fulfilled their responsibility as good stewards of creation (thereby glorifying God). In the words of Nehemiah, *the people had a mind to work* (Neh. 4:6).

Christians have also understood the relationship between economics and ecology. For instance, appreciating God's creation and exercising dominion of it was regarded as one of the most central biblical ideas affecting economic life. Although primarily written as an ecological response, the book *Earthkeeping*[17] gives great attention to economic theory since there is an obvious relationship. Dominion of creation belongs to all humanity.[18] Humanity is to exercise stewardship of creation by caring even as it is used. Although related, stewardship differs from private ownership since the former emphasizes responsibility to use God's resources in a manner consistent with God's purpose to meet the needs of all.[19] Therefore, there are certain limits upon mankind's use of God's resources.

During the time of the Industrial Revolution in Europe, there came a considerable development of the middle class and in a somewhat ephemeral time the desire of Chartism (a movement that developed as a protest against the injustices of the new industrial and political order in Britain) was realized. Chartist Joseph Rayner Stephens' speech at Kersal Moor, Manchester on 24 September 1838, encapsulated the biblical teaching of just and fair wages for work.

> ...every working man in the land had a right to have a good coat to his back, a comfortable abode in which to shelter himself and his family, a good dinner upon his table, and no more work than was necessary for keeping him in health, and as much wages for that work as would keep him in plenty, and afford him the enjoyment of all the blessings of life which a reasonable man could desire.[20]

An independent Methodist minister, Stephens would have known both the Old and New Testaments were in absolute harmony with his words. Truly, the doctrine of stewardship is consistent with the divine given right to private property. Under a communist regime, private property is held in common by society generally. Socialism is the view that private property should be used for the general good of all members of a community. Quite contrary to both systems, biblical teaching is private ownership of property, not community or state ownership. Biblical teaching is that property rights are private not public.

God owns all of creation, and he has graciously entrusted stewardship to humanity.[21]

Economic Theories

Arthur Young (1741-1820) was an English writer on agriculture and social economy. Prior to the French Revolution, he wrote extensive journals about his travels through France. Select phrases of frequently quoted by those advocating free enterprise. According to Young, it is the "magic of property" which "turns sand into gold." However, private ownership should not be understood as reason for abolishing rent or taxes. It does mean that a predetermined rate for rent should be established, and not prone to inflation against the proprietor by his own aggrandizement, or by the desire of the property-owner. A rent preserved in grants of land, by the compensation of which the tenant is resigned from other service (i.e. "quitrent" to use the medieval term) is a proprietor by all purposes (essentially, there are two owners: the freehold owner of the land and property and the copyhold owner of the property). The desired outcome is a fixed ownership on predetermined conditions, as Young stated, "Give a man the secure possession of a bleak rock, and he will turn it into a garden; give him a nine years' lease of a garden, and he will convert it into a desert."[22]

Representing the Austrian School of Economics, Ludwig von Mises wrote that economics "is a science of the means to be applied for the attainment of ends chosen, not, to be sure, a science of the choosing of ends. Ultimate decisions, the valuations and the choosing of ends, are beyond the scope of any science. Science never tells a man how he should act; it merely shows how a man must act if he wants to attain definite ends."[23] When economics is defined correctly as a set of propositions contemplating the logic of human choice, it is evident that Mises (knowingly or unknowingly) developed his analysis upon the biblical proposition of purposeful human action. The cognitive recognition of the essential relationship between moral laws and economic laws, according to God's Word, will result in the development of inexorable economic laws. James M. Buchanan Jr.,

1986 Nobel Laureate in Economics for his development of the contractual and constitutional bases for the theory of economic and political decision-making, stated, "What a science does, or should do, is simply to allow the average man to command the heights of genius. The basic tools are the simple principles. Without them, he is a jibbering idiot, who makes only noise under an illusion of speech."[24] Buchanan thought consideration of the Austrian School and Neoclassical School as two aspects of a single discipline would be beneficial. The Austrian School articulates the first aspect of the logic of human choice that deduces universal laws of human action from the necessity to generate maximum utility from a particular set of inputs. The Neoclassical School articulates the second aspect of the science of behavior that utilizes uses empirical data to test hypotheses about human action.[25]

> The insistence on the use of deductive reasoning alone is what separates Misesian economics from Chicagoan, Keynesian, Historical, or Marxist economics, to name some of the most influential schools of economic thought in the twentieth century. Every major school of economics except the Misesian seems to incorporate a reliance on empiricism or a study of history into its methodology. (The Austrian economist Murray Rothbard broke with Mises and tried to devise an Aristotelian foundation for his version of Austrian economics.) This makes Misesian economics the most promising rival to Christian economics.
>
> Because Misesian economics begins with axioms and proceeds by deduction, it bears a similarity to Christian theology, at least in form and method. Unfortunately, Misesian economics does not derive its economic postulates from the Bible; in fact, Mises could give no good account of why someone should accept his axioms and not those of another system of economics. Misesian economics has no "Thus says the Lord" at its foundation; in fact, its axioms do not even include a truth claim. But if the postulates of Misesian economics are actually found

in Scripture, or, to put it another way, if Mises borrowed his postulates from Christianity, perhaps unwittingly, then the epistemological basis for a deductive economics is present.[26]

Nevertheless, any problems that develop within Misesian economics are answered by Christian economics. For the propositions of economics to cease being subjective and become objective the statements must be established by the Bible. Robbins writes, "If they are, then while they may function as axioms for the discipline of economics, they do not function as axioms for the entire philosophy. Locating the postulates of economics in the Bible transforms them into theorems deduced by good and necessary consequence from the axiom of revelation. The axioms of economics then become theorems of Christian philosophy, and economics as a body of knowledge can proceed on the basis of divinely revealed propositions that do indeed make a truth claim."[27]

Work in the Millennium

Isaiah 65:13-16 begins with the *Lord GOD* addressing those who were not obedient to Him and did evil in His sight (65:12). God then contrasts the blessing for His *servants*. Five contrasts, the first four introduced by the emphatic *behold*, stresses the supreme joy of the servants of God in contrast to the miserable condemnation of the ungodly. Isaiah 65:17-25 closes the chapter with additional descriptions of millennial blessings. There has been some difficulty interpreting 65:17 as either a reference to the millennium or to the eternal state. Certainly, the second coming of Christ will reveal such blessings that it can only be described as *new heavens and a new earth*. Commenting on this verse, McGee wrote,

Here we have the creation of the new heavens and new earth. They seem to precede, chronologically, the setting up of the Kingdom here. It is equally clear in Revelation 21:1 that the new heavens and new earth follow the

Millennium. Radical transformation will take place on the earth during the Kingdom which is tantamount to a new earth. Such radical changes will take place on the earth with the rapture of the Church that it is difficult to be explicit as to the time that the new heavens and new earth come into existence. I have taken the position that the new heavens and new earth come into existence after the Millennium.[28]

Definitely, the greater part of the description pertains to the millennium since death (although the average lifespan is greatly increased; e.g. *For the youth will die at the age of hundred*)[29] is a reality in the time described which will not be a factor in the eternal state. It is challenging to understand the mind of those who discount a literal, earthly messianic reign here. Believing the current age is the kingdom is impossible to understand in light of Isaiah 65:20 since the conditions do not reflect present reality, nor could they possibly be a description of conditions in the eternal state. Ryrie's note is entirely accurate: it is "a description of the millennial kingdom, which is preliminary to the *new heavens and a new earth* (v. 17)."[30]

Henceforth, Isaiah 65:17-25 is understood to describe Paradise restored in the millennium. If economy is understood here as "house management" (οἰκονομία)[31] then one will enjoy the fullest extent of God's blessing as the inevitable result of one's work. Isaiah 65:21-22 describes a peaceful life as one works and enjoys the subsequent blessing from labor. The blessing of work, resulting in God's blessing, will characterize the millennium.

Isaiah first states the promise of prosperity in the millennium. *"Any they shall build houses and inhabit **them**; they shall also plant vineyards and eat their fruit* (65:21). The prophet then indicates what will not occur. *"They shall **not** build, and another inhabit, they shall **not** plant, and another eat* (65:22a; cf. 62:8-9). Private property is not regarded as evil since it will even be an aspect of the millennium. *For as the lifetime of a tree, **so shall be** the days of My people, and My chosen ones shall not wear out the work of their hands* (65:22b). The expression *lifetime of a tree* indicates fortitude and permanence (cf. Ps. 1:3; Jer. 17:1-8). God's *chosen ones* will enjoy the fullest manifestation of *the work of their hands*. Isaiah 65:21-22 communicates the innate relationship between work and its subsequent blessing.

"*They shall not labor in vain, or bear* **children** *for calamity; for they are the offspring of those blessed by the LORD, and their descendants with them* (65:23). McGee commented, "No fruitless effort and frustration. All efforts will be blessed."[32] Part of God's judgment upon man was to work *in toil* (Gen. 2:17-19), but during the millennium the work will not be *in vain*. All work will be for the glory of God and mankind will witness His incomparable blessing as the natural outcome of his labor. In the days of the millennium, God stated, "*It will come to pass that before they call, I will answer; and while they are still speaking, I will hear* (Isa. 65:24). Even the animal kingdom "*shall do no evil or harm in all My holy mountain,*" *says the LORD* (65:25).

Even in the millennium, private ownership is a blessing of work. Throughout the continuum of human history, mankind is responsible to God for the manner in which he works and uses his possessions. The privilege of work furnishes the right of private property thereby necessitating the proper use of one's possessions. Beisner aptly wrote,

> Biblical stewardship views God as Owner of all things (Psalm 24:1) and man—individually and collectively—as His steward. Every person is accountable to God for the use of whatever he has (Genesis 1:26-30); 2:15). Every person's responsibility as a steward is to maximize the Owner's return on His investment by using it to serve others (Matthew 25:14-30).[33]

The eternal state will surpass Paradise restored in the millennium. The preliminary stages of the millennium will not compare to the endurance of *the new heavens and the new earth*. "*And it shall be from new moon to new moon and from sabbath to sabbath, all mankind will come to bow down before Me,*" *says the LORD* (66:23). The saints of the Old and New Testament periods will worship God without end; such worship will be the enchanting business of eternity. The late David Breese wrote,

> The resolute man or woman is not easily persuaded to become a humble supplicant for government support. Being responsible, which is man's highest function, the strong human being does not concede to the proposition that the government owns, operates, and deserves it all. He lives and moves and has his being in a source other than the halls of a congress or parliament. He is a son of the living God. He is therefore confident that true riches are not the coins of the realm and that true government is the kingdom of heaven, which, despite temporary evidence to the contrary, rules over all. No...[a "mixed economy"—part free market, part government planning, and completely inflationary]...was but the catalyst whereby the incompetent majorities could subdue the competent minorities and use the government as a club to bring it to pass. Sensing the hopelessness of the course...we rejoice that the course of any individual can still be the pursuit of the will of the One whose kingdom is not of this world.[34]

PART 2

The Coming One World Government

CHAPTER 7

GOVERNMENT IN HISTORICAL PERSPECTIVE

Kerby Anderson

Every day of the week government affects individuals' lives. It tells them how fast to drive. It regulates their commerce. It protects them from foreign and domestic strife. However, most Christians fail to take time to consider the basic function of government. What is a biblical view of government? Why does government exist? What kind of government does the Bible allow?

Christian View of Government

Developing a Christian view of government is difficult since the Bible does not provide an exhaustive treatment of government. This itself is perhaps instructive and provides some latitude for these institutions to reflect the needs and demands of particular cultural situations. Since the Bible does not speak directly to every area of political discussion, Christians often accept different views on particular political issues. However, Christians are not free to believe whatever they want. Christians should not abandon the Bible when they begin to think about these issues, because there is a great amount of biblical material that can be used to judge particular political options.

The Old Testament teaches God established government after the flood (Gen. 9:6). Furthermore, the Old Testament does provide clear guidelines for the development of a theocracy in which God was the head of government. These guidelines, however, were written for particular circumstances involving a covenant people chosen by God. These guidelines do not apply today because modern governments are not the direct inheritors of the promises God made to the nation of Israel.

Apart from that unique situation, the Bible does not propose nor endorse any specific political system. The Bible, however, does provide a basis for evaluating various political philosophies because it clearly delineates a view of human nature. Every political theory rests on a particular view of human nature.

The Bible describes two elements of human nature. This viewpoint is helpful in judging government systems. Since humans are created in the image of God (Gen. 1:26–27), they possess the ability to exercise judgment and rationality. However, humans are also fallen creatures (Gen. 3). This human sinfulness (Rom. 3:23) has therefore created a need to control evil and sinful human behavior through civil government.

Many theologians have suggested that the only reason government exists today is to control sinful behavior because of the Fall. However, there is every indication that government would have existed even if man lived in a sinless world. For example, there seems to be some structuring of authority in the Garden (Gen. 1–2). The Bible also speaks of the angelic host as being organized into levels of authority and function.

In the creation, God ordained government as the means by which human beings and angelic hosts are ruled. The rest of the created order is governed by instinct (Prov. 30:24–28) and God's sovereignty. Insect colonies, for example, may show a level of order, but this is due merely to genetically controlled instinct. Human beings, on the other hand, are created in the image of God and thus are responsible to the commands of God. Humanity is created by a God of order (1 Cor. 14:33); therefore, mankind should also seek order through governmental structures.

A Christian view of government differs significantly from views proposed by many political theorists. The basis for civil government is rooted in man's created nature. Men are rational and volitional beings. He is not determined by fate, as the Greeks would have said, nor is man determined by his environment as modern behaviorists teach. Man possesses the power of choice. Therefore, man can exercise delegated power over the created order. Thus, a biblical view of human nature requires a governmental system which acknowledges human responsibility.

While the source of civil government is rooted in human responsibility, the need for government derives from the necessity of controlling human sinfulness. God ordained civil government to restrain evil (cf. Gen. 9). Anarchy, for example, is not a viable option because all have sinned (Rom. 3:23) and are in need of external control.

Notice how a Christian view of human nature provides a basis to judge various political philosophies. For example, Christians must reject political philosophies which ignore human sinfulness. Many utopian political theories are based upon this flawed assumption. Plato proposed, in *The Republic* (360 B.C.), an ideal government where the enlightened philosopher-kings would lead the country. The Bible, however, teaches that all are sinful (Rom. 3:23). Plato's proposed leaders would also be affected by the sinful effects of the Fall (Gen. 3). They would not always have the benevolent and enlightened disposition necessary to lead the republic.

Christians should also reject a Marxist view of government. Karl Marx believed human nature was conditioned by society, and in particular, the capitalist economy. His solution was to change the economy so that one would change human nature. Why is greed a common reality? According to Marx, greed exists because man lives in a greedy, capitalist society. If society changed the economy from capitalism to socialism, Marx taught, and then communism, greed would cease.

Christians should reject this utopian vision of Marxism because it is based upon an inaccurate view of human nature. The Bible does teach that believers can become new creatures (2 Cor. 5:17) through spiritual conversion, but that does not mean the effects of sin are completely overcome in this life. The Bible also teaches Christians will continue to live in a world tainted by sin. The view of Karl Marx contradicts biblical teaching by proposing a New Man in a New Society perfected by man's own efforts.

Since civil government is necessary and divinely ordained by God (Rom. 13:1–7), it is ultimately under God's control. It has been given three political responsibilities: the sword of justice (to punish criminals), the sword of order (to thwart rebellion), and the sword of war (to defend the state).

As citizens, Christians have been given a number of responsibilities. They are called to render service and obedience to the government (Mt. 22:21). Since it is a God-ordained institution, they are to submit to civil authority (1 Pet. 2:13–17), as they would to other institutions of God. As will be discussed later, Christians are not to give final and total allegiance to the secular state. Other God-ordained institutions exist in society alongside the state. Christians' final allegiance must be to God. They are to obey civil authorities (Rom.13:5) in order to avoid anarchy and chaos, but there may be times when they may be forced to disobey (Acts 5:29).

Since government is a divinely ordained institution, Christians have a responsibility to work within governmental structures to bring about change. Government is part of the creation order and a minister of God (Rom. 13:4). Christians are to obey government authorities (Rom. 13:1–4; 1 Pet. 3:5–6). Christians are also to be the salt of the earth and the light of the world (Mt. 5:13–16) in the midst of the political context.

Although governments may be guilty of injustice, Christians should not stop working for justice or cease being concerned about human rights. They do not surrender marriage as an institution simply because there are so many divorces, and they do not surrender the church because of many internal problems. Each God-ordained institution manifests human sinfulness and disobedience. The responsibility of the church is to call for a return of political leaders to this God-ordained task. Government is a legitimate sphere of Christian service, and so believers should not look to government only when individual rights are being abused. Christians are to be concerned with social justice and should understand governmental action as a legitimate instrument to achieve just ends.

A Christian view of government should also be concerned with human rights. Human rights, in a Christian system, are based on a biblical view of human dignity. A bill of rights, therefore, does not grant rights to individuals, but instead acknowledges these rights as already existing. The writings of John Locke along with the Declaration of Independence capture this idea by stating government is based on the inalienable rights of individuals. Government based on humanism, however, would not understand rights as inalienable, and thus opens the possibility for the state to redefine the rights its citizens may enjoy. The rights of citizens in a republic, for example, are articulated in terms of what the government is forbidden to do. Nevertheless, in totalitarian governments, while the rights of citizens may also be explained, power ultimately resides in the government not the people.

A Christian view of government also recognizes the need to limit the influence of sin in society. This is best achieved by placing certain safeguards on governmental authority. This protects citizens from the abuse or misuse of governmental power which results when sinful individuals are given too much governmental control.

The greatest threat to liberty comes from the exercise of power. History has demonstrated that power is a corrupting force when placed in human hands. In the Old Testament theocracy there was less danger of abuse because the head of state was God. The Bible amply documents the dangers that ensued when power was transferred to a single king. Even David, a man after God's own heart (1 Sam. 13:14; Acts 13:22), abused his power and Israel experienced great calamity (2 Sam. 11–21).

Governmental Authority

A key question in political theory is how to determine the limits of governmental authority. With the remarkable growth in the size and scope of government in the twentieth century, it is necessary to define clearly the lines of governmental authority. The Bible provides some guidelines.

Nevertheless, it is often difficult to place limits or express limits on government authority. As already noted, the Old Testament theocracy differed from the modern democratic government. Although human nature is the same, drawing biblical principles from an agrarian, monolithic culture and applying them to the technological, pluralistic culture requires discernment.

Part of this difficulty can be eased by separating two issues.

First, should government legislate morality? This question will be discussed in the section on social action. Second, what are the limits of governmental sovereignty? The following are a few general principles helpful in determining the limits of governmental authority.

Christians know God has ordained other institutions besides government which exercise authority in their particular sphere of influence. This is in contrast to other political systems which understand the state as the sovereign agent over human affairs, exercising sovereignty over every other human institution. A Christian view is different.

The *first institution* is the church (Heb. 12:18–24; 1 Pet. 2:9–10). Jesus taught that the government should work in harmony with the church and should recognize its sovereignty in spiritual matters (Mt. 22:21).

The *second institution* is the family (Eph. 5:22–32; 1 Pet. 3:1–7). The family is an institution under God and His authority (Gen.1:26–28; 2:20–25). When the family subsides, the government often has to intervene to protect the rights of the wife (in cases of wife abuse) or children (in cases of child abuse or adoption). The biblical emphasis, however, is not so much on rights as it is on responsibilities and submission (Eph. 5:21).

A *third institution* is education. Children are not the wards of the state, but belong to God (Ps. 127:3) and are given to parents as a gift from God. Parents are to teach their children (Deut. 4:9) and may also entrust them to tutors (Gal. 4:2).

In a humanistic system of government, the institutions of church and family are usually subordinated to the state. In an atheistic system, ultimately the state becomes a substitute god and is given additional power to adjudicate disputes and bring order to a society. Since institutions exist by permission of the state, there is always the possibility that a new social contract will allow government to intervene in the areas of church and family.

A Christian view of government recognizes the sovereignty of these spheres. Governmental intervention into the spheres of church and family is necessary in certain cases where there is a threat to life, liberty, or property. Otherwise civil governmental should recognize the sovereignty of other God-ordained institutions.

Moral Basis of Law

Law should be the foundation of any government. Whether law is based upon moral absolutes, changing consensus, or totalitarian impulse is of crucial importance. Until fairly recently, Western culture held to a notion that common law was founded upon God's revealed moral absolutes.

In a Christian view of government, law is based upon God's revealed commandments. Law is not based upon human opinion or sociological convention. Law is derived from God's unchangeable character and derived from biblical principles of morality.

In humanism, humanity is the source of law. Law is merely the expression of human will or mind. Since ethics and morality are man-made, so also is law. Humanists' law is rooted in human opinion, and thus is relative and arbitrary.

Two important figures in the history of law are Samuel Rutherford (1600-1661) and William Blackstone (1723-1780). Rutherford's *Lex Rex*, or *The Law and the Prince* (1644) had profound effect on British and American law. His treatise challenged the foundations of seventeenth century politics by proclaiming that law must be based upon the Bible, rather than upon the word of any man.

Until the time of Rutherford's writing, the king had been the law. The book created a great controversy because it attacked the idea of the divine right of kings. This doctrine contained the teaching that the king or the state ruled as God's appointed regent. Thus, the king's word had been law. Rutherford properly argued from passages, such as Romans 13, that the king (as well as anyone else) was under God's law and not above it.

Sir William Blackstone was an English jurist in the eighteenth century and is famous for this *Commentaries on the Law of England* which embodied the tenets of Judeo-Christian theism. Published in 1765, the *Commentaries* became the definitive treatise on the common law in England and in America.

According to Blackstone, the two foundations for law are nature and revelation through the Scriptures. Blackstone believed that the fear of the Lord was the beginning of wisdom, and thus taught God was the source of all laws. It is interesting that even the humanist Rousseau noted in his *Social Contract* (1762) that one needs someone outside the world system to provide a moral basis for law. He wrote, "Gods would be needed to give men laws."[1]

Unfortunately, the modern legal structure has been influenced by relativism and utilitarianism, in contrast to moral absolutes revealed in Scripture. Relativism provides no secure basis for moral judgments. There are no firm moral absolutes which allows society to build a secure legal foundation.

Utilitarianism examines mere consequences and ignores moral principles. This legal foundation has been further eroded by the relatively recent phenomenon of sociological law. In this view, law should be based upon relative sociological standards. No discipline is more helpless without a moral foundation than law. Law is a tool, and it needs a jurisprudential foundation. Just as contractors and builders need the architect's blueprint in order to build, so also lawyers need theologians and moral philosophers to construct good law. The problem is most lawyers today are extensively trained in technique, but little in moral and legal philosophy.

Legal justice in the Western world has been based upon a proper, biblical understanding of human nature and human choice. Western civilization detains criminals accountable for their crimes, rather than excuse their behavior as part of environmental conditioning. Individuals in the West also acknowledge differences between willful, premeditated acts (such as murder) and so-called crimes of passion (i.e., manslaughter) or accidents.

One of the problems in society today is that man does not function from assumptions of human choice. The influence of the behaviorist, the evolutionist, and the sociobiologist are quite profound. The evolutionist and sociobiologist teach human behavior is genetically determined. The behaviorist teaches human behavior is environmentally determined. Where does one find free choice in a system arguing that actions are a result of environment and heredity? Free choice and personal responsibility have been diminished in the criminal justice system, due to the influence of these secular perspectives.

It is, therefore, not by accident that the world today has witnessed a dramatic change in the outlook of criminal justice. The emphasis has moved from a view of punishment and restitution to one of rehabilitation. If man's actions are governed by something external and human choice is denied, then one cannot punish someone for something they cannot control. If the influences are merely environment and heredity, then society must rehabilitate them. However, such a view of human actions diminishes human dignity. If a person cannot choose, then he is merely a victim of circumstances and must become a ward of the state.

Christians must regard the criminal act seriously and punish human choices. While recognizes the value of rehabilitation (especially through spiritual conversion; v. Jn. 3:3), Christians also recognize the need for punishing crimes and offenses. The Old Testament provisions for punishment and restitution are more understandable in light of the biblical view of human nature. Yet today, there is a justice system operating which promotes no-fault divorce, no-fault insurance, and continues to erode the notion of human responsibility.

Civil Disobedience

But what should Christians do if government exceeds its authority? Do Christians have a responsibility and right to disobey? Those who would quickly dismiss this question as irrelevant should realize the implications of civil disobedience on Christian discipleship and obedience to God's law. If there is never a circumstance wherein a Christian would disobey God, then ultimately the state has become god. Therefore, civil disobedience must be permitted. However, if civil disobedience is permitted, under what circumstances may it be enforced?

The best articulation of these biblical principles can be found in Rutherford's essay *Lex Rex*. Arguing that governmental law was founded on the law of God, he rejected the seventeenth century idea of the "divine right of kings." The king was not the ultimate authority; God's law was the final arbiter (hence the title *Lex Rex,* "The law is king"). If the king and the government disobey the law, then they are to be disobeyed. He argued that all men, including the king, are under God's law and not above it. According to Rutherford, the civil magistrate is a "fiduciary figure" who possesses his authority in trust for the people. If that trust is violated, the people have a political basis for resistance. Not surprisingly, *Lex Rex* was banned in England and Scotland and was seen as treasonous and fomenting political rebellion.

The Bible provides a number of prominent examples of civil disobedience. When Pharaoh commanded the Hebrew midwives to kill all male Hebrew babies, they lied to Pharaoh and did not carry out his command (Exod. 1–2).

The Book of Daniel has a number of instructive examples. For example, when Shadrach, Meshach, and Abednego refused to bow down to Nebuchadnezzar's golden image, they were cast into a fiery furnace (Dan. 3). The commissioners and satraps persuaded King Darius to issue a decree that no one could petition any god or man for thirty days. Daniel nevertheless continued to pray to God three times a day and was cast into the lion's den (Dan. 6).

The most dramatic example of civil disobedience in the New Testament is recorded in Acts 4–5. When Peter and John were commanded not to preach the gospel, their response was, *"We must obey God rather than men* (Acts 5:29).

These examples each included at least two common elements. First, a direct, specific conflict arose between God's law and man's law. Pharaoh commanded the Hebrew midwives to kill male Hebrew babies. Nebuchadnezzar commanded his subjects to bow before the golden image. King Darius ruled that no one could pray. In the New Testament, the high priest and the Sanhedrin forbade the apostles from proclaiming the gospel.

Second, in choosing to obey God's higher law, believers paid the normal consequence for disobedience. Although several of them escaped the consequence through supernatural intervention, Christians know from biblical and secular history of many others who paid for their disobedience with their lives.

Some critics argue that civil disobedience is prohibited by the clear admonition in Romans 13:1 (*Let every person be in subjection to the governing authorities. For there is no authority except from God, and those which exist are established by God.*). Nonetheless, even this passage seems to provide a possible argument for disobeying government that has exceeded its authority.

The following verses speak of the government's role and function. The ruler is to be a "servant of God" and government should be rewarding good and punishing evil. Government failing to do so is outside of God's mandated authority and function. Government is not autonomous; it has delegated authority from God. It is to restrain evil and punish wrongdoers. When it does violate God's delegated role and refuses to reward good and punish evil, it has no proper authority.

The Apostle Paul called for believers to *be in subjection* to government, but he did not instruct them to obey every command of government. When government commands an unbiblical or unjust injunction, Christians have a higher authority. One can *be in subjection* to the authority of the state but still refuse to obey a specific law which is contrary to biblical standards.

Biblical Principles for Civil Disobedience

How should Christians engage in civil disobedience? Here are five principles that should guide an individual's decision about civil disobedience. *First*, the law (or injunction) being resisted should clearly be unbiblical and unjust. Christians are not allowed to resist laws merely because they disagree with them. The sin nature is a reality and man's natural tendency is toward anarchy, so it seems appropriate for Christians to make a strong case for civil disobedience before responding. The burden of proof should be on the person advocating civil disobedience. In a sense, one should be talked into disobedience. If the case is not compelling for civil disobedience, then obedience is required by default.

Second, the means of redress should be exhausted. One of

the criteria for a just war is that the recourse to war must be the last resort. Civil disobedience should follow the same rigorous criterion. When all recourse to civil obedience has been exhausted, then and only then can discussion of revolution begin. Even then, minimum resistance should be used if it can achieve a just result. If peaceful means can be used, then force should be avoided. Only when all legal channels for change have been closed or exhausted should civil disobedience be seriously considered. The only exception may be when the injustice is so grave and immediate that time for lengthy appeals is impossible.

Third, Christians must be willing to accept the penalty for breaking the law. The various biblical examples mentioned provide a model for Christian behavior in the midst of civil disobedience. Christians should submit to authority even when disobeying government. Such an attitude distinguishes civil disobedience from anarchy. By accepting the punishment, believers can often provide a powerful testimony to nonbelievers and awaken their concern for the injustice.

Fourth, civil disobedience should be accomplished in love and with humility. Disobeying government should not be done with an angry or rebellious spirit. Bringing about social change requires love, patience, and humility, not anger and arrogance.

A *fifth* and more controversial principle is that civil disobedience should be considered only when there is some possibility for success. Another one of the criteria for a just war is there be some reasonable hope of success. In the case of civil disobedience success is not an ultimate criterion, but it should be a concern if true social change is to take place. An individual certainly is free to disobey a law for personal reasons, but any attempt to change a law or social situation should enlist the aid and support of others. Additionally, Christians should prayerfully evaluate whether the social disruption and potential promotion of lawlessness which may ensue is worth the action of civil disobedience. In most cases, Christians will be more effective by working within the social and political arenas to affect true social change.

Biblical Principles for Social Action

How then should Christians be involved in the social and political arena? They should be distinctively Christian in their approach, and they should learn from the mistakes of other Christians in the past so they might be effective without falling into compromise or sin.

First, Christians must remember they have a dual citizenship. On the one hand, their citizenship is in heaven and not on earth (Phil. 3:17–21). Christians must remind themselves that God is sovereign over human affairs even when circumstances look dark and discouraging. Alternatively, the Bible also teaches that Christians are citizens of this earth (Mt. 22:15–22). They are to obey government (Rom. 13:1–7) and work within the social and political circumstances to affect change. Christians are to pray for those in authority (1 Tim. 2:1–4) and to obey those in authority.

Jesus compared the kingdom of heaven to leaven hidden in three pecks of meal (Mt. 13:33). The meal represents the world and the leaven represents the Christian presence in it. Christians are to exercise influence within the mass of society, seeking to bring about change in that manner. Though the Christian presence may seem as insignificant as leaven in meal, nevertheless the church is to bring about the same profound change.

Second, Christians must remember God is sovereign. As the Sovereign over the nations, He bestows power on whom He wishes (Dan. 4:17) and He can turn the heart of a king wherever He wishes (Prov. 21:1). Christians have often been guilty of believing they alone can make a difference in the political process. Christian leaders frequently claim the future of this country depends on the election of a particular candidate, the passage of a particular bill, or the confirmation of a particular Supreme Court justice. While it is important for Christians to be involved in social and political affairs, they must not forget that God is ultimately in control.

Third, Christians must use their specific gifts within the social and political arenas. Christians have different gifts and ministries (1 Cor. 12:4–6). Some may be called to a higher level of political participation than others (e.g., a candidate for school board or for Congress). All have a responsibility to be involved in society, but some are called to a higher level of social service, such as a social worker or crisis pregnancy center worker. Christians must recognize the diversity of gifts and encourage fellow believers to use their individual gifts for the greatest impact.

Fourth, Christians should channel their political and social activity through the church. Christians need to be accountable to each other, especially as they seek to make an impact on society. Wise leadership can prevent zealous, evangelical Christians from repeating mistakes made in previous decades by other Christians.

The local church should also provide a context for compassionate social service. In the New Testament, the local church became a place of training for social action (Acts 2:45; 4:34). Meeting the needs of the poor, the infirm, the elderly, and widows is a responsibility of the church. Ministries to these groups can provide a foundation and catalyst for further outreach and ministry to the community in general.

Christians are to be the salt of the earth and the light of the world (Mt. 5:13–16). In a needy society, Christians possess abundant opportunities to preach the gospel of Jesus Christ and meet significant social needs. By combining these two areas of preaching and ministry, Christians can make a strategic difference in society.

CHAPTER 8

SNARE OF WORLD GOVERNMENT

Phillip Goodman

The words came directly from Jesus Christ. There is a trap waiting at the end of human history. It is a trap awaiting a godless civilization at the second coming of Jesus Christ. "Be on guard, that your hearts may not be weighted down with dissipation and drunkenness and the worries of life, and that day come on you suddenly like a trap; for it will come upon all those who dwell on the face of all the earth" (Lk. 21:34-35).

The *Merriam-Webster Online Dictionary* defines trap as "something by which one is caught unawares; a position or situation from which it is difficult or impossible to escape."[1] Integral to this trap is the snare of a coming one world government which will appear in the form of ten kings, or nations. It was prophesied in the days of Daniel the prophet over 2500 years ago. *"The fourth beast will be a fourth kingdom on the earth...and it will devour the whole earth and tread it down and crush it"* (Dan. 7:23).

The *Merriam-Webster Online Dictionary* defines snare as "something by which one is entangled, involved in difficulties, or impeded; something deceptively attractive."[2] This one world government will be led by the Antichrist, an eleventh king who rises amid a ten nation restored Roman Empire to become the supreme world ruler. It will be a snare that involves the entire earth as part of a God-sent delusion. The divine delusion of a global government promising peace and prosperity, operating under the sovereignty of a "super" human being, will engulf the planet after all true believers in Jesus Christ are removed to

185

heaven—prior to the rise of the Antichrist— in an event called the rapture.

> And then that lawless one [the Antichrist] will be revealed whom the Lord will slay with the breath of His mouth and bring to an end by the appearance of His coming; *that is*, the one whose coming is in accord with the activity of Satan, with all power and signs and false wonders, and with all the deception of wickedness for those who perish, because they did not receive the love of the truth so as to be saved. And for this reason God will send upon them a deluding influence so that they might believe what is false, in order that they all may be judged who did not believe the truth, but took pleasure in wickedness (2 Thess. 2:8-12).

The modern world of 200 nations is destined to become a world of one super-government. In contrast to a benevolent government for the good of mankind, it will be responsible for the deaths of 50% of the earth's population within the short span of seven years; it will be a phenomenal catastrophe underscoring the deep wickedness of the coming one world government! This man-centered, Satan-controlled global government will be the polar opposite of the worldwide thousand year kingdom of righteousness (the millennial kingdom) that Jesus Christ will establish when He returns. The kingdom of Antichrist is a snare waiting to entrap a god-rejecting humanity.

Human Government: Established by God

Romans 13:1 states, *Let every person be in subjection to the governing authorities. For there is no authority except from God, and those which exist are established by God. Therefore he who resists authority has opposed the ordinance of God; and they who have opposed will receive condemnation upon themselves.* God, then, has established governments of men. No authority exists apart from the will of God. The Bible teaches, *That the Most High is ruler over the realm of mankind, and bestows it on whom He wishes* (Dan. 4:17) and *those* [governments] *which exist are established by God* (Rom. 13:1). Acts 17:26-27 also comments on divinely ordained government: *and He made from one, every nation of mankind to live on all the face of the earth, having determined their appointed times, and the boundaries of their habitation, that they should seek God, if perhaps they might grope for Him and find Him, though He is not far from each one of us.*

The passages above demonstrate God has not only authorized the existence of all human governments, but also He has actually determined their times of existence in history and their geographic boundaries of authority. Whether it be ancient Assyria, Babylon, Egypt, Greece, Persia, Rome, or modern China, France, Germany, India, or the United States (as sovereign entities exercising governing authority over subject populations), all have been *established by God.*

However, the story is not complete here. Acts 17:26-27 includes the phrase, *that they should seek God.* There is a divine purpose behind divinely-established human governments; they are intended to be based upon the Bible and expressing that worldview, thereby utilizing their powers as instruments of God! This is how governments and nations seek God. It has been the ideal since the original mandate for government following the global flood in the days of Noah. After the flood, God established the ultimate authority of government—capital punishment—and it was delegated to mankind within the context of the holy standard that "in the image of God He made man (Gen. 9:6). Governments are ordained and commissioned by God, but the goal is *that they should seek God* (a fact emphasized in Romans 13:1-14).

Clearly, when God ordains a government, He does so within the context of a holy purpose: the government is commissioned to be *a minister of God to you for good* (13:4). Government is to be *a minister of God, an avenger who brings wrath upon the one who practices evil.* Kings and presidents are called to be *rulers* [who] *are servants of God, devoting themselves to this very thing* [i.e., *a minister of God to you for good*] (13:6). Romans 13:3 communicates that when governments act in their divinely-authorized capacity, their *rulers are not a cause of fear for good behavior, but for evil* which is why every person is to *be in subjection to the governing authorities*.

It is only when a governing authority directly commands a believer to blatantly disobey a clearly revealed biblical command that a Christian would be disobedient. The disciples of Jesus in Acts 5:29 are an example when they said to the governing authorities, *"We must obey God rather than men."* In that instance, when the rulers commanded them to cease their public testimony about the risen Christ, in clear violation of the commands of the Lord (Mt. 28:18-20), they were acting beyond the bounds of their divinely ordained office (cf. Rom. 13:3). In the Acts 5:29 incident, however, the government was indeed *a cause of fear for good behavior*. As this author writes, this is exactly the direction of the uncontrollable trend toward a one world government.

Righteousness and Justice are the Foundation of Thy Throne

Behind every government there is a philosophy. Behind every philosophy there is a worldview. A worldview is the sum-total of one's view of reality. All worldviews are religious in nature since they deal with ultimate questions about reality, hence faith-based. The religious foundation for one's view of the world is grouped into three broad categories: (1) Theism: God is personal and uncreated, existing independent of His creation; (2) Pantheism: God is impersonal and uncreated; He is the creation, which is eternal; and, (3) Atheism: There is no God; the material world is all that exists.

In other words, theism states both God and creation exists. Pantheism teaches God is all that exists. Atheism proclaims the material world is all that exists. The world's five major religions (all others are by-products of one form or another) are Christianity, Judaism, and Islam (theism), and Buddhism and Hinduism (pantheism). Atheism, which proclaims "there is no God," is actually a sixth major religion because the arrogant assertion "there is no God" by necessity assumes an exhaustive knowledge of every sphere of the universe in order to exclude the existence of God. The atheistic assertion requires more faith than the other religions combined!

Relating to the religious worldviews is an interesting development which has resulted since World War II. Amazingly, it was the direct consequence of a government sponsored, "legal" injustice to the chosen people of God, the Jews. Responding to the unspeakable atrocities committed in the name of official Nazi government sanction, the international judicial tribunal, called the Nuremberg trials, was established by a world outraged by the Holocaust (the attempt to physically exterminate and medically eradicate perceived "inferior" races, especially the Jews). Geisler and Bocchino wrote, "This was something new; there had never been an international criminal court in all of history, and this event would set a precedent for the future."[3]

During the trials, the nations of the world (regardless of their particular worldviews, religions, or government systems) were forced to conclude there exists an absolute moral standard above the laws of nations, that is, a theistic worldview. There is an infinite standard of justice which all governments who administer "justice" must evaluate themselves. The international community was forced to acknowledge—at least implicitly—what the Bible had long declared, and what the Judeo-Christian based United States government acknowledged in the Declaration of Independence: "Natural [God-given] law supporters believe that [human] rights are not established by the positive [man-made] enactments of governments and are 'unalienable' in the sense that governments cannot take away what they do not bestow."[4]

According to the Bible, governments are not given a divine mandate to create justice; they are divinely ordained to secure God's standard of justice. *Righteousness and justice are the foundation of Thy throne; Loving-kindness and truth go before Thee* (Ps. 89:14). The question confronting the convening governments at the Nuremberg trials was "how can one nation (the United States) accuse another nation (Nazi Germany) of violating human rights if governments decide what a person is and determine what human rights are (if they are to be at all)?"[5] Scripture states, *Evil men do not understand justice, But those who seek the LORD understand all things* (Prov. 28:5). As Geisler and Bocchino wrote, "Without a standard of justice outside the world, how can someone logically point out injustice in the world?...Apart from an appeal to an objective, universal standard [God and the laws of God] that measures the laws of human governments, justice could not be served."[6]

According to Romans 2:14-15, God has placed knowledge of His absolute moral law within every human being. Romans 2:16 declares that such knowledge is so evident that humanity will be called justly to account for it in the day of judgment. C. S. Lewis aptly wrote, "A man does not call a line [justice] crooked unless he has some idea of a straight [absolute] line."[7] Just governments are established upon a preexisting eternal and unchanging just foundation, for indeed, *true and just are* [God's] *judgements* (Rev. 19:2). Evil governments, on the other hand, violate their own collective conscience.

Established By God: That They Should Seek God

It is a remarkable thing to contemplate a map showing the distribution of the world's major religions—Buddhism, Christianity, Hinduism, Islam, and Judaism. For instance, the western hemisphere is dominated by Christianity. Looking at a visual overlay of governmental systems from a political map, it becomes apparent that those nations dominated by the Protestant branch of Christianity are also characterized by governments valuing human freedom. These are the governments which in general have incorporated biblical principals into their governmental structures. The result has been the rise of societies valuing human justice and worth. The same overlay map reveals too obviously that the same is not true in the rest of the world; those other parts of the world are dominated by autocracies, dictatorships, and tyranny.

Daniel J. Boorstin, the director of the Library of Congress from 1975-1987, listed the ideal of "Individualism" as one of the "Ten Leading Ideas of the Second Millennium That Have Shaped Western Civilization and World History."[8] He wrote that individualism results "from the Protestant Reformation in the 16th century, and the rise of cities, commerce, and capitalism. [It is] the belief that the faith of the individual is essential to religious salvation, that the consent of individuals legitimates government, and that the worth of persons is to be measured by their worth as individuals and not by power or status." It is the presence of the true church as "salt and light" which made this possible. When Christ returns in the rapture for all true believers, the light reflected by His church in the world will be gone. However, even before that time, the degenerate effects of apostasy within the church are easing the path for the formation of the coming one world government. Early in the 20th century President Theodore Roosevelt made the statement, "I believe that the next half century will determine if we will advance the cause of Christian civilization or revert to the horrors of brutal paganism."9 The stage is being set for a "brutal paganism" without peer in the annals of history.

The Emerging Trend: One World Government

There are discernable trends in world history. The world's first history book, the biblical book of Genesis, records the breakdown of the world's primal international, political movement. At the Tower of Babel (Gen. 10-11) the trend toward a one world government was fragmented into 70 families when God divided the languages of the world into the root languages known today.10 As these families journeyed to various distant lands, they developed clans, nations, tribes, and eventually empires. The earliest recorded history supports this ancient scene of empires developing from the land of Babel (Babylon-Iraq) over time. Empires dominated the world until only recently. With the division of empires during the 19th and 20th centuries, nation-states emerged. Nationalism became the geopolitical shibboleth. Since World War II, the trend has been toward pan-nationalism and even globalism (and the trend is accelerating)!

The future of the world's current assemblage of sovereign states [nations] is also threatened by the trend toward globalization. All but a fraction of states have joined the United Nations, although it has limited authority. However, states are willingly transferring authority to regional organizations, established primarily for economic cooperation.[11]

Some of the other international coalitions in addition to the United Nations include the European Union, the North Atlantic Treaty Organization, the Organization of American States, the Arab League, and others. The tape of world history, in effect, is being rewound. The Bible predicts a return to "empire." The prophecies record a final, age-ending repeat of one world government with Babel at the center again (only this time on a global scale).[12] The empire of the Antichrist is coming.

A Misnomer: Revolt in the Kingdom of the Antichrist

To understand the dynamics of the rise and rule of the Antichrist during the end time, it is essential to address a widespread error popularized since the *Late Great Planet Earth* set the standard for pop-prophecy books in the late 1960s. It has been a dominant concept that, when Christ returns, the world will be in the midst of a revolt among the nations against the Antichrist, and the planet will be careening toward self-destruction from the effects of this "World War III." However, that is not the testimony of Scripture.

The start of this view is found by misapplying Revelation 9:13-21 to Revelation 16:12. The two passages are regarded as two closely related stages of a single event. When read in this context, it appears that an army of 200 million "kings of the east" (China and East Asian nations) will cross the Euphrates River during the last half of the tribulation period and begin a war with the Western alliance of the Antichrist. This will result in one-third of mankind being killed. Therefore, since these events involve the sixth trumpet and sixth bowl plagues, and are near the end of the tribulation, the world will supposedly be in the throes of a bloody civil war when Christ returns. Jesus has only to clean the area after this supposed self-destruction, except this is not the truth.

When the Revelation passages are understood as such, the

true scenario of the final three-and-one-half years of the reign of the Antichrist and the one world government is turned askew. In fact, the two passages are describing two separate events. The event of Revelation 9 does not describe a human military invasion. It involves a demonic invasion and deadly plague.[13] The Revelation 16 event occurs in conjunction with the Armageddon campaign in perfect agreement with the commands of the Antichrist. Critical to the correct understanding of the rise of the Antichrist and the onset of the one world government is the biblical sequence of those events as determined by contextual "time markers." Careful attention to these time markers will demonstrate the final one world empire of the Antichrist will be a global government which is supreme, unified, and unchallenged in the world of men. When Jesus returns, He will be confronting the solidarity of the nations, taking their stand *together Against the LORD and against His Anointed*. Then, the Lord will *laugh* at them, *scoff* at them, and *will speak to them in His anger and terrify them in His fury* (Ps. 2:1-5).

The Time Markers to the Sequence of Events

There exists in the text and context of Holy Scripture certain prophetic "time markers." These do not indicate times, seasons, days or hours, in fact, none are revealed in Scripture. However, they do serve as chronological keys to clarify the sequence of end time events.[14] The time markers that will be examined are essential to locating the sequence of the development, and thus the character, of the final one world government on the calendar of end time events. Four such time markers are especially important.

First, the catalyst for the final three-and-one-half years (herein referred to as the "end time") of the seven-year tribulation period will begin when the Antichrist enters the Temple in Jerusalem and declares to the entire planet that he is "God" on earth, and his kingdom is on earth. He will require worship as God by every person on the five continents. *And they worshiped the dragon* [Satan], *because he gave his authority to the beast* [Antichrist]; *and they worshiped the beast, saying, "Who is like the beast, and who is able to wage war with him?"* (Rev. 13:4).

The adulation of people in every nation means there are simply no challengers anywhere to the charismatic power and the war power of this mighty man of the ages.

Second, the absolute power of the Antichrist will remain intact by divine decree for the entire period of the end time until it is terminated by the return of Christ. *And there was given to him a mouth speaking arrogant words and blasphemies; and authority to act for forty-two months* [3 1/2 years] *was given to him* (13:5).

Third, the prophet Daniel wrote that during the entire period of the end time, the Antichrist will *prosper*. In other words, he will be successful until the Great Tribulation (*the indignation*) is completed, and Jesus returns. *"Then the king will do as he pleases, and he will exalt and magnify himself above every god, and will speak monstrous things against the God of gods; and he will prosper until the indignation is finished, for that which is decreed will be done"* (Dan. 11:36).

Fourth, at the terminal event of the end time period—that is, Armageddon and the return of Jesus Christ—all of the nations of the earth will be united with the Antichrist against the Jews and Jesus Christ. Scriptures, such as Joel 3:2, Zechariah 12:3; 14:2; Rev. 16:13-14; 19:19, are clear concerning this truth.

These four keystone truths of the Antichrist assuming supreme power, extending throughout the entire length of the end time, without human deterrence, with an iron-fisted control over all nations will enable the reader to understand a likely sequence of stages leading to the impending snare of the emerging one world government.

Nine Stages to the Snare of the Coming One World Government

Thinking on these four time markers, the reader can now begin to place the Scriptures detailing the rise of the Antichrist and the coming one world government on a sequential time-line. The key text is Daniel 11:36-45. Due to the detail in this passage and because of the extent of its time span, it will serve as the framework text. Other passages which bear on the development of the global end-time political system will be fit within the chronological framework. There are nine discernable stages to the arrival and growth of the coming one world government.

Stage 1: The Fall of Russia and the Islamic States

And the word of the LORD came to me saying, "Son of man, set your face toward Gog of the land of Magog, the prince of Rosh, Meshech, and Tubal, [Russia] *and prophesy against him, and say, 'Thus says the Lord GOD, "Behold, I am against you...and I will bring you out, and all your army...Persia* [Iran]*, Ethiopia* [Sudan-Ethiopia]*, and Put* [Libya] *with them, all of them with shield and helmet; Gomer* [Turkey] *with all its troops; Beth-togarmah* [Turkey-Armenia] *from the remote parts of the north with all its troops—many peoples* [other nations in the orb of these Islamic countries] *with you.... "After many days you will be summoned; in the latter years you will come into the land that is restored from the sword, whose inhabitants have been gathered from many nations to the mountains of Israel which had been a continual waste; but its people were brought out from the nations, and they are living securely, all of them. "And you will go up, you will come like a storm; you will be like a cloud covering the land, you and all your troops, and many peoples with you"* (Ezek. 38:1-9).[15]

Ezekiel 38-39 foretells of a massive invasion against Israel by a coalition of Russian and Islamic-allied states just prior to the seven-year tribulation period.[16] God will destroy the multinational invading forces supernaturally on *the mountains of Israel*. This will leave a gaping hole in the geo-political dynamics of the world. There will be a power vacuum in the Middle East. The Antichrist, who will arise out of the Assyrian realm of the reemerging Roman Empire, will rush to fill the void as a first step in his rise to power.[17] He will direct a covenant of peace (a false peace made to be broken) with Israel (Dan. 9:27). He will permit them to rebuild their Temple on its ancient site in Jerusalem. With his acknowledgment that Israel's God has acted (albeit not in true faith), and his rise to the politically expedient occasion amid the massive void created in the Russian and Islamic sectors of the world, his climb to power will be swift indeed.

Stage 2: The Rise of the King of the North

"As for the ten horns, out of this kingdom ten kings will arise; and another will arise after them, and he will be different from the previous ones and will subdue three kings" (Dan. 7:24). Ten leaders will arise who far surpass the other nations of the European Union (there are currently 25 member nations). By this time, the European Union will have taken its final form as the restored Roman Empire predicted in Daniel and Revelation. The key to this final form is the admission of Turkey into the European Union. It is the bridge state to the Middle East, which comprised the eastern sector of the ancient Roman Empire.[18] Appearing as a "belated" eleventh king among the new Roman Empire states of the Middle East will be the Antichrist. In the rise of God's overthrow of the mighty Russo-Islamic alliance, He will overcome Egypt, Greece, and Turkey by military might. In the process, the prophecy of the end-time restoration of Assyria, Egypt, Greece, and Turkey will be fulfilled (*in the latter period of their rule*; 8:23). At this point, the Antichrist will have essentially ascended to power over the eastern realm of the restored Roman Empire. He will establish slave governments loyal to him in these three countries.

"And at the end time the king of the South will collide with him, and the king of the North will storm against him with chariots, with horsemen, and with many ships; and he will enter countries, overflow **them,** *and pass through"* (11:40). The Antichrist, called *the Assyrian* in Micah 5:5-6, and identified with the geographic area of the Middle East as the *king of the North* in Daniel 11:40,[19] will surpass Egypt and *other countries* in the process of establishing his proxies in Egypt, Greece, and Turkey. Where will the Antichrist acquire his *many ships*, and his military might? By this time, he will have acquired control over the majority of combined forces of the Middle East, and will surely be in agreement with the leaders of the neo-Roman Empire. Every biblical indicator is that these military incursions will be unprecedented in human history in both their rapidity and scale of destruction. One-fourth of the earth's population will perish in the process (Rev. 6:8).

Stage 3: The Mantle of the New Roman Empire

"And the ten horns which you saw are ten kings, who have not yet received [at the time John wrote this passage] *a kingdom, but they receive authority as kings with the beast for one hour. These have one purpose and they give their power and authority to the beast. These will wage war against the Lamb...*[and] *will hate the harlot...For God has put it in their hearts to execute His purpose by having a common purpose, and by giving their kingdom to the beast, until the words of God should be fulfilled"* (17:12-17).

The *ten kings* are the ten nations that will be in power of the restored Roman Empire (European-Middle East Union) when the Antichrist first begins his ascendancy to power. As already mentioned, he will depose three of them, replacing them with his own proxy kings. Thus, there will still be *ten kings* over the new Roman Empire. However, the Antichrist will have a substantial advantage on the power mix. In light of the destruction of the Russo-Islamic coalition, the resultant power vacuum in the world, the military coup over the three proxy states, and the diplomatic coup of the Israeli "peace" covenant, something quiet remarkable will occur. The *ten kings* of the Roman Empire will actually bequest to the Antichrist for the throne of the end time Roman Empire. They will establish him as a single supreme ruler. The Antichrist will receive the mantle of New Rome.

Stage 4: The Fall of Countries

"...and he will enter countries, overflow them, and pass through" (Dan. 11:40). In stage four, the reader encounters the plural term *countries*, indicating that in the process of this swirl of activity the Antichrist will overthrow other nations. Some of these may be political reliefs of the previously fallen Russo-Islamic countries.

Stage 5: The Destruction of the Global Religious System

"And the ten horns which you saw, and the beast, these will hate the harlot [global religious system] *and will make her desolate and naked, and will eat her flesh and will burn her up with*

fire. For God has put it in their hearts to execute His purpose by having a common purpose, and by giving their kingdom to the beast, until the words of God should be fulfilled" (Rev. 17:16-17).

The true church will be raptured to heaven in the rapture before the Antichrist implements his false peace covenant with Israel. Millions of people will simply be gone. Just as a cesspool gushes in to fill a hole, so will the remaining religions of the world rush to fill the void, tying the knot of unity with the initial blessing of the Antichrist. This one world religious system will quickly become a liability to the emerging one world political system. In perfect agreement, not only among themselves, but also in unwitting compliance with God's plan and purpose, the Antichrist and the *ten kings* will destroy all vestiges of the one world religion and all of its trappings, churches, popes, prelates, mosques, and cathedrals. Thereafter, following his pattern of blitzkrieg, rapid-fire power inflation, the Antichrist will mimic his mentor and seek the ultimate display of power: *"I will ascend above the heights of the clouds; I will make myself like the Most High"* (Satan at the dawn of creation; Isa. 14:14). He will fill the religious void with worship of himself.

Stage 6: The Abomination in the Beautiful Land

"He will also enter the Beautiful Land [Israel], and many countries will fall; but these will be rescued out of his hand: Edom, Moab and the foremost of the sons of Ammon" (Dan. 11:41). Following the momentum of worldwide acclaim and adulation, the Antichrist will seize the moment. He will march victoriously into Jerusalem, cancel the covenant with the Jews, and enter the Temple of God declaring himself to be "God" on earth. He will demand not only economic, military, and political allegiance from the four corners of the earth, but also he will require worship as the divine incarnation from humanity in all places.

In the context of those days—when a fourth of humanity will fall dead at the feet of armies and plagues within three years or so, when countries will collapse like dominoes overnight, when millions of people simply disappear instantly in the rapture, when the earth itself will shudder under the weight of lawlessness through earthquakes and famines—sinful mankind will readily worship the Antichrist as their deliverer. Jesus called the act of the Antichrist desecrating the Temple and requiring self-worship *the ABOMINATION OF DESOLATION* (Mt. 24:15-21), and warned the Jews to flee the land because a *great tribulation* would begin. It is for this reason that the passage above indicates *Edom, Moab and the foremost of the sons of Ammon* [essentially Jordan] will be spared from the murderous destruction of the Antichrist. It will serve as a divinely provided safe haven for the fleeing Jews.

Stage 7: The Abdication of the Strongest Fortresses

*"And he will take action against the strongest of fortresses with **the help of** a foreign god; he will give great honor to those who acknowledge **him**, and he will cause them to rule over the many, and will parcel out land for a price"* (Dan. 11:39). In modern vernacular, the phrase *strongest of fortresses* would be rendered "superpowers." Daniel 11:39 is the strongest allusion in Scripture to the fate of the United States.[20] Other strong powers will subside to this volcanic-like concentration and rise of power in a single individual. It will be unprecedented among the annals of world history. Daniel 8:24 furnishes a sense of the military and political power of this individual: *"And his power will be mighty, but not by his **own** power, and he will destroy to an extraordinary degree and prosper and perform **his will**; he will destroy mighty men and the holy people."* Clearly, his power will come directly from Satan.

Stage 8: The Fall of Many Countries

*"He will also enter the Beautiful Land, and many **countries** will fall; but these will be rescued out of his hand: Edom, Moab and the foremost of the sons of Ammon* (11:41). Here the reader encounters the plural term *countries* again. However, this time it is *many*.

Stage 9: The Fall of Other Countries

*"Then he will stretch out his hand against **other** countries, and the land of Egypt will not escape. "But he will gain control*

over the hidden treasures of gold and silver, and over all the precious things of Egypt; and Libyans and Ethiopians **will follow** *at his heels"* (11:42-43).

Egypt, *the king of the South* throughout Daniel 11, will exert a prominent role against the Antichrist as he rises to the apex of his power. As one of the three proxy kingdoms among the ten-nation revived Roman Empire (which by this time will be under the control of the Antichrist), it will be victim to another military incursion as the Antichrist allocates the African continent for his control. Once again (viz. the third time in the Daniel 11 passage) there is mention of plural (i.e. *other*) *countries*. There are currently two hundred nations on the earth which will all align themselves, like lead filings to a magnet, at the footstool of the eschatological one world ruler.

Who Is Like Him?

And I **saw** *one of his heads as if it had been slain, and his fatal wound was healed. And the whole earth was amazed* **and followed** *after the beast; and they worshiped the dragon, because he gave his authority to the beast; and they worshiped the beast, saying, "Who is like the beast...?"* (Rev. 13:3-4). This one rhetorical question is truly a declarative statement implying its own answer: "No one is like the Antichrist!" The worldwide sentiment will sound loudly with enthusiastic approval across five continents. The apparent "reincarnation" of the Antichrist and the resurrection of the Assyrian Kingdom, and the restoration of the Roman Empire (all under his throne room) will be the explanation for the mysterious *fatal wound*.[21]

Who Can Make War With Him?

...and they worshiped the beast, saying..."who is able to wage war with him?" (13:3-4). This is another rhetorical question which also provides its own answer: "No one on earth can make war with the Antichrist!" That is the geo-political position of the nations by the midpoint of the seven-year tribulation (the

starting point of the end time).

Here it is important to note that kings and nations still exist within the one world empire of the Antichrist. However, these are subjugated, vassal states. As already demonstrated in the section on "time markers," the Antichrist will possess full authority for the entire end time period of forty two months, will prosper until the end, and will be joined in full compliance by all nations when he sets his countenance against Jesus Christ to *wage war with the Lamb* at the Battle of Armageddon (cf. Rev. 17:12-14; 19:19). His neo-Roman Empire will relate to the other kings and nations as vassal-states, which will comprise the one world government.

The Snare

Perhaps nowhere else is the nature of the coming one world government so concisely, yet so completely characterized as in Daniel 7:25. *'And he will speak out against the Most High and wear down the saints of the Highest One, and he will intend to make alterations in times and in law; and they will be given into his hand for a time, times, and half a time* [3 1/2 years].

The phrase *he will intend to make alterations in times and in law* is surrounded by the descriptions of the Antichrist's blasphemy against God and the persecution and murder of God's people. Thus, the *alterations in times and in law* must also be understood as a fundamental act to this attempted obliteration of God. The Antichrist will abolish all calendars (e.g. BC, AD, BCE, CE) and times (Jewish feasts and Christian holidays) which bring attention to the biblical God. He will change God's Law and the Ten Commandments, as understood by the great monotheistic religions, and as written on the hearts and consciences of every individual (Rom. 2:14-15). In summary, he will attempt to transfer society's understanding of the absolute attributes, decrees, and prerogatives of God to himself. Through the prophet Daniel and the Apostle Paul, the Holy Spirit warned,

"Then the king will do as he pleases, and he will exalt

and magnify himself above every god, and will speak
monstrous things against the God of gods; and he will
prosper until the indignation is finished, for that which
is decreed will be done" (Dan. 11:36).

Let no one in any way deceive you, for *it will not come*
unless the apostasy comes first, and the man of lawlessness is revealed, the son of destruction, who opposes and
exalts himself above every so-called god or object of
worship, so that he takes his seat in the temple of God,
displaying himself as being God (2 Thess. 2:3-4).

The Antichrist will attempt to create hostility between the
Creator and His creation; he will renew society under the
authority of *the god of this world*, Satan (2 Cor. 4:4). The
"snare" of the coming one world government will be the aboli-
tion of human rights for Christians and Jews. The Bible warns
repeatedly that the Antichrist and the iron fist of his enforcement
apparatus will wage war with the *saints of the Highest One*
(Dan. 7:25; 8:24-25; 11:44; Mt. 24:9, 21-22; Rev. 6:9-11; 7:9-
11). These *saints* are people (since the time of the rapture removing all church age believers to heaven) who are believing in Jesus
Christ as their Savior.

Multitudes of Gentiles will become Christians during the
tribulation period. Revelation 7 portrays 144,000 Jews believing
in Jesus Christ. This may happen as an aftereffect of the rapture,
or as a result of the northern invasion of Israel prior to the start
of the tribulation period. Many Jews will heed the call of Jesus
to flee to the mountains when the Antichrist enters the Temple
in Jerusalem, and will look to Jesus as their promised Messiah
and Savior.[22]

The numbers of believers who are pursued and martyred will
be immense. However, everyone of them will be released from
the temporal snare of this man-made hell by Almighty God at
the end of the age. He will rescue these martyrs through resurrection and He will rescue the saints who survive the tribulation
by divine intervention at the second coming of Christ.

Disturbing Rumors

"But rumors from the East and from the North will disturb him, and he will go forth with great wrath to destroy and annihilate many (Dan. 11:44). In light of previously enumerated time markers, this passage is revealing. Since, as already demonstrated, the Antichrist will have complete power extending for the entire span of the end time, and since this power will be unchallenged as he wields absolute control over all nations, what *rumors* could possibly disturb *him*? What kind of *rumors from the East and from the North* would cause him to *go forth with great wrath to destroy and annihilate many* [Jews].[23]

It cannot be a revolt against him from among the kings and vassal-nations of his empire, for, as demonstrated previously, they remain united until the second coming of Jesus. Furthermore, it cannot be an invasion of eastern Asian nations from beyond the Euphrates River (cf. Rev. 9:13-21), for it has already been stated these are not human armies but demonic forces. However, therein lies the key!

When God expresses His long delayed wrath on the earth without restraint, it results in cascades upon the last empire, that is, the one world government of the Antichrist. Additionally, it happens quickly, as all of the prophecies predict. [24] It also occurs with cosmic magnitude! The release of the angelic emissaries of Satan upon the world in the sixth trumpet judgment (Rev. 9:13-21), occurs near the very end of the reign of the Antichrist. One-third of mankind is killed which would result in a shock treatment to the psyche of even the Antichrist. It will certainly require his attention.

The directions given—*from the East and from the North*—are from the vantage point of Jerusalem[25] which identifies the activity in the direction of the Euphrates River, as indicated by the sixth trumpet. Furthermore, it is probable that a major portion of those killed by these demonic forces will be the populations of the far east, since the majority of the earth's population live there. This would also explain the rapid mobilization of the *kings of the east* to move toward the valley of Armageddon in accordance with the sixth bowl judgment.

The reader should understand that the bowl judgments result in a cascading crescendo as the heavens are opened in anticipation of the return of Christ. Although they are two separate events, there is a cause and effect relationship and only a short timespan between the sixth trumpet and the sixth bowl. The purpose of the *kings of the east* will be to do battle in *the war of the great day of God the Almighty*. The target for them, and all of the kings of the earth, is the chosen people of God, the Jews, in Jerusalem. It is this rumor that will ignite the Antichrist and the global armies into their facedown with Jesus Christ in Israel. After the *rumors from the East and from the North...disturb him*, and cause him to go *forth with great wrath to destroy and annihilate many...he will pitch the tents of his royal pavilion between the seas and the beautiful Holy Mountain; yet he will come to his end, and no one will help him* (11:45).

The Trap

There will be a double snare for the ungodly who follow the Antichrist. First, they will lose their God-given inalienable rights. They will be subjugated by the force of the state and will not *be able to buy or to sell* without being branded, earmarked, and numbered with the imprint of the Antichrist (Rev. 13:17). They will be forced into a worship routine focused upon *the image of the beast* (13:15). They will be murdered by state sanction if they do not worship the Antichrist. However, this one world government is a double snare for those *with the mark of the beast* for it will be a one way conduit to a terror far worse than any human can deliver. Scripture warns, *It is a terrifying thing to fall into the hands of the living God* (Heb. 10:31).

The second snare is infinitely worse than that imposed by the coming one world government. Even though the empire of the Antichrist will execute all who deviate from the satanic agenda of the powers that be, there remains a fate exceeding anything the Antichrist might do. Scripture states, the door was shut when the Lord will say, *"I do not know where you are from.... DEPART FROM ME, ALL YOU EVILDOERS"* (Lk. 13:25-27). Scripture also warns, *"And do not fear those who kill the body, but are unable to kill the soul; but rather fear Him who is able to destroy both soul and body in hell* (Mt. 10:28).

The second snare of the emerging one world government will become the trap of the Day of the Lord. When Jesus Christ returns to earth, He will judge the Antichrist and his legions and his subjugated-vassals and his global empire; those who are not slain and sent to hades will stand before the Judge of all the world and hear the pronouncement, *"Depart from Me, accursed ones, into the eternal fire which has been prepared for the devil and his angels* (25:41). The trap associated with the Day of the Lord is eternal.

Delay the Snare

Today the most significant trend toward a one world government is concentrated upon the development of the European Union (EU). The EU is the forerunner of the restored Roman Empire. The restoration of the Roman Empire is a clear prophecy for the last days (Dan. 2, 7; Rev. 17).

The amazing story of the formation of the EU is that since the post-World War II idea originally developed, its step-by-step organization has not missed a single opportunity. Each stage of the creation of European federation has met its target date. The founding ceremonies of EU development (first, the European Common Market, and now, the European Union Constitution) have occurred in Rome, as would be expected due to the prophetic Word.

EU foreign ministers have agreed Europe's first constitution will be signed in Rome. Italian Prime Minister Silvio Berlusconi had said last week that the document would be signed on 20 November. The new date would allow the outgoing EC President Romano Prodi to join in the ceremony two days before the end of his mandate, AFP news agency reports. The treaty will then have to be ratified in each country, either by referendum or a vote in parliament. The signing will take place in the same room where the original treaties which founded the EU were signed almost 50 years ago—in the Campidoglio Palace. In 1957, six nations signed the Treaty of Rome. The EU now has 25 members.[26]

Berlusconi, in Paris for a bilateral summit with French President Jacques Chirac, said the ceremony would take place in the same room where the Treaty of Rome, which established the EU's forerunner, was signed in 1957. "We will gather together on November 20 in Rome for the signing ceremony in the same palace, the same room as was used for the signature of the Treaty of Rome in 1957," Berlusconi told a joint press conference with Chirac. Chirac hailed the "decision, taken unanimously, to sign the constitutional treaty in Rome, making it the second founding treaty."[27]

As the rise of this neo-Roman Empire and the shadow of the coming Antichrist loom large, the best hope to forestall the one world government remains the true body of Christ, the Church. Christians must be vigilant to do as Christ commanded: *but you shall receive power when the Holy Spirit has come upon you; and you shall be My witnesses both in Jerusalem, and in all Judea and Samaria, and even to the remotest part of the earth* (Acts 1:8).

People must have their hearts changed by Christ before they can establish and operate a just society. Bible prophecy teaches, ultimately, this will not happen. Although the one world government of the Antichrist is coming, it may be delayed. Christians are also commanded to pray *for kings and all who are in authority, in order that we may lead a tranquil and quiet life in all godliness and dignity* (1 Tim. 2:1-2). Through the prayers of Christians, the world may be spared the snare of world government for a season.

"At one moment I might speak concerning a nation or concerning a kingdom to uproot, to pull down, or to destroy *it*; if that nation against which I have spoken turns from its evil, I will relent concerning the calamity I planned to bring on it. "Or at another moment I might speak concerning a nation or concerning a kingdom to build up or to plant *it*; if it does evil in My sight by not obeying My voice, then I will think better of the good with which I had promised to bless it (Jer. 18:7-10).

Christians should especially pray for the United States, which in spite of a horrific drift toward paganism, remains the primary nation in the world whose institutions are founded upon the "Ten Commandments [that] codify, in a handful of words, acceptable human behavior."[28] The United States of America was founded upon belief in the classical understanding of natural law that served as the basis for the fundamental principles (self-evident truths) proclaimed in the Declaration of Independence. Furthermore, in an effort to uphold and secure the axiomatic truths proclaimed in that declaration, the Founding Fathers chartered the Constitution and established a republic system of government.[29] Christians must pray for America as she is the world's best hope to forestall world government because "America is not only a religious nation but also an overwhelmingly Christian one."[30]

Escape the Trap

In conclusion, the Bible provides a simple formula for escaping the trap that will be triggered when Jesus Christ returns to judge and condemn the empire of the Antichrist and the one world government of autonomous man. *"Be on guard, that your hearts may not be weighted down with dissipation and drunkenness and the worries of life, and that day come on you suddenly like a trap; for it will come upon all those who dwell on the face of all the earth. "But keep on the alert at all times, praying in order that you may have strength to escape all these things that are about to take place, and to stand before the Son of Man"* (Lk. 21:34-36).

If one does not know Jesus Christ personally as Lord and Savior, he cannot *be on guard* or *keep on the alert*. Here is how a person can receive Jesus as Savior, and escape the coming snare of one world government, and the trap of the eternal judgment of the ungodly: *that if you confess with your mouth Jesus as Lord, and believe in your heart that God raised Him from the dead, you shall be saved* (Rom. 10:9).

CHAPTER 9

GOVERNMENT OF THE FUTURE

Ron J. Bigalke Jr.

Current events today in the political world should stimulate an interest in every introspective mind. Mankind is living in critical times as the attention of the world is being directed toward the East. Israel is truly the prophetic centre of the earth, as Bible prophecy is concerned with the destiny of the earth, and the destiny of the nations of the earth in relation to Israel. *"When the Most High gave the nations their inheritance, when He separated the sons of man, He set the boundaries of the peoples according to the number of the sons of Israel. For the Lord's portion is His people; Jacob is the allotment of His inheritance"* (Deut. 32:8-9).

Israel had been scattered throughout the earth, amongst the nations of the world; nevertheless, their national existence today is living testimony to the veracity of God's promises in His Word to fulfill all the promises He made with the nation. Of course, these promises are yet to be fulfilled *for the gifts and the calling of God are irrevocable* (Rom. 11:29). *A partial hardening has happened until the fullness of the Gentiles has come in; and thus all Israel will be saved; just as it is written, "The Deliverer will come from Zion, He will remove ungodliness from Jacob." And this is My covenant with them, when I take away their sins"* (11:25-27).

The destiny of the Jews, and the land of Israel, are central issues to world problems today for the destinies of the nations are inseparable from the destiny of the Jews and their land. Isaiah's distinctive title for God, the *Holy One of Israel*, is consistent with Zechariah's prophecy of judgment for those nations that would harm her (e.g. Zech. 12:2-9). Truly, the nations of the world are united to the future history of the Jews and Israel. The promised kingdom for the nation of Israel is a reality. The number of prophecies concerning the future blessings for the hardened nation is of such magnitude that it is difficult to understand how some Christians teach the church is Israel and the church is the kingdom which essentially means there is no objective standard for determining the fulfillment of Bible prophecy.

The prophets of both the Old and New Testaments foretold a one world government at the end of the age. This government of the future will be sustained by Satan himself. In the last days of the world's struggles, immediately preceding the millennial reign of Jesus Christ, a one world government will be in existence that will challenge the prophetic Scriptures regarding the Jews in the land of Israel. The wickedness of this government which be of such magnitude that the Lord Jesus Christ will return to Earth to destroy it and establish His earthly, millennial reign upon David's throne in Jerusalem.

The Gentile World Powers

The prophet Daniel describes the *times of the Gentiles* in great detail. His prophecy begins with the Babylonian Captivity of the Jews under Nebuchadnezzar and ends with the coming of the Son of Man in glory to destroy the last of the Gentile powers which have emerged in profane rebellion against God. The dominion of these powers will be removed and replaced by *an everlasting dominion which will not pass away* (Dan. 7:13-14). The metallic image of Daniel 2 in Nebuchadnezzar's dream details the course of the Gentile powers. Specifically, it concerns *what will take place in the latter days* (2:28). The Old Testament refers to two ages: the current age and the age to come. Between these two ages are *the latter days* which refer to the times immediately preceding the age to come.

Daniel 2:31-35 records the prophet's explanation to Nebuchadnezzar. In his dream, Nebuchadnezzar saw *a single great statute...which was large and of extraordinary splendor...and its appearance was awesome*. Although the image bore the appearance of a man, its various components included a head of gold, a chest and arms of silver, stomach and thighs of brass, legs of iron, and feet mingled with iron and miry clay. Nebuchadnezzar *continued looking until a stone was cut out without hands, and it struck the statue on its feet of iron and clay, and crushed them.* The remaining components *were crushed...like chaff from the summer threshing floors; and the wind carried them away so that not a trace of them was found.* Afterward, *the stone that struck the statue became a great mountain and filled the earth.*

Not only did Daniel reveal the dream to the king, but also God provided him with the *interpretation.* According to the interpretation, the head of gold symbolized the Babylonian Empire, controlled by Nebuchadnezzar (2:38). Formerly, God administered His purposes for an earthly rule through the Israelites, now He would execute His purposes through the Gentiles. Nebuchadnezzar, as the head of gold, would be the first of the Gentile rulers predestined by God to accomplish His purposes for human history (2:37-38).

Next, Daniel revealed *another kingdom* (2:39) to conquer the Babylonian Empire. It would be a *kingdom inferior*, as symbolized by the weaker metal, to the Babylonians. The Medo-Persian Empire is this second kingdom. It was inferior to the Babylonian since power was divided between the Medes and the Persians resulting in constant conflict.

The *third kingdom of bronze* (2:39) was the Grecian Empire. Although a weaker metal is used again, this kingdom would *rule over all the earth*. The head of the Greek Empire was, of course, Alexander the Great. The conquest of the known world was by Alexander the Great, and the kingdoms created by his generals after his death "Hellenized" the world. It was truly the first empire to *rule over all the earth*.

Great attention in the interpretation is now given to the *fourth kingdom as strong as iron* (2:40). The Roman Empire was this kingdom which crushed and broke the former three kingdoms *in pieces*. It wielded tremendous power in subjugating the nations of the known world. However, *it will be a divided kingdom* (2:41), as symbolized by the *legs of iron* (2:33).

The Roman Empire was established by Augustus in 27 B.C. and divided into the Western Roman Empire and the Eastern Empire in A.D. 395. When Theodosius died in A.D. 395, he divided the Roman Empire among his two sons, Honorius and Arcadius. Honorius ruled the West and Arcadius ruled the East. The Eastern Roman Empire, or Byzantine Empire, was a continuation of the Roman Empire in the Middle East after its division in A.D. 395. In the west, Rome did not exert much influence until Charlemagne was crowned Emperor of the Holy Roman Empire. The lands ruled by Charlemagne were a continuation of the Roman Empire in Europe. For these reasons most historians will agree that the Roman Empire never truly fell; rather, its power was distributed throughout the rising nations, that is, the toes *partly of iron and partly of pottery* [clay]. The toes symbolize the definitive severance of the fourth empire, or the Gentile nations as they will exist during the future tribulation period.

The feet of the image are mingled with iron and miry clay, *but they will not adhere to one another, even as iron does not combine with pottery* (2:43). The fact that the two components do not mix indicates the final form of Gentile government will be characterized by dissension. *Some of the kingdom will be strong and part of it will be brittle* (2:42). There will be an attempt to *combine with one another* (2:43), which is interpreted as a ten-nation confederacy (cf. Rev. 7:7, 24; Rev. 13:2). These Gentile world powers will attempt to unify and have a one world government. Scripture is not concerned here with geographical location, but primarily with the government of man. The stone *cut out of the mountain without hands* will utterly destroy all Gentile world government and *the God of heaven will set up a kingdom which will never be destroyed* (2:44-45). The image of Daniel 2 gives the final outcome of the Gentile powers as a whole, as opposed to their individual or sequential form.

The Beastly Empires

The most common biblical name for the ruler of the world government of the future is *beast* (Rev. 11:7; 13:1-4, 11-12, 14-15, 17-18; 14:9; 14:11; 15:2; 16:2, 10, 13; 17:3, 7-8, 11-13, 16-

17; 19:19-20; 20:4, 10). The only verse which calls this ruler "Antichrist" is 1 John 2:22. Throughout the history of the church, the term Antichrist has been used most frequently to designate the *beast*. The name *beast* is first used of the Antichrist in Daniel 7 where a description is given of the four successive Gentile powers. Each of these empires is pictured as beasts: Babylon *was like a lion and had the wings of an eagle* (Dan. 7:4), Medo-Persia resembles *a bear* (7:5), Greece was *like a leopard* (7:6), and Rome a beast with *ten horns* (7:7).

The Apostle John wrote, *And I saw a beast coming up out of the sea, having ten horns and seven heads, and on his horns were ten diadems, and on his heads were blasphemous names. And the beast which I saw was like a leopard, and his feet were like those of a bear, and his mouth like the mouth of a lion. And the dragon gave him his power and his throne and great authority* (Rev. 13:1-2). The *beast coming up out of the sea* is the Antichrist (Dan. 7:3; Rev. 17:15) for Revelation 17:15 delineates the sea as *peoples and multitudes and nations and tongues*. The Antichrist will emerge from the Gentile majority of humanity and will be the personification of the Gentile world empires. The *dragon* is Satan (12:9) who gives *his power and his throne and great authority* to the Antichrist. Receiving his power from Satan, the Antichrist will be more malevolent and merciless than the former beastly empires.

The four beasts in Daniel 7 symbolize four succeeding kingdoms, which parallel the four kingdoms of Nebuchadnezzar's image in Daniel 2. In his commentary on Daniel, W. C. Stevens wrote,

In connection with the explanation of verse 17 that these four beasts are four kings, we need to remember that we learned from the interpretation of Nebuchadnezzar's dream that the word "king" may be used for kingdom or empire; and not only covering the incumbency of a given king but also covering the entire duration of the empire itself. "Thou art this head of gold. And after thee shall arise another kingdom." And here in chapter 7, verse 23, we read: "And the fourth beast shall be the fourth kingdom upon the earth." Hence, it was made certain to Daniel that these four beasts represented the same procession of world-empires which the image of Nebuchadnezzar's dream portrayed.[1]

Daniel's vision gives God's perspective of the Gentile powers, whereas Nebuchadnezzar's dream provided the perspective of man. Man views history as evolving upward in majesty and power, but God views the history of man as a gathering of wild beasts consuming one another. Stevens comments,

> What are the attributes of beasts? To keep their own at any cost within their might: to quarrel over what they do not have but what they want; to fly easily into blood-thirsty rage at any affront, at any aggression, for any coveted object; under passion to take satisfaction in the blood, the agonies, the loss, the death of the objects of their rage; in a word, to be supreme in rule, in possession, in indulgence in so far as their power avails. God foresaw this spirit prevalent in the world empires down to their end. Indeed, it is the very spirit of world empire, and militarism is its indispensable element.[2]

The godless existentialist Nietzsche even admitted the fact that man's behavior is characteristic of a beast. In his *Will to Power*, he wrote,

> Man is beast and superbeast; the higher man is inhuman and superhuman: these belong together. With every increase of greatness and height in man, there is also an increase in depth and terribleness: one ought not to desire the one without the other—or rather: the more radically one desires the one, the more radically one perceives precisely the other.[3]

The Fourth Beast
Daniel 7 describes the same Gentile powers as the colossal image (i.e. Dan. 2), but in their individual and sequential form.

In other words, one replaces the next power. Although each kingdom succeeds the next, one should not assume the Gentile powers composing the various kingdoms disappear. *"As for the rest of the beasts, their dominion was taken away, but an extension of life was granted to them for an appointed period of time* (7:12). The fourth beast, the Roman Empire, will burgeon, and the life of the other beasts will be extended. The judgment of all the beasts will occur when the existing nations are also judged in the final conflict of world history.

One of the basic teachings of eschatology is there will be a revived form of the fourth Gentile world power (Dan. 2, 7). The Roman Empire is the fourth kingdom, and some form of that kingdom will be revived in the last days. The kingdoms will attempt to *combine with one another* (2:43) to form a ten-nation confederacy (cf. Rev. 7:7, 24; Rev. 13:2) which is the revival of the fourth beast. The revived Roman Empire will facilitate the worldwide control of the Antichrist. Dr. Walvoord explained,

> The prediction that there will be a ten-kingdom stage of the revival of the Roman Empire is one of the important descriptive prophecies of the end time. This prophecy anticipates that there will be ten countries originally related to the Roman Empire that will constitute the Roman Empire in its revived form.... Since the names of the countries are not given and there are many more than ten countries in the ancient Roman Empire, it leaves some flexibility in the fulfillment. The prediction, however, requires a political union and then a dictator over the ten countries.[4]

Contrary to any doubt concerning this fulfillment, the Roman Empire will be revived. *"The beast that you saw was and is not, and is about to come up.... And those who dwell on the earth will wonder...when they see the beast, that he was and is not and will come* (Rev. 17:8). Again, Walvoord provided clear explanation.

The reference to the beast as that which once was and

then did not exist, and then comes up again, as in verses 8 and 11, seems to refer to the world empire, the Roman Empire, which existed in the time of the apostles, seems to have gone out of existence, but is going to rise again and fulfill its role as a beast, or as a world government.[V]

The beast of Revelation 17:8, 11, which *was* in the time of the apostles *and is not* a world power today, will ascend *out of the abyss* prior to the second coming of Jesus Christ *and to go to destruction* when "*the sovereignty, the dominion, and the greatness of all the kingdoms under the whole heaven will be given to the people of the saints of the Highest One; His kingdom will be an everlasting kingdom, and all the dominions will serve and obey Him*" (Dan. 7:27). The revived Roman Empire within the European nations will be the absolute Western confederation.

The final form of the Gentile world powers will be *different from all the beasts that were before it, and it had ten horns* (7:7). The ten-horned beast is a confederation of ten kingdoms. The prophet explained, "*As for the ten horns, out of this kingdom ten kings will arise*" (7:24; cf. Rev. 17:12; 13:1). The *ten kings* will achieve world power when the fourth beast is revived during the future tribulation period. The ten-horned beast is the same as the toes *partly of iron and partly of pottery* in Daniel 2:42. The final form of the revived Roman Empire consists of ten kingdoms unified by *another horn, a little one,* which is the future world ruler (7:8, 23). The Antichrist is the ruler of the fourth beastly empire, and is simply called *the fourth beast.* The following quote is again from Walvoord.

Many have attempted to find the ten-horned stage of Daniel 7:7 fulfilled in ten kings of the Roman Empire, but there is nothing in history that corresponds to this.... The requirement for fulfillment of both Daniel 2 and 7 is a revival of the Roman Empire in relation to the end of the age. The New Testament adds many prophecies along this line. The final ruler will be politically Roman, as were the people who destroyed Jerusalem in A.D. 70

(Dan. 9:26). The Roman Empire fulfilled the prophecies precisely as in Daniel 2 and 7 right at the time of the first coming of Christ. From there on, however, there is no correspondence to history, and the final stage of the Roman Empire, which will be destroyed by the kingdom that comes from heaven, has never been fulfilled.[6]

The little horn (7:8) does not emerge until the ten-nation confederacy emerges. Daniel wrote, *"While I was contemplating the horns, behold, another horn, a little one, came up among them, and three of the first horns were pulled out by the roots before it; and behold, this horn possessed eyes like the eyes of a man, and a mouth uttering great boasts.* The little horn is an eleventh horn among the *ten horns* which will extirpate *three of the first horns*, that is, the beast assumed their power. The description *eyes of a man* is probably an indicator of intelligence, *and a mouth uttering great boasts* likely indicates his charisma.

Daniel's vision of the world empires is beastly (7:3-8). The *lion* (Babylon) is succeeded by *a bear* (Medo-Persia) to be conquered by *a leopard* (Greece), subdued by a *dreadful and terrifying and extremely strong* beast (Rome), and ultimately an inenarrable beast (a ten-nation confederacy). This last beast will have *ten horns* with one prominent horn who subdues the rest (7:24). The persecution of believers during this time will be intense: *"And he will speak out against the Most High and wear down the saints of the Highest One"* (7:25). The inenarrable beast is the Satanic Empire of the future tribulation period. The government of this future period will be as beastly as the empires.

The Ancient of Days and the Son of Man

Daniel 7:9-14 changes from a vision of four beasts to the glorious account of the reign of *the Ancient of Days* and the coming of the *Son of Man*. The throne scene in Daniel 7:9-14 is completely expanded in Revelation 4-20. In fact, these five verses in Daniel correspond with the 17 chapters of Revelation just mentioned.

The expression *Ancient of Days* is Aramaic[7] and only used in Daniel 7:9, 13, 22. Daniel 7:13, 22 are correctly translated with the article, but this is only the result of identifying the person designated by the anarthros expression in 7:9. In other words, the expression is not a name and should not be capitalized in 7:9 (the KJV, NKJV, NIV also capitalize the expression), although the adjectival expression is certainly a reference to God. Daniel *kept looking* and saw one *advanced in age* (cf. Gen. 24:1), hence, "ancient of days." The expression is meant to communicate symbolically the eternality of the Godhead.

God, *the Ancient of Days*, procures control of the earth's kingdoms through the Son of Man. According to Psalm 2, it is God the Father who will establish the Son of Man upon His rightful throne, but after He judges the little horn. The beast's kingdom is forcefully eradicated which is a fitting depiction of the swiftness in which the Lord judges the wicked at the end of the age (cf. Mt. 25). The heavenly, throne scene is a resplendent depiction the elect angelic creatures ministering before the *Ancient of Days*.

However, the vision of the heavenly throne room is also a scene of judgment. *"A river of fire was flowing and coming out from before Him; thousands upon thousands were attending Him, and myriads upon myriads were standing before Him; the court sat, and the books were opened* (Dan. 7:10). The corollary of this judgment is *the beast* [the little horn who was the ruling power of the Gentile powers] *was slain, and its body was destroyed and given to the burning fire* (7:11). Revelation 19:20 repeats Daniel's vision: *And the beast was seized, and with him the false prophet who performed the signs in his presence, by which he deceived those who had received the mark of the beast and those who worshipped his image; these two were thrown alive into the lake of fire which burns with brimstone.*

The destiny of the Gentile powers differs from the judgment of the beast. Their existence is prolonged for a predestined time, but the actual dominion of the Gentile powers is removed. *"As for the rest of the beasts, their dominion was taken away, but an extension of life was granted to them for an appointed period of time* (7:12). Daniel 7:12 seems to pose a difficult issue regarding the destruction of the previous three beasts.[8] If each of the Gentile world powers is succeeded by the fourth beast, then how are they granted *an extension of life...for an appointed period of time?*[9]

It is beyond question that *the rest of the beasts* will also experience judgment. Noted Old Testament commentator Keil wrote,

> ...not a definite time, the time of the divine judgment of the fourth beast, is meant, but the time of the continuance of the power and dominion for each of the several beasts (kingdoms), foreseen only in the counsel of the Most High, and not further defined. In accordance with this, the statement of v. 12 is that the first three beasts also had their dominion taken away one after another, each at its appointed time; for to each God gave its duration of life, extending to the season and time appointed by Him. Thus...the connecting of the end of the first three beasts with that of the last as denoting that in the horn not merely the fourth kingdom, but also the first three kingdoms, the whole world-power, is brought to an end by the last judgment. This thought, right in itself, and distinctly announced in the destruction of the image (ch. 2), appears, however, to lie less in the altogether loose connection of v. 12 with v. 11 than in the whole context, and certainly in this, that with the fourth beast in general the unfolding of the world-power in its diverse phases is exhausted, and with the judgment of this kingdom the kingdom of God is raised to everlasting supremacy.[10]

The curious thought regards the meaning of the *extension of life*. Larkin reminds his readers,

> It is well to recall that there is a **"Dispensation of Judgment"** between the Present Dispensation, and the Millennium, during which there shall be three

Judgments. (1) The **"Judgment of Believers for their Works"** at the "Judgment Seat of Christ." 2 Cor. 5:10. (2) The **"Judgment of the Jews"** during "The Great Tribulation." ...(3) The **"Judgment of Nations."** Matt. 25:31-46.[11]

The judgment of *all the nations* in Matthew 25:31-46 is to be understood as a judgment of individual Gentiles. The Greek word, *ethnos*, translated *nations* also means "*people* as distinguished from the Jews, *the heathen, Gentiles.*"[12] Benware wrote, "It is mainly used as a category of those people who do not belong to the chosen nation of Israel. So it would probably be clearer to speak of this judgment as the 'judgment of Gentiles' as these are set in contrast to the covenant people of Israel in both [Joel 3 and Matthew 25]."[13] One interpretation of Daniel 7:12 is "a general description covering the whole 'Dispensation of Judgment' period."[14] A second interpretation is to interpret the *rest of the beasts* as experiencing an *extension of life* beyond the judgment of Daniel 7:11 which would mean these have an opportunity to trust in the coming Messiah resulting in entrance into the millennium. The Aramaic, *'ad̲-zᵉmān wᵉ'iddān*, is adequately flexible to allow either interpretation. If the first interpretation is accepted, the *rest of the beasts* represent the unbelieving members of the Gentile world powers which will be judged in accordance with Matthew 25. The kingdoms of this world will be destroyed in terms of their dominion, but Gentile nations will still exist in the millennium. *The times of the Gentiles* will have ended and no longer shall they exercise authority over Israel.

The Aramaic word, *zᵉmān*, means "*to be appointed, fixed, determined*" (viz. "*time, appointed time*"),[15] translated as *kairos*, the opportune or right time (as opposed to measured time), in the Septuagint. However, *'iddān* refers to "*a prophetic period*"[16] or time as "duration,"[17] translated as *chronos* (measured time). Measured time is the interval between a *terminus a quo* (starting point) and the *terminus ad quem* (terminal point). The Aramaic, *'ad̲-zᵉmān wᵉ'iddān*, in Daniel 7:12 should be understood as a determined duration of time, and to the determined particular point in time, when the four beasts will experience the *terminus ad quem* of their *dominion*. Chafer commented on this verse as follows:

> With the death, resurrection, and ascension of Christ, and the descent of the Spirit, the door of gospel privilege was opened unto the Gentiles (Acts 10:45; 11:17-18; 13:47-48), and out of them God is now calling an elect company (Acts 15:14). Their new proffered blessings in this age do not consist in being permitted to share in Israel's earthly covenants, which even Israel is not now enjoying; but rather, through riches of grace in Christ Jesus, they are privileged to be partakers of a heavenly citizenship and glory. It is revealed that the mass of Gentiles will not in this age enter by faith into these heavenly riches. Therefore, this people, designated as "the nations," go on, and at the end of their stewardship as earth-rulers, which is the termination of "the times of the Gentiles" (Luke 21:24; cf. Dan. 2:36-44), they of that generation will, at the end of the tribulation period (cf. Matt. 24:8-31 with 25:31-46), be called upon to stand before the Messiah King, seated on the throne of His glory (Matt. 25:31-32) here on the earth…. The basis of this judgment and its disposition of each of these groups, who together represent the sum total of that generation of the Gentile nations, will be meritorious to the last degree.[18]

Daniel's vision ends with the presentation of the *Son of Man* (Dan. 7:13-14). The first coming of Christ to Earth was to be obedient unto death. Since Christ was obedient and faithful unto death, He became the sinner's substitute under the wrath of God, but He is sinless, and therefore, rose from the grave and ascended to the Father, returning to the glory which He had with the Father before the world was created (cf. Jn. 17:5). Following His ascension, Jesus Christ entered the heavenly throne room and was declared the *Son of Man* (i.e., the Son relating to mankind who was a partaker of humanity; Heb 2.14). The *Son of Man* approached the *Ancient of Days* to be

exalted and glorified (Jn. 13:31-32; cf. Phil. 2:8-11; Heb. 12:2).
Presently, the *Son of Man* is seated at His Father's right hand (Ps.
110:1) which occurred after Jesus was presented as the *Son of
Man* to His Father (Dan. 7:13-14).

Following the *Son of Man*'s presentation to the *Ancient of
Days*, Christ entered the Holy of Holies through (by means of)
His own blood, and is now seated at His Father's right hand. All
worldwide authority is given to Jesus, the *Son of Man*. The
Father has divinely directed for the *Son of Man* to co-reign with
Him over all creation (Ps. 110:1; Dan. 7:13-14; Eph. 1:20-22).
At the close of the tribulation, the *Son of Man* will depart from
the heavenly throne room of the *Ancient of Days* and will return
to Earth in power and glory to reign historically and visibly as
Messiah upon the throne of David.

Christ's current reign upon the Father's throne is not to be
confused with David's throne. At His ascension, Jesus was glorified with the glory which He had eternally with the Father
before anything existed; however, David's throne had a beginning in time and space. The fulfillment of the Davidic covenant
is yet future (cf. Rev. 5:2-5). In fact, Revelation 17:14 and 19:15-
16 is the fulfillment of Psalm 2. Revelation 22:16, reveals Jesus
as *the root and offspring of David, the bright morning star*.
When the New Jerusalem comes *down out of heaven from God*,
Scripture refers to Jesus as *the Alpha and the Omega, the beginning and the end*, and *the Lamb* (21-22). The title, *the Alpha
and the Omega, the beginning and the end*, refers to the eternality of God, and *the Lamb* refers to Jesus Christ as the sinner's
substitute. Scripture identifies *the Lamb* as co-reigning eternally
with the Father. Furthermore, Revelation 21:10-27 teaches the
names of *the twelve tribes of the sons of Israel* and *the twelve
names of the twelve apostles of the Lamb* are inscribed in a particular memorial on the walls of the New Jerusalem. The *holy
city* possesses *a great and high wall, with twelve gates* (21:12)
representing the twelve tribes of Israel. The twelve *foundation
stones of the city wall* arc inscribed with the *names of the twelve
apostles of the Lamb* (21:14). The unified memorial aptly communicates that the Lamb not only died for Israel and the church,
but for all humanity.

The Prophecy of the Seventy Weeks

Whereas the visions of Daniel 2 and 7 revealed the future for Gentile world powers, particularly over the nation of Israel, the prophecy of the seventy weeks in Daniel 9:24-27 is concerned with the future for the nation of Israel (the Jews) and the holy city (Jerusalem). The historical setting for the seventy weeks prophecy is the first year of the reign of Darius, the son of Ahasuerus, over the realm of Babylon. At this historical period, Babylon was conquered by the Medes and Persians. The Babylonian captivity for the Jews is reaching an end, and the prophecies of Jeremiah are soon to be fulfilled. Daniel studies the writings of the prophet Jeremiah and prays to God for revelation concerning the future of Israel (Dan. 9:1-23).

Daniel 9 is not clear concerning how Daniel became familiar with the writings of Jeremiah. Nevertheless, his prayer clearly demonstrates his knowledge concerning the coming punishment upon *the king of Babylon and that nation* (Jer. 25:11-12) and the return of the Jews to their land (29:10). The *seventy years* [had] *been completed for Babylon*, and Daniel wondered how God would *visit* the Jews and *fulfill* His *good word* to them. Perhaps the Jews would return to their land which would result in the coming of Messiah and the establishment of His kingdom. Daniel was not certain about the next event in Israel's history, but he knew confession was necessary if Messiah would come and the kingdom be established.

Daniel wrote, *Now while I was speaking and praying, and confessing my sin and the sin of my people Israel, and presenting my supplication before the LORD my God in behalf of the holy mountain of my God, while I was still speaking in prayer, then the man Gabriel, whom I had seem in the vision previously, came to me in **my** extreme weariness...and he gave **me** instruction and talked with me, and said, "O Daniel, I have now come forth to give you insight with understanding* (Dan. 9:20-22). God revealed a significant prophecy to Daniel through this Gabriel. Speaking to Daniel, the angel Gabriel indicated the prophecy pertained to *your people*, the Jews, *and your holy city*, Jerusalem (9:24).

The Seventy Weeks of Daniel 9:24-27

"Seventy weeks have been decreed for your people and your holy city…."

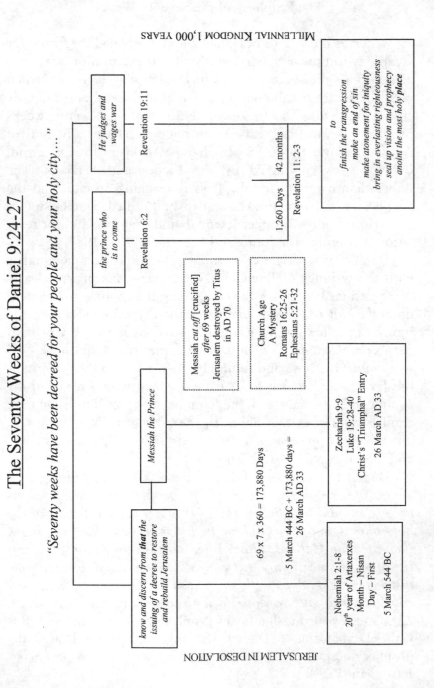

MILLENNIAL KINGDOM 1,000 YEARS

He judges and
wages war

Revelation 19:11

the prince who
is to come

Revelation 6:2

1,260 Days   42 months

Revelation 11: 2-3

to
finish the transgression
make an end of sin
make atonement for iniquity
bring in everlasting righteousness
seal up vision and prophecy
anoint the most holy **place**

Messiah *cut off* [crucified]
after 69 weeks
Jerusalem destroyed by Titus
in AD 70

Church Age
A Mystery
Romans 16:25-26
Ephesians 5:21-32

Messiah the Prince

Zechariah 9:9
Luke 19:28-40
Christ's "Triumphal" Entry
26 March AD 33

know and discern from **that** the
issuing of a decree to restore
and rebuild Jerusalem

69 x 7 x 360 = 173,880 Days

5 March 444 BC + 173,880 days =
26 March AD 33

Nehemiah 2:1-8
20th year of Artaxerxes
Month – Nisan
Day – First
5 March 544 BC

JERUSALEM IN DESOLATION

Whereas the prophecies in Daniel 2 and 7 revealed the prophetic history of the Gentiles, the intent of this prophecy is to reveal the future for the Jews and Jerusalem. Through this prophecy, God revealed the exact timing of Messiah's presentation of Himself to Israel as her King. It was this Messiah who would establish the prophesied kingdom to Israel and rule over her as King (9:25).

Before the kingdom of God would be established, Gabriel informed Daniel that *seventy weeks* must first occur. Following the *seventy weeks*, Daniel's prayers for God to fulfill His covenanted promises with Abraham and David would be answered. The Hebrew word for week is *shābu'îm* which means a unit of seven. Daniel's people were accustomed to the number seven in the same manner as Americans are accustomed to the number ten. A heptad ("seventy sevens") is any occurrence of seven, so it could refer to any appropriate units to measure time. In other words, "seventy sevens" (heptads) are decreed for the Jewish people and Jerusalem. In this passage, the proper understanding is to interpret the "seventy sevens" as weeks of years, that is, *seventy weeks* will transpire totaling four hundred and ninety years. Leviticus 25:8 demonstrates the concept of a week equaling seven years: *'You are also to count off seven sabbaths of years for yourself, seven times seven years, so that you have the time of the seven sabbaths of years, namely, forty-nine years.* When Scriptures refers to *seventy weeks* the meaning is weeks of years.

Gabriel proceeded to explain certain detailed events concerning the *seventy weeks*. For instance, the beginning of the period would be *from the issuing of a decree to restore and rebuild Jerusalem* (9:25). Recorded in Scripture are several commandments to rebuild the Jewish Temple (2 Chron. 36:22-23; Ezra 1:1-4; 6:1, 6-12; 7:11-26, but there is only one command to rebuild the city of Jerusalem. The command was given by Artaxerxes, king of Persia, in the 20th year of his reign (Neh. 2:1-12). *From the issuing of* this command, *until Messiah* is manifested as Prince of Israel, would be sixty-nine weeks. The first sixty-nine weeks are a combination of *seven weeks and sixty-two weeks*. The first *seven weeks* (forty-nine years) in addition to the next *sixty-two weeks* (four hundred and thirty-four years) is four hundred and eighty-three years *from the issuing of* [the] *decree to restore and rebuild Jerusalem* until the appearing of Messiah as Prince of Israel.

Two dates have been offered for the decree of Nehemiah 2. The majority view is that of Sir Robert Anderson in his classic and wonderfully meticulous work, *The Coming Prince*. Anderson dates the command on the first day of the Jewish month of Nisan, which he states as 14 March 445 BC.[19] Since each of the *seventy weeks* is seven years and the years are 360 days long, according to the Jewish calendar, then one calculates *sixty-nine weeks* by seven years in each week by 360 days per year which equals 173,880 days. Therefore, from 1 Nisan (14 March) 445 BC to 6 April AD 32 is 173,880 days. The first *sixty-nine weeks* concluded when Christ rode into the city of Jerusalem on a colt, and was proclaimed King of Israel (cf. Lk. 19:28-44). Although this is the majority view, a major problem with the calculations is the placement of Christ's crucifixion on a Friday.[20]

Harold Hoehner gives an alternative view in his book, *Chronological Aspects of the Life of Christ*. Hoehner dates the command of Artaxerxes as 4 March 444 BC (1 Nisan) concluding with Christ's entrance into Jerusalem as King on 30 March AD 33. Hoehner dates Artaxerxes succession as December 465 BC,[21] yet other research has determined this date to be in the preceding August.[22] This leads to misplacement of Nisan as Artaxerxes 20th year in 444 BC rather than 445 BC.

Additional problems are that 1 Nisan 444 BC was not on the 4 or 5 March but 3 April.[23] Hoehner's calculations do not give the Julian equivalent of 1 Nisan on the Babylonian calendar, because he only provides the Julian dates of new moons.[24] The problem is that this gives 2 March as the date of a new moon, rather than the 4 or 5 March in 444 BC. The interval from the Julian dates of 5 March 444 BC to 5 March AD 33 is precisely 483 solar years or approximately 173,855 days.[25] Simply adding twenty-five days brings the calculations to a total of 173,880 days (equivalent to years of 360 days, according to the Jewish calendar), thus, the end of the sixty-nine weeks would be

30 March AD 30.[26] However, 483 Julian years are about four days longer than 483 solar years. Therefore, the *terminus ad quem* for the sixty-nine weeks (following a 5 March 444 BC dating) would be 26 March AD 33.

It is intriguing to ponder that when Jesus approached Jerusalem on 26 March AD 33 and the people shouted, *"BLESSED IS THE KING WHO COMES IN THE NAME OF THE LORD; Peace in heaven and glory in the highest!"* (Lk. 19:37-38), this was the exact day Daniel had prophesied about 500-600 years previous. Without doubt, Luke records the word of Jesus as fulfillment of the prophecy: *"If you had known in this day, even you, the things which make for peace! But now they have been hidden from your eyes* (19:42).

From the time of Artaxerxes' command to rebuild the city of Jerusalem until *Messiah the Prince* was to be a total of sixty-nine weeks. After the sixty-nine weeks, Messiah would be *cut off* [crucified] *and have nothing* [i.e. not for His own sins]. Daniel's prophecy anticipated Israel's rejection of the Messiah and the postponement of the kingdom.

After the crucifixion of the Messiah, Jerusalem and the second Temple would be destroyed by the Romans, *the people of the prince who is to come. The prince who is to come* is the eschatological Antichrist. This destruction would occur because of the nation's rejection of the Messiah (Mt. 24:1-2; Lk. 19:41-44). However, the prophecy also stated *even to the end there will be war; desolations are determined.* In other words, the AD 70 destruction of Jerusalem by Titus and his armies was not the final destruction of the holy city (Zech. 9:11-17). The reference to *the end* extends the prophecy to the seventieth week. However, there is a temporal interval between the sixth-nine and seventieth weeks, which is the dispensation of the church.

The particular idiom for the time interval in the accomplishment of the messianic program for Israel is derived from the Greek verb *apotelō* [*apo*, "away from"; *telos*, "end"][27] meaning "to bring to an end, finish, complete" in the sense of "consummation that comes to prophecies when they are fulfilled."[28] Therefore, the apotelesmatic interpretation recognizes the development of the messianic program in the Old Testament as a single event, that is, "a near and far historical fulfillment is intended, separated by an indeterminate period of time." This period of time has been termed an "intercalation" or a "gap," however, the term "prophetic postponement" is more desirable. Postponement is an intercalation in fulfillment, which conveys a temporal delay, hence prophetic, since there is a purposeful and preordained work in God's decree. A parenthesis in God's messianic program was implied in the Old Testament concerning Israel's hardening (Isa. 6:9-13; Zech. 7:11-12), judicial exile (Deut. 4:27-30; 28:36-37, 49-50, 64-68); however, God did reveal completely this postponement in His divine decree until the time of the New Testament (Jn. 12:37-40; Acts 28:25-28; Romans 11:25-26).[29]

It is prophesied that the Antichrist *will make a firm* [false] *covenant with the many* [the Jewish people] (Dan. 9:27; cf. Ezek. 38-39). The same covenant is mentioned by the prophet Isaiah (28:14-22). The enforcing of the *firm covenant* will mark the beginning of the seventieth week, or seven years commonly referred to as the tribulation, or time of God's wrath. Daniel wrote, *in the middle of the week he will put a stop to sacrifice and grain offering.* Thus, Daniel 9:27 teaches the tribulation is divided by the abomination of desolation into two three-and-one-half year periods; the midpoint of the tribulation period is the time when the Antichrist demands universal worship as God (cf. 2 Thess. 2:3-4; Mt. 24:15-16; Rev. 13:8).

According to the divine program of Daniel 9 and 2 Thessalonians 2, the tribulation period will follow the rapture of the church. The rapture will terminate the present prophetic postponement of the church age between the sixth-ninth and *seventy weeks.* Shortly after the rapture, the tribulation period will begin with the enforcing of the false covenant between Israel and the Antichrist. It is this event that will set into motion the countdown of the final events of Daniel 9:24-27.

The nature of the tribulation period will focus on Israel. Jeremiah 30:7 refers to the tribulation as *the time of Jacob's distress.* During this period, God will prepare Israel for restoration and conversion (Deut. 4:29-30; Jer. 30:3-11; Zech. 12:10). God will also judge an unbelieving world during this time for sins against God (Isa. 13:9; 24:19-20; Rev. 4-19). All nations and communities will be affected by this judgment. However, there will be salvation for those who trust in Messiah. This time of wrath will result in worldwide evangelization and mass conversions (Mt. 24:14; Rev. 7:1-17).

The tribulation will conclude with the return of Christ to this earth. He will descend upon the Mount of Olives, cross the Kidron Valley, and enter the Eastern Gate (Zech. 14:4; Mt. 24-25). Although this gate is now sealed, it will be opened by the Messiah. When Christ establishes the millennial Temple, it will be filled with His glory and *the increase of His government* (Isa. 9:7). During the millennium, the six purposes of the *seventy weeks* will be fulfilled, Israel will be exalted among the nations, and Christ will rule the world through a theocracy from Jerusalem. This glorious sight, as described by Ezekiel (40-48), will complete the 490 years of the *seventy weeks* prophesied to Daniel by the angel Gabriel. Concerning this future period, Ice and Demy wrote,

> Isaiah 60-61 describes the glory of Jerusalem and Israel during the millennium and the ministry of Jesus during this period. It is during this time that Jerusalem will finally be a true city of peace (Isaiah 60:17,18).
>
> It will be from Jerusalem that Jesus Christ will establish a theocracy and reign throughout the millennium. Beginning in Jerusalem, there will be universal justice and peace (Isaiah 2:34; 11:2-5). Jeremiah recorded God's promises of this era that a Messiah-King would emerge from the Davidic dynasty and rule in righteousness and justice (Jeremiah 33:15,16).[30]

The Millennial Government

Once He has destroyed the wicked governments of mankind, Christ will establish His own government upon Earth. *"Behold, the days are coming,"* declares the LORD, *"When I shall raise up for David a righteous Branch; and He will reign as king and act wisely and do justice and righteousness in the land* (Jer. 23:5). Ryrie wrote,

Concerning the character of Christ's reign, the Scriptures teach that it will be in the plenitude of the Spirit (Isa. 11:2-5), that it will be in equity and justice (Jer. 23:5-6), that sin will be punished (Psa. 2:9; 72:1-4; Isa. 65:20; Zech. 14:16-210, that it will be prosperous and glorious (Jer. 23:5; isa. 24:23), and that it will be a reign of peace (Isa. 2:4; 11:5-9; 65:25; Mic. 4:3).

The center of government in the millennium will be Jerusalem. "For out of Zion shall go forth the law, and the word of the Lord from Jerusalem" (Isa. 2:3)...if interpreted literally the Scripture teaches this fact. Jerusalem will be a holy place (Isa. 4:3-5); a place of great glory (Isa. 24:23); the site of the future temple (Isa. 33:20); a praise in the earth (Isa. 62:1-7); rebuilt (Jer. 31:38-40); the spiritual center for the whole earth (Zech. 8:20-23); the city to which Christ returns (Zech. 14:4); and the joy of the whole earth (Psa. 48:2).[31]

There will be three groups of people to experience the millennial government of the King, Christ Jesus. Israel will be regathered to her land in belief of Messiah. The promise of a land, or Land [Palestinian] Covenant, by God promised Israel would return to her land after being scattered throughout the world. The Land Covenant (Deut. 29:1-30:10) reaffirms Israel's title deed to the land originally promised in the Abrahamic Covenant (Gen. 12:1-3, 7; 13:14-17; 15:1-21; 17:1-21; 22:15-18). The content of the covenant is found in Deuteronomy 29:1-30:10; it is a covenant distinct from the Mosaic Covenant (Deut. 29:1) made between God and the nation of Israel.

According to Deuteronomy 29:1-30:10, eight provisions are expected as fulfillment of the Land Covenant. *First*, the disobedience of Israel to the Mosaic Law and subsequent worldwide scattering was prophesied (Deut. 29:2-30:2). *Second*, after her disobedience, Israel will eventually repent (30:2). *Third*, the King, Christ Jesus, will return (30:3). *Fourth*, after being dispersed, Israel will be regathered to her land (30:3-4). *Fifth*, Israel will possess the land promised to her (30:5). *Sixth*, Israel will be regenerated (30:6). *Seventh*, Israel's enemies will be judged. *Eighth*, Israel will receive the blessings of the Davidic Kingdom (30:8-10).[32]

The second group of people to experience the millennial government is the nations. Ryrie wrote, "The nations will be subjects of the King during the millennium. 'Yea, all kings shall fall down before him: all nations shall serve him" (Psa. 72:11; *cf.* 86:9; Dan. 7:13-14; Mic. 4:2; Zech. 8:22)."[33]

The third group in the millennium is the church, *heirs of God and fellow heirs with Christ* (Rom. 8:17). The church will not be subordinate to King Jesus; her experience is "as one who rightfully shares the rule (2 Tim. 2:12; Rev. 5:10; 20:6)."[34]

The establishing of the government of the Messiah was the longing of the prophet Isaiah (11:1-5; 55:1-3). The same longing belongs to believers today for the second coming of Jesus Christ to fulfill the earthly, political promises of the Davidic covenant and as *the root and offspring of David* to be seated on David's throne in Jerusalem to rule in peace and righteousness. The kingdom of the Messiah is *an everlasting dominion which will not pass away; and His kingdom is one which will not be destroyed* (Dan. 7:14). The vision in Daniel 2 and 7 prophesies that human history will move toward a one world government which will culminate in an *everlasting dominion* of the King Jesus. The kingdom of Messiah will be established after the Gentile world powers are destroyed.

The Davidic covenant is an eternal, literal, and unconditional covenant. It still awaits fulfillment and is confirmed in numerous biblical passages (Ps. 89; Isa. 9:6-7; 11:1; Jer. 23:5-6; 30:8-9; 33:14-17, 19-26; Ezek. 37:24-25; Hos. 3:4-5; Amos 9:11; Lk. 1:30-35, 68-70; Acts 15:14-18). The eternal promises of the Davidic covenant will be mediated through the Messiah. The longing of an earthly kingdom characterized by faithfulness, peace, and righteousness is an eternal promise based on God's faithfulness to fulfill His covenant with David (2 Sam. 7:11; 1 Chron. 17:10).

CHAPTER 10

NATIONS' ROLE IN WORLD GOVERNMENT

Arno Froese

The nations belong to Satan, the god of this world. Therefore, it is only natural for the people to rebel against their Creator. Since the beginning of time, man has sought to be the master of his own destiny. In this chapter, the reader will learn how this tendency will lead to a one world government.

Why do the heathen rage, and the people imagine a vain thing? The kings of the earth set themselves, and the rulers take counsel together, against the LORD, and against his anointed, saying, Let us break their bands asunder, and cast away their cords from us. He that sitteth in the heavens shall laugh: the Lord shall have them in derision. Then shall he speak unto them in his wrath, and vex them in his sore displeasure. Yet have I set my king upon my holy hill of Zion (Ps. 2:1-6). The Psalmist is not addressing one certain group, but *the kings of the earth* (2:2). In contrast to the world, there is another King and kingdom, which is identified geographically: *my king upon my holy hill of Zion.*

Therefore, the nations' role in world government is actually the opposite of what God decreed. However, this should not be understood as meaning God does not establish governments; in fact, all are established by Him. The Lord Himself authorizes and establishes governments. One can learn this from the example of King Nebuchadnezzar, ruler of the first Gentile superpower, who said, "*the most High ruleth in the kingdom of men, and giveth it to whomsoever he will, and setteth up over it the basest of men*" (Dan. 4:17). However, this does not mean these governments are benevolent toward God and His laws, as

233

learned from Psalm 2. Nevertheless, Christians are admonished to obey all governments. *Let every soul be subject unto the higher powers. For there is no power but of God: the powers that be are ordained of God* (Rom. 13:1).

Spiritual Truth

If the governments rebel against the Lord and His anointed, why are believers instructed to obey them? To understand this one must know what it means to live *in* the world without being *of* the world. For instance, the moment an individual is *born again* (Jn. 3:3) he becomes a *new creature* in Christ (2 Cor. 5:17) and is eternally perfect in Him (Rom. 8; Eph. 1:1-14). However, this *new creature* lives in the old body of flesh and blood (cf. Rom. 7). Second Corinthians 15:50 states, *flesh and blood cannot inherit the kingdom of God.* Those who are in Christ are temporary citizens of this world (Heb. 11:13; 1 Pet. 2:11); therefore, *flesh and blood* is subject to the duties, regulations, and rules of each respective government. The spirit, on the other hand, is subject to spiritual things, that is, heaven. Keeping that distinction in mind is vital.

Ephesians 2:6 (*And hath raised us up together, and made us sit together in heavenly places in Christ Jesus*) and Philippians 3:20 (*For our conversation is in heaven; from whence also we look for the Saviour, the Lord Jesus Christ*) are realities when viewed from a spiritual perspective. Nevertheless, it is unrealistic from an earthly perspective to assume that God has *raised us up together* and *made us sit together in heavenly places in Christ Jesus*. Furthermore, the heavenly conversation is yet future, *from whence* believers *look* for the return of the Lord. Therefore, one must judge spiritual matters on a spiritual scale and earthly matters on an earthly scale.

One Nation under Satan?

The heathen rage, and the people imagine a vain thing because they are ruled by the devil. This truth results in a sensitive subject, particularly for Americans. As a country, Americans have adopted many "religious" mantras such as "One Nation, Under God," "In God We Trust," and "God bless America." Can a nation really claim to be "Under God"? According to Scripture, the answer is no since every nation is ruled by the prince of darkness. The Bible states, *He that committeth sin is of the devil* (1 Jn. 3:8). Since *all have sinned* (Rom. 3:23), all must belong to the devil. The devil actually has a legal claim to every single person on earth; the only exception is those who have been redeemed by the blood of the Lamb. The believer has a heavenly citizenship and is not ruled by the god of this world, but the God of this universe!

Of course, the devil does not have the right to establish a government (at least not yet). He is subject to God and the world is subject to the devil. One must understand that sin separates the unbeliever from God. God is not a dictator; He will not act contrary to His own immutable nature (Mal. 3:6; Jas. 1:17) and "coerce a reluctant will by force." There is only one way to escape Satan's clutches: by grace through faith alone in the blood of the Son of God, the Lord Jesus Christ. For the sinner to be liberated from the legal claim Satan has on him, he must trust in Jesus Christ alone (apart from any works) who paid for the sins of humanity with His own blood on Calvary's cross.

God's righteousness remains: *the soul that sinneth, it shall die* (Ezek. 18:4, 20). His purpose in redemption, however, was not decreed by His righteous power but by His love. *For God so loved the world, that he gave his only begotten Son* (Jn. 3:16). God's righteousness was satisfied by the sacrifice of His Son, activated by His love. The repentant sinner can now have fellowship restored with God by faith in Jesus Christ, the perfect Lamb of God. Although, still living in the sinful tabernacles of flesh and blood, which are subject to death, disease, and sickness, the believer's perishable body is indwelt by the Holy Spirit making it possible to serve God, and with the body to be obedient to government.

The Governments of the World

Often Christians pray for the results of an election. Many

sincere men and women actually believe they can change God's plan and intention for their country. Many people expend too much energy, finances, and time on political activities, hoping God will then demonstrate His favor upon their selection. For this writer, at least, he wonders if these dear Christians read their Bible for they would know only God decrees the establishment of governments.

Matthew's Gospel account contains the devil's temptation of Christ in the wilderness. *Again, the devil taketh him up into an exceeding high mountain, and sheweth him all the kingdoms of the world, and the glory of them; And saith unto him, All these things will I give thee, if thou wilt fall down and worship me* (Mt. 4:8-9). It is obvious from these words that all the kingdoms of the world are subject to the devil.

Switzerland, the World's Greatest Country

Another important aspect in relation to world government and the nations is the devil's amazing ability to deceive people, including numerous Christians. Consider Switzerland, the most prosperous and secure country in the world. The Swiss are extremely proud of their nation because they have achieved more than any other country in the world. This small country with a population of less than 7.5 million prides itself as being the most benevolent nation on the face of the earth.

No flag is as popular, beloved and respected as Switzerland's Red Cross flag. The Red Cross was founded in 1864, in Geneva, Switzerland by Swiss doctor Henri Dunant. Switzerland is special among the nations, as was evident when it joined the United Nations. Only Switzerland received special permission to display its square flag, which is contrary to United Nations regulations specifying all flags must be rectangular. The Swiss flag displays the white cross on a red background, while the colors on the Red Cross' flag are red on white.[1]

The Country of Peace
When the First and Second World War raged around it, Switzerland remained neutral and unscathed. The Swiss

demonstrated to the world that they were a peaceful people. If the Swiss claimed to be blessed by God with freedom, prosperity, security, and—most important—friendship with the rest of world, then there would be little opposition to such a claim. However, what does the Bible say? The prophet Isaiah wrote the following about the nations: *All nations before him are as nothing; and they are counted to him less than nothing, and vanity* (40:17). Thus, Switzerland is not so special after all. From a biblical perspective, one can proclaim there is no such thing as a "special" country. All countries belong to the prince of darkness.

In light of this, one is forced to examine the religious slogans from a much different perspective. Who is this god men ask to bless the country? Who is this god men say they trust? Who is this god men claim the nation is under? Obviously, it is not the God of the Bible, for He is identified by name: Jesus Christ! *Neither is there salvation in any other: for there is none other name under heaven given among men, whereby we must be saved* (Acts 4:12). Regardless of the good intentions, the pride of a nation is really the "raging" of the heathen, the "imagination of vain things" *against the LORD, and against his anointed.*

The True Special Nation

However, there is one nation that Scripture describes as different, special, unique, and guaranteed to be eternal: Israel. Below are just a few verses of Scripture demonstrating the uniqueness of Israel in comparison to all the nations of the world.

And I will bless them that bless thee, and curse him that curseth thee: and in thee shall all families of the earth be blessed (Gen. 12:3).

[God revealed His will to Abraham's son Isaac] And I will make thy seed to multiply as the stars of heaven, and will give unto thy seed all these countries; and in thy seed shall all the nations of the earth be blessed (26:4).

[God confirmed the promise above to Abraham's

grandson Jacob] And thy seed shall be as the dust of the earth, and thou shalt spread abroad to the west, and to the east, and to the north, and to the south: and in thee and in thy seed shall all the families of the earth be blessed (28:14).

For thou *art* an holy people unto the LORD thy God: the LORD thy God hath chosen thee to be a special people unto himself, above all people that *are* upon the face of the earth (Deut. 7:6).

For thou *art* an holy people unto the LORD thy God, and the LORD hath chosen thee to be a peculiar people unto himself, above all the nations that *are* upon the earth (14:2).

For the LORD thy God blesseth thee, as he promised thee: and thou shalt lend unto many nations, but thou shalt not borrow; and thou shalt reign over many nations, but they shall not reign over thee (15:6).

[Before his death, Moses revealed Israel's incomparability to all the other nations] Happy *art* thou, O Israel: who *is* like unto thee, O people saved by the LORD, the shield of thy help, and who *is* the sword of thy excellency! and thine enemies shall be found liars unto thee; and thou shalt tread upon their high places (33:29).

These statements are unconditional, based on the will of the God of Israel, Creator of heaven and earth.[2] One will have a much deeper understanding of the deep love God has for His people when contemplating these passages of Scripture. God has placed this special nation above all others. Christians must not forget that their nations are insignificant when compared with the only nation—Israel—chosen by God Himself.

Jewish Nationalism

Paul, the apostle to the Gentiles, is an excellent illustration of the action believers should exercise in relationship to their nation. Perhaps the reader just learned that Israel is the only nation in the world chosen by God. Now consider what the apostle Paul wrote about his nation.

> Though I might also have confidence in the flesh. If any other man thinketh that he hath whereof he might trust in the flesh, I more: circumcised the eighth day, of the stock of Israel, of the tribe of Benjamin, an Hebrew of the Hebrews; as touching the law, a Pharisee; concerning zeal, persecuting the church; touching the righteousness which is in the law, blameless (Phil. 3:4-6).

Paul was an Israelite, born into the greatest nation in the world. He came from the *tribe of Benjamin*, the first to be integrated into Judah (i.e. the chosen tribe). He was a Hebrew who identified himself with *Abram the Hebrew*[3] (Gen. 14:13), who is called *the father of all them that believe* (Rom. 4:11). He is *the* example of righteousness by faith (cf. Rom. 4). Moreover, Paul was a Pharisee. Although this term has a negative connotation in the Christian world because of Jesus' opposition to the Pharisees, the Pharisees did defend God's law. They taught with conviction that God controls history and He is above all things. *Unger's Bible Dictionary* states the following:

> "If we strip off its Greek form, from what Josephus says, it is nothing more than this, that according to the Pharisees *everything* that happens takes place through God's providence, and that consequently in human actions also, whether good or bad, a cooperation of God is to be admitted. And this is a genuine OT view."[4]

Commenting on being a Pharisee, Paul testified, *touching the righteousness which is in the law, blameless*. This man truly had reason to take pride in himself. He belonged to the greatest nation, born of the preferred *tribe of Benjamin*, *an Hebrew* and *a Pharisee*, and according to *the law*, *blameless*. Hardly anyone could make such a statement today.

What did Paul say when he compared all of these advantages to his belonging to Christ? *But what things were gain to me, those I counted loss for Christ. Yea doubtless, and I count all things but loss for the excellency of the knowledge of Christ Jesus my Lord: for whom I have suffered the loss of all things, and do count them but dung, that I may win Christ* (Phil. 3:7-8). Truly, Paul knew how to position nationalism in its proper place.

Government is "Minister of God"

Paul's attitude does not mean one should reject the authority of their nation, or even despise or ridicule its leaders since there are still duties and obligations. God's Word instructs believers to obey the government.

However, the government believers are to obey is not the government of God, it is a government allowed by God, placed under Satan's jurisdiction. This may be difficult for many to comprehend, but the Bible clearly instructs believers to be obedient to all governments, including communists, dictatorships, monarchies, or socialists to the extent that such obedience does not contradict God's commands. Obedience to government makes no difference to God *for all have sinned, and come short of the glory of God* (Rom. 3:23). All have sinned and are entirely depraved, prideful, and selfish. Thus, Satan has a legal claim to all.

Scripture confirms mankind is to be subject to the government. The Romans ruled the world during Paul's time and their forces occupied the land of Israel. The Jews were subject to the powers of Rome. Paul wrote to the church, *Put them in mind to be subject to principalities and powers, to obey magistrates,.to be ready to every good work* (Tit. 3:1).

One of the clearest descriptions of Gentile power structure came directly from Jesus when He answered Pontius Pilate. Jesus answered, *Thou couldest have no power at all against me except it were given thee from above: therefore he that delivered me unto thee hath the greater sin* (Jn. 19:11). This confirms the political authority Pilate possessed had been *given...from above.* Also significant is that neither Jesus, the apostles, nor the early church protested or rebelled against any government, nor did they attempt to change the prevailing law. The early church recognized that it was subject to government in the flesh, but in the spirit, it served Jesus Christ, the Son of God.

The Coming World Government

Since there is no special nation among the Gentiles, then how are the nations working toward a government that will herald the kingdom of Antichrist? The answer is through money! The *sine qua non* in most conflicts is money. Daniel described the Antichrist as follows

> And the king shall do according to his will; and he shall exalt himself, and magnify himself above every god, and shall speak marvellous things against the God of gods, and shall prosper till the indignation be accomplished: for that that is determined shall be done. Neither shall he regard the God of his fathers, nor the desire of women, nor regard any god: for he shall magnify himself above all. But in his estate shall he honour the God of forces: and a god whom his fathers knew not shall he honour with gold, and silver, and with precious stones, and pleasant things (Dan. 11:36-38).

During Daniel's time, money was translated into gold, silver, precious stones, etc. Accordingly, the reader should understand that economy, finance, and religion were integrated to honor an unknown god, but money was fundamental. When one reads articles in the daily newspaper concerning the United States' conflicts with its trading partners and vice versa, the main dispute always involves money. Years ago it was a matter of military power. If one country did not agree with another, swords were raised. The winner took the spoils and the loser paid the taxes. Money was the issue.

War is no longer an option among the industrialized nations. The nations have become integrated to such an extent that even the slightest conflict could prove to be catastrophic for all nations. President Bush tried to protect the United States steel industry from foreign competition by enforcing a firm tariff on all steel imports. This caused a global uproar with threats of multiple countermeasures, and as a result, the United States quietly cancelled the tariff. This is just one example among literally hundreds of conflicts occurring around the world daily.

Which Form of Government for the World?

There is little doubt that the Greek-Roman form of democracy is the only viable form of government accepted throughout the world today. The industrial world is governed by democracy and its success is virtually inconceivable. In the September 2002 issue of *Eternal Value Review*, financial analyst Wilfred Hahn wrote,

> ...rich Christendom (*countries that are historically Christian in the widest sense of this definition*)...today accounts for greater than 60% of world wealth, though only representing 10% of the world's population. These nations have average per-person incomes 13 times greater than the rest of the world. Without a doubt, the *Age of Global Capital* is a phenomenon of Christendom. To be more correct, it is a development of apostate or carnal Christendom, its societies largely having given themselves over to materialism and humanism. It could never have happened in Muslim countries....
>
> People living in nations that are predominately Muslim have an average income of $1,145 (*Year 2000 statistic in US dollars. Source: The World Bank and various.*) That compares to a world average for the rich Christian nations (*45 high-income countries as categorized by the World Bank*) of $27,033. Put another way, the people of the rich Christian nations have 23 times the average income of Muslims.
>
> Though the populations of the Muslim nations (approx. 1.1 billion) are some 50% greater in number than the rich Christian nations, as a group they only

account for 4.0% of world economic output (2000)....
The Muslim countries hardly have any presence in the
modern financial world. The stock markets of these
countries barely account for 1% of the total value of
world equity markets. Not surprisingly, the outstanding
bonds of Muslim countries amount to less than one-
tenth of 1% of the global bond market value (which at
last count tallied to more than $40 trillion). And lastly,
Muslim nations account for virtually zero of the notional value of world derivative markets. (*The Bank of
International Settlement reports this value at $115 tril-
lion at mid-year 2002.*) The picture couldn't be clearer.
The Muslim world is a non-entity in terms of the power
structure of the *Age of Global Capital.*[5]

The "Christian" countries represent democracy which
requires a world government.[6] Democracy dominates the world,
which is natural, because man wants to rule himself. "We the
people...by the people...for the people." That being the case,
nothing good can result since man is in opposition to God.
Currently and in the near future, democracy will be the epitome
of global success and, without exception, nations will become
subject to it.

First World Government

The desire of the nations for a global government is nothing
new. Even before Abraham is mentioned in Scripture, there is a
report of the first global government.

And the whole earth was of one language, and of one
speech. And it came to pass, as they journeyed from the
east, that they found a plain in the land of Shinar; and
they dwelt there. And they said one to another, Go to, let
us make brick, and burn them throughly. And they had
brick for stone, and slime had they for mortar. And they
said, Go to, let us build us a city and a tower, whose top
may reach unto heaven; and let us make us a name, lest

we be scattered abroad upon the face of the whole earth (Gen. 11:1-4).

Those who built the Tower of Babel opposed God, who instructed man to replenish the earth (Gen. 9:1-7). They said, *"let us make us a name, lest we be scattered abroad upon the face of the whole earth."*

Not only did this democratic society assume control of their fate here on earth, but also the citizens intended to *reach unto heaven*. It is unreasonable to assume they thought they could literally build a tower to *reach unto heaven*. What they did, however, was express their desire to have their own religion and their own plan of salvation, which is so typical of mankind.

All religions strive to reach God by various means, whether by buildings, music, prayer, sacrifice, or countless other religious activities. Man wants to communicate with God. However, God did not allow man to *reach unto heaven*. He came to earth becoming a man in the flesh. Jesus Christ said, *"I am the door...no man cometh unto the Father, but by me"* (Jn. 10:7, 9; 14:6). The building of the Tower of Babel stopped. The language of the people building the *city and a tower* was confounded. The Bible states, *So the LORD scattered them abroad from thence upon the face of all the earth* (Gen. 11:8).

First World Power

Later in history, there is the record of a revelation given to Nebuchadnezzar, the first ruler of Babylon. He had a dream but his *spirit was troubled to know the dream* (Dan. 2:3). None of his advisors could help him. A Jewish man named Daniel interpreted King Nebuchadnezzar's dream and thereby revealed the structure of the Gentile world from that time until the end of the world. *Then was the iron, the clay, the brass, the silver, and the gold, broken to pieces together, and became like the chaff of the summer threshingfloors; and the wind carried them away, that no place was found for them: and the stone that smote the image became a great mountain, and filled the whole earth* (2:35). None of the nations have a promising future; all will become *like the chaff of the summer threshingfloors; and the wind carried them away, that no place was found for them.*

United in Diversity

It is possible to witness the development of the nations working together for world government? There is no doubt in this author's mind that such is the case, but there are still many problems to be resolved. In the Western world, the United States attempts separatism with little success. This became obvious with the recent Iraq conflict. In the future, the United States will have to submit to the prevailing global spirit, "Unity through Diversity." Nevertheless, the Arab world has tried to build a Muslim world where all nations are brought together under the authority of the Koran. To the East is China, the great communist giant that is slowly drifting toward European social/capitalism, surprising the world with a phenomenal economic growth each year.

It may be necessary to explain the term "social/capitalism." The reader should know that capitalism, communism, and socialism are the three major philosophical forms of political economy. For all practical purposes, communism ceased to exist with the fall of the Soviet Union. Although, when one examines capitalism with a critical mind, it becomes evident that there really is not any such economic system. By definition, capital is limited to the possession of assets, which in turn should be the only measure for economy, finance, and government.

Social/Capitalism

After the September 11th terrorist attacks on New York and Washington, the United States airline industry suffered tremendously and several airlines filed for bankruptcy. However, the government gave $15 billion—not counting all the other benefits—to the airlines to help them survive. Incidentally, this was also the case with many other important industries in the United States that the government assists. However, the government got the money from tax revenues! The money the government received is social/capital, thus, socialism supports capitalism.

Global corporations such as General Electric, General Motors, and Microsoft have received enormous sums of social/capital (tax money), sometimes in the form of tax credit, tax relief, or "research grants." Such a system clearly proves the motivation behind capitalistic enterprises is tax money, or social/capital. Thus, the American system is actually modeled after the three major philosophies: capitalism, communism, and socialism. Moreover, it works!

Agricultural Socialism

The agricultural industry is designed to operate on capitalist principles, but the government controls and subsidizes the agricultural industry not only in the United States but also in all progressive countries. The American government controls it with taxes, a subsidy from the working class, tax-paying citizens. Large sums of money are paid to the farm industry for planting certain crops or raising specific breeds of livestock. Some farmers receive tax money *not* to plant their fields. The only term for such situations is social/capitalism. In the business section of *The State*, South Carolina's local newspaper, the headline was "S.C. Tobacco Farmers Closer to $700 Million in Payments." One part of the article stated, "If the bill ultimately becomes law, farmers would receive $10 for each pound of tobacco grown in 2002. South Carolina grew more than 68 million pounds— meaning a payment of $680 million or so over five years."[7] Using tax dollars to pay farmers who grow tobacco has nothing to do with capitalism, but is actually socialism.

The system of social/capitalism is extremely successful. In spite of the global population explosion, never before has man witnessed such an abundance of food production; even the poorest of countries seek to export food. The European Union's greatest problem was the addition of ten strongly agricultural nations on 1 May 2004. The European Union pays many of these farmers to leave their ancient trades and join the industrial revolution. Truly, such actions are social/capitalism at work!

Agriculture in Africa

Africa is the only continent where severe famine is reported on a regular basis. What is wrong with the agricultural industry in Africa? It may be a surprise but the entire food industry works according to the capitalist manner. Farmers are independent and can grow crops and raise cattle according to their short-term need with the purpose of obtaining cash. The result is often overproduction which results in lowering prices to such an extent that farmers do not have enough money to plant next year's crops. Thus, famine is the sad effect.

Global Power

The few examples given should prove sufficiently that capitalism does not actually exist, at least not in its original form. Nevertheless, the same can be thought regarding communism, which died when the Soviet Union—its main promoter—went bankrupt. The political economic philosophy of capitalism and communism can be discovered in all the nations of the world.

The economic philosophy described is termed "social/capitalism." In other words, socialism (tax-based assets) is the capital of the ten wealthiest countries in the world. Only the United States practices social/capitalism, which means the main beneficiaries are those who have the capital. The core of support is aimed at the employers (viz. those who create the jobs).

It is not surprising that a statistic from the late '90s revealed that foreign companies created 4 out of 5 new jobs in the United States. Such a statistic was observed when BMW announced its intent to build an assembly plant in the United States. BMW now successfully builds vehicles in South Carolina because of the excellent incentives the firm received from the government. Millions of dollars in tax credits, and multiple other advantages, were granted to BMW to establish the manufacturer in this state.

Alternatively, social/capitalism works to help the employees, so the average worker in a social/capital country enjoys a larger percentage that translates into more freedom and security. The author is not seeking partiality in either direction, but is simply

trying to demonstrate that the tendency of world government is
the direction of social/capitalism.

The *Ten Horns* and *Ten Kings*

A reasonable number of Bible scholars agree that ten nations
within Europe will arise to fulfill Daniel 7:24 (*and the ten horns
out of this kingdom are ten kings that shall arise*). Similarly,
Revelation 13:1 reads, *and saw a beast rise up out of the sea,
having seven heads and ten horns, and upon his horns ten
crowns, and upon his heads the name of blasphemy*, and 17:12
states, *and the ten horns which thou sawest are ten kings*.

The theory that the *ten horns* and *ten kings* will arise from
Europe became popular when the European Common Market
(based on the Treaty of Rome) was founded in 1957 with six
founding countries: Belgium, Germany, France, Italy,
Luxemburg, and the Netherlands. Denmark, Ireland, and the
United Kingdom gained entrance in 1973. Subsequently, Greece
was added in 1981 which brought the total to ten European
nations. Spain and Portugal were added in 1986. Austria,
Finland, and Sweden joined the European Union in 1995. Ten
new nations joined in 2004. The number *ten* is mentioned
repeatedly in prophetic literature. In the '60s, Midnight Call
founder Dr. Wim Malgo said, "Let us not look for ten countries
as members of the European Common Market constituting the
fulfillment of Revelation 17:12; rather, we must look for ten
power structures that will develop through the European initiative but will be worldwide."

The main reason for this author's objection is the *ten horns*
and *ten kings* power structure encompasses the entire globe;
therefore, it is not limited to Europe. Furthermore, one must also
consider that Scripture prophecies of *kings* and *horns*, not
"nations" or "countries." What is so unique about a king? He is
sovereign in his country and not dependent upon the democratic process of the people. Each king is unique, incomparable to
any other. *Horns* generally depict power in Scripture; thus, it
seems reasonable to conclude that these ten powerful kings are
uniquely identifiable power structures. They must be global and

represent the entire economic, financial, and political world. In order to be truly global, the following theory was proposed in another publication.[8]

Europe
Far East
Mideast
North America
South America
South Asia
Central Asia
Australia and New Zealand
Southern Africa
Central Africa

If the author is correct, the above proposal includes the entire globe. Nevertheless, he will emphasize that these are only suggestions that do not have any direct Scriptural basis other than comprising the entire world. It can be certain that the people on the European continent have conquered the world.

Is Europe the Model?

At one time or another, virtually all nations have tried to be greater, to expand their borders, to dominate more people and more territory. It is this tendency which led to World War I and World War II. During the time of the world wars, the European colonial powers withdrew their forces from their colonies as they became independent. Europe was literally flooded with war experts, trained soldiers, and an abundant supply of war material. A war was almost certain to rupture in Europe.

As the reader has now learned, when something happens in Europe, it becomes global in its effects. Why was it called a "world" war? It is because the whole world was involved. Remember, Europe is responsible for the implementation of civilization around the world. Therefore, it stands to reason the former colonies naturally had to participate when war occurred.

Final Borders?

Today's national borders are permanent. It is absolutely unthinkable that Mexico would declare war to recapture part of the territory conquered by the United States. It is out of the question for any European country to change its geographical boundaries. However, there is a distinct difference between the nations of the world and Europe. While other borders are being fortified, particularly since the September 11th terrorist attacks, European borders are being opened.

Something is occurring which has not transpired since the days of the Roman Empire. The nations that have become members of the European Union not only are working feverishly to prevent the dismantling of their borders, but also they are encouraging the eradication of borders within Europe.

The Growing European Union

In May 2000, ten nations received full membership to the European Union. Not one shot was fired. No propaganda was generated and no hate speeches were spoken. Willingly, and in most cases, joyfully, this still unidentifiable economic, financial, militaristic, political, and religious union devoured the new countries. Other nations are eagerly anticipating their acceptance by this exclusive club of free, prosperous, and secure people.

What is the European Union?

Unlike all other power structures, the European Union is a group of nations united by diversity. It may appear a contradiction because one cannot be diverse and united at the same time. However, therein lies the great difference. The United States, for example, promotes the slogan, "United We Stand." Europe, as already mentioned, is just the opposite. Its motto is "Unity in Diversity." Note the European Union's official statement posted on the Internet.

The European Union (EU) is a family of democratic European countries, committed to working together for peace and prosperity. It is not a State intended to replace existing states, but it is more than any other international organization. The EU is, in fact, unique. Its Member States have set up common institutions to which they delegate some of their sovereignty so that decisions on specific matters of joint interest can be made democratically at European level. This pooling of sovereignty is also called "European integration."

The historical roots of the European Union lie in the Second World War. The idea of European integration was conceived to prevent such killing and destruction from ever happening again. It was first proposed by the French Foreign Minister Robert Schuman in a speech on 9 May 1950. This date, the "birthday" of what is now the EU, is celebrated annually as Europe Day....

Initially, the EU consisted of just six countries: Belgium, Germany, France, Italy, Luxembourg and the Netherlands. Denmark, Ireland and the United Kingdom joined in 1973, Greece in 1981, Spain and Portugal in 1986, Austria, Finland and Sweden in 1995. In 2004 the biggest ever enlargement took place with 10 new countries joining....

The European Union has delivered half a century of stability, peace and prosperity. It has helped to raise living standards, *built a single Europe-wide market*, launched the single European currency, the *euro*, and strengthened *Europe's voice in the world.*

Unity in diversity: Europe is a continent with many different traditions and languages, but also with shared values. The EU defends these values, it fosters co-operation among the peoples of Europe, promoting unity while preserving diversity and ensuring that decisions are taken as close as possible to the citizens.

In the increasingly interdependent world of the 21st century, it will be even more necessary for every European citizen to co-operate with people from other countries in a spirit of curiosity, tolerance and solidarity.[9]

Every nation in the European Union is to keep, practice, and respect its own and other nations' cultures, holidays, languages, and traditions. The procedures of the European Union is unlike the nations of the new continents where culture, holidays, language, and tradition had to be sacrificed on the altar of unity. Immigrants from Europe who came to the United States had to abandon everything, separate themselves from their culture, customs, heritage, and even sacrifice their most precious possession, that is, their language.

The New Global World

Before this chapter concludes, it needs to be emphasized that the Bible—not the interpretations or theories of the author—is the ultimate source of truth. Regardless of the type of government one favors, how one participates in the political world, or what principles one obeys, the main point is the reality of the introductory Scripture. *Why do the heathen rage, and the people imagine a vain thing? The kings of the earth set themselves, and the rulers take counsel together, against the LORD, and against his anointed, saying, Let us break their bands asunder, and cast away their cords from us* (Ps. 2:1-3).

In unison the world is saying, *Let us break their bands asunder, and cast away their cords from us.* What are these *bands* and *cords*? God's law for all people.

As already stated, the devil has legitimate claim to all nations and all people, but he is not allowed to implement his own *cords* and *bands* (at least not yet). The God of Israel, the Creator of heaven and earth, still and always will overrule. Nevertheless, one day in the not-too-distant future, what is written in 2 Thessalonians 2:11 will be fulfilled. *And for this cause God shall send them strong delusion, that they should believe a lie.* What will be the result? The Antichrist will be revealed *who opposeth and exalteth himself above all that is called God, or that is worshipped; so that he as God sitteth in the temple of God, shewing himself that he is God"* (2:4).

Is it possible to identify the *bands* and *cords*? The author believes they are the nation of Israel. She stands in contrast to all the nations of the world. Even in this very day one witnesses the entire world condemn Israel for employing the same principles that nations have long used to establish their own borders: force. The world unanimously agrees that Israel does not have the right to the Promised Land (extending from the river of Egypt to the Euphrates River) as defined in Scripture. The world also agrees that Jerusalem cannot be the united capital city of a Jewish state. Although the Jews conquered that territory fairly, they are not allowed to settle there. Such unrighteous restrictions scream to heaven and condemn every single nation on the face of the earth.

In contrast to the nations' rebellion and opposition, the Lord said, "*Yet have I set my king upon my holy hill of Zion*" (Ps. 2:6). In summary, a world government is happening at this moment. All nations will become subject to it. However, that world government will be destroyed by the King of kings and the Lord of lords, the one who will sit upon *the holy hill of Zion* and rule the nations *with a rod of iron* (Ps. 2; Rev. 17:14; 19:16).

CHAPTER 11

THE CHURCH AND WORLD GOVERNMENT

Mal Couch

For a brief moment in church history there was an explosion of interest in the proper balance of end-time prophecy. Approximately the time of the beginning of the twentieth century, dispensationalism (and with it premillennialism) was the dominant theological view and greatly influenced Christianity in the Western world. The church longed for Christ to return and establish his government throughout the world. Godly scholars returned the church to normal/literal interpretation resulting in understanding of the Word of God becoming clear to many for the first time in centuries! The names of Darby, Larkin, Scofield, and Chafer are brought to mind. These two theological understandings (dispensationalism and premillennialism) gave the church a meaningful biblical framework resulting in a near-complete understanding of prophecy to the entire Bible.

What are the issues when examining end-time and prophetic interpretations? Why is it important to have in mind clearly how the end of history will come? Could a great majority of people in Christendom be fooled by anti-biblical and false views of eschatology? Could aberrant teachings about the return of Jesus Christ leave the church asleep regarding what is now before human history on the international front? Would false ideas about prophecy hide the truth in regard to the rapture of the church, the horrible worldwide tribulation, and the historic return of the Lord Jesus to the earth to reign? Beginning with amillennialism, and the current preponderance of the false

255

teaching of preterism, the church has always wallowed in views that have diverted attention from the truth. However, now, such diversion is truly deadly.

The Warning of Heresy

The apostle Paul wrote, *there must also be factions* (Gk *haireseis*; i.e. heresies) *among you, in order that those who are approved may become evident among you* (1 Cor. 11:19). In other words, Paul is saying error helps identify true biblical doctrine. Such error reveals who is teaching the truth or not. Peter seems to expand upon this thought. *But false prophets also arose among the people, just as there will also be false teachers among you, who will secretly introduce destructive heresies, even denying the Master who bought them, bringing swift destruction upon themselves* (2 Pet. 2:1).

Peter stated one of the proofs of *destructive heresies* is a denial of the literal return of Christ to judge the earth. Peter wrote, *in the last days mockers will come with **their** mocking, following after their own lusts, and saying, "Where is the promise of His coming? For **ever** since the fathers fell asleep, all continues just as it was from the beginning of creation"* (3:3-4). Eschatology, or prophecy, then becomes a test of false teaching. Much of the test has to do with the "shaking" of the pages of history, and with those who either affirm or deny Christ's literal return to earth. While there are many who embrace strange and foreign views of the return of Christ, this does not automatically mean they are heretics of the first order, but it does mean they have accepting a clearly unbiblical teaching. If a person is a little off center theologically, it can adversely affect one's view of the whole, that is, the entire body of biblical doctrine!

The Amillennial Disaster

Amillennialism rewrites the Word of God. It destroys the great promises of the Old Testament concerning the coming reign of the Messiah over the nation of Israel, and the world. The prefix *a* in *amillennial* means *no*, thus it is the rejection of a literal thousand-year kingdom reign. According to amillennialists, the kingdom promises of the Old Testament are fulfilled spiritually in the New Testament church. Most amillennialists would teach the promises are fulfilled only in an allegorical sense. Amillennialists also believe the kingdom of God is now present in the church age. Additionally, when Christ returns there is a judgment, and then eternity begins.[1]

Amillennialism

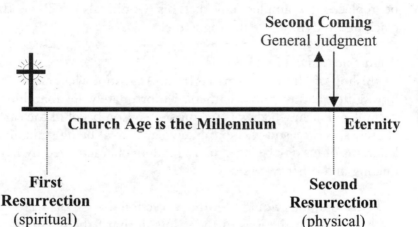

Second Coming
General Judgment

Church Age is the Millennium | Eternity

First Resurrection (spiritual)

Second Resurrection (physical)

All of the kingdom promises are ignored or applied now to the church by spiritualizing Scripture. This means the promises are allegorized or re-interpreted to mean something beyond a common sense interpretation. Such allegory began in the times of the rabbi Philo (ca. 15/10 B.C.-A.D. 45/50). The rabbis of Alexandria, Egypt, began to teach allegorically to counter what they believed to be Gentile criticism of the Old Testament.

Origen (ca. 185-ca. 254)

It is certain that Origen of Alexandria adopted his allegorical interpretation from Philo. A Christian theologian, he developed a theoretical three-level understanding of the meaning of Scripture: the literal, typological, and spiritual. The literal method was considered too simplistic. Mystical, or spiritualized, theological speculation was typical of Origen's eschatology.

The allegorical method of interpretation of Origen included his views regarding Bible prophecy. Allegoricism received wide acceptance in his day because the early church (around A.D. 200 and later) believed it had indeed replaced Israel as God's favored people. In other words, God was finished with any program for the Jews! Origen's views on prophecy (after becoming widely accepted), followed by Constantine's embracing of Christianity, are given as the central reasons that caused premillennialism to be replaced by amillennialism. This would also include the teachings and influence of Augustine.

Augustine (A.D. 354-430)

Bishop of Hippo in North Africa, Augustine was one of the most gifted Latin Church Fathers. Unfortunately, he abandoned premillennialism which was the most common belief of the early churches. His reason was extremely superficial being some millenarians of his day believed in a kingdom characterized by banqueting and other excesses.

> This opinion would not be objectionable, if it were believed that the joys of the saints in that Sabbath shall be spiritual, and consequent on the presence of God; for I myself, too, once held this opinion. But as they assert that those who then rise again shall enjoy the leisure of immoderate carnal banquets, furnished with an amount of meat and drink such as not only to shock the feeling of the temperate, but even to surpass the measure of credulity itself, such assertions can be believed only by the carnal. They who do believe them are called by the spiritual Chiliasts, which we may literally reproduce by the name Millenarians (*City of God* 20.7).[2]

Augustine and others were repelled by a perceived carnality among premillennialists, and began teaching the millennium mentioned in Revelation 20 must be spiritualized to signify the time of Christ's reign with the saints in the church age. During this spiritual millennium, Augustine taught Satan was bound or limited in power, but still able to seduce and deceive the church.

With seeming contradiction, Augustine still held to some kind of millennial reign; nevertheless, he believed there would be a thousand year kingdom to transpire between Christ's first and second comings. However, when the year 1000 arrived and past without Christ's return, Augustine's chronology was discredited. It became clear that amillennialists needed to spiritualize the duration of the millennium, in addition to its meaning. The thousand years were represented as an indefinite period of time between the first and second advents of Christ.[3] Cohn summarizes this view well.

> For a collective, millenarian eschatology Origen substituted an eschatology of the individual soul. What stirred his profoundly [Greek] imagination was the prospect of spiritual progress begun in this world and continued in the next; and to this theme theologians were henceforth to give increasing attention. Such a shift in interest was indeed admirably suited to what was now an organized Church, enjoying almost uninterrupted peace and an acknowledged position in the world. When in the fourth century Christianity attained a position of supremacy in the Mediterranean world and became the official religion of the Empire, ecclesiastical disapproval of millenarianism became emphatic. The Catholic Church was now a powerful and prosperous institution, functioning according to a well-established routine; and the men responsible for governing it had no wish to see Christians clinging to *out-dated and inappropriate dreams of a new earthly Paradise* [emphasis added].[4]

Such interpretation could be expected, and as a result of the departure from a literal interpretation (hermeneutic) in prophetic sections of the Bible, it is little wonder that liberal and amillennial views affirm the Apostle John wrote Revelation for the purpose of making martyrdom attractive. It is this kind of allegorical thinking, and theory, which has resulted in speculative (but unsuccessful attempts) to correspond the events of Revelation with the present church age. It represents a serious neglect of a consistent system of theology and allows opportunity for individual speculation regarding the meaning and application of any given passage of the Word of God.

One of the main points that unify amillennial thinking is the denial of the earthly thousand-year reign of Christ. By denying the literal sense of Bible prophecy, amillennialism teaches "one of the great lessons of the Apocalypse is its unfolding of such a bright view, not of a world beyond the grave, but of this present world—when it is contemplated with the eye of faith."[5]

What conclusions can be deduced concerning amillennial beliefs of the relationship of the church to the establishment of the government of Jesus Christ? It sows the seeds of liberal theology. It distorts almost half of Scripture and makes the Bible a confusing read because of the spiritualization of passages that should be interpreted in a literal and normal sense. In so many manners, the kingdom is now. There is no future for the nation of Israel. Furthermore, the present troubles in the Middle East have no present biblical implication.[6]

If part of the Bible can be spiritualized, such as the rapture of the church, the tribulation, and the world rule of the Antichrist, and the kingdom reign of Christ, then, other portions can be likewise spiritualized, such as the virgin birth, the resurrection, and miracles of Jesus. Allegorical interpretation, and amillennialism, produces the detrimental fruit of liberalism!

The Liberalism of Postmillennialism

Although there are initial aspects of this view articulated by Joachim of Floris, an earlier Roman Catholic writer, postmillennialism was first systematized by Daniel Whitby (1638-1725). Church historians agree that this view was not apostolic since there is no evidence of this belief in the early church. Though postmillennialism is developed from the allegory advocated by Origen, he was not postmillennial.

Teachings of Postmillennialism

As is common with most views departing from clear normal

teaching of Scripture, postmillennialists understand prophecy to be mostly allegorical. Postmillennialist have adopted an optimistic view about the technical capacity of mankind, thereby denying the total depravity of humanity, and believe the world is becoming better and better. Such views are illustrative of the liberal aspects of this teaching.

Postmillennialists believe in a growing triumph and final victory of Christendom that will climax before the second coming of Christ. The prefix *post* conveys the thought that Christ returns *after* the church has established the kingdom and made it influential worldwide. In other words, the church is building the kingdom, and when this task is completed successfully, then, Christ returns to reign over the kingdom of the church universally.[7]

Postmillennialism

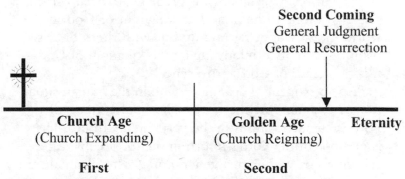

Whereas postmillennialism (as a theological system) has a liberal foundation due to the manner by which it destroys the teaching of Scripture and denies human depravity, not all the advocates of this system were liberal. However one wonders how the "conservative" teachers could embrace such a view and not be illuminated in their thinking! For example, the advances made in medicine and technology at the beginning of the 20th century resulted in postmillennialism becoming very popular.

However, following World War I, and the horrors of the war, postmillennialism experienced a decline.

Though certainly not theologically liberal, Princeton's Charles Hodge affirmed a postmillennial view of eschatology. He embraced the following teachings: (1) the universal propagation and spread of the gospel; (2) the conversion of many Jews who would become part of the church; and, (3) the coming of Antichrist and the attending events before the second advent. He also believed in (a) the resurrection of both the just and the unjust; (b) a general judgment; (c) the end of the world; and, (d) the consummation of Christ's kingdom. Although Hodge was more literal in his views, most postmillennialists embraced a spiritual view of eschatological events. Walvoord offered the following summary of postmillennialism.

> The kingdom is spiritual and unseen rather than material and political.
>
> The throne which Christ is predicted to occupy is the Father's throne in heaven. The kingdom of God in the world [now] will grow rapidly but with times of crisis. All means are used in advancing the kingdom of God— it is the center of God's providence.
>
> Any providential dealing of God in the human situation is a coming of the Lord. The final coming of the Lord is climactic and is in the very remote future. There is no hope of the Lord's return in the foreseeable future, certainly not within this generation. Postmillennialism, like amillennialism, believes that all the final judgments of men and angels are essentially one event and will occur after a general resurrection of all men and before the eternal state. Postmillennialism is distinguished from premillennialism which regards the millennium as future and after the second advent.[8]

Israel is the Church – the Church is Israel

Postmillennialism teaches the church is composed of all believers of all generations. With the call of Abraham and the founding of the people of Israel, the church was the outward form identified with the Jewish people. From Moses to Jesus Christ, the church was in its outward visible form in the nation of Israel. Since Israel was the people of God, it was also the church. Fruchtenbaum commented on the future of Israel in light of postmillennialism:

> The preaching of the gospel will have a steady growth, but at some point it will produce a massive revival among the Gentiles, resulting in the majority of the Gentiles being saved. This is the fullness of the Gentiles. When that fullness comes, a similar mass revival will occur among the Jews, resulting in the majority of the Jews being saved. In that way, all Israel will be saved. This will not result in a restoration of Israel to the land but in Israel's amalgamation into the Church. The fullness of the Gentiles and the saving of all Israel will result in a long period of peace and prosperity. It will last for a very long time, though not necessarily one thousand years. At the end of this long period will come a great apostasy and rebellion that will terminate with the second coming, a general resurrection, a general judgment, and the eternal state.[9]

What conclusions can be deduced concerning postmillennial beliefs of the relationship of the church to the establishment of the government of Jesus Christ? If there is ever a serious revival of postmillennialism, it would prepare the world for even wider anticipation of the arrival of the Antichrist. There are movements that could come together quickly with a postmillennial mindset which are active now in fooling people concerning the truth of the last days. Any event or any man who can accelerate the development of the so-called "present kingdom/church" will cooperate with the agenda of the world deceiver! Any teaching that would create a positive outlook as to how the last days will occur could be part of a postmillennial occurrence. In the international turmoil that will come in the final hours, anyone with a positive message will be welcome. This is just what the Antichrist will foster. He is the "counter-messiah," or "false-messiah," who will offer a peace plan to stop the earth from the brink of disaster.

The Seduction of Dominion Theology

In the past few decades, a new movement has developed within postmillennialism known by different names, such as "dominion theology," "theonomy," and "reconstructionism." These designations emphasize the major ideas found in postmillennial dominion theology.

Dominion

The teaching of dominion implies the church should control and dominate all areas of society, including the social structures, laws, and all aspects of public and private morality. The Christian dynamic should invade the court system, control legislation, the police forces, and the welfare system. The Christian goal is for universal development of biblical mores, and especially Old Testament principles, and for making all nations Christian republics with the Law of Moses serving as the governing covenant with the people. The further goal is to subdue sin in all spheres.

Theonomy

Theonomy is derived from two Greek words, *theos* (God) and *nomos* (law). Theonomists desire application of all legal aspects of the Mosaic covenant to the church today. There would even be death for violation of the Sabbath and stoning for some of the most serious crimes, such as homosexuality, kidnapping, murder, robbery, and even stoning for rebellious children. The Mosaic Law then becomes the constitution determining how all of mankind should be legally administered in government. The biblical, moral framework then is forced upon believer and unbeliever alike.

Reconstruction

The word, reconstruction, implies that enforcing the Mosaic

Law upon all the nations would result in the various societies becoming "reconstructed" and therefore Christianized. The church and the world would be changed and God's law would rule, resulting in the Lordship of Christ over the planet.[10]

This new form of postmillennialism is similar to the classic teaching on the subject, except the advocates are more militant in their determination to put these principles into practice. Reconstructionism is "a takeover" and a "power play" in order to force both Christian and non-Christian to accept the Old Testament order of things.

> Dominion theologians believe that it is the clear responsibility of the church to move beyond the matter of individual salvation and holiness and actively enter into the realm of public and social responsibility. Christians are to become activists and "promote and enforce obedience to God's law in society." They often chide premillennialists and amillennialists for manifesting in their theology "a desire to escape personal and corporate responsibility in an increasingly complex and threatening world."[11]

It is easy to understand how such a position could give impetus to an order that would be perfect for a dictator. He would have a system established that was recognized as intending to "save" society from chaos. The world desires a strong leader, and a powerful government established to control evil. Turmoil results in a suitable climate for autocracy, both spiritually and politically.

The Deception of Preterism

Preterism is the theological belief about eschatology teaching Christians can have it all! It promotes the idea that the second coming has taken place. Christ indeed did return in A.D. 70, but He also *returned literally* yet also in a *spiritual* sense. Preterists actually argue that "Christ did return" though one cannot see Him now sitting on the throne in Jerusalem!

New Preterism (that is, the preterism of today) was actually developed due to a fear of liberalism. R. C. Sproul admits that as a young theologian he was disillusioned by the liberal argument that Christ promised in Matthew 24-25 to "soon" return, but He did not. "How do evangelicals answer that?" he and other conservatives asked. To some the most obvious answer is that He did return at the time of the destruction of the Temple in A.D. 70! On the contrary, the return is taught to be spiritual.[12] Concerning Sproul and the preterist view, Ice wrote,

> Sproul says he believes he is helping to save biblical Christianity from liberal skeptics like Bertrand Russell and Albert Schweitzer by adopting a preterist interpretation of Bible prophecy: "One of Russell's chief criticisms of the Jesus portrayed in the Gospels is that Jesus was wrong with respect to the timing of his future return," notes Dr. Sproul. "At issue for Russell is the time-frame reference of these prophecies. Russell charges that Jesus failed to return during the time frame he had predicted." Dr. Sproul, along with many other preterists, answers this charge from liberals by saying that Jesus did return—in the first century. He returned spiritually through the acts of the Roman army, who destroyed Jerusalem and the Temple in A.D. 70.[13]

As Ice noted well, this approach is like fighting liberalism with liberalism.[14] Christians do not need to restructure the theology of the church in order to answer the foolish critics who detest the Bible and do not accept it as inspired by the Holy Spirit. Surprisingly, many pastors and Bible teachers are drifting from literal premillennialism and accepting the preterist view. LaHaye offers some valid questions that preterists cannot answer. He asked,

1. How can preterists possibly prove Jesus came back in A.D. 70?
2. How do they prove Satan was bound for a "thousand years"?
3. How do preterists explain that none of the events of the "end of the age" have ever taken happened?

4. What evidence can preterists marshall to show that Christ has been in charge of this world over the last 2,000 years?

5. How can preterists prove that the destruction of Jerusalem in A.D. 70 was the fulfillment of Jesus' description of the Great Tribulation?

6. How can the preterists prove that Nero was the Antichrist, as they claim?

7. How can the preterists prove that the 21 judgments of Revelation took place in A.D. 70?

8. How can preterists explain the fact that their theory was never taken seriously until the seventeenth century?

9. How can preterists show that "all the nations of the world" fought against Jerusalem and were then destroyed in A.D. 70?

10. What do preterists say about the fact that Jerusalem was not delivered in A.D. 70 as it was supposed to be by the arrival of the Messiah from glory?[15]

Seven other such questions demonstrate the preterists have not studying Scripture well enough in explaining Bible prophecy. It is because the Christian public is often gullible and uninformed on issues of eschatology that the average untrained Christian is susceptible for the deception found in preterism. The average layman is too often coerced into confusion and does not understand how to begin a response to such outrageous views. Preterists appear to have other agendas rather than bringing understanding to the clear and readable Word of God.

Concluding Thoughts

If preterism, or any of the other views addressed, are correct, then the Bible cannot be understood with any systematic meaning whatsoever. The early church must have been fooled by its mistaken premillennial views, though primitive and limited. The church has replaced Israel, and Israel as a nation has no future. Furthermore, the obvious fact that the world is becoming more and more sinful is denied. Certainly, there will be no actual rescue (the rapture) for the believers of the church dispensation. If the world is seen as progressing in its wickedness, Christianity will somehow "evolve" itself into something better.

Why do so many believers become confused as to the biblical scenario of what biblical prophecy is making so clear? The answers could be multiple, but the most basis response is the growing hatred for premillennialism and dispensationalism. There is the disintegration of Bible training and doctrine is being marginalized and discounted (which also includes the field of prophecy, in other words, eschatology).

As prophesied, Europe is being united into one nation, the Middle East is aflame, and true believers in Christ (in many societies such as America) are becoming targets of hatred. All of the above false views about prophecy have part in the hands of deceivers. Bigalke explained,

> Although the wording for a chapter identifying Christian movements who may actually be working toward the kingdom of Antichrist (e.g. amillennialism, postmillennialism, dominion theology, etc.) may seem a little harsh, there is great need to give warning concerning the teaching of certain theological systems which deny the literal establishment of the government of the Lord Jesus Christ on earth. If the church is the kingdom now, then there is no literal millennium to accommodate the government of Jesus Christ. Furthermore, some Christians seem to think things would be different in this country if only more Christians could be elected to office. Of course, it is wonderful to have Christians in government positions, but the Christians who believe the focus of the church is to fill the Congress and the courts and the White House with born-again believers in order to build a government wherein the church rules the country is a grievous doctrine. Such mentality actually attempts to deploy a key aspect of Christ's kingdom prematurely *without the King Himself*.[16]

They accost the church as to the actual events of the future making the church more at home in the world and comfortable in the present evil culture. Christianity has become simply some kind of "happy" metaphysical and mystical experience. Emotion and the expending of "spiritual" energy are now the tests of maturity and walking with God.[17]

Dispensational Premillennialism

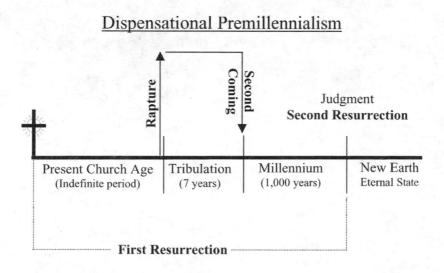

On the other hand, premillennialism and dispensationalism is understood when the interpreter uses the clear, literal, and normal hermeneutic of Scripture—from Genesis to Revelation. These systems are indeed Scriptural and are consistent with biblical realism. The Bible predicts an age of apostasy, a pretribulational rapture of the church, a horrible worldwide tribulation, and the premillennial return of Christ to bring in peace and godliness. Antichrist will establish an oppressive world government which Jesus Christ will destroy so that He alone establishes a government of peace and righteousness. While some accuse this view of being negative, the opposite is true. The Jews will be regathered to their homeland and will receive their Messiah as Savior and King. The human ingenuity of the world will fail, but God and His plans will not. The Lord Jesus Christ wins in the end!

CHAPTER 12

THE MILLENNIAL GOVERNMENT

Larry Spargimino

On a chilly day in 1607, three small ships—each hardly larger than a modern-day cabin cruiser—appeared on the coastline of North America, the area known now as Virginia Beach, Virginia. After landing and enjoying respite from many months of sea travel, Reverend Robert Hunt suggested they memorialize their landing in the New World by erecting a seven-foot oak cross brought from England, and claim the new land for the glory of God and the conversion of the indigenous peoples of the area.

Thirteen years later, another group of English settlers sailing on the *Mayflower*, arrived at Cape Cod, in what is now the State of Massachusetts. After coming ashore, these settlers drafted a foundational document, labeled by historians as one of the first documents "that helped establish the principle of self-government in America." Here are a few brief lines from this document:

> Having undertaken, for the glory of God, and advancements of the Christian Faith and honor of our king & country, a voyage to plant the first colony in the Northern parts of Virginia, do by these presents solemnly & mutually in the presence of God, and one of another, covenant & combine our selves together into a civil body politick; for our better ordering & preservation & furtherance of the ends aforesaid....[1]

America was founded on Christian principles by Christian people. The earliest settlers realized a godly government based upon Scripture was the only hope for order, peace, and prosperity. As can readily be seen from today's headlines, however, Christian influence in America is rapidly waning. With the legalization of abortion-on-demand, the frenzied drive to legalize same-sex marriages, a dramatic rewriting of history by revisionist historians, and a judiciary that is uncontrolled, the "civil body politick; for our better ordering & preservation & furtherance of the ends aforesaid" is becoming an evil body politic for the destruction of the ends envisioned by the founding fathers.

Will there ever be a godly government on planet earth or is it just a dream entertained by a few visionaries who need a reality check? This chapter will seek to demonstrate, from the Word of God, that indeed there will be a godly government on earth, and such a belief, though scorned by some, is well attested in Scripture.

Peering Into the Future

From the time of His initial promises to Abraham, God committed Himself to establishing a theocratic kingdom on earth. Since the paradise lost through Adam's disobedience was an earthly one, God revealed His plans to re-establish worldwide peace and righteousness in a future reign that would boldly declare His Sovereign Lordship over all creation. This theocratic kingdom "is necessary to accomplish God's purpose of demonstrating His perfect government over the earth."[2]

The kingdom age is a thousand year period (Rev. 20:1-6) during which Christ rules and reigns from Jerusalem, and brings in peace and righteousness upon the earth (Isa. 2:1-4). It is a time when the natural world, groaning under the Edenic curse (Gen. 3:17-19), will experience release from bondage (Rom. 8:20-22), with peace in the animal kingdom (Isa. 11:6-9) and great abundance in the earth's harvests (Amos 9:13-15).

While there are many outward and material blessings that will come upon the world during this future age, it will also be a time of spiritual renewal, a time when the law of God is written on the hearts of God's ancient covenant people (Jer. 31:33-34). God will take away the sins of Israel (Rom. 11:26-27) and pour forth His Spirit so that Israel will walk in ways that are pleasing to God (Ezek. 36:26-31). It is at this time that God will institute a special government and rule so both His glory and His righteousness will be demonstrated on all the earth.

Christ's role in this future government is articulated in Scripture: *For unto us a child is born, unto us a son is given: and the government shall be upon his shoulder...of the increase of his government and peace* **there shall be** *no end* (Isa. 9:6-7). While globalists have been seeking to institute a "new world order" by stealth, the rule of Christ will come publicly and dramatically bringing God's *true* new world order.

God's order is not some type of man-made utopian rule, which is the product of eons of evolutionary development, but a glorious divine rule. Pentecost quotes William Newell approvingly, as follows: "The thousand year's reign is the direct administration of divine government on earth for one thousand years by our Lord and His saints."[3]

God's Kingdom Rule

When one refers to God's kingdom rule it is not to be understood as God's general governance over all things. While God's government extends over all things—from things so small they are only visible under special magnification, to things so far away they can be seen only through the largest telescopes—His theocratic rule in the millennial kingdom is "God's rule thus specially manifested through one nation, and finally embracing all nations." Through this theocratic rule, God's *"Redemptive Purpose shall be accomplished and God's Sovereignty in all its fullness be recognized by every creature."*[4] The "one nation" referenced is Israel; the city of Jerusalem is its seat of government (Is. 2:1). "Jerusalem is also to be exalted as the governmental center of the earth," wrote Unger.[5]

The term "kingdom" is often employed with regard to different spheres of divine kingship. There is God's kingly rule over all creation whereby through His providence He directs and guides history to its appointed end. On the other hand, there are also specific manifestations of God's kingdom rule at different times in redemptive history. Roy E. Beacham wrote, "God's kingdom appears to be portrayed in two overlapping yet distinguishable realms. In the broadest sense, the Scriptures teach that God rules at all times over every aspect and entity of the created order. On the other hand, the Bible speaks of a limited rule of God, a rule that is localized on earth, framed within time, and centered on a select human constituency."[6]

The Government of the Millennium

When one refers to a "government" it should be understood as referring to an orderly and established system of administration and control over a given area. However, will a system of administration and control be needed during the millennium?

Government will be needed for at least two reasons. *First*, the population will be unusually large (Jer. 30:19-20; Zech. 8:4-5). In early America, when the population was scattered and settlements were few and far between, life was generally unregulated, but when the population began to increase then more regulation was necessitated. With the burgeoning of the human population during the millennium, certain laws and restraints will be needed to accommodate such a large population.

Secondly, there will still be sinners whose rebellious hearts will lead them to do evil things. LaHaye explained, "When the kingdom begins, all natural men, both Jews and Gentiles, will be believers. The Jews in their entirety will be saved just prior to the second coming of Christ. All unbelieving Gentiles (goats) will be killed during the 75-day interval between the tribulation and the millennium, and only believing Gentiles (sheep) will be able to enter the kingdom." With the course of time, however, "newly born, natural people will continue to inherit the sin nature from their natural parents...although Satan is confined, thus reducing temptation, the sin nature is quite capable of rebelling against God apart from Satanic activity."[7]

There are many proofs of the doctrine of human depravity

and the poignant effects of the sin nature. As a result of the reports of prisoner abuse at Abu Graib prison in Iraq, many were asking, "How could such a thing happen?" An equally-important question is: "What does this communicate about human nature and peer pressure?"

Several years ago a professor of psychology conducted a series of experiments at Yale University. Professor Stanley Milgram would tell a test subject, "the teacher," to give an electric shock to another subject, "the learner," whenever the learner made a mistake on a word-matching test. The voltage was increased with each error, rising to a potentially lethal 450 volts. However, there was no electricity and the learner was really an actor who knew all about the experiment. Milgram found that 60% of his "teachers" went to the maximum voltage despite the blood-curdling screams from the "learners." Milgram concluded "that with a little bit of coaxing, the majority (60%) of subjects would administer shocks right through to 450 volts."[8] Milgram's experiments revealed basic human nature which necessitates government, even during the millennium.

There will still be evil people in the theocratic kingdom. Isaiah 32:5 reveals that in the kingdom *the vile* [*nabal*, "fool," "ungodly person," cf. 1 Sam. 25:25; Ps. 14:1] *person shall no more be called liberal, nor the churl* [*kilay*, "rogue"] *said **to be** bountiful.*" In the kingdom, there will be such people, though they will be recognized for what they are.

The millennial era will witness utopian conditions that will be maximized by a well-fed and prosperous society, but men will still be sinners and sinners do dangerous and destructive things. The millennial government has been conceived by God for optimum results and proficiency. Nevertheless, what type of a government will there be in the kingdom?

While the republican form of government enjoyed in America today is the best form of *human* government, it falls far short of the theocratic government planned by God for the kingdom age. In a perceptive paragraph, Peters described the uniquely theocratic nature of the millennial government.

It is not a Republic, for the legislative, executive and

judicial power is *not potentially* lodged in the people, but in *God the King*; and yet it embraces in itself the elements both of a Monarchy and of a Republic;—a Monarchy in that *the absolute sovereignty* is lodged in the person of *the One great King*, to which all the rest are subordinated, but Republican in this, that it embraces a Republican element in preserving *the rights of every individual*, from the lowest to the highest, and in bringing the people, in their individuality, *to participate in the government* by the nation, as such, originally choosing the form of government, showing themselves to be "a willing people," and aiding in electing the subordinate rulers.[9]

While conditions are somewhat ideal during the millennium, conditions are, by no means, perfect. The strong will prey on the weak, and justice may be lacking in some measure. Moreover, the full blessings of the millennial rule will not be realized unless the millennial Ruler is able to exercise effectively His righteous rule. It is for these reasons that there will be a government during this period. Some characteristics of this government will not be provided.

Justice Instead of Injustice

Governments exist, at least in theory, so the rule of law, instead of the rule of the jungle, will be maintained. The millennial government is characterized by righteousness and justice which will result from the suppression of the wicked and the imposition of God's righteous law. *But with righteousness shall he judge the poor, and reprove with equity for the meek of the earth: and he shall smite the earth with the rod of his mouth, and with the breath of his lips shall he slay the wicked* (Isa. 11:4). This passage cannot refer to the first coming of Christ, or Christ's present rule over His people as Lord of the church. The millennial rule of Christ is not a rule of grace, but of law and judgment. Those who oppose Messiah's rule are not invited into a kingdom of grace; rather, they are slain, according to Isaiah 11:4, by the One who rules.

Isaiah 2:3 states, *for out of Zion shall go forth the law, and the word of the LORD from Jerusalem.* The law is the revelation of the will of God and the rule of behavior instituted throughout the earthly kingdom reign of Messiah. Without question, this rule will be enforced. Psalm 2:9 and Revelation 2:27 teach Christ will rule *with a rod of iron.* Walvoord taught that this represents "unyielding, absolute government under which men are required to conform to the righteous standards of God."[10] There cannot be anything but justice in the theocratic government because the millennial government is characterized by holiness which always produces equity and fairness in all of man's relations, both individually and nationally.

Peace Instead of War

The prophet Isaiah wrote, *they shall beat their swords into plowshares, and their spears into pruning hooks: nation shall not lift up sword against nation, neither shall they learn war any more* (Isa. 2:4). When Messiah comes He will not only bring peace but also *he shall speak peace unto the heathen: and his dominion shall be from sea even to sea, and from the river even to the ends of the earth* (Zech. 9:10). This speaks of a worldwide reign of peace instead of a reign of terror.

Order Instead of Disorder

Governments often bring order through totalitarian rule, a rule in which a dictator has ultimate power and authority. Given fallen human nature, power and authority concentrated in one individual can become a dangerous thing. However, Jesus Christ is without sin. He is therefore perfectly suited to exercise absolute rule over all of creation.

The messianic King possesses all power and authority to impose and maintain order. Christ will rule *with a rod of iron; as the vessels of a potter shall they be broken to shivers* (Ps. 2:8-9 quoted in Rev. 2:27). This is particularly applicable to those who rebel against Messiah's rule and reign. "The imagery," according to Ross, "is probably drawn from Egyptian execration customs in which the Pharaoh used his scepter to smash votive jars (pottery) that represented rebellious cities or nations."[11]

Liberty Instead of Bondage

Bondage is the fruit of oppression and injustice, but with the coming of Christ's equitable rule, there will be true liberty. Violence, oppression, and governmental corruption will be at a minimum. Even the natural world will turn against the transgressor. *And it shall be, **that** whoso will not come up of **all** the families of the earth unto Jerusalem to worship the King, the LORD of hosts, even upon them shall be no rain* (Zech. 14:17).

Truth Instead of Falsehood

Isaiah 2:3 promises God *will teach us of his ways, and we will walk in his paths: for out of Zion shall go forth the law, and the word of the LORD from Jerusalem*. Today, mankind is witnessing an unprecedented suppression of truth. The U.S. Postal Service, for example, does not allow parents and loved ones of service men and women in the Middle East to send Bibles and Christian literature, or anything contrary to the Islamic faith.[12] Moreover, the general media is fixated on promoting everything that is anti-Christian, such as Islam, homosexuality, and pornography.[13] However, during the kingdom age truth will receive its rightful place and will be presented without distortion or bias. In the kingdom, there will be a new and radical zeal for truth. Commenting on Zechariah 13, Fruchtenbaum wrote,

> In the process of Israel's regeneration and new prophetic manifestations, the false prophets who have led Israel astray during the course of the tribulation will be executed (Zech. 13:2-6). At the time of Israel's national cleansing from sin (v. 2) the false prophets will be sought out and executed. Often the parents of the false prophets will themselves be the ones to carry out the execution (vv. 2-3). Though many of these false prophets will attempt to hide the fact that they were formerly prophets, the scars on their bodies, a symbol of the prophetic office, will betray them for what they were. Their denials will not be able to save them (vv. 4-6).[14]

Vicegerents in the Theocratic Kingdom

While Jesus Christ is the messianic Lord and Ruler of the theocratic kingdom, the prophetic Scriptures indicate there will be other officials, or vicegerents, operative under His Lordship and subordinate to the Lord Jesus Christ. In a passage clearly testifying to a new order upon the earth, one discovers:

> In the land shall be his [the prince's] possession in Israel: and my princes shall no more oppress my people; and *the rest of* the land shall they give to the house of Israel according to their tribes. Thus saith the Lord GOD; Let it suffice you, O princes of Israel: remove violence and spoil, and execute judgment and justice, take away your exactions from my people, saith the Lord GOD. Ye shall have just balances, and a just ephah, and a just bath (Ezek. 45:8-10).

The following is a brief survey of the civil and religious leaders that will constitute the millennial government.

Princes

Isaiah 32 describes millennial blessings. In particular, verses 15-18 reveal there will be: (1) blessings from heaven; (2) a restoration of the natural world; (3) justice, implying a just government; and (4) peace for God's people. Nevertheless, in addition to a king, there will be princes. *Behold, a king shall reign in righteousness, and princes shall rule in judgment* (Isa. 32:1).

The Prince

This is an enigmatic figure mentioned in connection with the millennial Temple (Ezek. 44:3; 45:7, 16, 17, etc.). The prince's identity is not revealed, though Ezekiel wrote as though his readers know his identity. Who is the *prince*?

He is certainly not Jesus Christ, because the prince has to offer sacrifice for his own sin (44:22-23) and also engages in acts of worship (46:2). Moreover, in Ezekiel 46:16, the reader is informed that the prince divides an inheritance with his sons.

Such a statement leads the expositor to the conclusion that Jesus Christ is not the prince.

Ezekiel 34:24 states, *And I the Lord will be their God, and my servant David a prince among them; I the LORD have spoken it.* David is *a prince* but he is not "the prince." The prince is apparently some type of a religious leader. Ezekiel 45:13-17 indicates that specific dues are to be paid him by the people of the land and he will have the responsibility of providing the offerings and sacrifices at the religious festivals.

David

Hosea 3:5 reveals that the children of Israel will return *and seek the LORD their God, and David their king.* Numerous other prophecies also mention David in the context of the theocratic kingdom. The reader is told that God's people *shall serve the LORD their God, and David their king, whom I will raise up unto them* (Jer. 30:9).

Some believe the reference to *David* in these passages is really a reference to Christ, or to a literal son of David. Pentecost, however, argues "David means *the historical David,* who comes into regency by resurrection at the second advent of Christ." Pentecost demonstrates that, according to the New Testament (Mt. 19:28; Lk. 19:12-17), resurrected saints are to enjoy positions of responsibility as a reward. Since David was a man *after God's own heart,* a resurrected David would appear to be a proper understanding of these references.[15]

Others would answer that when Hosea 3 states the children of Israel will *seek the LORD their God, and David their king,* the idea of seeking the Lord and David would suggest that David in this passage is more than a mere mortal. Luke 1:32 reveals that the Lord shall give to Jesus Christ *the throne of his father David.* As Jesus Christ occupies the Davidic throne, He does so as the promised Davidic king. The children of Israel can properly be said to *seek the LORD their God, and David their king.* It is difficult to believe that during the theocratic kingdom anyone would sit on the throne other than the King Himself.

Allegorizing the Hope

While premillennial commentators may disagree on some details, all employ a grammatical-historical hermeneutic when interpreting prophecy. This approach has been used in the Christian church since its earliest history. Eusebius, citing Papias (c. 160), wrote, "Among these things, Papias says that there will be a millennium after the resurrection from the dead, when the personal reign of Christ will be established on this earth."[16]

Historically, Roman Catholic theology has allegorized Scripture so it can equate itself as the recipient of God's kingdom promises. In a *Catholic Answers* web article that is highly critical of the theology of the *Left Behind* series, the author stated the Roman Catholic Church "adheres to what has been the dominant view throughout Christian history—that the Millennium is going on *now*. It equals, or is roughly equal to, the Christian age."[17]

"But how can this be?" one should ask. "Does not the Bible speak about the earth being full of the knowledge of God as the waters cover the sea (Isa. 11:9)?" Indeed it does, argues the author of the web article.

> This prophecy was fulfilled by the coming of Christ and the inauguration of the Christian age. Today a third of the human race is Christian, and fully half of the human race worships God in one way or another. The remainder has—with few exceptions—at least heard of the true God, and by the standards of biblical history, knowledge of the Lord does indeed cover the earth like the waters cover the sea. The light has dawned, and the darkness has been dispelled.[18]

Contrary to what the Catholic author has written, this has not been "the dominant view throughout Christian history" and the darkness has not "been dispelled." Such shallow optimism is nothing more than wishful thinking made sacrosanct by heretical theology. LaHaye wrote, "With secular humanists in control of our educational system, our national media, and the Supreme

Court, and our government and moral perverts in control of our entertainment industry...it is obvious our country is far from 'getting better and better.' And this country is the best the world has."[19]

However, how does one explain such an approach to prophecy, and such an obviously erroneous sugar-coating of contemporary events, as in the above cited Catholic statement? Peters' comments are most insightful.

> It was only *when* the Scriptures and the promises were spiritualized, *when*, under the influence of release from persecution and incoming churchly prosperity, the church itself was exalted through civil patronage, that the Primitive doctrine was gradually but surely set aside, and *the church itself* was made (as by Origen) "*the mystic Kingdom of heaven*," or (as by Eusebius) "*the very image* of the Kingdom of Christ," or (as by Augustine) "*the City of God*."[20]

In other words, a literal millennial kingdom, far more glorious than all the pomp and grandeur of the Roman ecclesiastical organization, could not be tolerated when the temporal supremacy of an ecclesiastical organization that could depose monarchs and declare war was seen as the fulfillment of the reign of Christ on earth.[21]

Allegorizing Scripture is regarded as a great evil even by most evangelicals—yet many evangelicals allegorize prophecy and seek to justify the practice! Does God really mean what He says about the kingdom of Christ in the future, or do those passages refer to the church in the present age? What about the wolf dwelling with the lamb, and the lion eating straw like an ox, as described in Isaiah 11:6-8? Does this happen in today's world? Does one really see wolves dwelling with lambs? George Zeller tells an amusing story of a Russian zookeeper who boasted, "In our zoo here in Moscow, the wolf dwells with the lamb in the same cage, something which you Americans do not have." However, the zookeeper failed to mention that a new lamb had to be put in the cage every day![22]

What about the Church Today?

Will church age Christians have any role in the millennial government? Several New Testament Scriptures address this issue. *To him that overcometh will I grant to sit with me in my throne, even as I also overcame, and am set down with my Father in his throne* (Rev. 3:21). Revelation 2:26-27 is similar. *And he that overcometh, and keepeth my works unto the end, to him will I give power over the nations: And he shall rule them with a rod of iron; as the vessels of a potter shall they be broken to shivers: even as I received of my Father.* A note in the *Tim LaHaye Prophecy Study Bible* on this latter passage states, "Overcomers even in this unfaithful church are promised to be a part of that kingdom over which Jesus shall reign when He comes again."[23]

The apostle Paul also connects faithfulness in the church age and reigning with Christ. According to 2 Timothy 2:12, *If we suffer, we shall also reign with him: if we deny him, he also will deny us.* Does this mean if a Christian denies Christ he will lose his salvation? No, because Paul is not speaking about salvation, but about reigning with Christ, that is, if we suffer for Christ. The millennial government should be of interest to Christians today. It is an inspirational study to realize that the world, though seemingly out of control, is waiting for His full control.

PART 3

The Coming One World Religion

CHAPTER 13

RELIGION IN HISTORICAL PERSPECTIVE

Ron J. Bigalke Jr.

What is religion? It is defined as "the personal commitment to and serving of God or a god with worshipful devotion, conduct in accord with divine commands esp. as found in accepted sacred writings or declared by authoritative teachers, a way of life recognized as incumbent on true believers, and typically the relating of oneself to an organized body of believers."[1] According to the given definition, religion includes the worship of the true God and the worship of all false gods. Adam and Eve were created to serve and worship the one true, living God. How then did the worship of false gods develop? The origin of corrupt religion is found in the early pages of Scripture. Genesis 10:8-10 reads,

> Now Cush became the father of Nimrod; he became a mighty one on the earth. He was a mighty hunter before the LORD; therefore it is said, "Like Nimrod a mighty hunter before the LORD." And the beginning of his kingdom was Babel and Erech and Accad and Calneh, in the land of Shinar.

God's comments concerning Nimrod and Babel are found in Genesis 11:1-4.

> Now the whole earth used the same language and the

same words. And it came about as they journeyed east, that they found a plain in the land of Shinar and settled there. And they said to one another, "Come, let us, make bricks and burn *them* thoroughly." And they used brick for stone, and they used tar for mortar. And they said, "Come, let us build for ourselves a city, and a tower whose top *will reach* into heaven, and let us make for ourselves a name; lest we be scattered abroad over the face of the whole earth."

The Beginning of False Religion

The Tower of Babel is an attempt to found a religion apart from God. It demonstrates man's basic insecurity in needing to establish such a tower for protection (11:4). It also reveals an attitude of rebellion and a desire for independence. Of course, God would not allow this act of rebellion to His command to Noah and his sons, "Be Fruitful and multiply, and fill the earth" (Gen. 9:1). The "Table of Nations" (10) attests to the obedience of mankind to God's command in Genesis 9:1. It also gives the account of the end of the dispensation of conscience (8:15-9:7) resulting in the judgment of the confusion of languages (11:5-9) because the people filled the earth, but did not scatter (11:1-4). This account provides an important answer as to why the nations scattered and filled the earth. The dispersion at the Tower of Babel, whereby the people scattered into many different areas with differing languages, was the result of God's judgment.[2] God said,

> "Come, let Us go down and there confuse their language, that they may not understand one another's speech." So the LORD scattered them abroad from there over the face of the whole earth; and they stopped building the city. Therefore its name was called Babel, because there the LORD confused the language of the whole earth; and from there the LORD scattered them abroad over the face of the whole earth (11:7-9).

God moves in judgment and confuses their language. This forces the human race to scatter abroad, which they were unwilling to do themselves. This *toldot*[3] ends with the people of the earth separated from one another and separated from God.

The main figure of Genesis 10 is Nimrod, and *the great city* is Babylon. Nimrod is represented as establishing Babylon (10:8-12), which is both a type and prophecy of an evil, religious system (Isa. 21:9; Jer. 50:24; 51:64; Rev. 16:19; 17:5; 18:2-3). Both Nimrod and Babylon foreshadow the eschatological *man of lawlessness* and his city (2 Thess. 2:3; Rev. 13; 17). Although the name "Babylon" is derived from the Akkadian word *babilu* meaning "gate of god,"[4] it will become evident that it is a counterfeit to God's eternal city, *a house not made with hands, eternal in the heavens* (2 Cor. 5:1).

As a grandson of Ham (Gen. 10:6-8), Nimrod was likely born soon after the Flood (cf. 11:10-16). His name is derived from the Hebrew word *mârad*, which means "to be obstinate, to resist, to disobey, to rebel."[5] Genesis 10:8 describes Nimrod as *a mighty one on the earth*; it is a reference to his mighty influence. Genesis 10:10-14 records the extent of his earthly endeavors. The extent of his kingdom nearly occupied the whole region. Moses wrote aptly, "[Nimrod] *was a mighty hunter before the LORD*" (10:9). He was a mighty rebel against God. Seiss referenced the Targum of Jonathan which interprets the verse "to mean that he was *a mighty rebel before the Lord, the mightiest rebel before the Lord that ever was in the earth*. He also referenced the Jerusalem Targum which "reads it that he was *mighty in sin* before the Lord, a hunter of the sons of men...."[6]

According to Genesis 10:10, *the beginning of his kingdom was Babel*. Nimrod was not merely content to rule Babylon or the region; Scripture records, *from that land he went forth into Assyria, and built Ninevah* (10:11). Genesis 10 is not the mere record of one man's ambitions himself to build a kingdom; it is also the record of the great city and tower that was built in organized rebellion against God. Both the city and tower were made with human hands as man's strained attempt to act independent of God; they were poor counterfeits for the heavenly city. Ross wrote,

> It was at Babel—that city founded by Nimrod, a descendant of Ham through Cush; that city known for its pride and vanity; that seat of rebellion toward the true God and pagan worship of the false gods—that the Lord turned human ingenuity and ambition into chaos and confusion so that the thing the people feared most came on them and that their desire to be people of renown was suddenly turned against them.[7]

Genesis 11:4 reads, *Any they said, "Come, let us build for ourselves a city, and a tower whose top **will reach** into heaven, and let us make for ourselves a name, lest we be scattered abroad over the face of the whole earth."* The words *will reach* are italicized since they are not found in the Hebrew, and the translators have added the words due to implication. However, the verse is best understood with the words omitted. The people were building a tower whose top was equal to the heavens. In building the Tower of Babel, man did not desire to reach God; rather, the desire is to find a means of equality with God for man's own glory. Clearly, the construction of the Tower of Babel is the beginning of idolatry and all paganism. From this point, man would not only worship the creation but also seek to defy the self. The beginning of the Babylonian cult was the deification of Nimrod.

The Mother and Child Cult

All false religions began at Babylon and extended to Nineveh. Secular history affirms the subsequent division of this idolatry throughout the entire earth. God destroyed the wicked men in the Flood (6:1-12), and Nimrod's idolatrous tower and city (representative of organized religion) was the revival of wickedness and corruption. Just as the whole earth (excepting Noah and his family) was of one accord before the Flood, so man again was unified in rebellion against God. *The same language and the same words* in Genesis 11:1 could be interpreted as the unified, idolatrous attitude of mankind. *The whole earth* sought a means to strengthen and disseminate their organized religion. Reminiscent of Satan's organized rebellion (Isa. 14:11-14), wicked man's goal aspiration was to *make for ourselves a name* (Gen. 11:4). All false religion and idolatry, after the Flood, is revived though Nimrod's leadership.

By dropping the vowels and the first consonant of Nimrod's name, the remaining letters, m, r, d provide the basic etymology of the chief god of the Babylonian pantheon, Marduk (Heb. Merodach; Jer. 50:2). In his classic apologetic, Hislop wrote, "There is no doubt that Nimrod *was* a rebel, and that his rebellion was celebrated in ancient myths; but his name in that character was not Nimrod, but Merodach...."[8] In the Babylonian religion, the wife of Nimrod was Semiramis. Nimrod and Semiramis were the ancient god and goddess of Babylon. Commenting on the historical period, Hislop recorded,

> Now the period when Semiramis lived,—a period when the patriarchal faith was still fresh in the minds of men, when Shem was still alive, to rouse the minds of the faithful to rally around the banner for the truth and cause of God, made it hazardous all at once and publicly to set up such a system as was inaugurated by the Babylonian queen. We know, from the statements in Job [31:26-28], that among patriarchal tribes that had nothing to do with Mosaic institutions, but which adhered to the pure faith of the patriarchs, idolatry in any shape was held to be a crime, to be visited with signal and summary punishment on the heads of those who practised [sic] it.[9]

According to the Babylonian mythology, Semiramis claimed to have a virgin-born son, after Nimrod's death, which was the beginning of the mother and child cult. The worship of the goddess and her son was the fundamental character of the religion of ancient Babylon. The corrupt religion is a perversion on the part of Satan to counterfeit the genuine virgin birth of the Messiah, and to cause disrepute upon the actual historical event in the Gospels. Hislop provides the following commentary about the worship of Semiramis and her alleged virgin-born son.

In Papal Italy, as travelers universally admit (except where the Gospel has recently entered), all appearance of worshipping the King Eternal and Invisible is almost extinct, while the Mother and the Child are the grand objects of worship. Exactly so, in this latter respect, also was it in ancient Babylon. The Babylonians, in their *popular religion*, supremely worshipped a Goddess Mother and a Son, who was represented in pictures and in images as an infant or child in his mother's arms. From Babylon, this worship of the Mother and the Child spread to the ends of the earth.[10]

Hislop's work, *The Two Babylons*, chronicles the spread of the ancient Babylonian cult of the mother and child throughout other divisions of the earth. The following chart indicates the proliferation of the cult throughout these other localities.[11]

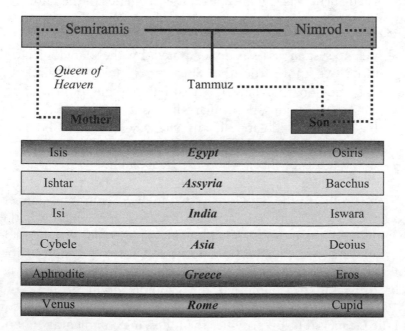

Mother		Son
Isis	**Egypt**	Osiris
Ishtar	**Assyria**	Bacchus
Isi	**India**	Iswara
Cybele	**Asia**	Deoius
Aphrodite	**Greece**	Eros
Venus	**Rome**	Cupid

The prophet Jeremiah warned the Israelites against offering sacrifices to *the queen of heaven* (7:18; 44:17-19, 25). Hislop researched the Babylonian worship of *the queen of heaven* and found its inception to follow the death of Nimrod. After Nimrod died, Semiramis did not want to love her power and wealth, so she claimed to have a virgin-born son who would be the salvation of mankind. Scripture refers to this son as Tammuz (Ezek. 8:14). "In life her husband had been honoured as a hero; in death she will have him worshipped as a god; yea, as the woman's promised seed, "Zero-ashta," who was destined to bruise the serpent's head, and who, in doing so, was to have his own heel bruised."[12] It is obvious that Satan attempted to counterfeit the true prophecy concerning Jesus Christ. *The queen of heaven* is Semiramis, the wife of Nimrod, who is the original mother of the mother and child cult. The cult continues in Roman Catholicism and is the basis for Mariolatry wherein mother and Child are worshiped as co-redeemers.[13]

> Among all the women who have ever lived, the mother of Jesus Christ is the most celebrated, the most venerated, the most portrayed, the most honored in the naming of girl babies and churches. Even the Koran praises her chastity and faith. Among Roman Catholics, the Madonna is recognized not only as the Mother of God but also, according to modern Popes, as the Queen of the Universe, Queen of Heaven, Seat of Wisdom and even the Spouse of the Holy Spirit.[14]

Whereas Roman Catholicism regards the title "Queen of Heaven" positively, it is actually a pagan title and continues the idolatry to this day. Hislop asked, "But if the guilt and danger of those who adhere to the Roman Church, believing it to be the true Church where salvation can be found, be so great, what must be the guilt of those who, with a Protestant profession, nevertheless uphold the doomed Babylon?"[15] The idolatrous mother and child cult culminates in the Book of Revelation. *THE MOTHER OF HARLOTS*, whose name is *a mystery,* "*BABYLON THE GREAT* (Rev. 17:5)," is the source of all harlotries and corrupt religions of the earth. According to Scripture, the essence of the cult is the endeavor to gain earthly power and wealth through religious authority. Babylonianism continues today in the Buddhist shrines, Hindu temples, Mohammedan mosques, and the Word of Faith movement to name a few.

From Monotheism to Polytheism

The organized, universal rebellion against God at Babel is clearly the beginning of idolatry; it was also a universal rejection which is evident in the thoughts of mankind and his worship. God revealed Himself *so that they are without excuse. Because that which is known about God is evident within them; for God made it evident to them. For since the creation of the world His invisible attributes, His eternal power and divine nature, have been clearly seen, being understood through what has been made, so that they are without excuse* (Rom. 1:19-20). Rebellious mankind *did not honor Him as God, or give thanks* (1:21). Instead of honoring God, mankind rejected Him universally and *worshipped and served the creature rather than the Creator* (1:25). The rejection of God not only affected man's worship, but also it affected his reasoning abilities. *Professing to be wise, they became fools* (1:22).

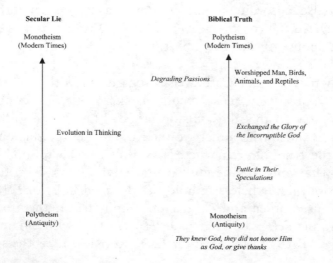

Secular Lie		Biblical Truth
Monotheism (Modern Times)		Polytheism (Modern Times)
	Degrading Passions	Worshipped Man, Birds, Animals, and Reptiles
Evolution in Thinking		*Exchanged the Glory of the Incorruptible God*
		Futile in Their Speculations
Polytheism (Antiquity)		Monotheism (Antiquity)
		They knew God, they did not honor Him as God, or give thanks

In contrast to the secular view of religion, which teaches ancient man evolved in his thinking from polytheism to monotheism, man's worship has continually degraded. Worship of God has steadily degenerated from monotheism to polytheism. The biblical and historical truth is, prior to the organized rebellion against God at Babel, man was monotheistic. As mankind followed their sinful nature, *they became futile in their imaginations, and their foolish heart was darkened* (1:21).

Babel is the beginning of polytheism and its ecumenical spirit continues in the present day. The culmination of man's idolatry is still future until *the man of lawlessness is revealed, the son of destruction* (2 Thess. 2:3). The organized rebellion of Nimrod is a mere foreshadow of things to come. Genesis 10-11 records the inception of Satan's counterfeit system of spirituality. The embryonic emergence of organized lawlessness and recalcitrance at Babel will reach its complete development in Satan's absolute counterfeit, the Antichrist, who will make the effects of his counterfeit spirituality extend worldwide. Similar to Nimrod, the mighty rebel, Antichrist, *the man of lawlessness...the son of destruction*, will be known for his recalcitrance also (2 Thess. 2:3).

Religious Worldviews

How is counterfeit spirituality represented today? Generally, seven worldviews have been recognized: atheism (disbelief in the existence of any God), deism (belief in a transcendent God, or First Cause, substantiated only by reason not faith), finite godism (limited knowledge of God because the future is unknowable and conditioned upon other events undeterminable to man and even God), panentheism (belief in a God immanently contained within all creation meaning the universe is the animating force of God), pantheism (belief in a universe of an all-encompassing immanent God), polytheism (belief in several Gods), and theism (correct belief in the existence of an immanent and transcendent God). All of the seven worldviews have permeated the culture and taught at practically every secular institution of higher learning throughout North America and virtually throughout the world. If one were to study comparative religions at a secular university, Christianity would be taught as an equally viable belief as other world religions. Of course, Christian theism should be taught as truth at Bible colleges and universities. Since atheism, pantheism, and theism are the foremost worldviews the charts below will illustrate the fundamental beliefs of each. Although theism could include some non-Christian beliefs, the charts will only reflect theism according to Scripture.

	WORLD	GOD	SIN	SALVATION	TRUTH
ATHEISM	Eternal; Uncreated; Evolved	Does Not Exist	Body Mortal; Human Ignorance	No Eternal Destiny; Annihilation	Relative; Situational
PANTHEISM	Immaterial World is God; *Ex Deo*	Infinite; "Impersonal All"	Evil is Illusion; Ignorance	Oneness with God	Relative; Subjective
CHRISTIAN THEISM	Created; *Ex Nihilo*	Immanent; Personal Transcendent	Total Depravity	Grace Through Faith Alone	Absolute

	ULTIMATE REALITY	HUMAN NATURE	HUMAN DESTINY	MORAL AUTHORITY	GOAL OF HISTORY
ATHEISM	No God; World is All That Exists	Body Mortal	Annihilation	Relative; Determined by Humanity	No Purpose or Meaning; No Goal
PANTHEISM	God is All; All is God	Body Mortal; Soul Immortal	Oneness with God; Reincarnation	Relative; Determined by Lower Manifestations of God	Merge with the Divine
CHRISTIAN THEISM	Infinite, Personal God	Body and Soul Immortal	Resurrection to Eternal Life or Damnation	Absolute; Determined Solely by God	Eternal Kingdom of God

The reader should recognize the most fundamental disagreement among the three major worldviews is the existence and nature of God. In fact, belief in the existence and nature of God has deceived or provided positive instruction for more people than anything real or imaginary. Religious beliefs have changed history—positively and negatively—and are the major content of all forms of communication. Nothing on the planet has impacted more people collectively and individually than belief in the existence and nature of God. After examining the charts, another obvious conclusion must be that the worldviews are mutually exclusive. The essential beliefs of the three major worldviews (and the other four worldviews if they were included) regarding the world, God, sin, salvation, truth, ultimate reality, human nature, human destiny, moral authority, and the goal of history negate each other. It is logically impossible for all religions to unite as one, or to teach all world religions propose varying ways of reaching the same destiny. It is crucial for Christians to affirm the uniqueness of God's revelation to Israel in the Old Testament, and the uniqueness of Jesus Christ, as made known in the New Testament (cf. Heb. 1:1-3).

Why do these negating beliefs exist? False beliefs escalate for several reasons, but specifically Scripture declares that Satan *the god of this world has blinded the minds of the unbelieving, that they might not see the light of the gospel of the glory of Christ, who is the image of God* (2 Cor. 4:4). The strategy of Satan, the enemy of mankind, is to delude *the minds of the unbelieving* from understanding the *light of the gospel.*

At the risk of oversimplifying the reasons for one adopting one of the varying worldviews, two reasons will be asserted as the cause. The first cause is one's heredity, that is, the belief of one's family or culture. The second reason is experience, either positive or negative. A negative experience with a perceived form of Christianity may cause one to embrace atheism or pantheistic worldview. For example, in the 1820s and 1830s, western New York was called the "Burned-Over District." In contrast to the preaching of the First Great Awakening in America, Charles Finney, a "revivalist" of the Second Great Awakening, believed revival could be created apart from God's sovereignty by the right use of means. He would claim to have a stirring revival but would return to the same area a year later and find the state of religion to be worse than before his "revival." The problem was people would become excited during Finney's revival meetings, but after the experience dissipated the people would become disillusioned and would resort to even greater sin. Often the unsaved will believe they are having a genuine experience of God's presence, but after the initial excitement there is no change in their life so they believe that Christianity must not be true. Certainly, some people did become Christians during the Second Great Awakening, but it is also a lesson to the church that if preaching is void of God's Word even worse conditions may follow than previously. A bad experience with a perverted form of Christianity may cause one to embrace an atheistic or pantheistic worldview. Another reason for a person embracing a pantheistic worldview is a transformational experience. Consider the following example of a Hindu sect.

> *Stay high forever.* No more coming down.... Expand your consciousness by practicing the Transcendental Sound Vibration.... *Turn on* through music, dance, philosophy, science, religion, and prasadam (spiritual food). *Tune in.* Awaken your Transcendental Nature! *Drop out* of movements employing artificially induced states of self-realization and expand consciousness.... End all bringdowns, flip out and stay for eternity.[16]

In a post-materialistic society, people are searching for meaning and fulfillment in life. Blaise Pascal if often credited for saying, "There is a God-shaped vacuum in every man that only God can fill." Augustine wrote, "Thou hast made us for Thyself, O God, and our hearts are restless until they find their rest in Thee." People know they need divine guidance and are accountable to their Creator. Christians need to respond boldly and loudly, as the Apostle Paul said, *For I am not ashamed of the gospel, for it is the power of God for salvation to everyone who believes...for in it* **the** *righteousness of God is revealed from faith to faith; as it is written, "BUT THE RIGHTEOUS MAN SHALL LIVE BY FAITH"* (Rom. 1:16-17). The following chart demonstrates several prominent beliefs (atheistic, pantheistic, or theistic) contrary to Christianity. It should be recognized that false beliefs can be easily identified by claims for authority outside and addition to the Bible, denial of the tri-unity of God, denial of the deity of Jesus Christ, an idealistic view of man and sin, and a system of salvation obtained through works resulting in no assurance of salvation.

	AUTHORITY	GOD	JESUS CHRIST	MAN/SIN	SALVATION
CHRISTIANITY	Bible	Self-Existent; Tri-unity	Redeemer; God Incarnate	Totally Depraved	Grace Through Faith Alone
BAHA'I	Writings of Baha'u'llah	Unknowable	One of Many Manifestations of God	Perfection Possible; Unlearn Sin	Baha'i Law
BUDDHISM	Buddhist Writings	Siddhartha Guatama	Manifestation of Maitreya Buddha	Suffers Due to Karma	Four Noble Truths; Eightfold Path
HINDUISM	*Bhagavad Gita*; *Vedas*	Brahman-Atman	Avatar	Divine Essence	Reincarnation; Self-Enlightenment
ISLAM	Koran	Allah	Ascetic Prophet	Original Sin	Five Pillars; *Jihad*
JUDAISM	Torah; Oral and Written Traditions	Yahweh; Denies Tri-unity	Deceiver; False Messiah	Deny Original Sin	Mosaic Law
NEW AGE	Various; Relativistic	God is All; All is God	Guru; Enlightened	Basically Good; Evolve Into God	Occult Discipline; Self-Enlightenment
SATANISM	Mostly *Satanic Bible*	Deny Anything Supernatural	"Artisan of Hoaxes"	Unbridled Human Potential	Atheistic; Hedonistic

The Bible alone is the Word of God![17] Therefore, Christianity teaches that only one God who is immanent (personal) and transcendent (beyond His creation) exists. Scripture reveals three distinct personalities in the Godhead—the Father, the Son, and Holy Spirit—and these three Persons are one God, the same in substance, eternally equal in power and glory (Deut. 6:4; Isa. 6:8; Mt. 28:19; 1 Cor. 8:6; 2 Cor. 13:14; 1 Jn. 5:7). The atheist makes an absolute statement that there is no God, which he cannot make because he does not possess absolute knowledge of this world or the universe. The best that an atheistic could be is an agnostic (i.e. a person skeptical about the existence of God). Nevertheless, even the atheist's skepticism is denied by Scripture: *The fool has said in his heart, "There is no God"* (Ps. 14:1a; cf. Rom. 1:20). The battle against false religious systems concerns the Holy Bible alone as God's authoritative revelation of His existence and nature.

East Meets West

As already demonstrated, the Babylonian religion which began in Genesis 11 has permeated the entire culture throughout the world. The foundational ideas of Western civilization are the theology and values of the Bible. Therefore, any "seduction" of Western thinking must challenge the logical and true propositions of Scripture. Of course, the seduction must be subtle which is precisely the role of Eastern mysticism.

The word occult comes from the Latin, *occultus*, meaning "hidden" or "concealed." Occult philosophy teaches there are unexploited powers within mankind that will allow him to discover what is hidden in the material world. The underlying theme of occult philosophy is being promoted in a subtle way at every level of culture. Many believe the only hope for human survival is a revival of Eastern mysticism, a derivative of paganism and Gnosticism diverting understanding of the Gospel. In other words, the hope is in mankind. It is no coincidence that humanism is fundamentally identical to the occultism associated with Eastern religious practices, such as, meditation, visualization, and yoga.

Ecologists and others believe the only formidable enemy of this pagan revival is Christianity with its "narrow minded and out-dated beliefs" as recorded in the Holy Bible. Furthermore, the fact that salvation is by grace through faith in Jesus Christ alone is reprehensible to those who anticipate an Eastern revival. Mankind is encouraged to embrace the New Age, or dawning of the Age of Aquarius. However, history demonstrates the New Age movement is not new in any way. It is the same old lie of the serpent in the Garden of Eden (cf. Gen. 3:1-5) which is being presented in new forms for contemporary culture.

Esoteric disciplines such as alchemy, astrology, Kabbalism, Taoism, yoga, witchcraft, and Zen are penetrating Western society. The New Age movement is largely responsible for the influence of Eastern mysticism in the West. Today, the practices of Eastern mysticism are being aggressively promoted for the proselytizing of a transformation in human consciousness to serve as an initiation for every cultural institution.

It is important to know that the common experiences of mysticism are not intellectual; rather, they are focused on a cosmic totality. German philosopher, Johann Gottlieb Fichte, had a profound influence on philosophers Schelling and Hegel. It was Hegel's influence that almost made pantheism the agreed philosophy of even the highly educated. Fichte believed the mind is the fundamental nature of the universe. In other words, man's thoughts are not the result of experiences occurring within the material world; rather, thought is part of the one universal mind. Self-consciousness is the principal metaphysical reality whereby one finds the road to cosmic totality, which is "the Absolute." Henceforth, morality is the principal quality of the self and it also acts as the activating rule of the material world. One goal of the New Age movement is to clarify self-consciousness. The highest degree of self-consciousness is achieved when one recognizes "Mind" or "Spirit" as the fundamental principle of reality.

Hinduism teaches the existence of a partial experience of multiple forms of God. For instance, each Hindu deity is part of a complex. If "the Absolute" is to be located in any way, then it is within a complex and not one or another of its own members. In this sense "all the gods are merely forms of Brahman." The Hindu belief is a vision of cosmic totality, that is, a related consciousness of a larger whole manifesting on different fractal-like levels. The fractal-like nature proves the experiences are false, since all are abbreviated forms of Satan's lie in Genesis 3.

The synergetic principle of the universal mind is for all individuals to identify their separate experiences within the cosmic totality. The goal of Eastern mysticism is to reinterpret human experience as a need for personal and social transformation. Though there are innumerable initiations within Eastern mysticism, all involve a direct link to the demonic. The person experiences a spiritual transformation with the prince of this world (i.e., the arch-enemy of mankind who is none other than the devil, Satan himself) through powerful experiences of bliss, joy, and love. All the experiences seem to confirm the profound spiritual growth toward enlightenment. The same occurs in many "Christian" revival meetings wherein doctrine is discarded and the common experience unites those involved with a pantheistic

savior who is immanent in all things but not the transcendent
God of the Holy Bible.

The main idea of Eastern mysticism is all mankind is divine
and possesses unlimited potential. Mankind only needs to
become aware of his potential through mind-altering experiences, which would include any form of occultism to make this
happen. Once mankind realizes his unlimited potential, it is
believed he can create a new world of peace, prosperity, and harmony. Eastern mysticism seeks to reinterpret common experiences into related systems of thought, such as "all is one," "man
is god," "the need for enlightenment," and "self-realization."

All is One

The "all is one" declaration seeks to explain experiences
resulting in an altered state of consciousness. The idea is disso-
lution of any distinctions between the individual and the experience. Since only one Reality is believed to exist, then any good
or evil manifestations all belong to the same Reality. Faith is in
an all-encompassing Reality. "All roads lead to Rome," since
there is one ultimate Reality, or true consciousness. Hinduism
refers to this as *Sat-Chit-Ananda*, which is the "ecstasy of consciousness aware of itself" (interestingly, Nobel prize-winning
physicist, Erwin Schrödinger, received much of the inspiration
for his work in quantum mechanics from the Hindu *Vedas*).

The "all is one" proposition confounds the *imago Dei* with
the *essentia Dei*. The *imago Dei* does not mean that man possesses even an ember of divinity nor the *essentia Dei*. Peter did
write, Christians are *partakers of the divine nature* (2 Pet.1:4),
but his statement is referring to the transformation of the
Christian to reflect the attributes of God not union with the
essentia Dei.

The Divinity of Man

The next proposition that "man is god" assumes the
inevitable based on the experience of "the ecstasy of consciousness
aware of itself." Since there is one single Reality, all humanity is

an emanation of the one Reality; therefore, man only needs to realize that he is god. Man's own consciousness provides the inevitable link. The Harmonic Convergence is the attempt to mobilize people throughout the world to unite for the purpose of meditating and visualizing peace so the consciousness of the planet will be increased thereby averting the Apocalypse. One way to accomplish this is by thinking positively, and hence, connecting with the ultimate Reality underlying the universe. This is also the idea of monism, that is, everything (God, man, and nature) is all one single Reality.

The theoretical system of Cistercian abbot Joachim of Fiore (ca. AD 1135-1202) included three ages of "historical evolution." The first age was the Age of the Father, which corresponded roughly with the time of the Old Testament, or Law. The second age was the Age of the Son, which related with the time of the New Testament, or Gospel era. The last age would be the Age of the Spirit, which was a future time of peace and knowledge of God throughout the earth.[18] The New Age movement believes that some aspects of Joachim's Age of the Spirit will correspond with the Age of Aquarius.

History can be divided into one of two models: linear or cyclical. The majority of Eastern worldviews believe history is cyclical, whereas the majority of Western worldviews represent history as linear. The cyclical model is not characterized by apocalyptic thinking, although this does not mean that cataclysmic thinking is entirely absent. The Eastern worldview would understand the timing of biblical prophecies as timeless (i.e., idealism). Nietzsche is an example of Western philosophy encouraging a cyclical view of history since his "*over*man" or "superman" is eternally overcoming himself throughout history over, and over, and over again.[19]

The Hebrews, and their surrounding neighbors, articulated the linear model of history. Although this model primarily views history as progressing in one direction, it also views history as somewhat repetitive. "The present is not a replay of the past. Rather, history moves from one event to the next until it reaches its final goal."[20] Therefore, the apocalyptic will view history as progressing linearly. In other words, history itself is progressing

toward a climactic end of time that will be preceded by cataclysmic judgments. The linear view of history may appear to be
entirely pessimistic since there will be a definite judgment in the
Apocalypse, but it is actually optimistic in the end since cataclysmic events will be followed by victory. The cyclical view of
history only pictures things as worsening since there is no intervention within history.

Enlightenment and Self-Discovery

Enlightenment is what helps raise one's awareness of the
interrelation to everything. Such a belief denies the distinction
that God gave to each thing after its own kind (Gen. 1-2).
Eastern religions are stating that everything is one and everything is really God, and man is actually a god who possesses
unlimited potential. Man is responsible for his actions, but then
he is accountable only to himself. Eastern mysticism does not
sing "glory be to God" but it is "glory be to me." Since salvation in Eastern philosophy is the realization of the one true
Reality, it does not require man to be accountable to God as his
Creator and Savior. Through hidden knowledge (*gnosis*), one
experiences "enlightenment," "self-realization," "union," or
"at-one-ment."

Interestingly, Eastern mysticism is believed to be scientific
rather than religious. By trying to explain its beliefs in scientific
terms, Eastern Mysticism seeks to gain credibility. For instance,
using religious terms New Age evangelist Maharishi Mahesh
Yogi[21] introduced his Transcendental Meditation to the West in
1959, but it was excluded by the government as a religious practice. Therefore, he simply renamed the practice as "The Science
of Creative Intelligence" which would then offer respectability.
Transcendental Meditation is one of the most popular means of
mental and physical relaxation, stress relief, self-realization, and
human evolution among New Agers.

Transcendental Meditation is one of many yoga techniques
imported from the East. Yoga is literally "yoking" or "union"
with the one divine Reality. There are eight stages to yoga: moral
restraint (*yama*), self-culture (*miyama*), posture (*asana*), breath

control (*pranayama*), control of the senses (*pratyahara*), concentration (*dharana*), meditation (*dyhana*), and a state of elevated consciousness (*samadhi*).[22] The techniques of Transcendental Meditation involve emptying one's mind of distracting influence by reciting a Sanskrit word known as a "mantra," and to engage in an initiation rite which is essentially a Hindu worship ceremony. Transcendental Meditation is a Hindu-based practice masquerading as science.

Maharishi originally introduced Transcendental Meditation as a religion in his book, *The Science of Being and Art of Living*,[23] published in 1963. Later when the government excluded it as a religious practice, Maharishi began presenting Transcendental Meditation as scientific. He called it "The Science of Creative Intelligence,"[24] substituting the term "creative intelligence" for "Being" (or Brahman). Self-realization is to result by realizing one's innermost nature as identity with the Being.

The scientific nature of TM was questioned in the 1977 Federal Court Case of *Malnak v. Yogi*. One of the most important stages in the initiation ritual of TM is the *puja*, a Vedic hymn.[25] Concerning the puja, Judge H. Curtis Meanor of the US District Court at Newark, New Jersey wrote, "The puja chant is an invocation of a deified human being who has been dead for almost a quarter of a century…. It cannot be doubted that the invocation of a deity or divine being is a prayer."[26] The teaching of "creative intelligence" as science was not validated and the religious nature of Transcendental Meditation was emphasized. The teaching of the course in New Jersey public schools was ruled to violate the First Amendment.[27]

Scripture never encourages one to stop thinking in order to concentrate on a mantra. On the contrary, the exhortation is to be sober and alert, actively resisting the wiles of the devil (1 Pet. 5:8-9). Christian meditation focuses not on the vain repetition of a mantra, but on the solid foundation of God's Word (e.g. Ps. 1:1-2; 19:7-14). The underlying premise is that man needs to be united with the divine principles through enlightenment and the use of meditative techniques; however, regardless of the terminology it is religion.

The advancement along the path of *gnosis* ("knowledge") reveals increasing familiarity with the one Reality and the illusion of the realm of the material. The material relationship to the divine One is a manifestation that, in a sense, denies the reality of matter. The monistic idea that all is one and God is all, leads to the conclusion that spirit is the only life. Therefore, everything not part of God is an illusion. Hence, it is due to a faulty consciousness that man does not understand this reality.

Through further enlightenment and utilization of spiritual laws, man becomes capable of creating his own reality by manipulating the progress of his own evolution toward godhood. Anything real is composed of consciousness, therefore, man learns to control and master reality by deepening his consciousness. Since negative thinking is the result of faulty consciousness, this is one of the reasons why positive thinking is so important. Clement Stone, author of *Success through a Positive Mental Attitude* (co-authored by Napoleon Hill), stressed the power of the mind and tried to make a science of faith. Hill was not the only one who embellished this concept. Robert Schuller's "possibility thinking," Norman Vincent Peale's "positive thinking," Clement Stone's "positive mental attitude," Charles Capps' "positive confession," and Oral Roberts' "seed-faith" principles all teach the same thing: the power of faith as a force to change one's environment, including God.

Possibility thinking is nothing short of humanistic psychology stressing the power of the mind. Faith is a force that Christians and even non-Christians can utilize to manipulate reality. By following the techniques of possibility thinking, one is able to become a co-creator with God. "Possibility thinking" is essentially the same belief of Eastern practitioners.[28] Christian faith does not work miracles by "the operation of spiritually scientific laws," and prayer is not a force underlying the universe.[29] Mankind is believed to possess a power within himself which is the continuous flow of energy in the mind. Positive thinking is believed to unlock man's unlimited potential and allow the mind power to flow through him.[30] Negative thoughts would not exist apart from the unenlightened; they are the ones who create negativity by developing harmful patterns of thinking. At this point, mysticism merges into magic. Man now possesses unlimited potential reminiscent of the Tower of Babel (Gen. 11:6).[31]

The influence of Eastern mysticism in society is attested by the rise in the belief that man is god. Among mystics, God is not the personal Creator of the Bible. Eastern mysticism teaches there is an impersonal god-force (as in *Star Wars*), the "force" or "god within." The distinction between black magic and white magic is firmly fixated in the modern mind. The propaganda of the New Age movement and the influence of Jungian psychology through the *Star Wars* "Force" have effectively promoted this alleged distinction.

Although the belief that white magicians use magical power for blessing and benefit and black magicians use magical power for damage and harm is popular in modern culture, this distinction is not found in occult history. Historian Jeffrey Burton Russell wrote, "Necromancy…was understandably regarded by nonmagicians as the most sinister aspect of divination. In Medieval Latin, the original Greek root (*nekros*: a corpse) was corrupted to the Latin *niger* ('black'), whence *nigromancy*, the 'black art.' It is largely from this etymological confusion that the term 'black magic' derives."[32]

Likewise, the Force in *Star Wars* utilized the distinctions. The "dark side" of the Force is used for evil and the light side is used for good. Nevertheless, the Force is the power of both good and evil. The Force is not personal; it is an impersonal energy field permeating all of life. Although the Force is not omnipotent, it is omnipresent; it is the equivalent of a Supreme Being.[33] Actually, the *Star Wars* movie is an elementary teaching on initiation into witchcraft. The Force is the product of Eastern mystical philosophy and, as such, is an abomination to God because it usurps His sovereignty and leaves mankind in darkness rather than Christ's *marvelous light* (cf. 1 Pet. 2:9). George Lucas even admits to the syncretism of religious beliefs in the *Star Wars* saga. His invention of the Force is "an almost 'academic' exercise in refashioning ancient myths for modern audiences…. It's a distillation of a lot of mythological religious teachings."[34] Rather than an objective faith based upon *many convincing proofs* (Acts 1:3), the Force is an existential "leap of faith" into the dark.[35] Scripture warns man of the danger of trusting his feelings, which are deceitful (Jer. 17:9), but to heed the instruction of God's Word (Jn. 17:17).

The impersonal god-force was nothing more than a sleeping mass of energy exploding into billions and billions of individualized parts of consciousness. All these points of consciousness had become souls entering the material world but they themselves are not material. By entering the astral plane, immaterial souls are able to come to the understanding that all is illusory. Metaphysical ignorance results from believing man is not god. Hence, sin is non-existent; it is metaphysical ignorance.

However, the presence of sin is substantiated by death in the world *because all sinned* (Rom. 5:12). *And inasmuch as it is appointed for men to die once and after this* **comes** *judgment* (Heb. 9:27). Although man believes he is a little god on earth, the true God said, *"you will die like men"* (Ps. 82:7). Possessing the mind of Christ does not mean becoming a god, but demonstrating the "self-emptying" of Jesus as a suffering servant (Phil. 2:5-11); it is the result of humble self-renunciation to follow God's will. Eastern mysticism in any form is incompatible with true biblical faith. Though mysticism embraces the lie that there is one ultimate Reality in existence, and all points of consciousness belong to that same reality, Jesus declared there is only one Truth. It is the lie that takes many forms. The broad road has many paths leading to destruction and the narrow road has one way that leads to eternal life: Jesus Christ.

The "god power" movement is embedded in pantheism. God is not an individual, but a force of infinite intelligence and consciousness. Since man is part of that force, god is within him, hence, man is god. In an interview with Bill Moyers on PBS, Joseph Campbell was quoted as saying, "Heaven and Hell and all the gods are within us."[36] Man creates his own universe by revolutionizing his thinking thereby manifesting the early stages of consciousness rising. Superconsciousness is full awareness of the self.

The New Age teaching of "god within us" causes New Agers to believe they are gods and can exert power over all things. Human potential is unlimited, and as Shirley MacLaine stated, "you are unlimited."[37] Man ignores his sinful condition and any awareness of personal sin. Since there is only one Reality, man is not under a moral law. To believe in good or evil is a dualistic concept that the New Ager finds repulsive. The world will not accept negativity because New Agers are optimistic about their evolution. By realizing god is within all, man is able to raise his consciousness and combat the Apocalypse. By waking the divine within each person, man can herald the New Age. It is believed that man is at an exciting crossroad presently where he can actually control his own evolutionary progress. Of course, to inaugurate the New Age there needs to be complete unity, that is, a one world economy, government, and religion.

Scripture records a different destiny for those who believe they can attain their full potential without Christ. Roman 3:12, Psalm 39:5, and Isaiah 64:6 teach that man's true nature is complete emptiness; there is no good in man unless the Father draws men unto Himself by the Holy Spirit through the accomplishments of the death and resurrection of Christ. The true Christian obeying God's will is promised strength to overcome all things in this world (Phil. 4:13). The anticipation in history for the church is the return of her Lord. Scripture is clear that the only way to a true utopia is to enter the Kingdom of God by way of the cross (Jn. 3:3; 14:6).

Eastern Missionary Groups

A "paradigm change" (a term introduced by scientist Thomas S. Kuhn in 1962) in the religious beliefs of Western culture is evident by the stylish embrace of Eastern mysticism and fashionable paganism. The meaning of paradigm in a standard dictionary is "an example" or "a model." However, this is not the meaning of the word today. When one speaks of a paradigm shift this means that one interprets reality as he believes it to be. In other words, truth is within one's own mental formation. Of course, in order to reach this state of belief one must discard all sound logic and reason. Originally, the initial establishment of Europe and North America was based upon a religious belief in one Almighty God and belief in His standards of right and wrong, and His provision and intervention in the affairs of mankind. These once prominent beliefs have largely been replaced with the mythical belief of gods and goddesses, paganism, evolution, and a lack of morality in society.

One such example is the YMCA and Scouts of America. George Williams founded the YMCA in 1844 to meet the needs of young men in the city. Williams wanted to provide a location where young men could exercise and socialize within a Christian environment. The YWCA was started in 1866 to meet the similar needs of young women. Following the mission of the YMCA, the Boy Scouts of America was founded in 1910 and the Girl Scouts of America followed in 1912. Whereas the original intent of these organizations was to pursue Christian ideals, they have now added an amalgamation of Buddhist and Hindu rituals (e.g., tai chi and yoga).

The promise of unlimited human potential is the foundation of Eastern mysticism, the New Age movement, occultism, paganism, Satanism, and witchcraft. The promise of empowerment is very seductive for often naïve practitioners. It is this promise that is continually presented in various forms in businesses, churches, education, and health care. Bookstores tout elaborate New Age sections to titillate their unsuspecting readers with Eastern philosophies. However, the lurid promises of Eastern religion ultimately fail. For instance, the Eastern worldview of Hinduism has completely twisted the value system of India. Nevertheless, the consequences of such a worldview seem to elude Westerners who are viewing these beliefs as charming and chic.

Is there a movement powerful enough to influence this Eastern seduction of the Western mind? Yes. The largest missionary organization in the world is the Vishva Hindu Parishad. The Vishva Hindu Parishad was founded on 8 July 1966 at an international Hindu conference. While missionaries are excluded from evangelizing Hindus in India, the Hindus send their gurus to the West in an effort to proselytize Westerners to accept Eastern mysticism. In fact, it was at the international conference that the Hindu gurus were chosen to be the first crusaders.

According to Paragraph 4 of the Vishva Hindu Parishad's constitution their chief goal is "to establish an order of missionaries, both lay and initiate, the purpose of propagating dynamic Hinduism." In other words, the aim of this organization is an aggressive strategy to convert the world to Hinduism. Naïve Westerners naïvely believe these Eastern gurus have come to the West by mere happenstance and have nothing to do with "dynamic Hinduism." Frequently, these gurus have tried to misrepresent their Hinduism with scientific terms, but this would be much like the Catholic Pope saying he represents a group of scientists just happening to have their headquarters stationed in Rome.

One of the most aggressive missionaries was Maharishi Mahesh Yogi. Eastern mysticism impacted millions in the 1960s through the Transcendental Meditation Movement. The Hare Krishna gained prominence chanting in the streets. Swami Prabhupada was a Sanskrit scholar and the guiding spirit behind the Hare Krishna Movement. Prabhupada translated and interpreted the ancient language of India for the West. Noted celebrities, such as George Harrison, have composed songs as dedications to the Hare Krishna. The International Society for Krishna Consciousness (ISKCON) has established a temple in New York City and numerous ISKCON centers throughout other cities. Sometimes the Hare Krishna is called the "fundamentalists" of the Hindu missionaries.

There are literally thousands of religious cults and sects that have been influenced by Eastern mysticism. Werner Erhard is the founder of both EST (Erhard Seminars Training) and The Forum seminars, which were the result of his influence by Hindu guru, Swami Muktananda.[38] The Theosophical Society began particularly in India between the Vedanta and Sankhya. The Upanishads taught theosophy as well. H. P. Blavatsky's books made the teachings popular in modern culture. Blavatsky even confessed that she received her teachings from Indian masters.[39]

Many mystics like Paracelsus accepted the belief that there is an all-pervading spirit, the life force behind all life and energy. Anton Mesmer developed this belief in the *anima mundi*, or "life force," hoping to explain the forces he believed to be working during hypnotism. The combinations of mesmerism, Eastern mysticism, and Swedenborgism led to the development of the New Thought teachings of Phineas P. Quimby. Consecutively, Mary Baker Eddy's Christian Science and Charles and Myrtle Fillmore's Unity School of Christianity were deeply influenced by the occult, yoga, meditation, Spiritism, and mysticism.[40]

Paul Twitchell, who said he received his commission by Tibetan monk Rebazar Tarzs who allegedly appeared in spirit form while Twitchell was in the mystic Himalayas and the Kush mountains, brought the popular occult religion of Eckankar to the modern world. Not only was Twitchell influenced by Tarzs, but also by Hindu guru Sudar Singh. Singh provided Twitchell with the foundation of Eastern mysticism for the new religion of Eckankar. Later in life, he was initiated into *Ruhani Satsana*, the "Divine Science of the Soul." The development of his involvement with Eastern and occult practices led to the start of his movement which is a plagiarism of the Hindu sect Radhasoami.[41]

Not only is Hinduism influential in religious movements, but also in the schools and universities. Aurobindo, Da Free John, Krishnamurti, Rajneesh, Ram Dass, and Yogi Bhajan are a few of the Hindu gurus influencing this movement. Swami Vivekananda, Paramahansa Yogananda, Ram Dass, Meher Baba, Da Free John, Bhagwan Shree Rajneesh, and Shree Aurobindo promoted the rejection of all religious and moral principles as the only means of social progress.[42] At the present time, Hinduism is experiencing a revival in India and is spreading to other countries as well. In North America, Hinduism is often popular on college campuses claiming to offer personal peace, tranquility of mind, harmony with nature, and victory over fleshly appetites. Hare Krishna, Transcendental Meditation, and other Eastern religious movements have their foundation in Hinduism.

While the Vishva Hindu Parishad is influential as a missionary organization, there is one individual who is the most prominent of the proselytizers of Eastern mysticism: the Dalai Lama, Tenzin Gyatso. Believed to be the reincarnation of the 14th Dalai Lama, he finds himself appealing more and more to those who know nothing of his philosophy based on the noblest of Buddhist principles and unadulterated sorcery. Tantric practices of magic and sexuality are presented as spirituality without the need for faith.[43] He receives much help for his cause from The Gere Foundation. Hollywood actors, Richard Gere and Harrison Ford, once hosted an event that raised $650,000 for Tibetan causes. Among the 1,000 guests were such Hollywood luminaries as Meg Ryan, Dennis Quaid, Steven Segal, Sharon Stone, Oliver Stone, Leonard Nimoy, and Shirley MacLaine.[44] Just as the serpent beguiled Eve, Satan is actively working to corrupt further the already depraved minds of the world through his subtlety (2 Cor. 11:3).

Eastern Practices

Monism is a metaphysical theory that attempts to explain the nature of being and reality as a unified whole. The more mankind experiences this oneness, the less likely the chances are for mankind to destroy each other and the world. The monistic theory is in stark contrast to the diversity of created things that God, as Creator, brought into existence. For instance, creation is not the same as the Creator for He is transcendent. The belief that "all is one" leads to the inevitable conclusion that man is god since he is part of the one divine Reality. As well-known New Ager, Shirley MacLaine said, "I know that I exist, therefore I AM. I know that the God-source exists. Therefore IT IS. Since I am part of that force, then I AM that I AM."[45] MacLaine's blasphemous statement is rampant among those involved in Eastern religious practices and mocks the true God who said, "I AM who I AM" (Exod. 3:14).

The ancient practice of Eastern meditation comes from belief in former lies. Both Hindus and Buddhists teach meditation; it involves emptying the conscious mind to awake the god consciousness ("divine within"). The most common method of accomplishing this is by reciting a mantra. Letting go of all conscious thoughts and chanting a mantra supposedly attunes the mind to what mystics call the higher self or cosmic oneness. However, such beliefs are in direct contrast to prayer. Prayer is a communication with God by the efficacious sacrifice of Christ Jesus. Prayer to God does not involve emptying the mind to become attuned with the divine spark believed to be resting dormant in man. Eastern meditation directs one into an altered state of consciousness that may cause an intense religious experience. The experience, however, is contrary to biblical teaching. Man is embracing error he believes is truth. Herein is the danger because Satan masquerades as an angel of light (2 Cor. 11:14).

Eastern meditation involves a deep state of relaxation, intense concentration on a mantra, and high suggestibility. The altered states of consciousness result from physiological reactions in the brain. Sometimes the experiences are terrifying, but there are also times when the experiences are exhilarating. Eastern meditation provides religious ecstasy that always directs one to occult power. Christian meditation involves conscious thoughts. The moment a person empties his mind that person is allowing himself to be possessed by a spirit outside of himself which he cannot identify objectively. The result is Satanic influence and widespread deception.

How Should Christians Respond?

The fundamental beliefs of Eastern mysticism began in the Garden of Eden and developed even more at the Tower of Babel. Occult beliefs are not new for they have been around since the beginning of time. The lie of the devil that mankind can be as gods is always undergoing revision by the archenemy of mankind (cf. Gen. 3:1-15). An awareness of the wiles of Satan in the affairs of the world should not cause one to be surprised since Scripture has already declared that Christians are to *be of sober spirit, be on the alert. Your adversary, the devil, prowls about like a roaring lion, seeking someone to devour* (1 Pet. 5:8). It is entirely possible that many who worship false gods of the current time do so quite ignorantly (cf. Acts 17:23). Nevertheless, regardless of the level of deception or sin in one's life, the Word of God still stands true. If anyone will believe that salvation is a free gift of God given solely by His grace through a faith relationship with Jesus Christ alone then he will be saved for it is the good news of Christ's death and resurrection for sinners that is *the power of God for salvation to everyone who believes* (Rom. 1:16). The spiritual battle will rage onward until Christ returns to this present earth in all His glory to judge the devil and all wickedness. In the meantime, the Word of God must be preached and the good fight of faith fought vigilantly (2 Tim. 4:1-8).

CHAPTER 14

SNARE OF WORLD RELIGION

Andy Woods

Prior to Christ's second coming, Scripture predicts a global religion will capture the hearts and minds of all humanity. This religion will be so pervasive in influence that it will persecute and, in most cases, exterminate all nonconformists. Various trends proceeding in today's world are obviously setting the stage for this coming world religion. As these "pieces of the puzzle" are gradually assembled, it is making the coming religion more and more of a reality in today's world; those holding to a biblical worldview will find themselves increasingly out of harmony with the philosophy and way of life of the modern age. Thus, believers living on the eve of the coming world religion need to be aware of its soon entrance into the world, as well as how to respond to it once it arrives. Although the body of Christ will not be on earth when this world religion reaches its zenith in the coming tribulation period, it is still likely that the church will experience much of the initial stage setting for the universal religion before the rapture occurs.

With due consideration of the above, this chapter is designed to educate believers concerning the snare of the future world religion. Three points will be made. *First*, the biblical predictions of a coming world religion will be examined. *Second*, the disturbing trends taking place within our world potentially setting the stage for the coming world religion will be explored. As will be demonstrated, these trends encompass not only events taking place outside the church but also within it as well. *Third*, biblical advice will be given regarding how Christians and spiritual leaders living on the

317

eve of this predicted worldwide apostasy should respond.

Scriptural Predictions of the Coming Global Religion

The Tower of Babel

The Bible is unmistakably clear that a global religion focusing on the person of Antichrist will exist upon the earth just before the return of Christ. A proper understanding of the final global religious system first requires an analysis of the first world wide religious apostasy. The end time religious system has its foundation in the historical account of the Tower of Babel recorded in Genesis 10–11. This section of Scripture is significant because it records humanity's first worldwide rebellion against God. Here, one learns of mankind's rebellion against God's command to *fill the earth* following the flood (Gen. 9:1, 7). Under the leadership of Nimrod (10:8–12), mankind instead gathered *in the land of Shinar* (11:2) for the purpose of building *a city, and a tower whose top **will reach** into heaven* (11:4).

While the political components of this apostasy are evident in the tangible manifestations of *a city, and a tower* at Shinar, it is important not to underestimate the religious dimension of this rebellion. It is because of the desire to make a name for themselves (11:4), "Babylon is the city where mankind first began to worship himself in an organized manner."[1] Moreover, the "*ziggurat*, intended by them to reach the heavens, was no doubt intended to be a place of occult worship of the stars and heavens."[2] Babel is also the place of the origin of the infamous mother-child cult. According to extra-biblical tradition, Nimrod's wife, Semiramis had a son named Tammuz through an alleged miraculous conception. According to tradition, Tammuz was killed by a wild animal and miraculously restored to life.[3] Hitchcock explained the global influence of this mother child cult beginning at Babel.

> The legend of Semiramis and Tammuz spread around the world. Their names were changed in different places, but the basic story remained the same. In Assyria, the mother was Ishtar, the son was Tammuz. In Phoenicia, the

mother was Astarte and the son was Baal. In Egypt, she was Isis and her son was Osiris, or Horus. In Greece she was Aphrodite and her son was Eros. For the Romans, the mother was Venus and the son was Cupid.[4]

Overall, the Tower of Babel represents humanity's first collective rebellion against God. Genesis 11 emphasizes both the political and religious facets of this apostasy. Moreover, "this initial centralization, followed by the global distribution, *is the primary mechanism by which Babylon became the central influence in all cultures and civilizations which followed.*"[5]

God's response to this collective rebellion was swift and decisive. According to Genesis 11:5-9, God frustrated this worldwide apostasy by confounding human language thereby inhibiting the builders from communicating with one another. God's action had a purpose. When God noted *nothing…will be impossible for them* (11:6), He was referring to the virtual unlimited potential for evil with the existence of a single religion and government. Satan's capacity to lead humanity away from the truth is enhanced if only one government exists, and this single government happens to be in the hands of anti-God forces. No opposition to an anti-God agenda is even possible under this scenario. However, with the existence of multiple nations, those nations that reject anti-God agendas can work to oppose those nations embracing such agendas. Consequently, evil is restrained at least to some extent.[6] Thus, ever since the Tower of Babel incident, God has decreed that humanity be ordered according to national boundaries, rather than global government (Deut. 32:8; Isa. 2:4; 66:18; Acts 17:26; Rev. 12:5; 20:3; 21:24, 26).[7]

However, one of Satan's purposes throughout history has been to subvert this divine ordering of nations. His desire is instead to reunite the world so he once again can have unlimited control of it through one man. Thus, Satan's ambition has always been "to bring man back to Babylon under his rule. This will finally happen according to Revelation 17–18. Both the city of Babylon and the false religious system of Babylon will be resurrected in the end times."[8] In other words, global government and religion will reappear in the very geographic locale where it first began. The fact that human rebellion will one day cycle back to where it all began comes as no surprise to diligent Bible students due to numerous parallel themes (or common denominators) revealed through both the books of Genesis and Revelation. Concerning this phenomenon, Henry Morris observed, "The Book of Revelation is the sequel to the Book of Genesis, the two books together bounding all history and bounding all of God's revelations to mankind. They constitute the alpha and omega of God's written word, the Book of Beginnings and the Book of Unveilings."[9] Examples include the thematic parallels between the probationary world of Genesis 1-2 and the eternal state of Revelation 21–22, as well as the parallels between the cursed world as depicted in Genesis 3 and the eternal state of Revelation 21–22.[10]

Now that the reader has understood that the coming world religion has its foundation in the Tower of Babel incident, let him now turn attention to some of the biblical predictions of a revived Babylon. These predictions should be understood in a twofold manner. Not only do they predict the reemergence of the literal city of Babylon on the Euphrates, but they also predict the reemergence of the global religious influence that the city enjoyed in Genesis 11. -

Zechariah 5:5-11

A key example of evidence directly predicting a futuristic religion emanating from Babylon is a prophetic vision found in Zechariah 5:5-11. This vision was given in 519 BC and is the seventh of Zechariah's eight night visions recorded in Zechariah 1:7–6:8. First, the contents of the vision will be described and then an interpretation provided. In order to understand the meaning of the vision, the following five elements must be understood.[11]

First, Zechariah saw a basket for measuring grain (otherwise known as an ephah). It is because an ephah was the largest measure in the Old Testament and was typically used for measuring flour and barley, that the basket signifies commerce. Second, in the basket, Zechariah saw a woman signifying wickedness. Third, Zechariah saw the woman being pushed back into the basket and a heavy lid was closed on top of her. This incarceration of the woman in the basket signifies that God is in control and He will release her from the basket only in accordance with His timetable. Fourth, Zechariah saw the basket being transported to the land of Shinar. This part of the vision identifies the specific geographic locale that one day the woman will exercise authority whence she is released from her incarceration. The Old Testament repeatedly identifies Shinar as the exact same portion of real estate where the Tower of Babel, as well as historic Babylon, once stood (Gen. 10:10; 11:2; 14:1, 9; Isa. 11:11; Dan. 1:2). Fifth, Zechariah was told the woman will be released one day and set upon the pedestal of a temple in Shinar. Since this part of the vision conscripts religious imagery, it communicates that the woman will be vested with future religious authority. It is this fifth facet of the vision that has the most relevance to the coming global religion.

By organizing all these five elements, Zechariah's vision teaches that once again, commerce, religion, and wickedness will return to the land of Babylon through God's providence. Historic Babylon fell in 539 BC and Zechariah's vision was given in 519 BC. Since Zechariah's prophecy was given 20 years after the historic fall of Babylon, it is clearly speaking of events still awaiting a future fulfillment. Revelation 17–18 record the circumstances by which this vision will ultimately be fulfilled. In the coming tribulation period, the literal city of Babylon (Rev. 17:18) will exert wicked influence (17:2), commercial power (18:10-18), and religious authority (17:2; Jas. 4:4) over all the inhabitants of the earth (17:15). The fact that Zechariah 5:5-11 and Revelation 17–18 are predicting the same event can be seen in the many parallels between the woman of Zechariah 5 and the harlot of Revelation 17–18.[12]

Zechariah 5:5-11	Revelation 17-18
Woman sitting in a basket	Woman sitting on the beast, seven mountains, and many waters (17:3, 9, 15)
Emphasis on commerce (a basket for measuring grain)	Emphasis on commerce (merchant of grain, 18:13)
Woman's name is wickedness	Woman's name is Babylon the Great, Mother of Harlots, and Abominations of the Earth
Focus on false worship (a temple is built for the woman)	Focus on false worship (17:5)
Woman is taken to Babylon	Woman is called Babylon

Overall, when one examines these prophecies in accordance with one another, he learns that global religion (headquartered in Shinar) will dominate the world during the coming tribulation period as global religion (headquartered in Shinar) dominated the world in the early chapters of Genesis.

Revelation 17–18

The clearest biblical prediction of a future religion influencing the world from Babylon is found in Rev 17–18. Revelation 17 features a woman named Babylon the Great. She is later identified as a city (17:18). Since all the other geographic locales and cites in Revelation are understood literally, it is best to understand this reference to the city of Babylon literally also. However, not only does John portray the woman as a literal city, but he also portrays her as a religious influence. There are several reasons for this assertion.

First, women in the Book of Revelation often symbolize religious systems. For example, in Revelation 2:20, the woman Jezebel is symbolic of a false religious system contaminating the church at Thyatira. The woman in Revelation 12:1-6 symbolizes the nation of Israel and the Jewish religious system (Gen. 37:9-10). The woman in Revelation 19:7 represents the bride of Christ, which is the church (Eph. 5:22-32). Second, the woman on the beast is referred to as a whore or a prostitute involved in sexual immorality (Rev. 17:1-2, 4, 5, 15; 18:3, 9). In Scripture, false religion is often analogized to sexual sin. For example, Christians are the bride of Christ (Eph. 5:22-32, 2 Cor. 11:2), hence when they pursue other gods, Scripture calls them adulterers (Jas. 4:4). This designation is speaking of the act of spiritual adultery rather than physical adultery.

Third, Revelation 17:5 reveals the title "Mystery Babylon" is written on her forehead. Ancient Babylon was an empire heavily influenced by mystery pagan religion. When the Babylonian King Nebuchadnezzar was troubled by a dream, the first people he called to offer an interpretation to the dream were the astrologers, enchanters, magicians, and sorcerers (Dan. 2:1-3). The fact that these were the people the king immediately sought for help, in a moment of personal crisis, illustrates how dominated Babylon was by pagan religion. Fourth, the beast the woman is riding is adorned with blasphemous names (Rev. 17:3). The term *blasphemous* has definite religious connotations; it refers to heretical religious activity contrary to Scripture. The fact that the beast is covered with these names indicates he is influenced by heretical religion.

Revelation 17 also depicts the scope of the woman's religious influence. Revelation 17:1 describes her as sitting *on many waters*. Revelation 17:15 interprets these *waters* as the *peoples and multitudes and nations and tongues* that the woman will influence. In other words, the woman will have religious influence over the entire world in the coming tribulation period. Interestingly, these same four categories of *peoples and multitudes and nations and tongues* are nearly identical to the categories used in Revelation 5:9 to depict those for whom Christ died. Thus, to the extent that the benefit of Christ's death is interpreted universally, the woman's religious influence should be understood universally as well. This religion will eventually focus upon the Antichrist as its ultimate object of veneration (2 Thess. 2:4; Rev. 13:4, 8, 12, 14-15). Interestingly, as John emphasizes the veneration of the beast, he also reemphasizes the global aspects of the coming religion through his use of the phrase *all who dwell on the earth will worship him* (Rev. 13:8).

Overall, the woman in Revelation 17 will fulfill the identical role fulfilled by the Tower of Babel in the early chapters of Genesis. She will be a literal city *in the land of Shinar* who will exert a universal religious influence throughout the entire world. In fact, John draws a deliberate parallel between the Tower of Babel and the future global religion through his use of the phrase *MOTHER OF HARLOTS* (17:5). The word "mother" conveys the notion that she is the one who ultimately gave birth to all harlotry. Only the Tower of Babel fits this description.[13] Since the Tower of Babel incident occurred before God had established national divisions through the creation of languages, this event stands in its own unique category as the first and only collective rebellion against God by mankind ever to have occurred in past history. As previously indicated, this initial apostasy in one centralized locale "followed by the global distribution, is the primary mechanism by which Babylon became the central influence in all cultures and civilizations which followed."[14]

World Events

Now that the biblical foundation for the coming world religion has been established, let the reader now direct attention to events occurring in the world today which are setting the stage for this coming world religion. The architects of globalism have traditionally recognized the existence of divergent religious beliefs in the world as perhaps the greatest hindrance toward the establishment of a new world order. In 1953, internationalist Charles P. Schleicher observed, "There are those who believe that only a universal religion to which men are fervently devoted, one which unites men in devotion to a single god and in a common brotherhood, will serve to overcome divisions among men and the worship of the secular nation-state."[15] Thus, the new world order cannot come into existence unless certain trends preceding it have the effect of bringing all religious beliefs under a common unity. As one examines the world scene, it is evident such trends are becoming more and more prevalent. These trends include the New Age movement, the Gaia Hypothesis, a selective application of the separation of church and state doctrine, the ecumenical movement, and the doctrinal "dumbing down" of evangelicalism. It should be observed that the first three trends on this list depict events occurring in the world generally, while the last two items depict events occurring within the four walls of the church.

New Age

Many people have questioned whether one religion can universally impact the world today. The world religions today represent wide divergence in theological thought. For instance, a Hindu, a Buddhist, a Muslim, and the Mormon cult have very little common theological ground. However, the recent rising popularity of the New Age Movement makes the possibility of a world religion more palpable. The genius of the New Age lies in its ability to unite divergent religious worldviews into a coherent whole. The basic premise of the New Age is that every member of humanity has the ability to evolve into deity or toward enlightenment.[16] New Ager John White explained, "sooner or later every human being will feel a call from the cosmos to ascend to godhood."[17]

Since one can choose his own route to deity through any religion, the underlying premise of the New Age is that all religions are right and every religion leads to enlightenment. Thus, the Christian Scientists are progressing toward enlightenment through their chosen route. The Hindus are progressing toward enlightenment through their chosen route. The Muslims are progressing toward enlightenment through their chosen route, etc. New Age critic Johanna Michelsen best summarized this inclusive mentality when she observed, "The New Age is the ultimate eclectic religion of self: Whatever *you* decide is right for you is what's right, as long as you don't get narrow-minded and exclusive about it."[18] Under this rubric, spirituality is in vogue; however, biblical Christianity, with its emphasis on doctrine, dogma, and exclusiveness is less attractive. Since all religions are as valid as any other and all religions lead to enlightenment in New Age theology, today's New Age movement may very well be the common thread by which all the religions of the world will unite.

The relationship between the New Age movement and the coming globalism should not be underestimated due to the movement's repeated claim that it will lead humanity into utopia. Just as humanity supposedly evolved upward from the lower animal species, New Agers promise to lead humanity through the next evolutionary phase from its current state into the new world order. According to Ferencz and Keyes, "Despite all of the contemporary stresses and strife, an objective analysis of the historical record will show that humankind is experiencing a continuous—though wobbly—movement toward a more cooperative world order."[19] Elsewhere, these same authors indicated, "We have seen that humankind is not simply moving in a vicious killing circle; it is on *an upward climb* toward completing the governmental structure of the world. We are inspired by our great progress toward planethood."[20]

Gaia Hypothesis

Not only is the advent of the New Age movement setting the stage for the coming one world religion but the prospect of global religion is also greatly enhanced with the rapid spread of the Gaia Hypotheses, otherwise known as mother earth theology. According to this belief, the Earth itself is an actual living, thinking entity. In the words of Thomas Berry, "One of the finest moments in our sensitivity to the natural world is our discovery of the earth as a living organism."[21] Thus, if one does not respond to "Mother Earth" in the proper way, she will "retaliate" against mankind by causing earthquakes and climate problems.[22]

Gaia hypothesis advocate Vaclav Havel explained, "According to the Gaia Hypothesis, we are parts of a greater whole. If we endanger her, she will dispense with us in the interest of a higher value—that is, life itself."[23] James Lovelock similarly argued,

> Gaia is Mother Earth. Gaia is immortal. She is the eternal source of life. She does not need to reproduce herself as she is immortal. She is certainly the mother of us all, including Jesus...Gaia is not a tolerant mother. She is rigid and inflexible, ruthless in the destruction of whoever transgresses. Her unconscious objective is that of maintaining a world adapted to life. If we men hinder this objective we will be eliminated without pity.[24]

Such a belief stands in stark contrast to divine order as revealed in Scripture. "Mother Earth" theology is pantheistic since it confuses the creation and the Creator (Rom. 1:26-27). On the other hand, the Bible teaches the earth is merely an inanimate object. God gave man dominion over the Earth (not the opposite) so he could exercise stewardship over it on God's behalf (Gen. 1:28-30).

Moreover, if "Mother Earth" theology continues to proliferate, it has the potential of doing more to unite the planet than any other belief. It could single-handedly cause the type of totalitarian control prophesied in Revelation 13:16-18. For example, if man should become convinced that his economic activity needs to be regulated in order to prevent "Mother Earth" from retaliating against him, he will submit to control of virtually every aspect of his life. Where men work, what men drive, what type of fuel he uses for transportation, what men eat, and what kind of hair spray is used, etc., will all be subject to international control thereby removing political and economic freedom. According to former Vice-President Al Gore, "we must make the rescue of the environment the central organizing principle for civilization."[25] Coffman noted the corresponding deterioration of human rights if the environment is indeed made "the central organizing principle for civilization." He observed:

> If everything is equal, then everything has equal, intrinsic value. Hence, mankind must change from looking at the world from a "man centered" point of view...to looking at it from a "life centered" perspective...If everything is equal because it is equally god, then man has no more value than a tree, rock, water, mouse, mosquito, rattlesnake, or bubonic plague virus.[26]

Selective Application of the Separation of Church and State Doctrine

Not only are the New Age and Gaia theologies setting the stage for the coming world religion, but the selective application of the separation of church and state doctrine is an equally significant stage setting trend. However, in order to understand this trend one first needs some historical perspective. In 1962 and 1963, the Supreme Court removed voluntary public school prayer and Bible reading, and has subsequently used the precedent established in these cases to eliminate virtually all forms of Christian expression in public life. However, an honest appraisal of these initial decisions shows them to be inconsistent with the vision of the constitution's authors. Consider the following six facts.

First, the court based its ruling on the "wall of separation of church and state" yet none of these words actually appear in the actual language of the First Amendment. The religion clauses of the First Amendment simply read, "Congress shall make no law respecting an establishment of religion, or prohibiting the free exercise thereof." Interestingly, the words "separation of church and state" are actually found in a letter Thomas Jefferson wrote to the Danbury Baptist Association in 1802 as opposed to the First Amendment itself. It is strange to connect Jefferson's words in this letter to the First Amendment since Jefferson was outside the country serving as America's ambassador to France when the Constitution was debated, ratified, and adopted.[27]

Second, the court assumed Jefferson's "wall of separation of church and state" was intended to prohibit the practice of Christian principles in government. However, this historical analysis is suspect. In writing to the Danbury Baptists, Jefferson used this expression to assure them that the federal government would not interfere with their private free exercise of religion. The letter did not address government sponsored religious activity.[28] The wall prevented the government from interfering with Christianity rather than preventing Christianity from influencing government. Moreover, as President, Jefferson supported and signed into law a treaty with the Kaskaskia Indians providing a stipend from the federal treasury to support a missionary to minister to the Kaskaskia Indians.[29]

Third, regarding the issue of religious practices in public schools, the court confidently asserted that the framers of the Constitution would have opposed such a practice. However, the court conveniently ignored the legislative activities of the first congress, which was comprised of those who wrote and adopted the Constitution and the Bill of Rights. This first congress passed the North West Ordinance, which was signed into law by President Washington. Article III of the Northwest Ordinance reads, "Religion, morality, and knowledge being necessary to good government and the happiness of mankind, schools and the means of education shall forever be encouraged."[30] Moreover, it was those who wrote the First Amendment that also placed government-subsidized chaplains into the congress and the military.

Fourth, the court applied the First Amendment's prohibition

of a government-established religion to religious activity occurring at the state level. Such an application contradicts the articulate wording of the religion clauses of the First Amendment, which read, "*Congress* shall make no law respecting an establishment of religion, or prohibiting the free exercise thereof." The First Amendment places the prohibition of establishing a religion on Congress rather than upon the state governments.

Fifth, the court used the Fourteenth Amendment as the medium for making the First Amendment's religion clauses applicable to the states. However, the Fourteenth Amendment has nothing to do with religion. Historically speaking, the Fourteenth Amendment was passed in 1868 during the post-Civil War era to guarantee certain rights to the recently emancipated slaves.

Sixth, by banning voluntary prayer in public schools, the court made the radical move of overturning a 340-year-old tradition in American educational history. The court did so without citing a single precedent. Interestingly, the court later called attention to the non-existence of any precedent cited when it noted, "Finally, in *Engel v. Vitale*, only last year, these principles were so universally recognized that the court, without the citation of a single case...reaffirmed them."[31] Nevertheless, following established precedent is one of the cornerstones of American jurisprudence. Overall, the preceding facts demonstrate how severely the court violated the original intent of the framers of the Constitution in order to remove Christian principles from the public square.

Despite the court's willingness to violate the intent of the Constitution in removing Christianity from public school classrooms, the same court has shown reluctance toward applying the same standard to pagan religious practices. Since nature abhors a vacuum, pagan religious practices quickly filled the void created by the banished Judeo-Christian value system. Consequently, many public school children are still exposed to religious practices. However, these practices are now in the form of New Age visualizing and channeling.[32] In fact, New Agers are quite open in their conviction that the public school classroom is an appropriate venue for proselytizing and evangelizing the next generation with the New Age worldview. Note the words of New Ager John Dunphy.

> I am convinced that the battle for humankind's future must be waged and won in the public school classrooms by teachers who correctly perceive their role as proselytizers of a new faith: a religion of humanity that recognizes and respects the spark of what theologians call the Divinity in every human being. These teachers must embody the same selfless dedication as the most rabid fundamentalist preachers.[33]

Regarding such practices, the court suddenly turned a deaf ear to its cherished separation of church and state doctrine. While one religion was banished from government, another religion was allowed entrance. Thus, separation of church and state has been used selectively to remove Christianity from the public square while simultaneously preparing the way for tax subsidized New Age and occultic practices.

   All of this sets the stage for the coming global religion. In Revelation 17, the woman represents a religious system emanating from Babylon and the beast represents coming global government. The fact that the woman is riding the beast demonstrates the interrelationship that government will have with religion during the tribulation period. However, in order for this scenario to become a reality, Christianity had to have first been banned from public life while being replaced by an alternative belief system. The judiciary's selective employment of the separation of church and state doctrine since the early 1960's has made such an exchange of religions possible. Let the reader now turn attention to some stage setting events taking place within the church.

Ecumenism

   The ecumenical movement seeks to unite all Christendom, whether liberal or conservative, protestant or Catholic, under one common rubric. This concept is nothing new as far as those outside of evangelicalism are concerned. Liberal groups, such as the National Council of Churches, have been traditional advocates of ecumenism. What is new, however, is the recent willingness of evangelicals to support the ecumenical agenda. Nothing epitomizes the new spirit of ecumenism sweeping through evangelicalism more than the 1994 accord known as Evangelicals and Catholics Together. This document, signed by numerous leading evangelicals, called for the recognition of unity between the Catholic and Protestant movements, even to the extent of promising not to proselytize one another. Thus, the document seeks common ground between Catholicism and Protestantism while simultaneously ignoring the insurmountable theological differences between the groups. Such differences include salvation by faith alone, Scripture alone as the sole source of authority for faith and practice, veneration of Christ alone, Christ as the sole mediator between God and man, Christ's effectual once for all death, the exclusion of the non canonical literature, etc.[34]

Evangelical flirtation with ecumenism is also evidenced through the desire of many evangelicals to embrace the creeds of the church as the *sine qua non* of Christianity. If evangelicals can produce a creedal "short list" of what constitutes Christianity, then it becomes possible for them to merge with other groups who believe differently on many other issues while still holding to the same "short list." Charles Colson offers the following definition of "mere Christianity": "Articulated in the classic confessions and creeds, it embraces such fundamentals as the Virgin Birth, the deity of Christ, the Atonement, the Resurrection, the authority of Scripture, and the Second Coming."[35] However, this list omits references to the way of salvation, justification by faith alone, and the sufficiency of Scripture alone as the sole rule of faith and practice.[36] "What in this brief list of doctrines would exclude Mormonism?"[37]

Moreover, using the confessions and creeds of the church as the bare essentials of Christianity is a sketchy proposition. First, it involves a shift in authority from divinely authored Scripture to humanly authored creeds. Second, most of the creeds were originally written for the purpose of dividing by confronting a particular heresy of the day, rather than producing a "short list" for the sake of unity.[38] Third, many of the creeds simply are not complete enough to constitute an exhaustive statement of faith.

For example, the Apostle's Creed does not even address the issue of Christ's deity. Therefore, there is no basis for a Jehovah's Witness who denies Christ's deity not to give full assent to the creed.[39] The creed also omits *sola Scriptura, sola fide,* and the Trinity.[40]

The ecumenical movement is fundamentally flawed because it emphasizes love and unity at the expense of doctrinal truth. Biblical unity centers on truth (Acts 2:42-47) while false unity sacrifices truth (Gen. 11). The first Christians had no interest in the type of ecumenism so rampant in today's church. Mike Gendron explained,

> Jesus brought division, not unity with the Jewish leaders for their pride and spiritual blindness (Mt. 23). Paul did not unite with the Judaizers who loved Jesus but preached another gospel (Gal. 1:6-9). Jude refused to unify with those who crept into the church to pervert the grace of God (Jude 4). John did not seek unity with those who went out from us because they were never really of us (1 Jn. 2:19). Peter never joined hands with false teachers who had forsaken the right way to follow the way of Balaam (2 Pet. 2:15). The writer of Hebrews did not purse unity with those who ignored such a great salvation (Heb. 2:3).[41]

However, as the spirit of ecumenism continues to grow in today's evangelical church, the greater the possibility that evangelicalism could eventually merge with other groups that believe differently and thus find itself as a mere member of the coming global religion.

Doctrinal "Dumbing Down" of Evangelicalism

Perhaps the primary reason why so many believers see themselves on common theological ground with those who have divergent beliefs is because they are unfamiliar with what biblical Christianity actually teaches. Such ignorance can be traced to the fact that very few "conservative" churches emphasize doctrinal teaching. Many of them have fallen prey to the new "seeker friendly" approach to doing church. The main emphasis in seeker-oriented churches[42] is to attract the unsaved to church by offering sermon topics which appeal to the "felt needs" of the unregenerate.[43] Thus, the Bible is used selectively to preach a variety of pragmatic "how to" messages. Those topics that risk offending the unchurched, such as sin, hell, the second coming, etc., are omitted from the church's Sunday morning diet. Such a selective approach creates "canon with the canon" by teaching philosophy that robs the church of the spiritual knowledge necessary to reach maturity. When seeker advocates are confronted with the lack of doctrinal and expositional teaching in their churches, their standard answer is that such teaching occurs at the midweek service or during small group ministry. However, as explained by T. A. McMahon, theory and practice are often two different things.

> As we've noted, most seeker-friendly churches focus much of their time, energy, and resources on accommodating unchurched Harry and Mary. Consequently, week after week, the entire congregation is subjected to a diluted and leavened message. Then, on Wednesday evening, when a fellowship is reduced to a quarter or a third of its normal size, would it be reasonable to assume that his remnant is served a nourishing meal featuring the meat of the word, expositional teaching, and an emphasis on sound doctrine and discipleship? Hardly. We've yet to find a seeker-friendly church where that takes place. The spiritual meals offered at midweek services are usually support group meetings and classes for discerning one's spiritual gifts or going though the latest psycho-babelized "Christian" bestseller...rather than the study of the Scriptures.[44]

Thus, this type of ministry approach inevitably fosters doctrinal ignorance and biblical illiteracy. In fact, seeker advocate Rick Warren seems to minimize unnecessarily the significance of doctrine and exposition. Note the following quotes from his writings: "God won't ask you about your religious background or doctrinal views;"[45] "Jesus said our love *for each other*—not our doctrinal beliefs—is our greatest witness to the world;"[46] "Today many assume that spiritual maturity is measured by the amount of biblical information and doctrine you know;"[47] "The Bible is far more than a doctrinal guidebook;"[48] and, "The last thing many believers need today is to go to another Bible study. They already know far more than they are putting into practice."[49]

It is difficult to harmonize these statements with the priority the early church had for learning apostolic doctrine (Acts 2:42), as well as the constant emphasis Paul gave to doctrine in his Pastoral Epistles. Warren wants to see mature Christian living, but the fact of the matter is the Christian cannot live what he does not know. Although the seeker orientation may represent good marketing, it is poor ecclesiology. The movement finds itself to be inconsistent with God's purpose for the church which is to equip believers to live the Christian life (Eph. 4:11-16). The net effect of the seeker movement is to foster ever continually a lack of discernment in the Body of Christ, thereby making evangelicalism increasingly susceptible to the siren song of the ecumenical movement.

How Then Shall We Live?

Throughout this chapter, the reader has been made aware of the biblical predictions concerning a coming world religion, as well as obvious stage setting occurring both outside and inside the church which are preparing the way for its soon arrival. How should Christians live as they see the seeds of global religion coming to fruition? Christians must take their primary cues from 2 Timothy. The purpose of this book was to admonish Timothy to adhere to the divine pattern of ministry even in the midst of growing opposition and apostasy (2 Tim. 3:1–4:6). It is as if this book was written primarily for today's believers and spiritual leaders living on the eve of the greatest apostasy the world has ever seen. There are three pieces of advice from 2 Timothy this author would like to leave the reader.

First, believers should expect opposition. Paul warned

Timothy that all *who desire to live godly in Christ Jesus will be persecuted* (2 Tim. 3:12). Interestingly, during the tribulation period the global religion is portrayed as being drunk with the blood of Christian martyrs (Rev. 17:6). The global religion will oppose believers because of the natural conflict between the "every road is right" mentality of the global religion and the exclusive claims of Christianity. Nevertheless, Jesus said, "*I am the way, and the truth, and the life; no one comes to the Father, but through Me* (Jn. 14:6). Likewise, Peter said of Jesus Christ, "*And there is salvation in no one else; for there is no other name under heaven that has been given among men, by which we must be saved.* First Timothy 2:5 states, *For there is one God, and one mediator also between God and men, the man Christ Jesus.* In Galatians 2:21, Paul explained if righteousness could be obtained by any other means than faith in the Son of God alone, *then Christ died needlessly.* Jesus said, "*Enter by the narrow gate; for the gate is wide, and the way is broad that leads to destruction, and many are those who enter by it. "For the gate is small, and the way is narrow that leads to life, and few are those who find it* (Mt. 7:13-14). Christianity does not claim to be one among many options, but the only hope for the lost soul. Adherence to these claims will result in believers being in opposition with the wisdom of the global age that says everyone is right as long as one is sincere.

Second, spiritual leaders must restore the priority of doctrine and exposition in their ministries (a message that is clear in 2 Timothy). New Testament scholar Dan Wallace observed that of the 27 commands given in 2 Timothy, 18 of those commands relate in some way to the ministry of the Word. Thus, exactly two thirds of the commands given in the book pertain to doctrine and the ministry of the word.[1] These figures demonstrate the priority that Timothy was to give to doctrine and the Word even in the midst of growing apostasy. Today's spiritual leaders, living on the eve of the coming global religion, should do no less.

Third, spiritual leaders are to give proper attention to the totality of biblical revelation rather than just portions of it. Before Paul commanded Timothy to *preach the word* (2 Tim. 4:2), he first explained that *all Scripture is inspired by God and profitable for teaching* (2 Tim. 3:16). By harmonizing these texts, it should be clear to the reader that Paul admonished Timothy to communicate everything that God has revealed rather than only some aspects of the Word. In ministry, there is always a temptation to speak on those subjects that are pleasant to the listener and minimize those subjects that are unpleasant. As already noted, the seeker approach to ministry seems to advocate such a selective teaching approach. Here Paul explains to Timothy that his focus should not be on what pleases and displeases people; rather, he is to give priority to everything God has revealed. Not only does such attention encompass the pleasant biblical subjects, but the unpleasant ones as well. As ministers obey this admonition, they will find their congregations more discerning, healthy, mature, and equipped to resist the allurement of the coming global religion.

CHAPTER 15

RELIGION OF THE FUTURE

Roger Oakland

*Tell us, when shall these things be? and what **shall be** the sign of thy coming, and of the end of the world?* the disciples asked Jesus (Mt. 24:3). He responded to this question by giving them a number of answers. While the signs that He gave are now setting the stage for prophetic fulfillment, indicating we are indeed living in the last days, there is one sign above all others taking precedence in the list. It was the very first sign that Jesus mentioned. He said the terminal generation could expect widespread deception in His name. This chapter is written with the intent of warning the church concerning this end-times deception which will precede the return of Jesus Christ.[1] At times, this author has attempted to write as a journalist examining the spiritual environment of the times from a biblical perspective. The author's own personal concerns are given regarding the deception that is masquerading in the church in the name of Christ.

Signs, Signs, Everywhere are Signs

Signs and wonders are happening all over the world! Are they genuine? On the other hand, could these be the signs Jesus said would occur before His Second Coming? If these signs and wonders are of God, who would want to be against them? If the signs and wonders were deceptive, then why would anyone want to be for them? Any attempt to answer these questions will naturally invite great controversy.

The Bible states believers should *mark them which cause*

divisions (Rom. 16:17). The Bible also teaches that unity within the body of Christ is very important. However, what is the biblical definition of unity? Can Christianity be based on false ideas, error, deception, or lying signs and wonders? What does the Bible claim? Should the Bible be overlooked in order to fabricate a false unity in the name of Christ? Is it not critical for Christian unity to be based always on the truth?

While those who question ecumenism are often labeled divisive and narrow-minded, the Bible does command that the Word of God be carefully presented. While this author has often been accused of being divisive, he wonders sometime if this is due to misunderstood. For instance, if Romans 16:17 is read in its entire context the reader will see the whole picture. Paul wrote, *Now I beseech you, brethren, mark them which cause divisions and offenses contrary to the doctrine which ye have learned; and avoid them.* According to Paul, those who teach contrary to what the Bible teaches cause divisiveness.

Before writing this chapter, God's help was sought, as the author is not looking for more controversy. However, what is a Christian to do when witnessing an ongoing trend that the Bible warns would occur? On the other hand, what should the response be when some are saying "these are the signs and wonders that we have been anticipating that will now prepare the way for Jesus to come?" One of these two views must be wrong. If the signs are from God, then warning people against them would be blasphemous. If the signs are false, then the consequences are very serious and many people could be deceived if they are not warned.

Supporters of the "signs and wonders" are convinced they are right. They often question those who say they are wrong? Is it not unbiblical to attack a well-known pastor or a famous evangelist? What about the healings and people being raised from the dead? Did not Jesus say His church could do what He did? Is this author saying that "signs and wonders" do not follow the preaching of the gospel?

Oftentimes, another argument is given. Why would anyone be so bold to speak out against a revival? Is the person more interested in eschatology than knowing the truth? Another one of the author's critics actually said, "No wonder you suffer so much hardship and your son was killed in an accident—you are guilty of blaspheming the Holy Ghost." Yes, this author has heard all these questions, comments, and accusations. People write or call the ministry everyday. One brother actually said, "The whole world is coming to Jesus whether you believe it or not. If you do not stop what you are doing, I am predicting God will take you out."

Of course, this author regards such claims seriously. Who would want to blaspheme God? Who would want to be personally responsible for holding back a genuine revival? This is a serious matter! If the critics are right, then this author is wrong and a tool of the devil as they say. As well, hell is a real place, and this author does not want to go there, nor anyone else that he knows.

"Signs and wonders are following the preaching of the simple gospel," many say. Could this be the great revival the "New Wine Movement" has been predicting? Alternatively, is there a possibility the world is being prepared for a final grand delusion mentioned in the Bible (cf. 2 Thess. 2)? While many have contacted the author expressing appreciation for his biblical position on the New Wine Movement, others have indicated disappointment and have stated that such criticisms are dividing the body of Christ and blaspheming the Holy Spirit. One person told this author, he had no right to say the New Wine Movement is connected with the apostasy the Bible teaches will happen before the Antichrist is revealed. By boldly proclaiming, "this is that," this author was told, he would someday stand before God and answer for having prevented people from becoming part of the great end-times revival that is supposedly underway in the world today.

Broad is the Road and Narrow is the Way

Many are saying that a global manifestation of "signs and wonders" will be essential for the spreading of the gospel on a worldwide scale. Over the past several decades, experience-based Christians have been promoting a style of evangelism that requires "Christian unity" as the prerequisite. Unity in the name of Christ, they say, produces miracles that are attributed to Christ. These methods, better known as "power evangelism," are based upon the premise that "signs and wonders" bring about conversions to Christ which are necessary to usher in the second coming of Jesus Christ.

However, a careful study of the Bible indicates before the return of Jesus to earth there will be a time when people should be cautious about signs and wonders. Jesus said the signs and wonders at this time would be of the deceptive variety (Mt. 24:24). Paul also warned about such supernatural phenomena as part of a grand delusion that would deceive many and prepare the way for the Antichrist (2 Thess. 2: 9). Jesus also proclaimed a warning about a faith focused primarily on the miraculous. He said many would be deceived and spend eternity in hell; even though they had experienced supernatural phenomenon in His name, they had never understood the simple gospel (Mt. 7:21-23).

On another occasion Jesus warned about the dangers of seeking after signs and wonders. He said, *Why doth this generation seek after a sign? verily I say unto you, There shall no sign be given unto this generation* (Mk. 8:12). Later in the same chapter, Jesus made it clear to His followers that they should understand the true reason for following Him. He declared, *Whosoever will come after me, let him deny himself, and take up his cross, and follow me. For whosoever will save his life shall lose it; but whosoever shall lose his life for my sake and the gospel's, the same shall save it* (8:34-35).

It is obvious that Jesus placed a high priority on understanding the gospel. He did not seem to promote the idea that people should seek Him for signs and wonders alone. Therefore, what is more important: to experience healing, then later die and go to hell, or to understand the gospel and live forever?

One final example from the Scriptures confirms Jesus was not supportive of people following Him for the sake of miracles. Although Jesus is the God of true miracles, and it is true that signs and miracles followed the good news of His preaching, people must not follow miracles for the sake of following miracles. They must understand the gospel. If they do not, there is great potential for deception in Christ's name. John 2:23-25 reads, *Now when he was in Jerusalem at the passover, in the feast day, many believed in his name, when they saw the miracles which he did. But Jesus did not commit himself unto them, because he knew all men. And needed not that any should testify of man: for he knew what was in man.*

Based on the words and actions of Jesus, as recorded in the Bible, it would seem that signs and wonders are secondary to the preaching of the true gospel. Should believers not pay attention to what Jesus has said and done? Furthermore, how can one know for sure if the reported miracles are genuine or counterfeit? Is Satan deceiving the masses and is mankind experiencing a preview of a future delusion that will send many to hell? Before making a judgment, it would be important to check out the facts. Remember, the road to hell is wide and many are those who travel on it. While the way to heaven is a narrow way, it is possible to travel this road if you understand the gospel. There is one thing the reader can know for sure: believing in the gospel of Jesus Christ is the means to enter heaven not "signs and wonders." Of course, time will tell who is right and who is wrong. Meanwhile, remember that the consequences of being wrong are very serious. Eternity is a long time to spend in hell and there are no second chances to escape.

Revival or Apostasy?

This author is not convinced the Bible teaches there will be a great revival in the last days before Jesus returns. Jesus commissioned his church to preach the gospel worldwide (Mt. 28:18-20). Many in the church, of course, are being faithful to the Great Commission. There are many around the world today who are responding to the gospel and becoming genuine believers and followers of Jesus Christ. As this author has traveled throughout the world over the past two decades, it has become obvious that God is touching many lives. Those who were once in darkness have been delivered and are now in the Kingdom of God. However, to say that a massive revival is occurring and that nearly the whole world will embrace Jesus as their true

Savior is not found in the Scriptures (cf. Mt. 7:13-14). Instead, there seems to be strong evidence indicating that Satan will be the inspiration behind a great end-times delusion that will lead many people into eternal damnation.

The Bible teaches ever since Adam and Eve's disobedience, Satan has been active with his scheme to deceive mankind. One of his techniques is to fool people into believing there is more they need to know than what God has revealed to man through His Word. One of the devil's favorite tactics is combining God's Word with extra-biblical revelation or experience. Since the time that Satan deceived Eve to eat from the forbidden tree, mankind has been vulnerable to his deceptive plan.

The Bible is also clear that God has always been faithful to warn the world about the dangers of seeking experiences which can lead people astray. In the Old Testament era, God used the prophets to warn His people. As God has warned mankind in the past, so too, His warnings are still relevant today. Today is a time for people who love God to scrutinize all they are being taught and to be certain the teaching is faithful to God's Word.

A Battle Is Raging

In the Book of Ephesians, Paul, writing by the inspiration of the Holy Spirit, clarified that our battle as humans is not against fellow humans. There are forces at work in an unseen realm, or spiritual dimension, whose plan is to separate mankind eternally from the God of the universe. Paul also stated that Satan is a master schemer and a clever manipulator (Eph. 6:10-12). Knowing that Satan has a scheme to deceive the world, should not believers be alert to his devices? If the most important truth found in the Bible is God's plan of eternal salvation through Jesus Christ, would it not be reasonable to assume Satan would try to convince people they were going to heaven by using Christ's name, when in reality they were not?

The Battle Plan

Today many people are redefining the term "salvation." The way to heaven, which Jesus said is narrow (Mt. 7:13-14), is becoming wider every day according to them. There are many who believe salvation is based upon tradition or what some man or organization claims as truth. Others are already convinced they are believers because they have experienced the miraculous in Jesus' name. However, Jesus said he will judge the entire world one day, and many people will be surprised to discover they are not true Christians (instead they will have been deceived to think they were believers because they had a supernatural experience in the name of Jesus). As opposed to entering heaven, they will spend eternity in hell (7:21-23).

With this portion of Scripture in mind, it is clear that Christianity based on teachings that are extra-biblical can be misleading (even damning; 2 Pet. 2:1). Certainly, Christians can have experiences, but the experiences must be based on the Bible. Satan is a master at counterfeiting the spiritual gifts God has given to His church. When people seek after extra-biblical experiences or use these practices as a focus to draw people together in unity for the sake of unity, the resulting unity may be spiritually catastrophic.

The Bible teaches true faith is based upon hearing God's Word (Rom. 10:17). Therefore, apostasy (a falling away from the cardinal teachings of the Christian faith) must be a faith that is not based on the Bible. If someone is an apostate, he has fallen away from a faith in God and His Word for a faith in something else.

Thy Word is Truth

This chapter has been written as a love letter and a call to awake all people who profess the name of Jesus Christ. Therefore, this chapter has been written to all Protestants and Roman Catholics. It is also the author's desire that others who do not profess to be Christians would also read this chapter.

It needs to be clearly stated here that not all who are in the New Wine Movement and are embracing extra-biblical experiences are apostates. In fact, many people who are part of this group are sincerely God-loving people. They desire to live effective lives for Jesus Christ. However, many of these same people say they have discovered new manifestations of the power of

God, when there is no basis for these manifestations in the Word of God.

As this chapter was being written, daily prayer for wisdom and the ability to present what God had placed upon the author's heart in a way that would not offend readers was exercised. It is because of the controversial nature of this chapter, the author recognizes that some who read it will undoubtedly still be offended. The challenge then to the reader is that every page be examined according to the Word of God. Anything in this chapter that is not biblically based should be rejected.

The Counterfeit Bride

The author has made a connection between the New Wine Movement, and what he calls the "Babylonian Vine" from the words written by the apostle John, found in the Book of Revelation. In the seventeenth chapter, John wrote:

> And there came one of the seven angels which had the seven vials, and talked with me, saying unto me, Come hither; I will show unto thee the judgment of the great whore that sitteth upon many waters: With whom the kings of the earth have committed fornication, and the inhabitants of the earth have been made drunk with the wine of her fornication. So he carried me away in the spirit into the wilderness: and I saw a woman sit upon a scarlet colored beast, full of names of blasphemy, having seven heads and ten horns. And the woman was arrayed in purple and scarlet color, and decked with gold and precious stones and pearls, having a golden cup in her hand full of abominations and filthiness of her fornication: And upon her forehead *was* a name written, MYSTERY, BABYLON THE GREAT, THE MOTHER OF HARLOTS AND ABOMINATIONS OF THE EARTH (Rev. 17:1-5).

Throughout the New Testament, the true church is represented as the bride of Christ. The reader should know that the only way to become a part of this true church is by the narrow path which is the gospel of Jesus Christ. In the Book of Revelation, the harlot represents a counterfeit bride, or movement, that prepares the way for a counterfeit Christ. Although this ecumenical religion will be in the name of Christ, it will be based upon a religious worldview that embraces many of the pagan practices that originated at Babylon (as recorded in Genesis 11).

In the eighteenth chapter of the Book of Revelation more detail is given concerning the incredible impact this false religious movement is going to have upon the whole world. John stated, *For all nations have drunk of the wine of the wrath of her fornication, and the kings of the earth have committed fornication with her, and the merchants of the earth are waxed rich through the abundance of her delicacies* (18:3). Then, in the nineteenth chapter of Revelation, John explains what will happen to the counterfeit bride. In his own words: *And after these things I heard a great voice of much people in heaven, saying, Alleluia; Salvation, and glory, and honor, and power, unto the Lord our God: For true and righteous are his judgments: for he hath judged the great whore, which did corrupt the earth with her fornication, and hath avenged the blood of his servants at her hand* (19:1-2).

Judgment is Coming

The Bible states that a terrible time of judgment is coming upon this earth for those who have willingly rejected the true gospel of Jesus Christ. While many have said they have joined a new movement, tasted of the "new wine" and know that it is real, because they have "become drunk in the Spirit," the present author is concerned these same people may have become spiritually intoxicated. This is a time for sober contemplation. *Therefore let us not sleep, as do others; but let us watch and be sober. For they that sleep sleep in the night; and they that be drunken are drunken in the night. But let us, who are of the day, be sober, putting on the breastplate of faith and love; and for a helmet, the hope of salvation* (1 Thess. 5:6-8).

Searching for the Truth

True believers should demonstrate a God given passion for the truth and a compassion for the deceived. Whenever something is read or taught, it needs to be compared with Scripture. One of the author's favorite verses is found in Matthew 22:29. Jesus said to the Sadducees, *Ye do err, not knowing the scriptures, nor the power of God.* It is not a matter of just the "Word" or just the "Spirit." The Christian's spiritual lifeline should be based upon a balance between the Word and the Spirit, and this balance only the Word can reveal.

What a great privilege it is to know believers have been given God's Word and His Spirit to reveal His truth! The Word of God has been given to believers by God and will help them to understand Satan's deceptive plan for the last days. The author's prayer is that everyone who reads this chapter will do so with reverence and trust the Bible more than before and see the danger of tasting the new wine from the Babylonian vine before it is tragically too late.

Deception in His Name

Although the New Testament was written almost two thousand years ago by men inspired by God, every Bible-believing person knows the words are still relevant and applicable to spiritual matters today. On one occasion, when Paul was writing the church at Corinth, he warned them about leaving the simple truth of the gospel and getting caught up in deception that would attack them three different ways. *But I fear, lest by any means, as the serpent beguiled Eve through his subtlety, so your minds should be corrupted from the simplicity that is in Christ. For if he that cometh preacheth another Jesus, whom we have not preached, or if ye receive another spirit, which ye have not received, or another gospel, which ye have not accepted ye might well bear with him* (2 Cor. 11:3-4). If one were to translate what Paul wrote to the Corinthian church into modern-day language, it would sound something like the following:

Do not complicate the gospel. Keep it simple. Watch out that the same devil that tricked Eve does not trick you.

Just because one is a Christian does not mean he is immune to deception. Satan likes to trick people in the name of Christ, and in order to do so, he makes people think they believe in Jesus, when in reality they do not know Jesus at all. Rather than being led by the Holy Spirit, an unholy deceptive spirit can delude one into believing in a counterfeit gospel instead of the true gospel.

Correction or Compromise

The trend preparing the world for an experience-based Christianity continues to escalate. More people are traveling to an increasing number of places where they say God is manifesting Himself through signs and wonders. Those who caution others to beware of deception in the name of Christ are now becoming a minority.

Christianity that is biblically based must always be focused on a personal relationship with Jesus Christ. However, history reveals there has always been a tendency for Christians to stray away from this essential tenet of the faith. There are many ways to have worship and devotion to Christ diverted. Seeking after extra-biblical revelation from angels, or placing too much emphasis on a biblical personality like Mary, are two examples that start the list. Although the gospel is not complicated, it is easy to complicate.

Satan, God's adversary, is a master at deceiving mankind. It is because the gospel is a narrow way that is predicated upon faith in Jesus Christ alone that Satan has numerous schemes for inspiring people to believe in a counterfeit form of Christianity. The imitation may look and feel like the real thing, but in reality it is an abomination to the One who shed His blood on the cross.

A study of the Apostle Paul's writings is clear that the early church was constantly falling into Satan's plan to complicate the gospel or pervert the basic message in some way. After warning the Corinthians about leaving the simple gospel for another gospel, he told them why the church was being led astray. He wrote, *For such **are** false apostles, deceitful workers, transforming themselves into the apostles of Christ. And no marvel; for Satan himself is transformed into an angel of light. Therefore **it is** no great thing if his ministers also be transformed as the ministers of righteousness; whose end shall be according to their works* (2 Cor. 11:13-15).

It is obvious Paul was concerned about false doctrines that were being propagated by false teachers who were Satan's agents masquerading as followers of Jesus Christ. In his letter to Timothy, Paul warned that these *doctrines of demons* would intensify in the last days as part of the apostasy to impact the body of Christ (1 Tim. 4:1). Nowhere in any of Paul's writings can one find a precedent that permits believers to compromise and embrace teachings that are not biblically based.

Although Paul wrote about the importance of unity and brotherly love, neither he nor any other writer whose words were inspired to appear in the Bible, give authority to seek after unity for the sake of unity and forsake the truth. The Scriptures teach that Paul corrected the church when it embraced error. He never made a practice of dialoguing or entertaining the false doctrines that were propagated by false teachers. He always corrected false teaching with a passion for the truth and a compassion for the deceived. Is the church, both corporately and individually, willing to follow Paul's example? Although confronting this heresy may not be popular, it is biblically correct!

The Serpent's Lie

A foundational principle of Christianity is the Bible is true. Hence, if the Bible is true and the Bible states that God has an adversary, would it not be reasonable to believe that Satan—God's adversary—would do everything possible to deceive people from coming to the knowledge of the truth? What methods does Satan use to accomplish his plan? Are these methods still in effect today?

The Bible, consisting of the Old and the New Testament, contains the good news of the gospel of Jesus Christ. The gospel of Jesus Christ proclaims that individuals can be reconciled to

God and spend eternity with Him if they will acknowledge their sin and believe that Jesus died in their place on Calvary's cross. The Bible is also clear that Satan has an agenda to blind mankind from understanding this plan. Since the rebellion of man in the Garden of Eden, hundreds of millions of people throughout the generations have fallen into Satan's plan.

Although the Bible teaches hell was prepared for the devil and his angels, man who willfully rejects God's plan of salvation has the same destiny (Mt. 25:41). The apostle Peter warned about Satan's tactics. He wrote, *Be sober, be vigilant; because your adversary the devil, as a roaring lion, walketh about, seeking whom he may devour* (1 Pet. 5:8). John described Satan's agenda in the Book of Revelation by stating Satan was the one *who deceives the whole world* (Rev. 12:9). Satan is alive and well and his plan to deceive is still very effective.

He is a Schemer

How does Satan intend to deceive mankind, and how can believers identify when someone has been deceived unknowingly? Does the Bible indicate what to notice that will help prevent self from falling into the same trap?

The best manner to understand man's vulnerability to deception is to review briefly what happened when man was first deceived. Satan, whom the Bible calls the father of lies (Jn. 8:44), came to the first woman, Eve, and initiated a conversation that triggered man's rebellion.

> Now the serpent was more subtle than any beast of the field which the LORD God had made. And he said unto the woman, Yea, hath God said, Ye shall not eat of every tree of the garden? And the woman said unto the serpent, We may eat of the fruit of the trees of the garden: But of the fruit of the tree which *is* in the midst of the garden, God hath said, Ye shall not eat of it, neither shall ye touch it, lest ye die. And the serpent said unto the woman, Ye shall not surely die: For God doth know that in the day ye eat thereof, then your eyes shall be opened, and ye shall be as gods, knowing good and evil (Gen. 3:1-5).

It is obvious that Satan caused Eve to doubt the words of God. Additionally, he suggested to her that extra revelation was the key for her successful future. It was this lie that brought about the fall of mankind. Certainly Satan's deceptive methods have not changed to this day.

Nothing New Under the Sun

According to the inspired words of Solomon, *there is no new thing under the sun*. Whatever has occurred in the past will reoccur. History merely repeats itself in cycles (Eccl. 1:9-10). Therefore, if Satan has a master plan to deceive mankind, and if his plan has been successful in the past, should one not expect that he is still at work today?

Secondly, the Bible reveals that an understanding of the physical realm is not complete unless one considers the spiritual dimension that God also created. All of mankind has grown accustomed to analyzing the world around him through the use of the five senses. Man can touch, feel, smell, taste, and hear what occurs in the surrounding world. Although the spiritual dimension is just as real, one is not able to perceive its presence under normal everyday experiences.

To comprehend fully the history of mankind, it is necessary to understand the role the spiritual dimension has performed since the fall of man in the Garden of Eden. The Bible is clear that man is not the only intelligent being that exists in the universe. For example, God also created the angelic realm. These spirit beings are able to manifest themselves to humans and then dematerialize.

Satan, the leader of the fallen angelic realm, was the first spirit being to interfere in the affairs of mankind. He appeared to Eve in the form of a serpent and enticed her to disobey God and His Word. He suggested that there was another dimension available to her if she was to partake of the fruit of the forbidden tree. Instead of being confined here on earth with limited knowledge, man could know both good and evil and have the capability of being *as gods*, he said (v. Gen. 3:1-5).

Satan's claims were partially true. If he could cause man to disobey God and follow him, he would be able to take mankind captive as hostages with him on his way to eternal damnation. Certainly, biblical history reveals Satan's plan has been fruitful. There is a clear pattern repeated many times throughout human history. Although God has revealed His grace to mankind throughout the ages, fallen human beings still have a tendency to resist God's plan of salvation and instead follow the fallen angelic realm that has an objective to deceive mankind.

It Is Not Flesh and Blood

Writing to the Ephesians, Paul stated, *For we wrestle not against flesh and blood, but against principalities, against powers, against the rulers of the darkness of this world, against spiritual wickedness in high places* (Eph. 6:12). These words are absolutely true despite what many Bible skeptics would like some to believe. Yes, according to the Bible, intelligent spirit beings do exist. Some are holy and some are not. The unholy ones are commonly called demons (or fallen angels). When mankind attempts to communicate with this spiritual dimension he will be deceived.

The Bible prohibits believers from being involved in an attempt to contact the fallen spirit world. Paul wrote, *For there is one God, and one mediator between God and men, the man Christ Jesus* (1 Tim. 2:5). Are believers rejecting these words and being prepared for a final delusion? The Scriptures say yes! The experience-based Christianity is proof the delusion is presently underway.

Apostasy and Bible Prophecy

The Bible is a unique book. No other book has ever been written basing its entire credence upon the claim that the statements it contains about the future must occur with one hundred percent accuracy. While this statement may seem too incredible for skeptics who refuse to believe the Bible is the Word of God, there are many who study Bible prophecy that stand firmly behind this claim. History reveals countless Bible prophecies have already been fulfilled. The unfolding of current events demonstrates numerous prophecies are in the process of being fulfilled. This chapter will present the biblical foundation showing the Bible predicts great deception will take place in the name of Christ in the last days.

Deception in His Name

In Matthew 24, the Bible relates that one day Jesus' disciples approached Him privately and asked what signs would indicate His second coming was near. *Tell us*, they said, *when shall these things be, and what shall be the sign of thy coming, and of the end of the world?* (Mt. 24:3). Jesus responded to them by presenting a list of events that could be expected before His second coming. He mentioned there would be *wars and rumours of wars* and that nations would rise up against other nations (24:6-7). He said famines and earthquakes would be common all around the world (24:7). He claimed that human behavior would be characterized by lawlessness, and that society would be just like it was in the days of Noah (24:12). Additionally, Jesus said another sign His return would be soon would be the *gospel of the kingdom shall be preached in all the world for a witness unto all nations; and then shall the end come* (24:14).

While Jesus talked concerning all of these signs indicating His second coming was near, it seems He emphasized one sign above all others. The first sign that He mentioned is that there would be many who *shall deceive many* (24:3-4). More specifically, the last days would be a time when deception would take place in His name. He clarified this by saying, *For there shall arise false Christs, and false prophets, and shall shew great signs and wonders; insomuch that, if it were possible, they shall deceive the very elect. Behold, I have told you before* [in advance] (24:24-25).

This statement Jesus made was not just for the disciples gathered together with Him on the Mount of Olives. The statement is relevant and true for anyone who is willing to take His Word seriously today. If Bible prophecy concerns knowing the future in advance with absolute accuracy, then it would be wise to be attentive. It is obvious Jesus said what He said for the purpose of warning those who would live in the days before His return to beware of being deceived. Notice that He made it very clear that the deception to spread worldwide would be in His name. Obviously, the fulfillment of Matthew 24 will occur during the seven years of the tribulation, but it is appropriate to understand the current deception as setting the stage for this prophetic fulfillment.

Great Apostasy or Great Revival?

There is a much discussion today in Christian groups concerning "the great revival that must take place before Jesus can return." While every genuine Bible-believing Christian should have a desire to see unbelievers saved so they will not face judgment (not only regarding the temporal judgment of the last days scenario, but also the eternal judgment which will follow), it is equally important for them to be aware of the deception that Jesus said would even impact believers.

Jesus warned that lying signs and wonders would be instrumental in leading people astray before He returned (Mt. 24:23-25). Obviously, lying signs and wonders have the potential of deceiving people into a lost eternity. When Jesus was speaking at the Sermon on the Mount, He taught He would determine the eternal destiny of all mankind. As Judge of all humanity, Jesus said there would actually be individuals who believe they are believers when in reality their eternal destiny will be the Lake of Fire. In Jesus' own words: *Not every one that saith unto me, Lord, Lord, shall enter into the kingdom of heaven; but he that doeth the will of my Father which is in heaven. Many will say to me in that day, Lord, Lord, have we not prophesied in thy name? and in thy name have cast out devils? and in thy name done many wonderful works? And then will I profess unto them, I never knew you: depart from me, ye that work iniquity* (7:21-23).

It seems apparent that these words of Jesus should be taken seriously. The cost of being deceived into believing one is a Christian, when in reality he or she is not, is eternal separation from God. Believing in Jesus requires a true understanding of the gospel, not just an experiential encounter in the name of Christ.

The Miracle Man

The apostle Paul also warned that lying signs and wonders

in the last days would deceive people. This would occur as part of the delusion that would be the prerequisite for the Antichrist. The deluding influence would be part of Satan's strategy to seduce the world into the preparation for the counterfeit bride for the counterfeit Christ. As Paul stated: *Even him, whose coming is after the working of Satan with all power and signs and lying wonders, And with all deceivableness of unrighteousness in them that perish; because they received not the love of the truth, that they might be saved. And for this cause God shall send them strong delusion, that they should believe a lie* (2 Thess. 2:9-11).

Paul also stated that the church would play a key role in the prelude to the revelation of the man who will claim to be God. This whole scenario could not happen, Paul wrote to the Thessalonians, until after apostasy happened. He wrote, *Let no man deceive you by any means: for **that day shall not come**, except there come a falling away first, and that man of sin be revealed, the son of perdition; Who opposeth and exalteth himself above all that is called God, or that is worshipped; so that he as God sitteth in the temple of God, showing himself that he is God* (2 Thess. 2:3-4).

The word *apostasy* means a falling away from the faith.[2] The Bible states *faith **cometh** by hearing, and hearing by the word of God* (Rom. 10:17). Therefore, an apostate faith is a faith based on extra-biblical ideas, or experiences, to convince people they are genuine believers when they are not.

Doctrines of Demons

Although the Bible teaches the day is coming when *every knee should bow* (Phil. 2:9-11) to Jesus Christ, that day is still in the future. Satan and his followers still heavily influence the present world. The *god of this world* (2 Cor. 4:3-4) which Paul described is still alive and quite active.

In addition, the Bible teaches end-times deception is not an exception. Instead, it is the rule. Although God's power is greater than what the devil has to offer, this does not mean believers can ignore Satan's devices. The Bible warns that the great deceiver is *like a roaring lion seeking whom he may devour* (1 Pet. 5:8), and such deception can occur at any hour.

In other words, it is wise to be alert to biblical teaching about deception in the last days. Some have said, "We have to have more faith in God's ability to bless us than in Satan's ability to deceive us."[3] Although there is an element of truth in this statement, there is much more to be said. When people willingly ignore God's warnings in His Word, they become certain candidates for the doctrines devised by demons.

In light of Bible prophecy, believers need not speculate about Satan's ability to be involved in sowing the seeds for apostasy. This is merely a biblical fact. As Paul wrote to Timothy, *Now the Spirit speaketh expressly, that in the latter times some shall depart from the faith, giving heed to seducing spirits, and doctrines of devils* (1 Tim. 4:1). If this were the only verse in the entire New Testament indicating there would be spiritual deception in the last days, would that not be enough? However, there are numerous others that add to the deception complexion. Satan is the deceiver and deception is his strategy. In the last days, his agenda will certainly intensify.

Jannes and Jambres

A great word of warning concerning the danger of using signs and wonders as an end-times tool for evangelism needs to be emanated. It is clear from the Old Testament that Satan is a master of conjuring signs and wonders as a means of showing he can operate in the paranormal realm.

One example can be found in the Book of Exodus. There is a situation in which Moses, Aaron, and Pharaoh were involved in a supernatural signs and wonders demonstration. When Aaron's staff was turned into a serpent, the Pharaoh called for his sorcerers and magicians to repeat the same (Exod. 7:8-11). In the New Testament, Paul identifies these Egyptian signs and wonders experts by name. As part of his end-times dissertation to Timothy, he warned about the appearance of similar last day charlatans. *Now as Jannes and Jambres withstood Moses, so do these also resist the truth: men of corrupt minds, reprobate concerning the faith. But they shall proceed no further: for their folly shall be manifest unto all men, as theirs also was* (2 Tim. 3:8-9).

Once more it is evident the Bible teaches there will be a concentrated demonic effort in the last days to deceive people from the authentic faith which is based upon the Bible. With this in mind, it is interesting to note that mankind is living in a period of history when many people are talking about faith. However, what is this faith that is occupying their conversation? If the whole world is going to experience a biblical faith, then why would Jesus have said the following: *Nevertheless when the Son of man cometh, shall he find faith on the earth?* (Lk. 18:8)? Today is a time to be serious concerning the biblical faith. A faith based upon tradition or a belief system that has been introduced by some extra-biblical experience is most certainly not true biblical faith. If the church does not heed the warning from Scripture, then she could be fooling herself.

New Wine or Old Deception?

It is happening everywhere. Many are saying the church is living in the midst of a spiritual awakening. Such individuals declare God is pouring out His Spirit on believers and unbelievers, and the church is going to witness the greatest revival in history. Now is the time to "catch the wave" and renounce old religious ideas, they insist. The church has arrived. This is the new era that so many have been predicting for decades. Members of the church must embrace the Holy Spirit's new strategies for revival or be left behind.

A few years ago, *Charisma* featured a major article foretelling the future of the body of Christ. On the front cover, the following statement was made: "Fasten your seat belt. A Christian revival could sweep the world in the next 25 years."[4] Like others who espouse the final end-times great revival, *Charisma* has been promoting this idea that God is pouring out a new anointing to prepare an army of God to win the world for Jesus in these last days. Some are also saying, "Experiencing God's power by imbibing the new wine is proof one has enlisted as a member of God's army." The more unity there is in the body of Christ, the more signs and wonders will occur. According to the proponents of the New Wine Movement, more people will come to Christ when more signs and wonders are demonstrated.

The Fire is Spreading

A 1997 issue of *Charisma* contained a feature article called "The Blessing Spreads Worldwide." The leading paragraph stated, "Since an unusual spiritual renewal movement erupted in 1994, many Christian leaders have become convinced that a global revival is on the way."[v] According to this New Wine theology, a "fire" that was lit at the Toronto Airport Vineyard (now the Airport Christian Fellowship) in January of 1994 is now being transferred worldwide. Proponents say the Toronto "blessing" is transferable and contagious. Once a person receives "it," he can give "it" away to others.[6]

Writing for *Charisma*, Marcia Ford retraced the origin of the blessing back to Pastor John Arnott. He and his wife Carol claimed they received their anointing from Claudio Freidzon while in South America. Claudio Freidzon had received his anointing from Benny Hinn.[7] Hinn claims he received a special empowerment when he came in close contact with the bones of Kathryn Kuhlman.[8] Another source of this New Wine anointing for the Toronto church was St. Louis Vineyard pastor Randy Clark.[9] He received an "anointing" from self-proclaimed "Holy Spirit bartender" Rodney Howard-Browne.[10] Howard-Browne is convinced that God appointed him to light the fire of revival around the world.[11]

From Toronto this "blessing" has spread to many countries throughout the world. Recipients have taken the blessing to their homes in England, South Africa, Australia, and even Mainland China.[12] The Brownsville Assembly of God in Pensacola also received a double-dose of the blessing. Senior pastor John Kilpatrick's wife brought it from the Toronto Airport Christian Fellowship.[13] Evangelist Steve Hill received his "anointing" while attending the Holy Trinity Brompton Church in London, England, and then brought it to Florida.[14] Now, the Pensacola Assemblies of God church promotes a variation of the Toronto Blessing called "the river of God."[15]

The "river of God" has been the central focus of the teachings to emerge from the Brownsville Assemblies of God in

Pensacola. According to a full page advertisement in the December 1996 issue of *Charisma*, over one million people have traveled to Pensacola to receive a "touch from God." Afterwards they return home and "spread the fire" to their own churches.[16]

The fire that is being transferred, according to these enthusiasts, does not come from a burning flame. The method of receiving the "fire" comes by letting "the river of God surround, uphold, refresh and at times overwhelm you."[17] The biblical basis for this new doctrine, supporters say, can be found in Ezekiel chapter 47. According to this interpretation of Scripture, Ezekiel saw a vision of a river that flowed from the Temple of God. This river is supposed to be the river now flowing in churches where people are open to the "new thing" God is doing.

The Anointing

The New Wine Movement and the new "anointing" are inseparable. When a person is said to "catch the fire" he will receive "it." Nearly everyone who has received this experience has his own personal story. The following is an account given by John Arnott, senior pastor of the Toronto Airport Christian Fellowship.

> We heard about the revival in Argentina so we traveled there in November of 1993, hoping that God's anointing would rub off on us somehow. We were powerfully touched in a meeting led by Claudio Freidzon, a leader of the Assemblies of God in Argentina.[18]

According to Arnott, he was touched by an encounter with a spiritual leader who had some type of power which was apparently transferred to him. This occurred when Claudio Freidzon prayed and touched John and Carol Arnott. John fell and then was able to stand. At first, he questioned whether or not this experience was his own flesh or from God. Then something else happened. Freidzon asked Arnott if he wanted the "anointing." As Arnott described,

"Oh yes, I want *it* all right," I answered. "Then take *it*!"
He slapped my outstretched hands. "I will. I will take
it," I said. Something clicked in my heart at that
moment. It was as though I heard the Lord say, "For
goodness sake, will you take *this*? Take *it, it's* yours."
And I received by faith.[19]

The Transferable Anointing

One of the central themes of the New Wine Movement is the
idea that the Spirit of God is a transferable anointing. Once
received, it is commonly believed, this anointing can be given
away to others. Often the word "impartation" is used by those
who believe they have this God-given ability. However, it can
easily be documented that the concept of impartation is not new.
During the late 1940's, this doctrine was promoted by an aberrant group of experience-focused Christians from North
Battleford, Saskatchewan, Canada known as the Latter Rain
Movement.

The "impartation" concept that certain individuals are capable of receiving and then imparting an anointing was one of the
main reasons many church leaders declared the Latter Rain
teachings heretical. While this and other Latter Rain teachings
had a major impact throughout North America and some parts
of Europe, strong opposition by Bible teachers who supported
sound biblical doctrine, forced the "manifest sons of God" belief
underground. Richard Riss, a staunch supporter of the Latter
Rain Movement, writes about this in his book *The Latter
Rain*.[20]

At a General Council meeting held by the Assemblies of
God in Seattle, Washington, in the fall of 1949, a resolution
was adopted disapproving the practices of what was termed
"The New Order of the Latter Rain." A number of specific
concerns were listed in this document. Among these were "the
overemphasis to the imparting, identifying, bestowing and con-
firming of gifts by laying on of hands and prophecy" and "the
erroneous teaching that the Church is built upon the foundation
of the present-day apostles and prophets." The official disap-
proval concluded by stating,

Such other wrestings and distortions of Scripture interpretations which are in opposition to teachings and practices generally accepted among us. For it be further
resolved, that we recommend following those things
which make for peace among us, and those doctrines and
practices whereby we may edify one another, endeavor-
ing to keep the unity of the Spirit until we all come into
the reality of faith.[21]

Although the General Council of the Assemblies of God
rebuked the New Order of Latter Rain in 1949, time has a way
of deleting memories. Fifty years and a few years later, it is
apparent that things have changed. Impartations, the "transferable anointing," and the apostle and prophet movement have
now become acceptable. The difference today is that very few
are concerned. While in the past, most evangelical Protestants
would have considered such ideas heretical and the evidence of
a cult, there is a large trend underway today indicating many
evangelicals are embracing a similar view.

A myriad of well-known Christian leaders are claiming that
God is raising an elite group of supernatural prophets and apostles, reminiscent of the claims of the Latter Rain Movement of
the 1940s and '50s.[22] Called the Apostolic Movement (or the
New Apostolic Reformation) this mighty end-times army of
God, which consists of saints trained by specially commissioned
apostles, has been called to establish the Kingdom of God on
planet earth. Dr. Bill Hamon, a noted bishop, an apostle and a
modern-day prophet, has written a book on this subject.
*Apostles, Prophets, and the Coming Moves of God: God's End-
Time Plans for His Church and Planet Earth* is dedicated

...to the great company of Prophets and Apostles that
God is bringing forth in these days. May it be enlighten-
ing and enabling to all those who are called and chosen
to co-labor with Christ in fulfilling the coming moves of
God. It is for all those who are committed to making
ready a people, preparing the way by restoring all things.
This will enable Christ Jesus to be released from heaven

to return for His Church and establish His kingdom over all the earth.[23]

The New Apostles

The apostle John Eckhardt, pastor and overseer of Crusaders Ministries in Chicago, has traveled throughout the United States and around the world imparting spiritual truths. He understands his role as the business of "perfecting the saints." Eckhardt explains how vital his newly recognized office is to God's plan for the world in the last days. He discusses his role in a chapter of the book, *The New Apostolic Churches*, compiled by C. Peter Wagner.

> It was never the will of God for the Church to go without the apostolic dimension. Because of tradition and unbelief, this dynamic did not continue from generation to generation. The good news is, though, that we are now living in times of restoration. We view ourselves as being a part of prophetic fulfillment.[24]

According to Hamon, one of the first truths the Lord taught the church is the saints could not be fully perfected without the ministry of the apostle. The five ministry gifts given for equipping the saints (v. Eph. 4:11) include apostles and prophets. It takes all five of these ministry gifts operating in the church to mature properly God's people for the work of the ministry. When the apostle is absent, the saints will lack the apostolic character needed to fulfill the Great Commission.[25]

When most Christians hear the title "apostle" they most commonly think of the Apostle Paul or Peter, pillars of the Christian faith. Leaders of the New Apostolic Reformation believe this title is bestowed upon some today based on such concepts as "calling," "gifting," and "revelation." They say today's apostle has the responsibility to establish new churches, correct error, and oversee other ministries. Hamon adds to this description:

> The apostle has a revelatory anointing. Some major characteristics are great patience and manifestation of

signs and wonders and miracles. We will know more and see greater manifestations concerning the apostle during the peak of the Apostolic Movement.[26]

With the described mindset, the Apostolic Movement is said to be growing. Signs and wonders, and meetings characterized by prophetic utterances, allow these apostles and prophets militant urging for the church to renounce the encumbrances of traditional Christianity and follow wherever the Spirit leads. Gathering at well-organized and well-attended conferences, they have a strategy for spreading their theology around the world.

Fire and Rain

The "Catch the Fire: The Release of the Apostolic and the Prophetic Conference" was held at Harvest Rock Church in Pasadena on 12-16 November 1997, and hosted by Pastor Che and Sue Ahn. According to the brochure announcing these meetings, the host pastors have a heart for evangelism and "a vision to see a new generation saved, empowered, trained, and released to the nations for the coming harvest."[27] The roster of speakers over this five-day conference included John Arnott, Mike Bickle, Paul Cain, Gerald Coates, Frank Damazio, and Rick Joyner. The brochure gave background information and several reasons why the conference was going to be held.

> Revival fires are burning in hot spots around America and the world. There is hardly a day that passes when our email lines do not report a new outbreak of God's power somewhere. The Church of Jesus Christ is uniting in unprecedented ways for global prayer, fasting, and world evangelism initiatives. The zeal of God is crushing His enemies and His people are bursting with millennial expectation that a great worldwide awakening, the dawning of a new era of a church full of the glory of God, and a blazing revelation of Jesus Christ.[28]

The brochure offered an explanation for the current "worldwide awakening."

The Apostles and the Prophets, of whom the Book of Ephesians speaks, are arising as the foundation of the church, Jesus Christ Himself being the Chief Cornerstone. There used to be a day when little hope was offered for the fulfillment of the vision of the Ephesian Magna Carte of the Church. But God has spoken and a manifestation of true prophets and apostles will come forth to cause His church to reveal Christ in fullness to the world.[29]

The *Catch the Fire* brochure also presented a brief biography for each of the conference speakers. Regarding Paul Cain, the brochure stated:

With a life marked by the supernatural since he was in the womb, Paul Cain has been used of God since he was a boy; fulfilling the call of his life to "preach the gospel as the apostle Paul of old." After an almost thirty year hiddenness with the Lord, Paul emerged in 1988 with a message of holiness and revival; proclaiming the gospel of the Lord Jesus Christ to unbelievers and calling the church back to the New Testament standards of purity and power. In 1992, the Lord began to use Paul to minister prophetically to both national and international leaders at the highest levels of government. He has since been invited to meet with the Heads of State from several nations.[30]

Cain's biography mentioned his ministry had emerged from hiddenness with the Lord for over thirty years. This "hiddenness" seems to correspond to a period of time in his life when he was also embarrassed. In a message called "The Latter Rain," which Cain delivered at the Toronto Airport Vineyard on 28 May 1995,[31] he mentioned for a long time "he was embarrassed" to talk about the topic of "latter rain" in "certain evangelical circles." However, he is no longer embarrassed to talk about this latter rain doctrine since the new awakening popularized as the Toronto Blessing has been embraced worldwide.

Spread the Fire is the bimonthly newsletter published by the Toronto Airport Christian Fellowship. The purpose of this newsletter is to inform interested supporters of what God is doing through the Toronto Blessing. In the December 1996 issue, an article was written summarizing a Paul Cain prophecy called "From Appetizer to Main Course."[32] The article in this issue updated supporters of the Toronto Blessing with a prophecy Paul Cain had recently given. Cain, a former associate of William Branham and a bold advocate of the questionable doctrines of the Latter Rain Movement, claimed God had now given him some new insight regarding the future of the Toronto Blessing. According to Cain, another visitation in Toronto was to occur and the next wave of the "new thing" would soon be on its way.

> On September 14th the prophet, Paul Cain, delivered the following prophetic words to John and Carol Arnott according to the following main points. "The Lord has initiated the Toronto Blessing, not man.... He has refreshed His people in order to prepare them for the next level of visitation.... We are now at the place of the Lord's threshing floor. The Toronto Blessing has gathered the wheat and the chaff during this visitation.... God is preparing the wheat to go on to the next level."[33]

It is this "next level" (or "next wave") that so many supporters of experience-based Christianity are awaiting today. Cain and others believe only those whom he calls the "wheat" will move forward to the "next level." As he stated in his prophecy: "Others (the chaff) will be blown away by the next wind, or fall. You are to lead the people on to the next level, from appetizer to main course...the days ahead should be employed for preparation for the next thing God will do."[34]

Church historians who have studied the Latter Rain Movement will immediately recall this same kind of terminology used previously. The "new level" (or the "main course") which Cain is referring is supposed to birth the "new breed" of Christian which Latter-Rain advocates believed would be manifesting. In the '40s and '50s, they were called the "over-comers" (or the "manifested sons of God"). The elitist attitude to have emerged from the "overcomer" and "manifested sons of God" doctrines during the Latter Rain Movement produced divisions within families and resulted in numerous church divisions. Is this what will happen when the New Wine Movement adds the "full meal deal" to the menu?

Test the Spirits

Even New Wine promoters like John Arnott preach and teach certain spiritual experiences need to be tested biblically. However, it is apparent he is confused on this issue. It is easy to say one will base their teachings upon the Word of God, but it is quite another thing to understand what the Word of God actually teaches. Again, consider John Arnott's own words.

> These questions need to be asked when evaluating a spiritual experience: Is this in the Word of God? Is something similar in the Word? Does the Word of God prohibit this? Is it within the character of God as revealed through the Bible? When we ask if something is biblical, we're really asking if it is from God, aren't we? We don't want to be deceived. And we have the Bible to show us who God is, what He is like and what kinds of things He does. So we evaluate things according to the Bible, as we should. Yet as we see the Spirit of God doing more and more, we may see some things that no chapter and verse in the Bible specifically describes. Why? God did not intend to describe every act He would ever do in the Bible.[35]

The statement above by Arnott is the typical defense made by New Wine promoters. This author is convinced this brand of apologetics is based upon a desire to justify anything and everything in the name of God even though "it" cannot be found in the Word of God. It seems to be very possible that genuine sincere Christians who follow this kind of teaching could easily be led astray. If believers are not willing to be consistent concerning what to believe, then the church will be inconsistent. Inconsistency can easily lead to apostasy. Paul warned, apostasy is a key factor in preparing the way for the Antichrist (2 Thess. 2:3-12).

The author here is convinced a spiritual delusion is in progress presently in the name of Christ. Again, Scripture stated this would happen (2 Thess. 2:3-12) and the current trend indicates this is exactly what is occurring today. According to the Bible, if Christians are being deluded now, one can only expect the delusion will intensify. Arnott, of course, would disagree. He stated, "When we first experienced the increase of the Holy Spirit's power, the Lord told us, 'I am going easy on you now so that when the real power shows up, you will not be terrified.'"[36]

Although Arnott and his colleagues believe they have heard the voice of the Lord, it is obvious they have not. Many voices are being heard today. Does the church need to be reminded there are other spirits, another gospel, and another Christ (2 Cor. 12:3-5)? Would it not be wiser to be cautious knowing a strong delusion is predicted for the end of the age? Arnott argues, "Comparatively speaking, we have not really seen anything yet. If we can't participate when the power is low, what are we going to do when the real power shows up? Realize that God is awesome, and don't be surprised if His power overwhelms you."[37]

Doctrinal Differences

Bible doctrine is based on the idea that a particular tenet of faith must be established by the support of the whole council of God. Scripture must always provide the basis for biblical doctrine. All Scripture has been given by inspiration of God (2 Tim. 3:16).

Today, there are many church leaders saying Bible doctrine is not as important as once thought. Holding firm to biblical doctrine can divide the body and inhibit revival. Others have claimed not everything God has ever done is in the Bible. It is important then not to judge the new things God is doing. Let God be God, leaders of the New Wine Movement say, and just follow wherever the Spirit may lead.

Supporters of this brand of experience-based Christianity often use the Book of Acts to support their views of strange behavior and chaos occurring in the church as God distributes His Spirit. For example, Dick Reuben (a regular speaker at the Brownsville Assembly of God) said,

> If you read the Book of Acts, you will discover some pretty strange and abnormal things going on. People, they looked on and they marveled. Let me tell you, the church through the years, we've become organized, and we've learned how to do church, and we've depended upon the hand of the flesh, and we've devised programs.... But listen, when God shows up, it gets kind of chaotic. Did you know that?[38]

Then admonishing his critics and proposing a new doctrine based on what the Bible does not say, Reuben continued,

> You say, "Well, I don't see some of this happening in the Book of Acts." Listen. The Holy Spirit couldn't put everything that He did in the Book of Acts. As Steve [Hill] has said, "If God did everything He—if God had reported everything He did on the day of Pentecost in the Bible, you'd have to have a wheelbarrow just to carry Acts 2 around." And so God didn't put everything in the Bible that happened![39]

What should be the response of the church to this new doctrine designed to justify strange behavior in the name of Christ? Is it biblically accurate to teach new doctrines can be fabricated which justifies one's feelings and beliefs? What about the Berean style of Bible study mentioned in the Book of Acts? Why did Luke commend them for their diligence to examine *the scriptures daily, whether those things were so* (Acts 17:11)?

Of course, it would take a wheelbarrow to carry the Book of Acts if everything God did on the Day of Pentecost was recorded. However, God only inspired Luke to record all He wanted the church to know. The Bible indicates Christians should be more concerned about what the Bible teaches, rather than what the Bible does not teach. However, demonstrated in this chapter, the very opposite is happening within the New Wine Movement. God's Word is not only being ignored, it is being completely reinterpreted to justify the signs and wonders which are touted as a necessary prerequisite for revival.

Reformation before Revival

Since becoming a Christian, God has given this author a desire to witness for Jesus Christ and tell the lost about God's saving grace. His whole life is now dedicated to being a tool God can use in order for the gospel message to be shared wherever God leads. The author's primary objective for writing this chapter has been to direct people to the true gospel while reminding Christians that God has an adversary who has a plan to delude people in the name of the Savior. As the reader nears the end of the chapter, it will be prudent to provide some biblical solutions to the problems discussed.

Christian books are written and published primarily for two reasons. The first reason is for popularity. A second is to make a statement or a message the author feels compelled to communicate. This chapter (nor any of the author's other works), as readily understood, has not been written for the sake of popularity. The reason this chapter was written is due to a message burning in the author's heart which he believes needed to be shared.

A Biblical Exhortation

Why would anyone want to write against what is popular? Who would dare challenge a great end-time Christian revival which many insist is occurring in the name of Christ? The answer is quite simple. In order to please God, one must trust and believe in His Word. Every Christian longs to witness a great revival before the return of Jesus Christ. However, a revival based upon a unity not Bible-based is not a revival. If there is to be a genuine revival for the church, another Reformation would be required. It is imperative for people who profess to be

Christian, to return to the essentials of the gospel and glorify Jesus Christ.

When the discussion arises about whether or not one is experiencing a global revival in the name of Jesus, it is important to ask two questions. Is the revival in accordance with God's divine will? Is the revival based upon sound biblical principles found in His Word? If one is in violation of God's will, he will not please Him, no matter how sincere and well intentioned his objectives may be. For the purpose of illustrating this point, consider a biblical example. In the First Book of Chronicles, there is the account of David's attempt to please the Lord by bringing the ark of God to Jerusalem.

> And David said unto all the congregation of Israel, if it seem good unto you, and that it be of the LORD our God, let us send abroad unto our brethren every where, that are left in all the land of Israel, and with them also to the priests and Levites which are in their cities and suburbs, that they may gather themselves unto us. And let us bring again the ark of our God to us: for we inquired not at it in the days of Saul. And all the congregation said that they would do so: for the thing was right in the eyes of all the people (1 Chron. 13:2-4).

In this situation there was a decision to bring the ark to Jerusalem based on what seemed to be "the right thing in the eyes of the people." David consulted with the leaders of the Jewish nation. These chosen vessels of God believed they were making the right decision. It is beyond doubt that they were attempting to perform a service to their God to bring glory and honor to Him. It would appear then, from man's perspective, "the thing" that "was right in the eyes of the people" was the right thing to do.

When considering the full council of God the believer is able to understand what was right in man's eyes was totally wrong from God's perspective. In His Word, God had given specific instructions regarding how the ark was to be transported and who was allowed to touch the ark (Numb. 1:50; 7:9). God's divine and sovereign will had been recorded in advance. The decision seemed right to the leaders of Israel but it was the wrong decision according to God. As a result of man's disobedience, there was judgment.

> And they carried the ark of God in a new cart out of the house of Abinadab: and Uzza and Ahio drove the cart. And David and all Israel played before God with all their might, and with singing, and with harps, and with psalteries, and with timbrels, and with cymbals, and with trumpets. And when they came unto the threshing floor of Chidon, Uzza put forth his hand to hold the ark; for the oxen stumbled. And the anger of the LORD was kindled against Uzza, and he smote him, because he put his hand to the ark: and there he died before God. And David was displeased, because the LORD had made a breach upon Uzza: wherefore that place is called Perezuzza to this day. And David was afraid of God that day, saying, How shall I bring the ark of God home to me? (1 Chron. 13:7-12).

The consequences of being genuinely sincere, but sincerely deceived, were catastrophic for Uzza and the children of Israel. From this Old Testament example, there is a written record in the Word of God that should be helpful for believers today. It is always important to consider what God has revealed in His Word. If the church will not do this, there is a very strong possibility the church (and the world) will be led astray.

The Final Word

> And God spoke all these words, saying: "I am the LORD your God, who brought you out of the land of Egypt, out of the house of bondage. You shall have no other gods before Me" (Exod. 20:1-3; NKJV).

Beloved, while I was very diligent to write to you concerning our common salvation, I found it necessary to write to you exhorting you to contend earnestly for the faith which was once for all delivered to the saints (Jude 3; NKJV).

For certain men have crept in unnoticed, who long ago were marked out for this condemnation, ungodly men, who turn the grace of our God into lewdness and deny the only Lord God and our Lord Jesus Christ (4; NKJV).

But I fear, lest by any means, as the serpent beguiled Eve through his subtlety, so your minds should be corrupted from the simplicity that is in Christ. For if he that cometh preacheth another Jesus, whom we have not preached, or **if** ye receive another spirit, which ye have not received, or another gospel, which ye have not accepted, ye might well bear with **him** (2 Cor. 11:3-4).

Then one of the seven angels who had the seven bowls came and talked with me, saying to me, "Come, I will show you the judgment of the great harlot who sits on many waters, with whom the kings of the earth committed fornication, and the inhabitants of the earth were made drunk with the wine of her fornication." So he carried me away in the Spirit into the wilderness. And I saw a woman sitting on a scarlet beast which was full of names of blasphemy, having seven heads and ten horns. The woman was arrayed in purple and scarlet, and adorned with gold and precious stones and pearls, having in her hand a golden cup full of abominations and the filthiness of her fornication. And on her forehead a name was written: MYSTERY, BABYLON THE GREAT, THE MOTHER OF HARLOTS AND OF THE ABOMINATIONS OF THE EARTH (Rev. 17:1-5; NKJV).

Many will say to Me in that day, "Lord, Lord, have we not prophesied in Your name, cast out demons in Your name, and done many wonders in Your name?" And then I will declare to them, "I never knew you; depart from Me, you who practice lawlessness!" Therefore whoever hears these sayings of Mine, and does them, I will liken him to a wise man who built his house on the rock: "and the rain descended, the floods came, and the winds blew and beat on that house; and it did not fall, for it was founded on the rock. Now everyone who hears these sayings of Mine, and does not do them, will be like a foolish man who built his house on the sand: and the rain descended, the floods came, and the winds blew and beat on that house; and it fell. And great was its fall" (Mt. 7:22-27; NKJV).

But take heed to yourselves, lest your hearts be weighed down with carousing, drunkenness, and cares of this life, and that Day come on you unexpectedly. For it will come as a snare on all those who dwell on the face of the whole earth. Watch therefore, and pray always that you may be counted worthy to escape all these things that will come to pass, and to stand before the Son of Man (Lk. 21:34-36; NKJV).

Therefore take heed to yourselves and to all the flock, among which the Holy Spirit has made you overseers, to shepherd the church of God which He purchased with His own blood. For I know this, that after my departure savage wolves will come in among you, not sparing the flock. Also from among yourselves men will rise up, speaking perverse things, to draw away the disciples after themselves. Therefore watch, and remember that for three years I did not cease to warn everyone night and day with tears. So now, brethren, I commend you to God and to the word of His grace, which is able to build you up and give you an inheritance among all those who are sanctified (Acts 20:28-32; NKJV).

But you, beloved, remember the words which were spoken before by the apostles of our Lord Jesus Christ: how they told you that there would be mockers in the last time who would walk according to their own ungodly lusts. These are sensual persons, who cause divisions, not having the Spirit. But you, beloved, building yourselves up on your most holy faith, praying in the Holy Spirit, keep yourselves in the love of God, looking for the mercy of our Lord Jesus Christ unto eternal life. And on some have compassion, making a distinction; but others save with fear, pulling them out of the fire, hating even the garment defiled by the flesh. Now to Him who is able to keep you from stumbling, And to present you faultless before the presence of His glory with exceeding joy, to God our Savior, who alone is wise, be glory and majesty, dominion and power, both now and forever. Amen (Jude 17-25; NKJV).

I charge thee therefore before God, and the Lord Jesus Christ, who shall judge the quick and the dead at his appearing and his kingdom; Preach the word; be instant in season, out of season; reprove, rebuke, exhort with all longsuffering and doctrine. For the time will come when they will not endure sound doctrine; but after their own lusts shall they heap to themselves teachers, having itching ears; And they shall turn away their ears from the truth, and shall be turned unto fables. But watch thou in all things, endure afflictions, do the work of an evangelist, make full proof of thy ministry. For I am now ready to be offered, and the time of my departure is at hand. I have fought a good fight, I have finished my course, I have kept the faith: Henceforth there is laid up for me a crown of righteousness, which the Lord, the righteous judge, shall give me at that day: and not to me only, but unto all them also that love his appearing (2 Tim. 4:1-8; NKJV).

There are two more scriptures which apply to those who have been seduced by the New Wine Movement. The first comes is found in Isaiah 24, and concerns the final judgment of those on earth. The Lord warns,

The earth also is defiled under the inhabitants thereof, because they have transgressed the laws, changed the ordinance, broken the everlasting covenant. Therefore hath the curse devoured the earth, and they that dwell therein are desolate: therefore the inhabitants of the earth are burned, and few men left. The new wine mourneth, the vine languisheth, all the merryhearted do sigh (Isa. 24:5-7).

To those who have partaken in the New Wine, it is not too late to return to the Lord and His Word. It is the prayer of this author for those who have been deceived to hearken unto the voice of the Lord who offers deliverance and salvation. *Come out of her, my people, that ye be not partakers of her sins, and that ye receive not of her plagues* (Rev. 18:4).

CHAPTER 16

NATIONS' ROLE IN WORLD RELIGION

Arno Froese

"The world's religions are in turmoil," shout the headlines. Yet, according to the prophetic Scripture, one knows *all that dwell upon the earth shall worship him* (Rev. 13:8), that is, the Antichrist. The main purpose of this chapter is to demonstrate how this process will unify the world's religions. One can be certain that prophecy will be fulfilled and the entire world will worship Antichrist who will be Satan incarnate.

The Nations and World Religion

How are the nations working toward a world religion that will inaugurate the kingdom of Antichrist?[1] *And I saw one of his heads as it were wounded to death; and his deadly wound was healed: and all the world wondered after the beast. And they worshipped the dragon which gave power unto the beast: and they worshipped the beast, saying, Who is like unto the beast? who is able to make war with him?* (13:3-4). History testifies of great men who led their nations to victory and were subsequently honored, praised, and sometimes even worshipped. However, there are three remarkable aspects in Revelation 13:3-4.

1) The phrase, *wounded to death*, needs some explanation because some assume this means there will be a death, therefore, a subsequent resurrection, which will imitate the resurrection of the Lord. However, the verse states, *as it were wounded to death*, therefore, not actually

death. Nevertheless, this will be a great miracle apparently because *his deadly wound* [will be] *healed*. The false prophet is revealed later in this chapter: *whose deadly wound was healed* (13:12). The people of the world will consider this a miraculous healing.

2) *All the world wondered after the beast.* Numerous other leaders throughout history have been praised and honored beyond measure, but here Scripture identifies *all the world*. In other words, this will be a global event, indicating global systems such as economy and finance, government, and religion are already operative at that time. Often it is mistakenly assumed that the Antichrist will be the one to create the New World Order. However that will not be the case. As the reader learned in Chapter Four and Chapter Ten of this book, the New World Order is already under construction. It started 2,000 years ago with the Roman Empire and now is entering its final stages of completion.

3) *They worshipped the dragon...and they worshipped the beast....* This statement describes blatant unprecedented global worship of the devil. It will be a unique, one-time event.

To emphasize the point above, the Apostle Paul wrote, *But I say, that the things which the Gentiles sacrifice, they sacrifice to devils, and not to God: and I would not that ye should have fellowship with devils. Ye cannot drink the cup of the Lord, and the cup of devils. Ye cannot drink the cup of the Lord, and the cup of devils: ye cannot be partakers of the Lord's table, and of the table of the devils* (1 Cor. 10:20-21). In this passage, the correct translation is "demons" for there is only one devil. Satan's forces will infiltrate the church of Jesus Christ in *sacrifice, fellowship, the cup,* and *the table*. These things are precious to believers in the Lord Jesus Christ. Under the devil's leadership, demons will infiltrate the church to create an imitation of the true church.

Invisible Powers

Later the Apostle Paul wrote about the great deception, revealing there are *"another"* Jesus, *"another"* spirit, and *"another"* gospel. *For if he that cometh preacheth another Jesus, whom we have not preached, or if ye receive another spirit, which ye have not received, or another gospel, which ye have not accepted, ye might well bear with him* (2 Cor. 11:4).

Demons belong to the invisible world. Scripture states, *While we look not at the things which are seen, but at the things which are not seen: for the things which are seen are temporal; but the things which are not seen are eternal* (4:18). It is vital for Christians to recognize there is an invisible world. Eternal things are invisible so do not let anyone say he or she has seen Jesus, the Holy Spirit, or other heavenly beings, because the Bible says man cannot see these things. The Apostle Peter reinforced this teaching when he wrote, *Whom having not seen, ye love; in whom, though now ye see him not, yet believing, ye rejoice with joy unspeakable and full of glory* (1 Pet. 1:8).

Peter's teaching leads to another point relating to mankind on earth. *For we wrestle not against flesh and blood, but against principalities, against powers, against the rulers of the darkness of this world, against spiritual wickedness in high places* (Eph. 6:12). The *wrestle* has no relationship to earthly government for these are spiritual powers. Luther translated this verse a little more clearly: "Our battle is not against flesh and blood, but against princes and rulers with the lords of this world against the powers of darkness who rule this world by evil spirits under the heavens."

Ephesians 6:12 helps to understand the fulfillment of Bible prophecy. When the nations' role in world religion is examined, one must not mistakenly identify a number of false religions and practices. For example, the ordination of homosexuals, same-sex marriage, and abortion are only the visible manifestations of the powers of darkness at work. The ones who endorse and support these abominations are not themselves the powers of darkness, but they certainly have become servants to them.

The Glory of the Antichrist

The seven-headed, ten-horned world leader who will *rise up out of the sea* (Rev. 13:1) is the global leader destined to rule the world and lead the world to its greatest glory, and ultimately to its greatest catastrophe. During Election 2004, Americans will agree with favor or even vote for certain political leaders. In the Revelation 13 passage, however, it states people will *wonder* after this man. In other words, they will be amazed by him; they will identify no one on earth to be like him. The glory of the Antichrist is the great miracle to occur during the final stages of the end times.

The fact of the world wondering *after the beast* and worshipping him indicates the church of Jesus Christ, God's testimony on earth, is no longer present. Complete spiritual darkness will have spread across the entire world. Peace, brotherhood, and prosperity will become a reality. Political controversies will cease, racial issues will be solved, poverty will be eliminated, and most importantly, the world will have a leader it can admire, praise, and even worship.

Glorious Military Leader

Furthermore, the beast will also have complete military authority: *who is able to make war with him?* This seems to indicate some will not agree with him; however, one must remember that the overwhelming majority of "churchianity"[2] will become his followers. In theory, members of churchianity believe in the truth of Scripture; therefore, the Antichrist will be a substitute for Christ. He will be a false Jesus who will preach a false gospel inspired by a false spirit.

Those who embrace churchianity—the most powerful religious, political, and economic identity on the planet—will still be on earth. As discussed in Chapter Ten, there is no reason to believe this will change. Churchianity has dominated the world for 2,000 years and is identical to the fourth and final Gentile global superpower.

Enemies of Antichrist

Who will be the Antichrist's enemies? One can assume the cults will oppose churchianity and the Antichrist's rule. Consider the Jehovah's Witnesses who would rather be killed than change their beliefs. Many groups, movements, and denominations will not agree with the New World religion; they will oppose the worship of a human being. Nevertheless, they may still be in darkness. Satan and his demons have deceived the overwhelming majority of the world's population. *For such are false apostles, deceitful workers, transforming themselves into the apostles of Christ. And no marvel; for Satan himself is transformed into an angel of light. Therefore it is no great thing if his ministers also be transformed as the ministers of righteousness; whose end shall be according to their works* (2 Cor. 11:13-15).

Churchianity will be the Antichrist's power base because it presents a new Christ, one who is benevolent to all people. In 550 BC, Daniel identified him with the following words: *And through his policy also he shall cause craft to prosper in his hand; and he shall magnify **himself** in his heart, and by peace shall destroy many: he shall also stand up against the Prince of princes; but he shall be broken without hand* (Dan. 8:25). Scripture states, *he shall magnify **himself** in his heart* which is the gospel circulating within churchianity today. The church is no longer a minority consisting of insignificant, despised, rejected, persecuted people who are sometimes even killed. Today, the church is a powerful institution working cooperatively with the economic and financial, military, and political systems of the spirit of religious globalism.

More Enemies

Other groups will oppose the Antichrist. The Muslims automatically come to mind. While the majority of people will compromise with churchianity, using the same negotiation tactics and philosophies being used to unify Europe, a minority will refuse. There is no reason to believe all Muslims will follow the footsteps of Antichrist; there will always be an exception. The same applies to all other religious groups. Ultimately, however, they will not be able to oppose Antichrist because the Bible asks *who is able to make war with him?* He will seize all authority and inflict woe to those who will oppose him.

Hitler as Example

Generally, most people have heard negative thoughts concerning Adolf Hitler and his Nazi empire in Germany. Yes, they were brutal, destructive, and evil; for the Germans however, he was the great liberator. In fact, most people supported this extremely popular leader who transformed Germany and produced economic, financial, social, and military miracles. Hitler took advantage of man's self-righteousness by repeatedly appealing to the religious conscience of the nations: "With the help of God Almighty we shall…;" "With God on our side we will prevail…;" "The Lord our God will avenge us of our enemies." It was this type of rhetoric which solved the problem of the religious people.

So who opposed Hitler? God saved this author, a native of Germany, in 1967 and since then, he has made a habit of asking Germans if they knew anyone who hated Hitler. The question was asked after the war, after the Soviet Union defeated Germany with the help of the Allies and devastated the country. During all the years of questioning, this author has never met a single person who said they disliked Hitler. On one occasion even, the author asked his brother (who was born in 1938) if he knew anyone who hated Hitler. His wife quickly answered, "Uncle Jup was jailed by the Nazis." My brother responded, "He was jailed because he was a Communist."

Prior to God saved this author, he met a German engineer named Wolfgang Duwe in Melbourne, Australia. Wolfgang was a brilliant inventor and intellectual who hated Hitler and everything associated with Nazism. However, he was an atheist who rejected the Bible and the possibility of God's existence. My wife's grandmother was deeply involved in the occult. When Hitler became the leader of Germany, she said, "Just wait, you'll see what you get out of this bloodhound."

These few examples should be enough to show that most Germans supported Adolf Hitler. Not only did the workers fall

for the great deception, but also so did the majority of the intel-
lectuals. Even those of royal descent laid aside their titles for the
sake of their beloved Fuhrer. Friends, that is deception but mere
child's play compared to what the spirit of the Antichrist is doing
today. Hitler persecuted Jehovah's Witnesses, Mormons, homosexuals, Jews, Freemasons, gypsies, and many others. However,
for the Germans, Hitler was a beloved leader. Under his reign
they received freedom, hope for the future, and security.

Only One Escape

A great disservice will be given to the church if the evil
results of the Antichrist's rule during the *great tribulation* are
given without mentioning the advantages. The Bible uses the
word *deception* repeatedly because people cannot be deceived by
force. For example, deception is accomplished by making people
believe their church denomination, nationality, or tradition of a
good family and heritage will save them. There is no escape from
the clutches of the Antichrist; sooner or later, everyone will
become entangled in the cunning system of his deception and
will surrender without conscience. There is only one way of
escape, that is, genuine faith in the only way God has provided
for man to be saved: grace through faith in the Lord Jesus
Christ.

One More Group of Enemies

One group not yet mentioned is the one comprised of
Christians who will have accepted Jesus as their Savior after the
rapture. They will refuse the mark of the beast, jeopardize their
lives, and eventually be killed. This group of people is identified
in Revelation 7:9: *After this I beheld, and, lo, a great multitude,
which no man could number, of all nations, and kindreds, and
people, and tongues, stood before the throne, and before the
Lamb, clothed with white robes, and palms in their hands.*
Revelation 7:14 explains who these people are: *And I said unto
him, Sir, thou knowest. And he said to me, These are they which
came out of great tribulation, and have washed their robes, and
made them white in the blood of the Lamb.*

The Most Significant Enemy

The most significant enemy will be the Jews, who will initially accept the rule of the Antichrist. The Lord Jesus said, *I am come in my Father's name, and ye receive me not: if another shall come in his own name, him ye will receive* (Jn. 5:43). The Jews rejected Jesus and accepted a substitute: the Caesar of Rome. They deliberately, intentionally, and voluntarily chose the foreign dictator who occupied their country rather than Jesus, King of the Jews. Pontius Pilate offered them the choice: *and he saith unto the Jews, Behold your King!* How did the crowd reply? *The chief priests answered, We have no king but Caesar* (19:15).

Ultimately Israel will accept the Messiah for *they shall look upon me* [Jesus] *whom they have pierced* (Zech. 12:10). Almost 600 years before Christ's first coming, the prophet Jeremiah wrote the following about the day of the Lord: *Alas! for that day is great, so that none is like it: it is even the time of Jacob's trouble; but he shall be saved out of it* (Jer. 30:7). Israel will be saved from the greatest trials and tribulation.

The World Leader

How is it possible for the world to have one leader, one military power structure, and one person to worship? Today's religions are in disarray. While Churchianity is the world's largest religion, Islam—and its teachings intended for accomplishing world dominion—is diametrically opposed to churchianity. Furthermore, there is Hinduism which claims to be the oldest religion in the world. The Hindus do not want to embrace Christianity. What about Buddhism? Japan is probably the most successful country in the world. An estimated 93.1% of its population follows Shinto-Buddhism. Neither do these believers have any intention of converting to Christianity. Despite the odds, a great change must occur. Believe it or not, this change is taking place even as you are reading this book.

Unity Religion

It is this author's belief that the religions of the world will continue to exist. Europe serves as an example relating to political unity. Twenty-five sovereign nations belong to the European Union, and despite the uniqueness of each country, they all adhere to the same constitution and follow the same laws. The European Union is "unity in diversity" which is the key for globalization to unlock the door to the New World Order (in this case, a New World religion).

Babylon and the Jews

King Nebuchadnezzar of Babylon had a dream which the prophet Daniel interpreted by explaining the Gentile structure as beginning with Nebuchadnezzar and ending with the Antichrist of Rome. When Daniel finished speaking, *Then the king Nebuchadnezzar fell upon his face, and worshipped Daniel, and commanded that they should offer an oblation and sweet odours unto him. The king answered unto Daniel, and said, Of a truth it is, that your God is a God of gods, and a Lord of kings, and a revealer of secrets, seeing thou couldest reveal this secret* (Dan. 2:46-47). It is significant that King Nebuchadnezzar worshipped Daniel. Scripture does not say whether Daniel refused his worship or the sacrifices of oblation. Thus, Daniel responded to the king on his level since the king was a pagan and that is what pagans do.

The Golden Image

An important aspect of this dream and its interpretation was it indicated King Nebuchadnezzar was the greatest. *Thou, O king, **art** a king of kings: for the God of heaven hath given thee a kingdom, power, and strength, and glory. And wheresoever the children of men dwell, the beasts of the field and the fowls of the heaven hath he given into thine hand, and hath made thee ruler over them all. Thou **art** this head of gold* (2:37-38). Surely Nebuchadnezzar must have felt proud when he heard he was represented by the *head of gold*. Actually, the next chapter reads, *Nebuchadnezzar the king made an image of gold, whose height was threescore cubits, **and** the breadth thereof six cubits: he set it up in the plain of Dura, in the province of Babylon* (3:1).

purpose of building this great golden image is revealed in the next several verses.

Then Nebuchadnezzar the king sent to gather together the princes, the governors, and the captains, the judges, the treasurers, the counsellors, the sheriffs, and all the rulers of the provinces, to come to the dedication of the image which Nebuchadnezzar the king had set up. Then the princes, the governors, and captains, the judges, the treasurers, the counsellors, the sheriffs, and all the rulers of the provinces, were gathered together unto the dedication of the image that Nebuchadnezzar the king had set up; and they stood before the image that Nebuchadnezzar had set up. Then an herald cried aloud, To you it is commanded, O people, nations, and languages, *That* at what time ye hear the sound of the cornet, flute, harp, sackbut, psaltery, dulcimer, and all kinds of musick, ye fall down and worship the golden image that Nebuchadnezzar the king hath set up (3:2-5).

These verses describe religious unity, the beginning of the spirit of Antichrist! The height of this image was sixty cubits and *the breadth thereof six cubits*. Six musical instruments were listed: (1) *cornet*; (2) *flute*; (3) *harp*; (4) *sackbut*; (5) *psaltery*; and, (6) *dulcimer*. Nebuchadnezzar wanted to establish a united religion, visibly portrayed in this sixty by six image of gold and worshipped at the sound of these six instruments. Only three Jewish men refused when everyone else fell down and worshipped the image. *There are certain Jews whom thou hast set over the affairs of the province of Babylon, Shadrach, Meshach, and Abednego; these men, O king, have not regarded thee: they serve not thy gods, nor worship the golden image which thou hast set up* (3:12).

Where Was Daniel?

What happened to Daniel and the other Jews? Daniel 2:2 records that the prophet belonged to the intellectual elite. After the king's dream, *the king commanded to call the magicians, and the astrologers, and the sorcerers, and the Chaldeans, for to shew the king his dreams. So they came and stood before the king.* They could not interpret the dream so a decree was issued *that the wise men should be slain; and they sought Daniel and his fellows to be slain* (2:13). The escapade, as recorded in Daniel 2:46-47, has already been reference. Next, the reader is informed: *Then the king made Daniel a great man, and gave him many great gifts, and made him ruler over the whole province of Babylon, and chief of the governors over all the wise men of Babylon* (2:48). Daniel became the chief governor over Babylon's elite. *Then Daniel requested of the king, and he set Shadrach, Meshach, and Abed-nego, over the affairs of the province of Babylon: but Daniel sat in the gate of the king* (2:49). Shadrach, Meshach, and Abed-nego became politicians in Babylon; as politicians they were in the categories of *the princes, the governors, and captains, the judges, the treasurers, the counsellers, the sheriffs, and all the rulers* (3:3). Obviously, Daniel did not possess any of these titles because he was chief over the wise men as opposed to the politicians or the law enforcers. Therefore, one must assume the invitation to worship this sixty by six golden image was not addressed to the general public, but to the financiers, the law enforcers, the military, and the politicians, among whom were Shadrach, Meshach and Abed-nego. How did the episode end?

> *Then* Nebuchadnezzar spake, and said, Blessed *be* the God of Shadrach, Meshach, and Abed-nego, who hath sent his angel, and delivered his servants that trusted in him, and have changed the king's word, and yielded their bodies, that they might not serve nor worship any god, except their own God. Therefore I make a decree, That every people, nation, and language, which speak any thing amiss against the God of Shadrach, Meshach, and Abed-nego, shall be cut in pieces, and their houses shall be made a dunghill: because there is no other God that can deliver after this sort. Then the king promoted Shadrach, Meshach, and Abed-nego, in the province of Babylon (3:28-30).

Blueprint for World Religion

Genesis 11 contains the report of man's attempt to build the Tower of Babel. In that case, it was a democratic system; the people were in charge. God stopped the tower-building attempt by confusing the people's languages. Thus, the first democratic effort to establish a world religion failed. However, in Nebuchadnezzar's situation, the attempt to establish a unified religion was established through the law, which was reinforced by capital punishment in the event of disobedience. In the final analysis, the reader should understand that neither the people nor the law, but a manmade *image of the beast* become the authority, as it will be during the reign of the Antichrist. The refusal to worship the image of the beast will result in death (Rev. 13:15).

Global Rome

The guideline for religious unity originates from Rome which best represents churchianity. As previously demonstrated, Roman civilization and churchianity are leading the world which is true politically, financially, militarily, economically, and religiously. It is for this reason that only Europe is capable of making the necessary compromise to accommodate the remaining religions of the world.

From a political perspective, there is no alternative to Greek-Roman democracy. On an economic level, social/capitalism is the undisputed winner in the global race for economic dominion. Since the Soviet Union is not an issue, there is no significant military force outside of the European Union-United States alliance. However, there is a problem to the extent that religion is concerned. Churchianity does not have even a small possibility of converting the Muslim world or the Hindu and Buddhist nations. Although the church likes to boast of "reaching the world for Christ," such a statement is actually voicing empty words.

After becoming a believer, this author listened eagerly to Billy Graham and admired the simple way he proclaimed the Gospel. However, during a crusade in Japan, he said the church there was growing exponentially. He said within a few decades, Christianity would no longer be a minority religion. Graham's statement was an ambitious statement but far from reality. At that time, the *CIA Fact Book* indicated only 0.7% of Japan's population was Christian.

Although thousands of missionaries are scattered throughout the world (South Korea leads the world in hosting the greatest number of missionaries), Christianity's effort to spread the Gospel is small in comparison. Such a statement may sound discouraging to those involved in the work of the Lord, but there is comfort that Jesus said He would build His church. In other words, regardless of the developments and in spite of any vastly exaggerated statements by Christian leaders, the church is growing, being purified, and will be completed by Jesus Christ.

The Counterfeit Church

Outward Christianity is no longer identifiable which is not surprising because counterfeit Christianity was active during the apostles' time. For example, Acts 16:16-17 reads, *And it came to pass, as we went to prayer, a certain damsel possessed with a spirit of divination met us, which brought her masters much gain by soothsaying: the same followed Paul and us, and cried, saying, These men are the servants of the most high God, which shew unto us the way of salvation.* The statement is amazing because a demon-possessed person was telling the truth. *These men are the servants of the most high God, which shew unto us the way of salvation.* What would happen if this occurred today? It is probable that the majority of people within churchianity would wholeheartedly endorse this wonderful testimony for Jesus.

Nevertheless, what was the response of Paul? *And this did she many days. But Paul, being grieved, turned and said to the spirit, I command thee in the name of Jesus Christ to come out of her. And he came out the same hour"* (16:18). In other words, a person who has not been born again of the Spirit of God does not have the privilege to proclaim the Gospel of Jesus Christ. If that person does so anyway, then such is not the responsibility of the church. However, one must not allow that person into the fellowship of born-again Christians to preach a false gospel. Not everything appearing to be true, sounding wonderful, or even based on the Bible is true Christianity. With the exception of true believers, Christianity today can be defined at best as churchianity and at worst anti-Christianity.

Dedication, sacrifice, and service are no longer required of those who become missionaries or Christian witnesses today. Midnight Call founder, the late Dr. Wim Malgo, commissioned missionaries with the clear instructions that they were expected to leave their homeland, die, and be buried in the country they served. Today, a number of missionaries sent by Dr. Malgo remain on the field. Their children and grandchildren have been born, reared, and educated in the countries where they serve the Lord. Malgo represents the process which leads to the growth of the church of Jesus Christ, but that is not what the majority of Christians accept anymore. Today's Christians believe Christianity can spread by technology enabling millions to be reached at any given moment. For instance, turn on the radio or television to hear boasting voices preach that they are reaching the world for Christ, but apparently, and too frequently it is not true.

False Missionaries

Compromise is the key to world religion; therefore, preaching the true Gospel of Jesus Christ will be eliminated eventually. The Apostle Paul wrote a letter to the Corinthians stating, *For if he that cometh preacheth another Jesus, whom we have not preached, or if ye receive another spirit, which ye have not received, or another gospel, which ye have not accepted, ye might well bear with him* (2 Cor. 11:4). The statement here reveals the reality of another Jesus, another spirit, and another gospel, which is a very successful trio within Churchianity today. Its message converts millions, but the majority of those alleged conversions are not born-again believers. They are mostly converts to a system, success, and prosperity, or to another Jesus, empowered by another spirit through the preaching of another gospel.

Again, how did Paul react? *And this did she many days. But*

Paul, being grieved, turned and said to the spirit, I command thee in the name of Jesus Christ to come out of her. And he came out the same hour" (16:18). Why did Paul oppose this promotion of the Gospel? He opposed it because he recognized the proclamation was made by another spirit; although it was true in word, it was made with a deceptive intention.

False Christs

Mel Gibson's movie, *The Passion of the Christ*, has resulted in much controversy among churchianity. Having been asked many times for an opinion of this movie, this author would like to share some observations. No one in the film saw the historical Jesus, and no one was actually hurt, crucified, killed, or rose from the dead in the movie. The movie is not real. Therefore, the question is "Since when does fiction need to be used to tell the truth?" If someone wants to know about the crucifixion, he should read the Bible! Furthermore, Christians must be sober in their analysis. Occultists who have no relationship to the church of Jesus Christ produced this movie. Mel Gibson revealed his goal for the movie to the Eternal Word Television Network, the global Catholic network.

> It is crucial to realize that the images and language at the heart of "The Passion of the Christ" flow directly out of Gibson's personal dedication to Catholicism in one of its most traditional and mysterious forms—the 16th-century Latin Mass.
>
> "I don't go to any other services," the director told the Eternal Word Television Network. "I go to the old Tridentine Rite. That's the way that I first saw it when I was a kid. So I think that that informs one's understanding of how to transcend language. Now, initially, I didn't understand the Latin.... But I understood the meaning and the message and what they were doing. I understood it very fully and it was very moving and emotional and efficacious, if I may say so."
>
> The goal of the movie is to shake modern audiences by brashly juxtaposing the "sacrifice of the cross with

the sacrifice of the altar—which is the same thing," said Gibson. This ancient union of symbols and sounds has never lost its hold on him. There is, he stressed, "a lot of power in these dead languages."[3]

What has been the response by official representatives of Roman Catholicism[4] concerning the evangelical world watching their movie?

As someone involved in the distribution and marketing of the film, I noticed early on the fervor with which many Protestant communities were preparing to use the film for evangelistic purposes. Websites sprang up featuring downloadable materials about Jesus and the gospels. Marketing companies began churning out posters and flyers promoting the film and their own faith communities. Tracts poured into circulation making the case for Christ as the key to peace and happiness in life. In terms of effecting conversions and motivating people to weed out sin from their lives-which is what meditating on the Passion of Christ is all about-our evangelical brothers and sisters have been an inspiration. But can their theology adequately mine such cinematic gems as the Last Supper flashbacks or the deeply Marian themes presented in the movie?

And without an understanding of Mary as our model in true Christian faith, one cannot begin to understand her significant role in the film. Only the fullness of Catholic faith can help us grasp these essential elements that figure so prominently in the Scriptural record, the apostolic Tradition, and the film. The Passion of The Christ quite poignantly links the sacrifice of the cross with the Eucharistic sacrifice of the Mass. In doing so, it faithfully depicts biblical and Catholic teaching.[5]

Bible-believing Christians know Mary was a sinner in need of salvation like any other person on earth. In fact, she said, "*my spirit hath rejoiced in God my Saviour*" (Lk. 1:47). However, the basis for the movie was not Scripture but a book, *The Dolorous Passion of our Lord Jesus Christ*,[6] containing the revelations and visions of a 19th century Catholic mystic which influenced Mel Gibson.

THE DOLOROUS PASSION has been inspiring thousands since it first appeared in 1833—being based on the detailed visions of Our Lord's Passion and Death as seen by Venerable Anne Catherine Emmerich (1774-1824), a German Augustinian nun, and recorded by Clemens Brentano, a prominent literary figure of the day. A saintly person from her youth and a great mystic and victim soul, Sister Emmerich was privileged by God during almost a lifetime of ecstatic visions to see all the events of Our Lord's suffering and death, which visions we can now understand in hindsight were a great gift from God to the world. Her account of the Passion and Death of Our Lord Jesus Christ, while faithful to the Bible, is heart-rending, edifying and surprising—because of its intimate detail. THE DOLOROUS PASSION recounts with incredible precision the horrendous sufferings undergone by our Saviour in His superhumanly heroic act of Redemption. Also illuminating is its description of Mary's participation in the sufferings of her Son, so that this book gives the reader a poignant understanding of why Our Lady is often called our "Co-Redemptrix" and "Queen of Martyrs." THE DOLOROUS PASSION is a singular book that conveys a lasting impression of the terrible Agony of Our Lord, of His infinite love for us that motivated His Agony, and how his Passion and Death were brought on by each person's sins. Here is a book that gives one a holy feeling just to read it. Here is a book that will melt a heart of stone![7]

BLASPHEMY! The author even dedicated the book to Mary as follows: "To the Immaculate Heart of the Virgin Mary, Mother of God, Queen of Heaven and Earth, Lady of the Most Holy Rosary, Help of Christians, and Refuge of the Human

Race." Quite contrary, Scripture states, *For **there is** one God, and one mediator between God and men, the man Christ Jesus* (1 Tim. 2:5). Roman Catholics deny 1 Timothy 2:5, as the quote below indicates.

> ...the eve of the Passion and Death of the Savior, had arrived; at earliest dawn the Lord called his most beloved Mother and She, hastening to prostrate Herself at his feet, responded; "Speak, my Lord and Master, for thy servant heareth." Raising Her up from the ground, He spoke to Her in words of soothing and tenderest love: "My Mother, the hour decreed by the eternal wisdom of my Father for accomplishing the salvation and restoration of the human race and imposed upon Me by his most holy and acceptable will, has now arrived; it is proper that now We subject to Him our own will, as We have so often offered to do. Give Me thy permission to enter upon my suffering and death, and, as my true Mother, consent that I deliver Myself over to my enemies in obedience to my Father. In this manner do Thou also willingly co-operate with Me in this work of eternal salvation, since I have received from Thee in thy virginal womb the form of a suffering and mortal man in which I am to redeem the world and satisfy the divine justice. Just as thou, of thy own free will, didst consent to my Incarnation, so I now desire thee to give consent also to my passion and death of the Cross...."[8]

In spite of official Roman Catholic teaching, churchianity—including some Protestant preachers—has been mesmerized by the missionary tool of Roman Catholicism.

World Religion in the Making

The true church of Jesus Christ has no possibility of reaching the world for Christ. However, Christians continue to work, pray, and preach with sincerity of heart that God will continue to save sinners by the preaching of His Word. Not even churchianity with all its sophistication, glory, power, and political clout has the possibility to convert the Muslim world or change the hearts of the Hindu nations. Churchianity has already ceased preaching the Gospel to Roman Catholics, which according to their own official literature, claim salvation through the Catholic Church and a mediator named "Mary" who is certainly not the Mary as Scripture reveals her.

What must be done to create a world religion? Compromise! Churchianity has done that rather well. A powerful infrastructure and industry have been developed to promote this modern compromising gospel which will not offend any other religion. Global economy and government are setting the trend. The European Union demonstrates extreme tolerance to anyone and anything, and it is creating a model for churchianity to follow to create a New World religion. Just as individual nations in the European Union retain their languages, cultures, and customs (yet remaining 100% European), so too will the world's religions keep their identity as Catholics, "Protestants," Muslims, Buddhists, and Hindus. Unfortunately, they are uniting to fulfill what has been written in Scripture. *And all the world wondered after the beast. And they worshipped the dragon which gave power unto the beast: and they worshipped the beast...and all that dwell upon the earth shall worship him* (Rev. 13:3-4, 8).

CHAPTER 17

RELIGION OF THE FUTURE

Ron J. Bigalke Jr.

The purpose of this chapter is to provide a forewarning concerning unbiblical trends thereby encouraging discernment. The question is often asked of this author, "Will there be a one world religion?" According to Scripture, the answer is "Yes." The last 3 1/2 years of the tribulation period will be a time of intense persecution for the nation of Israel. It is at the midpoint of the tribulation period that the Antichrist will break his covenant with Israel (Dan. 9:27; Mt. 24:15). The results of the breaking of the covenant will be both political and religious. For instance, the Antichrist will make a stop of the Jewish sacrifices in the rebuilt temple (Dan. 9:27). At this point, the period of time called the *great tribulation* will begin (Mt. 24:15-16, 21).

Daniel 12:11 adds the following: *"And from the time that the regular sacrifice is abolished, and the abomination of desolation is set up, **there will be** 1,290 days.* In others words, from the time of the abomination of desolation until the beginning of the millennial reign of Christ will be 1,290 days. The extra 30 days after the time of Christ's second coming is to judge the sheep and goats to determine who will enter the millennial kingdom and who will condemned to eternal punishment (cf. Mt. 25). Therefore, the Antichrist will stop both worship of God, and the Jewish sacrificial system, to declare worship of himself (2 Thess. 2:4).

Scripture indicates the Antichrist (or Beast) will increase his rule from a revived Roman Empire to the entire world during the last half of the tribulation period (Rev. 13:12-17). Revelation 17-18 indicate the Antichrist's one world government will not only focus upon political concerns, but also economic and religious. The world today believes the only hope for mankind will be a one world economy, government, and religion which would certainly be logical in an unstable world. However, such attempts are an attempt of mankind to build heaven on earth thereby rejecting God's authority.

The move toward a global religion is stronger than ever today. For instance, the New Age movement has infiltrated every area of Western thought in the business world, health profession, education, and even the church occasionally. Organizational religious unity and theological heresy are rampant in the current day. Clearly, the setting of the stage for the rise of the Antichrist from a revived Roman Empire is developing. What will follow is evidence of this trend.

The Death of Materialism

The growth of modern science began with astronomers Copernicus (1475-1543) and Galileo (1564-1642), and anatomist Vesalius (1514-1564). From 1200 to 1600, science generally reflected a biblical world view. In addition to Copernicus and Galileo, Roger Bacon (1561-1626) and Tycho Brahe (1546-1601) acknowledged a universe with grand design. Following the 17th century, the Catholic Church was largely responsible for suppressing scientific knowledge. *Providentissimus Deus* (1893), the encyclical of Pope Leo XIII (1878-1903), proposed the idea that Scripture could err in regards to natural science.[1] During the 18th and 19th centuries, God and later modern science were generally considered antithetical which meant science became mechanistic, or materialistic. Mechanistic science was thought to explain everything that exists on the basis of matter and motion. Dr. Francis A. Schaeffer wrote, "Materialistic thought would never have produced modern science. Modern science was produced on the Christian base.... The materialistic-energy, chance concept of final reality...was a choice, in faith, to see things that way."[2]

Noted cult expert Dave Hunt wrote, "The acceptance of Darwinian evolution in the nineteenth century was the key development in moving the scientific world into hard-core materialism."[3] However, a two-dimensional mechanistic view of the universe does not adequately explain the existence of all things. Furthermore, it certainly does not explain the origin and final destiny of man in the universe. It is evident that the universe is not impersonal matter and energy with its current form due to impersonal chance. Rather than modern science leading people away from the Creator, it actually reveals His existence.

Today, materialism is being replaced with the idea of an entire universe beyond the material world. Life extends beyond the physical world. The contrast between mind and brain, remote viewing, mysticism, parapsychology, altered states of consciousness, etc. demonstrate the reality of entities beyond this world. A mechanistic view of the universe simply does not account for the evidence of a non-physical world.

It seems as though the old devil of an uncle, Screwtape, in C. S. Lewis' famous *Screwtape Letters* spoke prophetically: "We are really faced with a cruel dilemma. When the humans disbelieve in our existence we lose all the pleasing results of direct terrorism and we make no magicians. On the other hand, when they believe in us, we cannot make them materialists and skeptics. At least, not yet."[4] Hunt wrote,

> Unfortunately, while the delusionary lie of materialism has been largely discredited, it has been replaced by a new spirituality that still remains tied to this universe and to science. There is a belief in nonphysical "entities," including "angels," but their identity is decided entirely on the basis of what they say about themselves. At the same time, there is an even greater skepticism toward belief in demons, Satan, the God of the Bible, and Jesus Christ as the only Savior.[5]

Whereas "the delusionary lie of materialism has been largely discredited," there is "a new spirituality" developing which is seducing the world and churchianity. The evidence today is that professing Christians, and even the church, is enthusiastically embracing false teaching. It needs to be understood that a false teacher has knowledge of the truth but apostatizes from it, but false teaching is almost always a subtle combination of truth and error. Perhaps an example will help to illustrate the necessity of biblical discernment. Warfarin is a sweet clover proven to be nutritious as fodder, but in 1948, warfarin was first used as the ideal rat poison. It is only the 2% that is deadly. The example here is given to prove that a little error can be extremely danger-ous. Furthermore, the second most frequently mentioned subject statistically in the Epistles of the New Testament relates to apos-tasy. It is not an option to follow the example of the Bereans who *received the word with great eagerness, examining the Scriptures daily, to see whether these things were so* (Acts 17:11).

False Teaching in the Church

The need for Christians to exercise discernment as never before is evident in the following examples of false teaching in "popular" Christendom, or churchianity. Only the dominant false teachings in the church will be given here since an entire book could be written on this subject.

12-Step Program[6]

The beginning of the popular 12-step program was when Bill Wilson joined the Oxford Group, founded by Frank Buchman, a Lutheran minister. Later, it was known as Moral Rearmament (MRA). Members of the Oxford Group practiced divination and received their guidance similar in method to mediums who per-ceive messages from demons. Buchman, for instance, was known to spend "an hour or more in complete silence of soul and body while he gets guidance for the day."[7]

The founder of AA (alcoholics anonymous), Bill Wilson, was an alcoholic when he met another alcoholic, Dr. Silkworth. It was Silkworth who convinced Wilson that alcoholism was a dis-ease. Having accepted that lie, Wilson was relieved that he was not accountable to God for his mistakes. University of California professor, Herbert Fingarette, has written an entire book that proves alcohol/drug addiction is not a disease.[8]

There are two dangers of the twelve steps of AA and NA.

First, the beginning of the twelve steps is linked to the occult. *Second*, the belief in "God, as you understand Him" (according to Step 3 and 11) is a form of "spiritual" Russian Roulette. The twelve steps provide an appearance of godliness, but a closer examination reveals otherwise. Though the movement capitalizes the "h" in "Him" when referring to God, their god is not the God of the Bible. It is because one can believe in any god that many people have become worse through the twelve steps since they have become involved in spiritism and occultic practices through a god conceived in their own mind to help them with their alleged disease. Although the god may help them, he will never judge them since they are sick with a disease. The Bible, however, says the disease is sin, not addiction. The 12-steps program has a spiritual emphasis apparently giving some churches comfort to hold meetings for AA and NA and ignore the occult relationship. Rather than faith Jesus Christ—the way, and the truth, and the life (Jn. 14:6)—many choose the way that seems right and instead it leads to destruction (Prov. 14:12).

Course in Miracles

A Course in Miracles is said to be "a unique, universal, self-study spiritual thought system that also teaches the way to Love and Inner Peace." It claims to be a mind-awareness text, but it was spirit dictated to a now deceased Jewish psychologist, Helen Schucman.[9] The *Course* promises spiritual self-betterment through practical exercises to enhance the subject's perception of reality.

One must realize the *Course* divides reality into the real and the illusion. The real is the realm of God. The *Course* reflects a monistic view of an undivided oneness of Being where there is no separation. On the other hand, the illusory is the realm, which is experienced everyday. The world seems real, but this is only because man is closely identified with his separatistic ego and physical body.

The chief disciple and promoter of the *Course* is Marianne Williamson. She is the "guru of the moment in Hollywood." Williamson is available for lectures on everything from intimacy and relationships to money and careers. Though her talks frequently mention Jesus and the Holy Spirit, the *Course* is not Christian. Nevertheless, the *Course* quietly claims to be Christian. The opening pages imply Jesus Christ is the author. Williamson's book, *A Return to Love*, elicits a return to love of God, but how is this possible if God is an impersonal oneness and man is absorbed into basically nothingness? Furthermore, she writes, "the most important revelation, the crux of the Course, is that in reality it [separation from God] never actually happened at all...."[10]

Not only does the *Course* deny sin, the reality of death, and the devil, but also it diminishes the crucifixion and resurrection of the Lord. Though *A Course in Miracles* may claim to have all of life's answers, there is nothing new under the sun (Eccl. 1:9). Its followers have embraced the devil's lie and denied the efficacy of Christ's atonement. The *Course*, as such, has no answers to life.

Ultimately, Williamson has synchronized Christianity, Buddhism, pop psychology, and the 12-steps of AA/NA into her lectures.[11] Since reality is one, then it must be logical to assume all religions are one, and lead to the same destination. Both the workbook[12] and the text[13] for the *Course* state, "The Final Judgement on the world contains no condemnation." However, Jesus said, "Therefore just as the tares are gathered up and burned with fire, so shall it be at the end of the age (Mt. 13:40). The unbeliever cannot attempt to deny God's judgment, but the Son of man will purge the world of the wicked and will reign in righteousness with His saints.

Robert Schuller

Any analysis of the teachings of Robert Schuller will reveal serious errors with biblical teaching. The first problem with Schuller's teaching is that he has a man-centered theology as opposed to a God-centered theology. With subtlety, Schuller wrote that God is not glorified until man is glorified. In fact, he writes, "...it is impossible to glorify God until we glorify his children."[14] In the beginning of his book, *Self Esteem: The New Reformation*, Schuller quotes from an associate professor at the University of Pennsylvania. The professor's comments regarding Schuller's book are shocking: "It is surprising how our minds have come to a similar position—you have pursued a religious route and I have pursued a scientific path, and we have both arrived at the same bottom line: unconditional self-esteem."[15]

Schuller has redefined salvation, as well, teaching "to be born again means that we must be changed from a negative to a positive self-image...."[16] Hell is redefined as "the loss of pride that naturally follows separation from God.... A person is in hell when he has lost his self-esteem."[17] His statements are major alterations of God's Word because Jesus taught hell is a literal place of torment (Mk. 9:47-48).

Certainly, one of the most blasphemous teachings of Schuller is that Christ's death on the cross was solely for protection against His perfect self-esteem being turned into sinful pride.[18] According to Schuller, Jesus would not even tell mankind they are miserable sinners.[19] Quite contrary, Jesus said, *"I have not come to call the righteous but sinners to repentance"* (Lk. 5:32). Rather than the cross sanctifying the ego trip, it is a testimony of man's utter depravity and the horrible price God paid to redeem fallen mankind.

Another dangerous aspect of Schuller's teaching is "possibility thinking," which is essentially humanistic psychology stressing the powers of the mind. Faith is a force or power for Christians and even non-Christians to use for the manipulation of energy. By following these techniques man can become co-creators with God.[20] Fundamentally, Robert Schuller's "possibility thinking" is the same as Eastern practitioners.[21] The church must not tolerate Schuller's teachings. One should not seek fellowship where these false teachings are taught (Rom. 16:17) for they will lead to dangerous consequences (Mt. 7:17; 24:11-12; Acts 20:30).

Norman Vincent Peale

Although highly regarded in many churches primarily through his magazine, *Guideposts*, Norman Vincent Peale embraced a heresy called New Thought. One of the developments from New Thought is Ernest Holmes' United Church of Religious Science. Although Holmes was an occultist and believed in spirit guides,[22] Peale said, "Only those who knew me as a boy can fully appreciate what Ernest Holmes did for me. Why, he made me a positive thinker."[23] New Thought was rejected as heresy by the church when it first originated, nevertheless, the mind science cults developed from it. Through the writings of Norman Vincent Peale, this New Age movement of its day has kept its teaching in the church.

Peale was a 33rd degree Mason and was even on the front cover of two Masonic publications, *The New Age* (May 1986) and the *Scottish Rite Journal* (March 1991). Peale has written many forwards to occultic books including Helen Keller's *My Religion*[24] and John Marks Templeton's *Discovering the Laws of Life*.[25] As a guest on the Phil Donahue program, Peale was asked of the need to be born again. He replied, "Oh, no, you've got your way to God, I've got mine. I found eternal peace in a Shinto temple in Japan."[26]

Although Peale referred to God, it is clear from his writings and testimonies that Christ is only a principle. Peale's influence by the occult is detected by his understanding of faith. Faith works miracles by "the operation of spiritually scientific laws" and prayer is a force underlying the universe.[27] The problem is that faith is not exercised towards an impersonal principle, but in the person of Jesus Christ.

The power innate in humans is the constant flow of energy in the mind, according to Peale. More mental power can be acquired by saying "With the mind of Jesus I can do all things." Positive thinking is the means for releasing man's abilities and allowing power to flow through him.[28] Biblically, possessing the mind of Christ is the "self-emptying" of Jesus as a suffering servant (Phil. 2:5-11). To have the mind of Christ is to be in humble self-renunciation in doing God's will. Peale's versions of faith and true biblical faith are as incompatible as grace and works.

Napoleon Hill

Napoleon Hill wrote one of the most popular books for personal achievement, *Think and Grow Rich*. Both Andrew Carnegie and "the Venerable Brotherhood of Ancient India" inspired this book.[29] The author's purpose in the book is for the reader to "find the magic of self-direction, organized planning, auto-suggestion, master-mind association, an amazing revealing system of self-analysis, detailed plans for selling your personal services, and a wealth of other specific helps from the experience of great men who have proved their value."[30]

Clement Stone, author of *Success through a Positive Mental Attitude* (co-authored by Hill),[31] stressed the power of the mind and tried to make a science of faith. Hill was not the only one to embrace this concept completely. Robert Schuller's "possibility thinking," Norman Vincent Peale's "positive thinking," Clement Stone's "positive mental attitude," Charles Capps' "positive confession," and Oral Roberts' "seed-faith" principles all teach the same, that is, the power of faith as a force that can change one's environment and even God. Not only is this "doctrine of demons" taught widely to leaders in the business world, but also it pervades churchianity.

Napoleon Hill received his "guidance" from "unseen, silent forces"[32] and "Invisible Counselors" (Emerson, Paine, Edison, Darwin, Lincoln, Burbank, Napoleon, Ford, and Carnegie).[33] He wrote, "I was astonished by the discovery that these imaginary figures became apparently *real*...."[34] Not only did Hill become exceedingly fearful of the meetings with his "Invisible Counselors," but also—by his own admission—he confessed, "The experiences were so uncanny, I was afraid if I continued them I would lose sight of the fact that the meetings were *purely experience of my imagination*.[35]

Obviously, demonic spirits were influencing this author's famed Law of Success. Hill quoted Henley as follows: "I am the master of my fate, I am the captain of my soul." He then stated that Henley should have informed mankind that such is true for all men "*because* we have the power to control our thoughts.[36] Actually, what Hill considers a liberating concept is actually one of man's problems, that is, man wants to be captain of his own soul, master of his destiny. Sinful humanity attempts to usurp God's sovereignty. Even Stanford Graduate School of Business has a course entitled, *Creativity in Business*,[37] which teaches these occult beliefs. Mankind is indeed acting like little gods on earth, but the true and only God has said, *"you will die like men"* (Ps. 82:7).

Positive Confession

Positive confession is one of the most distinctive doctrines of the Word of Faith Movement. Such televangelists as Charles Capps, Paul Yonggi Cho, Kenneth Copeland, Kenneth Hagin, Benny Hinn, Frederick C. Price, Robert Tilton, and many others are responsible for this teaching that originated with occultist E. W. Kenyon. The basic teaching of positive confession is given in the saying, "What I confess, I possess." It is the belief that a person can bring into existence what he speaks with his mouth. Faith is nothing more than confession; hence, the power of the tongue is the key to positive confession. Charles Capps wrote, "I [God] am not the one that is causing your problems. *You are under an attack of the evil one* and I can't do anything about it. *You have bound me by the* [negative] *words of your own mouth.*"[38]

Positive confession teachers believe they have creative power similar to God and claim by "divine right" they can manipulate reality. By agreeing with God's Word, in confession, the humanistic ideals of these teachers is said to follow.[39] However, belief in positive confession is the same as in witchcraft. Benny Hinn even appealed to witchcraft as proof that the power of the spoken word (*rhema*) works.[40] Pragmatism does not make the practice biblical (Mt. 12:22-28; Deut. 13:1-5). These teachers promote pagan practices which are pantheistic (all is God) since faith is not in a personal God, but it is an untouched power even witches can use.

Paul Yonggi Cho teaches the power of positive confession is the ability to incubate the third dimension by entering the fourth dimension, the spiritual realm, as opposed to the mere three material dimensions. Cho's fourth dimension is unproven by science or logic. He wrote, human beings become like God "through the fourth dimension" by "incubat[ing] the third dimension, and connect[ing] it." Mortals have a power comparable to God's ability to "give the word" and "speak forth" in order to create.[41]

The common response given to this author for denouncing these practices as unbiblical is that he is trying to understand it logically. In the forward to Cho's book, Robert Schuller wrote, "Don't try to understand it. Just start to enjoy it!"[42] Such advice has been given by many occultists, but for a "Christian" to make such requests is deplorable. God tells His children, *test the spirits* (1 Jn. 4:1). A personal God predestines the events of a believer's life and not some impersonal power in one's words manifested through positive confession.

Although positive confession adherents claim supernatural inspiration for their teachings, the source of revelation contradicts God's Word. Interestingly, many spirit guides encourage their mediums to promote positive confession. The popular craze in angels has also given credibility and endorsement to the teachings of positive confession. Many of these mediums and angels refer to the same biblical proof texts as the faith teachers.[43]

Rather than finding support from the Bible for positive confession, the teachings of the movement can be linked to the Mind Sciences. The cults of Armstrongism and Mormonism also believe in the divine power of man and believe man can become a god (the next logical step if positive confession were legitimate). In fact, Benny Hinn,[44] Morris Cerullo,[45] Paul Crouch,[46] Earl Paulk,[47] Kenneth Copeland,[48] and many others believe they are gods.

The common source of power among positive confession teachers is the demonic. D. R. McConnell is a historian on the Charismatic movement and did graduate work at Oral Roberts University. He knows the teachings of positive confession directly. He wrote, "E. W. Kenyon...formulated every major doctrine of the modern Faith Movement.... The roots of Kenyon's theology may be traced to his personal background in the metaphysical cults, specifically New Thought and Christian Science.... Kenyon attempted to forge a synthesis of metaphysical and evangelical thought.... The resultant Faith theology is a strange mixture of biblical fundamentalism and New Thought metaphysics."[49] Clearly, the connection between Word of Faith theology and occultism is not accidental. Anthropologist Michael Warner reported, "many techniques long practiced in shamanism, such as visualization...positive attitude...and mental and emotion expression of personal will for health and healing...are being reinvented in the West precisely because it is needed."[50]

Reducing Prayer to Science

A 1997 poll found that 82% of Americans believe in the "healing power of prayer," 64% believe doctors should pray with their patients if they request it, 28% believe faith healers have the ability to heal, and 28% believe in therapeutic touch.[51] Prayer is popular in the fields of herbal medicine, naturopathy, and holistic practices. New Age physician, Deepak Chopra offers his healing approach as an alternative to biblical prayer: "I satisfy a spiritual yearning without making [people] think they have to worry about God and punishment."[52]

Robert Schuller claims possibility thinking is a form of prayer. However, what is basis for believing one could think their desires and through believing actually receive those things? Michael Harner, a practicing shaman, demonstrated that positive attitude to actuate a universal force is a technique "long practiced in shamanism." Likewise, mental and emotional expressions of personal will for health and healing is a shamanistic practice reinvented, in the field of holistic practice, for Western acceptance.[53] It does not matter what religion or spiritual approach works, providing it produces results. Robert Schuller repeated this idea: "You don't know what power you have within you...! You make the world into anything you choose."[54] There simply is no power of belief in prayer; it is belief in the One who hears one's prayers.

The "scientific" benefit of prayer is a placebo effect at best and demonic manipulation at worst. Largely through the writings of Norman Vincent Peale, Robert Schuller, and the Word of Faith teachers, "faith" has become a scientific term. God has an extremely minor part in answering prayer, since one only needs to believe enough to receive the desired results. Peale was one of the first clergymen to consult with a doctor in hopes of bridging the gap between science and religion. He was not concerned with the particular faith of the doctor; his only concern was for "a psychiatrist who was a man of faith." Peale found his answer in doctor Smiley Blanton. The Blanton-Peale Institute was founded on the uniting of "pastoral counseling with psychological medicine."[55]

The scientific belief in prayer is classic pantheism. The idea is that mankind is a part of the whole. Quantum physics asserts that matter and energy are interchangeable, hence, man is a manifestation of the infinite universe, not an individual. The material is only illusion because mankind's material bodies are part of the universal body, which is spirit, and mankind's mind is part of the universal mind. Man only needs to realize the divine within him and tap the vast reservoir of energy already present in his true self.

Mental attitudes can trigger the brain to release chemicals into the blood stream, and bring physical healing. A relaxed and joyful attitude can stimulate the brain and nervous system to begin a process of self-healing, but this is quite distinct from the belief that man possesses unlimited potential. Psychosomatic problems can be healed with a placebo, but to mix science and religion will produce grand deception. Christians should not take a "leap of faith" into occultism, but should know what and why they believe (1 Pet. 3:15). Genuine biblical faith results from a relationship with the true God. God grants prayers only as they coincide with his will, not the power of belief in something. Christianity is not true because it works, but because it is based on the evidence of history (Lk. 1:1-4; Acts 1:3; Rom. 1:4; 1 Thess. 2:5; 2 Pet. 1:16).

Near-Death Experiences

Among the best-selling authors in the field of near-death experiences is Raymond A. Moody, who wrote two books on the subject, *Life after Life* and *Reflections on Life after Life*, both of which were published by Bantam Books in 1975 and 1976 respectively. The other author is Elisabeth Kübler-Ross, who wrote *Questions and Answers on Death and Dying*, published by MacMillan in 1974. Following closely behind Moody and Kübler-Ross is Ralph Wilkerson, pastor of Melodyland Christian Center in Anaheim, California and author of *Beyond and Back* in 1977. Mormon Betty J. Eadie had her experience published in 1992 as *Embraced by the Light*. Two major motion pictures, *Brainstorm* and *Flatliners*, were based on near-death experiences.

It is vital to remember that no matter how real an experience may be, it must not be given the same authority of Scripture. Scripture says much about death, but says little about the actual process of death, that is, what actually happens at the exact moment of death. Genesis 35:18 gives the first reference to a soul departing the body in death. Whereas, 1 Kings 17:21 records God granting the soul of a child to return to his dead body. Ecclesiastes 12:7 offers a clue as to what happens at death.

The problem with near-death experiences is the person claims to have died and returned from the dead to share a vision or message with the world. The obvious needs to be stated though, namely, the experience is called "near-death" so the person was not clinically dead. There are abundant accounts of people being resuscitated after long periods of time during which no vital signs registered, indicating the soul never left the body, but the body merely ceased to function. Many people have waked from these states and have no conscious recollection.

Normally, the near-death experience begins with a roaring sound, followed by the sensation of traveling quickly down a dark tunnel towards a distant light at the end. Oftentimes the being of light embraces the person in love or the being claims to be Jesus. The being never condemns the person and never mentions the need of salvation. It would make perfect sense for Satan to take great pleasure in convincing souls not to fear the judgment of God. Douglas Groothuis, professor of philosophy at Denver Seminary, rightly concluded, "the disembodied soul is still subject to the deception wrought by the 'ruler of the kingdom of the air' (Eph. 2:2) and his minions, who are not above appearing as angels of light (2 Cor. 11:14)."[56] God said, *And inasmuch as it is appointed for me to die once and after this comes judgment* (Heb. 9:27), which would mean the person's experience was not what it was believed to be, especially when the messages frequently conflict Scripture.

Shaktipat and Charismania

Shaktipat is a term used to describe the touch of a guru. The guru is considered to be a manifestation of the one divine Reality: Brahman. Usually the guru will place his hand to the worshipper's forehead, resulting in the worshipper falling down to the ground in a state of ecstasy. The ecstatic state is a powerful manifestation of what is believed to be a divine encounter. Kali, the wife of Shiva the destroyer, is the most feared and revered deity in Hinduism. Her power is greater than any Hindu deity, including Shiva, Ganesh, and Hanuman. Kali is also known as Shakti, which literally means power. The demonstration of power in the touch of a guru is believed to manifest Brahman, the one force in the universe. It is believed that the *shaktipat* must come through a channel of power, the underlying force of the whole universe, embodied in Shiva's consort Shakti (Kali). The tremendous experience of power from the goddess Shakti, administered through the guru's touch, causes the worshipper to fall to the floor in a state of ecstasy, or he may see a bright light, experience a trance vision, whereby he receives an experience of enlightenment or inner illumination, or else may experience some other mystical or physic experience.

In his book, *Feast of Fire*, John Kilpatrick, former pastor of Brownsville Assembly of God in Pensacola and now fulfilling his "apostolic calling" throughout the world, believes such experiences are proof of revival. Whether the experience is called *shaktipat*, resting in the Lord, or slain in the spirit, the source is the same. Kilpatrick believes otherwise and wrote, "something is happening inside those 'horizontal before the Lord.'"[57] The experiences of the charismatic, who claims the phenomenon is from God, must explain the remarkable identity with the world of the occult. Only the spiritually inept would not recognize the occult influence.

The emphasis in charismatic revivals is on fire and power. In the occult, the *kundalini*, or serpent force, changes into fiery form, or "shakti." The manifestation of *kundalini* awakening is characterized by "a rich spectrum of emotional and bodily manifestations" and "sensations of energy and heat." Violent shaking, jerking, and twisting often overcome the person's body. The manifestations are uncontrollable and are usually followed by unnatural laughter, speaking things previously unknown, and a variety of animal sounds. The experiences can range from visions of the divine and demonic.[58]

Clearly, the experience called "slain in the spirit" is not of God, but it is a counterfeit experience of a true fellowship with God through His Word. Certainly some of the experiences are real, but the phenomenon itself is wholly demonic. Scripture proof texts are commonly given for support of the phenomenon, but none are valid. For instance, the disciples at the transfiguration fell on their faces in fear when God spoke (Mt. 17:6). The Philippian jailer fell on his face because he feared for his eternal life (Acts 16:29). Men will fall on their face because of reverence for God and never were they unconscious or touched by a guru. ...*And so he will fall on his face and worship God, declaring that God is certainly among you* (1 Cor. 14:25).

Toronto Blessing

The Lester B. Pearson Airport in Toronto, Canada is the location for the Toronto Blessing. The movement itself did not begin in Toronto. Randy Clark, a St. Louis Vineyard pastor, attended a conference in Tulsa, Oklahoma, which was conducted by Rodney Howard-Browne, a South African Pentecostal minister. When Clark first heard Howard-Browne, his life and ministry were at a low. Similarly, John Kilpatrick described the same experience prior to the start of the "revival" at Brownsville Assembly of God.[59] Clark claimed his life was changed at the conference, which was the result of the manifestations occurring during the service. In January 1994, Clark was scheduled to speak at the Airport Vineyard in Toronto. The services were scheduled for a few days but developed into several weeks. Since that time, the Airport Vineyard Church has become headquarters of the "blessing" resting in Toronto. Many attempt comparisons of the "blessing" to the Azusa Street Revival in 1906.

John Arnott, pastor of the Airport Vineyard, would be the first to acknowledge the strange manifestations occurring at his church. It is not uncommon to find church members and guests laughing uncontrollably, falling on the floor, people roaring like lions, loud weeping, and violent shaking. None of these manifestations are new to the Vineyard Movement. The late John Wimber, founder of the Vineyard Movement, witnessed all the above manifestations as characteristic to the Vineyard churches.

Those involved do not see a problem with people falling down in a prolonged state of ecstasy, identical to Hindu worshippers who feel the power of *kundalini* energy. According to these charismatics, whether one attributes the source to God or the devil is not as important as the experience. Those that would criticize the movement are called heresy hunters and accused of being unspiritual for criticizing this so-called "move of God." Holy Laughter is also commonplace. The result of being "soaked in the spirit," losing consciousness after being "slain in the spirit," is uncontrollable laughter called "holy" because it is alleged to come from God. In the *Stormy Search for the Self*, Christina and Stanislav Grof, foremost authorities on spiritual crises resulting from occult practice, state one of the results of awakening *kundalini* energy is unmotivated and unnatural laughter or crying.[60]

Any consideration of the Toronto Blessing, should ask why there is no biblical precedence. The identical—not similar—experiences are from the pagan world. One need only watch the documentary film, *Fear is the Master*, and observe Bhagwan Shree Rajneesh produce the same effects as the Toronto Blessing by the power of the devil. Furthermore, in his book, *Dance your Way to God*, he encouraged his disciples "just be joyful.... God is not serious...this world cannot fit with a theological god...laugh your way to God."[61] Both the "Holy Ghost Bartender" Rodney Howard-Browne and Rajneesh encouraged their followers to be "drunk on the divine." The people involved in these manifestations are not experiencing God, but have been seduced by the wiles of the devil.

Apparitions

Medjugorje, Yugoslavia, a village in Bosnia-Herzegovina, is supposedly the location for the daily appearance of the Virgin Mary to four visionaries in 1981. Those who have heard her messages, report she is calling sinners to repentance and prayer. These visions are called apparitions. Over 30 million people have visited Medjugorje, and there are even Medjugorjan prayer groups and retreat centers ever multiplying. Other appearances have been occurring throughout the world. In Vienna, over 1,000 people gather weekly to pray the rosary and meditate on the latest message from Mary received by her visionaries at Medjugorje.

The phenomenon in Medjugorje started when a farmer's irreligious children caught a glimpse of Mary and heard her speaking. The children had never heard of the other apparitions of Mary in places like Lourdes, France in 1858, and Fatima, Portugal in 1917. Thousands have since come and claim to witness strange lights and smelled heavenly perfumes. Many pilgrims visiting the site claim physical healing, deliverance from addiction, and a renewal of Catholic piety.

The apparition of Mary rejects the word of Jesus that salvation is only through Him. "Our Lady of Medjugorje" also commended the doctrine of purgatory, ceremonialism, and works as opposed to grace.[62] The "Lady of Guadeloupe" and the Fatima apparition have rejected Christ's sufficiency; even the Denver apparition claimed to offer sacrifices for the sins of the world. If only people would read the Word of God (cf. Col. 2:13-14, etc.), they would not fall prey to such false gospels. The sources of the Marian apparitions are clearly demonic. The message they give is another Jesus and another gospel. The current Pope and millions of others declare, "Totus tuus Sum Maria" which means "Mary, I am totally yours." The unprecedented Mariolatry within Catholicism is based on two documents: Pope Pius IX's *Ineffabilis Deus* and Pope Pius XII's *Munificentissimus Deus*. Both documents are as anti-biblical as the Marian apparitions.

The Roman Catholic teaching on Maryology is leading many gullible souls into darkness. Exodus 20:3-5 states only God is to be worshipped. Worship of Mary is neither logical (since she is not omnipresent) or biblical (since God alone is worshipped), therefore, these apparitions may only be understand as the result of the demonic. Though Mary was a wonderful woman, and Christians honor her as the mother of Jesus, she has passed from death into heaven. Attempts to communicate with her is an abomination (Deut. 18:10-12). Necromancy (*nekros*, "dead," and *manteia*, "divination") is an abomination to God. It does not matter how wonderful a person was on this earth, when they are dead, it is an abomination to seek contact with him or her. However, demons will communicate with those who ignore God's Word.

In these last days [God] *has spoken to us in **His** Son* (Heb. 1:1-2) not through Mary. If the apparitions are not from God, then logically they are demonic or a natural phenomenon, such as the water stain on the office building (formerly belonging to Seminole Finance Corporation) in Clearwater, Florida. Whenever the apparitions are worshipped and obeyed, they are a tool of Satan to deceive people to have faith apart from Jesus Christ and trust a lie instead. Commenting on the Marian apparitions, Timothy Kauffman wrote, "I can say that none of the apparitions of Mary have done any violence to Rome's lofty view of her. But the apparitions have done violence to the little we know of Mary from the Scriptures. They have also done violence to the Gospel of Christ."[63]

Channeling is another form of necromancy. A channeler is believed to receive information from a reality other than the physical one. The channeler's information does not come from himself in any psychological or unconscious manner; the messages are received outside the channeler's ordinary conscious or unconscious mental state. The source is completely divorced from a physical level of reality.[64] Former New Age leader, Randall Baer, expressed the true agenda of the channeled spirits. He wrote, "They come with an olive branch of peace, love, and universal brotherhood in one hand, and a smoking gun concealed behind their back in the other."[65]

The most famous instance of contacting the dead is recorded in the First Book of Samuel (28:1-25). Saul sought to contact the spirit of Samuel through a witch at Endor. The witch is said to have *a familiar spirit* (KJV) meaning the medium is controlled by a divining demon. The biblical example reveals the common contact with the dead is an impersonation through the power of demons. The biblical record of the medium's terror at the appearance of a real spirit demonstrates the fraudulence of spirit contact.[66] Though most contacts with the dead can be dismissed as pure fraudulence, there are times when real communications with the spirit world occur. The primary reason for Christians to reject contact of the dead, including an apparition, is that Scripture condemns the practice (Deut.

18:11; Gal. 1:6-8). God is thought to be untrustworthy or Scripture is not sufficient for man's knowledge. Why seek contact with the dead when God has provided *everything pertaining to life and godliness* (2 Pet. 1:3) in His Word? For a Christian to seek an apparition, or form of necromancy, for counsel is to call God a liar. Furthermore, either the Bible is true *inasmuch as it is appointed for me to die once and after this **comes** judgment* (Heb. 9:27) or else the deceased are returning to earth on some astral plane to guide man in defiance of God's revelation. Not only has God forbidden such practices, but also the message undermines the true biblical faith.

Postmillennialism and New Age Thinking

Modern postmillennialism is generally attributed to Daniel Whitby (1638-1725), a Unitarian minister. Whitby was the first to challenge the amillennial interpretation of Revelation 20 that was quite prevalent in the church at the time. Both conservative and liberal theologians were influenced by Whitby. The late John Walvoord explained,

> The rising tide of intellectual freedom, science, and philosophy, coupled with humanism, had enlarged the concept of human progress and painted a bright picture of the future. Whitby's view of a coming golden age for the church was just what people wanted to hear. It fitted the thinking of the times.... It was attractive to all kinds of theology. It provided for the conservative a seemingly more working principle of interpreting Scripture. After all, the prophets of the Old Testament knew what they were talking about when they predicted an age of peace and righteousness. Man's increasing knowledge of the world and scientific improvements that were coming could fit into this picture. On the other hand, the concept was pleasing to the liberal and skeptic. If they did not believe the prophets, at least they believed that man was now able to improve himself and his environment. They, too, believed a golden age was ahead.[67]

Whitby's system of interpretation resulted in two types of postmillennialists: "(1) a Biblical type of postmillennialism, finding its material in the Scriptures and its power in God; (2) the evolutionary or liberal theological type which bases its proof on confidence in man to achieve progress through natural means."[68] The mission of the liberal theological type was to liberate mankind from social injustices, and is generally associated with the social gospel.

Liberal postmillennialism regarded man as essentially good and life on earth as getting better which would lead toward a golden age for humanity. Two things were essential to this position: (1) there was no gospel; (2) there was much hope in evolutionary progress. Conversely, the biblical type of postmillennialism was also optimistic concerning the future, but it is committed to "a glorious age of the church upon earth through the preaching of the gospel under the power of the Holy Spirit."[69] Gary Scott Smith demonstrated that the inspiration for the social gospel came from evangelical postmillennialism.

> Failing to recognize its roots in the evangelical social concern of the eighteenth and nineteenth centuries, historians have usually described the Social Gospel as a radically new departure. During the one hundred years prior to the development of this movement in the 1870s and 1880s, however, many evangelicals labored vigorously to improve social conditions. Through the Bible, missionary, education, temperance, anti-slavery, and peace societies of the Benevolent Empire and through their work among America's poor, soldiers, and handicapped during the mid-nineteenth century—as in the earlier labors of John Wesley, William Wilberforce, and the Clapham Sect in England-evangelical Christians provided the example, inspiration, and principles for much of the Social Gospel.[70]

Rousas John Rushdoony's work, *The Messianic Character of American Education*, is an attempt to address some of the mistakes Puritan eschatologists made which resulted in their influence of the social gospel. Not only has postmillennialism had an influence in liberalism, but also it has been influential in the charismatic movement. Gary North responded to Dave Hunt's work, *The Seduction of Christianity*, which gave attention to this influence.

> Mr. Hunt points out that the language used by other "positive confession" ministers is similar to the man-deifying language of the New Age "positive thinking" theology.... He implicitly associates New Age optimism with an optimistic eschatology. He recognizes (as few of the "positive confession" leaders have recognized) that they have become operational postmillennialists. They have abandoned the mind-set of premillennial, pretribu-lational dispensationalism, even though they have not made this shift known to their followers, who still profess faith in dispensationalism. He sees clearly that a new eschatology is involved in "positive confession," a *dominion eschatology*.
>
> ...he is worried, not just because a few charismatic preachers who are sloppy in their wording *appear* to have adopted New Age theology, lock, stock, and barrel. They have no more self-consciously adopted New Age theology than they have self-consciously adopted historic postmillennialism.[71]

The optimism of both charismatics and postmillennialists allows them to collaborate. The only difference between the two is that the charismatics are optimistic in regards to their own well-being, whereas the postmillennialists are optimistic in regards to society's eventual well-being. Such mistaken optimism allows postmillennialism to collaborate with unorthodox groups for the sake of building the kingdom. One of Hunt's points in his book is that this relationship is a "seduction" resulting from the postmillennial vision for the future.

The New Age Movement
The New Age movement first gained popularity in the early

70s. During the 80s, New Age beliefs permeated almost every aspect of culture. The New Age movement is regarded as "a meeting of three cultural forces: the Judaic and Christian traditions, Western occult mysticism, and Eastern religions."[72] The primary emphasis of the New Age movement is transformation; therefore, it is quite millennial. A major tenet of New Age thinking is the current Age of Pisces (the Age of Christianity) is diminishing and the Age of Aquarius (the New Age) is impending. The Age of Aquarius will come when the world experiences spiritual and psychological transformation.

Since the New Age is optimistic, it thoroughly rejects premillennialism since the teaching of an apocalypse prior to the time of blessing is anathema. In some aspects, the New Age is similar to postmillennialism because mankind will establish the New Age when the mass of society experiences radical transformation. Therefore, mankind will become a "world savior"[73] and all consciousness will be united. Since the New Age is based on a new paradigm, changes must occur. While elements of the old order will be retained, there will be a convergence of East and West. Rationalism will be balanced by intuition. God, humanity, and nature will no longer be regarded as distinct entities. The environment will be nurtured because humanity will be one with nature.[74]

Many New Agers anticipate a coming "Christ" who will establish this New World Order. However, the Christ of the New Age movement is completely separate from the Christ of the Bible. The Christ in the New Age movement is a spirit separate from a historical figure. Many religious leaders are said to have possessed the "Christ-spirit" (even Jesus). There is an obvious inconsistency here among New Agers since some believe the Christ is spirit only, whereas others anticipate a coming Christ who will manifest his presence and guide humanity in both spiritual and psychological transformation.

Occult Influence in the World

Having addressed some of the major delusions in churchianity, attention will now be given to occult influence primarily in the secular world.

Ecology and the Occult

Former vice-President Al Gore has received applauds from both gurus and shamans for his book, *Earth in the Balance*, even though he is deeply critical of conservative Christians. Gore demonstrates his fervent support of Buddhism, Hinduism, Native American Spiritism, and the "global environment crisis." The need for a balance between mankind and his environment is due to "an outer manifestation of an inner crisis that is for lack of a better word, spiritual!"[75]

While Christianity is deplorable, Native American religions offer "a rich tapestry of ideas about our relationship to the earth." When President Franklin Pierce wanted to buy the land of Chief Seattle and his tribe, the Chief wanted to know, "Will you teach your children what we have taught our children. That the earth is our mother? This we know: the earth does not belong to man, man belongs to the earth."[76]

Even former President Bill Clinton embraced the eco-agenda to prevent the apocalypse said to be threatening mankind. To prevent an apocalypse, Americans have to be educated so the public understands the threat of global warming.[77] However, as scientists have consistently proven, the supposed global warming threat is itself nothing more than foolish speculation. Reports from the National Climactic Data Center stated that there is no substantial proof of global warming. One scientist concluded, "There are simply too many natural climate variations—which have nothing to do with humans...."[78]

Essentially, the environmental movement is not about social concerns, rather it is a spiritual movement. God warned mankind about those who have *exchanged the truth of God for a lie, and worshipped and served the creature rather than the Creator, who is blessed forever* (Rom. 1:25). Instead of worshipping the creation, the Creator commanded, *Let all the earth fear the LORD; let all the inhabitants of the world stand in awe of him* (Ps. 33:8). The environmental movement seeks to unite all religions to save the planet which means world's religions must ignore doctrinal differences and unite as one to inaugurate a new spirituality. Christians can be concerned for the environment, but must not let ecology take precedence over the Great Commission. The concerns of the environmental movement should be an opportunity to explain the cause and only solution that is Jesus Christ.

Of course, anyone that disagrees with ecologists is thought as a hindrance to the evolution of mankind. Gore wants mankind to embrace a goddess religion, which was "eliminated by Christianity," because such an understanding of Mother Goddess "offers us new insights into the nature of the human experience."[79] Gore's statement is completely anti-Christian. His philosophy denies the eternal Fatherhood of God. God does not create *ex deo* as a woman's body does, rather he creates *ex nihilo*. Tal Brooke, president of the Spiritual Counterfeits Project in Berkeley, wrote that the ethical and moral issue raised by ecology is "an anti-Christian program that would further erase God while polluting the souls of the collective.[80] Is this not what Paul called *oppositions of science falsely so called?* (1 Tim. 6:20; KJV).

Drugs and the Occult

Commenting on the affects of drugs, Dr. Peter R. Breggin made the following observation: "At the root lies a dangerous assumption that it is safe and effective to tamper with the most complex organ in the universe."[81] When the normal connection between man's brain and mind is loosened, the opportunity is given for demonic spirits to control the brain. Nobel Prize winner, Sir John Eccles, did research on the brain leading to his conclusion that the brain can be operated by a nonphysical entity in the same manner that a human being manipulates a machine for his purposes.[82]

Craving for transcendence, or wholeness, many people become involved in drug usage. The spiritual dimension is oftentimes obscured by the physical dimension. The quest for deeper spirituality has to be satisfied by more drugs, while many do not realize their chemical dependence is the result of a spiritual problem. The Psalmist cried, *As the deer pants for the water brooks, so my soul pants for Thee, O God* (Ps. 42:1). Pascal described this thirst as the "God-shaped vacuum" within each and every person, and unless God fills the void man will resort to all manner of wickedness.

It is undeniable that drugs do become a substitute for dependence on Christ. Even the secular world recognizes the dangers of drug usage. It is through the use of drugs that many become involved in the occult. For instance, the Beatles friendship with Maharishi Mahesh Yogi followed the recording of the album *Sergeant Pepper's Lonely Hearts Club*, the band's testimony to LSD influence. Later, these same drug induced states were found to intensify with the practice of Eastern mysticism.

God has condemned the use of mind-altering drugs. The New Testament mentions sorcerers twice (Acts 13:6, 8) and sorceries four times (Rev. 9:21; 18:23; 21:8; 22:15). Both are condemned in the Old Testament (Ex. 7; Isa. 47; Jer. 27; Mal. 3). The Greek word for sorcery in the New Testament is farmakeiva (*pharmakeia*) which is the equivalence of today's shaman or sorcerer, who experience altered states of consciousness to contact spirits. One reason for the judgment in the Book of Revelation upon an evil and unrepentant world is due to their drug usage: *and they did not repent...of their sorceries* (Rev. 9:21).

UFOs and the Occult

The UFO connection is a perfect explanation for the rapture of the church and also for divine guidance into the New Age. The belief that other beings in the universe have evolved in the same manner as human beings is exciting to those who believe man is at the verge of becoming a god. Belief that UFOs evolved into supernatural beings has encouraged mankind to think the same is possible. If only man could contact the UFOs, they would reveal the process of evolution to godhood. Dr. Jonathan Henry, professor at Clearwater Christian College, wrote,

> Just as Nimrod led the people to worship the heavens, we are seeing a virtual worship of the heavens arising in our culture today. It is not merely that evolutionism and other false systems place human opinions ahead of what God says. The fact is that the New Age, Hinduism, and

evolutionism are all promoting a single theme which, it is claimed, will lead man to higher development, and eventually to godhood. That theme is...The Search for Extraterrestrial Life.[83]

The experiences of the UFO contacts reveal a demonic encounter, rather than contact with a higher intelligence in the universe. Consider the words of Shirley MacLaine: "I found people had experiences similar to mine: people involved with trance channeling, past life recall, growing spiritual awareness, and even contact with UFOs."[84] There is an obvious connection between the world of the occult and UFO encounters. Whitley Strieber is just one example. His best-selling books, *Communion* and *Transformation*, chronicle his supposed abductions by UFOs. Strieber, who has a strong background with occult practices (Zen, witchcraft, Gaia worship, mysticism, Gurdjieff),[85] provides a chilling description of the true identity of the UFOs. He wrote, "Increasingly I felt as if I were entering a struggle that might be even more than life-or-death. It might even be a struggle for my soul.... Alone at night I worried about the legendary cunning of demons. At the very least, I was going stark raving mad.... He looks mean. Is this the devil? What the hell is this?"[86]

The mechanistic scientist will not find such conclusions very convincing. Agnostics and atheists feel they are too sophisticated for such archaic encounters with the demonic. The identity of UFOs is not "little green men" but demons, masquerading as angels of light (2 Cor. 11:14) which is obvious when comparing close encounters of the fourth kind and higher with encounters of occult experiences. The demonic forces are working to deceive mankind to find hope somewhere else in the universe other than God. It is likely that these same demons will provide a rational explanation for the rapture of the church when it happens. In her book, *Aliens Among Us*, Ruth Montgomery quoted the message of one channeler who received a message from "space brother," Andromeda Rex. "The Great Evacuation will come upon the world very suddenly. The flash of emergency events will be as the lightening that flashes in the sky. Our rescue ships will be able to come in close enough in the twinkling of an eye to set the lifting beams in operation in a moment."[87]

The purpose of transformation in the UFO movement is to prepare mankind for the Age of Aquarius. The Piscean Age, beginning with the time of Christ, is thought to be diminishing. To be ready for the New Age mankind will have to experience dramatic changes in consciousness. The stage is certainly set for mass delusion. The UFO phenomenon thrives on creating a perfect disguise to delude the world into thinking there is a salvation outside of Jesus Christ. Dr. Henry concluded his chapter as follows: "Yet the Bible tells us that those who have come to Jesus Christ alone for personal salvation can have wisdom and intelligence simply by asking Him for it (James 1:5). Why should we search anywhere else?"[88]

Rock Music and the Occult

In Greek mythology, the Muses were the daughters of Zeus and Mnemosyne. The Muses were nine in number. Hesiod said they were all one in mind, heart, and spirit. If the Muses loved someone he was at once said to forget his worries when one of the Muses' servants sang. Each field of the arts was under the direction of the Muses. Hesiod said the Muses revealed to him their ability to make falsehood seem to be truth as they so desired. If the Muses inspired a man, he was considered to be more sacred than a priest.

It is noteworthy that many musicians have claimed to receive their inspiration from the supernatural. Perhaps the most popular musician to credit his influence from the spirit world was the "electronic shaman," Jim Morrison. Jim Morrison called the spirits "The Lords,"[89] Joni Mitchell called her muse "Art,"[90] Jimi Hendrix did not call his influence by name but he knew he was possessed by something,[91] and the list could continue.

Obviously, it is in the realm of the spirit that music reaches its greatest heights of influence and power. It is not just the Greeks who are inspired by spirit beings today. Most rock musicians admit their creativity arrives in somewhat unusual manners. Music, which certainly relates to man's spirit, is among the most potent techniques of Satan to empower the lusts of man's heart. Satan does not just use a Hitler or Manson to accomplish his goals; he can use a pretty singer or amazing guitarist to disguise his presence and purposes.

Mick Jagger was quoted as follows: "Who's dead this week then? Roy Orbison? Hard to tell these days, innit! Pop star! They're droppin' like flies! Droppin' all over the place, mate!"[92] It seems as though the muses do inspire many musicians with fame and fortune, but the price to pay is one's own soul. Pamela Des Barres' book, *Rock Bottom*,[93] documents the high number of rock related deaths. The message in popular rock music today is completely anti-Christian, and the demonic influence is all too rampant. The Scripture warns, *Do not be deceived, God is not mocked; for whatever a man sows, this he will also reap* (Gal. 6:7).

A Tale of Two Cities

"It was the best of times, it was the worst of times, it was the age of wisdom, it was the age of foolishness, it was the epoch of belief, it was the epoch of incredulity, it was the season of Light, it was the season of Darkness," wrote Charles Dickens in his classic *A Tale of Two Cities*. The Bible presents another tale of two cities from Genesis to Revelation identified as Jerusalem and Babylon. Jerusalem is the city of God and Babylon is the city of Satan. Both oppose each other.

The Bible depicts Babylon as the beginning and continual nurturing of the kingdom of man (Gen. 11:1-9). The Satanic reign of Antichrist incorporates all economical, political, religious, and social aspects identified with Babylon. Daniel described Babylon as the beginning of the Gentile kingdoms to dominate earth's history during *the times of the Gentiles* (Dan. 2, 7; Jer. 30:7; Lk. 21:24). Babylon will be revived in the end times for a significant role in the tribulation (Rev. 14:8; 16:19; 17-18). The period of Gentile domination will not end until Christ returns to the earth in judgment.

Revelation 17-18 depicts Babylon as the origin of all godless economy, government, and religion. Nearly all ungodliness during the tribulation period is connected to Babylon. The Apostle John prophesied of *BABYLON THE GREAT, THE MOTHER OF*

HARLOTS AND OF THE ABOMINATIONS OF THE EARTH (Rev. 17:5). Babylon, or Antichrist's harlot, is the "mother" of all false religion in the end times from Genesis 11 to Revelation 18. All the religions of the world, including an apostate form of Christianity, will unite with ecclesiastical Babylon during the tribulation period (Rev. 17). Nevertheless, at the end of the tribulation, God will judge these false religions forever.

The Satanic Trinity

The Satanic trinity will be a counterfeit of the true and living God. Satan (representing God the Father), Antichrist (representing God the Son), and the False Prophet (representing God the Holy Spirit) will comprise this false trinity. The Antichrist and the False Prophet will collaborate to control a one world economy, government, and religion. The False Prophet (or *another beast*) will be the spokesperson for the Antichrist (Rev. 16:13; 19:20; 20:10). It is written of the False Prophet, *he deceived those who had received the mark of the beast and those who worshipped his image* (Rev. 19:20). He deceives the world to worship the first beast, Antichrist, through *signs and wonders*. Near the end of the tribulation, the Antichrist grows weary of the counterfeit religion and *will make her desolate and naked, and will eat her flesh and will burn her up with fire* (Rev. 17:16). The destiny of the Antichrist and the False Prophet, however, is to be cast into the lake of fire at the return of Jesus Christ (Rev. 19:20).

Great discernment needs to be exercised today in light of the occult influence in the church and world and the things still to come. Furthermore, any so-called "Christian" movement working toward a kingdom on earth is to be seen as working toward the kingdom of Antichrist. The responsibility of each and every Christian is to share the Gospel with the lost, defend the faith, and to be looking for the glorious hope of Christ's return.

Biblical Role of Experience

Much of churchianity is dominated by man-centered evangelism and experience-based Christianity. Certainly, man has a role in evangelism, but he is not the emphasis; it is God alone who is the focus of the Gospel, since it is the good news of *His* holiness, love, and sovereignty. Similarly, experience has a necessary role in the Christian faith, but it is not the foundation for belief. The basis for experience always needs to be the truth of God's Word. Doctrine and application cannot be separated; orthodoxy produces orthopraxis.

Individual accounts of experiencing the presence of the Lord are as various as there are Christians. There are numerous nations, *tribes and peoples and tongues* that will stand *before the throne and before the Lamb* (Rev. 7:9). The experience of redemption verifies what has occurred as a person is born again by grace through faith in Jesus Christ. The changes to follow redemption are fundamental since all Christians are involved, and no Christian can deny what has occurred in a personal sense. It is this same experience working in the life of every Christian since the birth of the church. Old Testament saints testified of a salvation experience stating their sin had been removed as far as the east is from the west (Ps. 103:12), and as a result, testified of a change in the quality of their lifestyles. Paul testified that he was once the foremost of all sinners (1 Tim. 1:12-13), but through grace and mercy in Jesus Christ, his life was forever changed.

However, as already demonstrated, there is a caution to be exercised in the role of experience. For example, the influence of personal experience in Eastern religions upon Western society has led to a questioning of what types of experience are unbiblical. Irresponsibility occurs when all experience is accepted as valid, since that would ignore the reality of Satan and his demons, and the deceitful of one's own flesh. A biblical experience is verifiable, but a non-biblical experience is predisposed to a mysticism that is difficult to test. Therefore, Christians need to be careful when sharing testimonies with non-Christians because they also have experiences of denying self which will challenge the validity and uniqueness of the Christian's experience. It is not wise to use experience as the basis for Christian beliefs since only God's Word is truth, but Christians can explain their experience because of divine revelation which proponents of other religions do not have.

Defining Biblical Experience

E. Y. Mullins defined biblical experience as follows: "It is the state or condition produced in the mental, moral and spiritual nature of man when he conforms to the conditions which Christianity declares to be necessary to have union and fellowship with God."[94] Biblical experience "is the state or condition" of being *born again*, or regenerated (Jn. 3:3, 5). John instructs his readers that the born again experience is only through the work of God regenerating a child of wrath into a new creature. The experience is not the result of church membership, heredity, positive thinking, or self-effort. Salvation is initiated by God and secured by the power of God.

Mullins proposed the question "Is the Christian conscious of a change?"[95] Repentance (*metanoia*) is a change of mind. Sorrow and repentance are different (2 Cor. 7:9). The Greek word *metamelomai* ("to regret") is never used in a passage referring to salvation. Therefore, repentance and living godly is different (Acts 26:20). As evidence of repentance, *bring forth fruit* (Mt. 3:8; cf. Lk. 17:1-4). Repentance is entirely inward; confession of sin and living godly are bringing *forth fruit*. Repentance and faith then are not synonymous, but repentance alone assumes the presence of faith just as faith alone assumes repentance. True repentance does not occur without faith, so even though they are not synonymous they cannot be separated. Similarly, faith and hope are separate but one cannot be present without the other, and so it is with repentance and faith. Repentance and faith are inseparable, but to say which occurs first this author does not know. Therefore, when regeneration occurs the Christian is knowledgeable of repentance, and the surrender of the will. The danger of experience alone is that it does not affect the will. Preaching of God's Word can be *both* emotional and intellectual, but when an appeal for change is made, the message must be intended for the will since it is the greatest resistance to the truth. A Christian then recognizes this surrender of the will, and that he or she has truly been *born again*. Furthermore, the consciousness feels the presence of Jesus Christ through the indwelling of the Holy Spirit.

The consciousness recognizes the affects of being *born again* and the presence of the Lord Jesus Christ which affects the countenance of the Christian in every sphere of life. The first recognition of change is spiritual transformation. When believers are justified by grace through faith, *we have peace with God through our Lord Jesus Christ* (Rom. 5:1). Justification includes a *walk in newness of life* (6:4) which produces tension between the flesh and the spirit for the new Christian (7:14-25). The life of the flesh once loved is now hated, and the life of the Spirit once hated is now loved. The difference between the experience of the Christian and other religious experiences is the ministry of the Holy Spirit providing the dynamic to live a new life that is evidence of no longer being in condemnation but now giving evidence of the righteousness of God.

Not only is there a moral and spiritual change for the Christian, but also there is an intellectual change. *The fear of the LORD is the beginning of knowledge; fools despise wisdom and instruction* (Prov. 1:7). The intellectual change is not solely rationalistic, but it is wisdom from God through His Word. Rationalism is completely man-centered. The wisdom of God also uses the mind, but it is God-centered. Rationalism will always result in self-righteousness and the absence of repentance (Isa. 47:10). The wisdom of God begins with *a humble spirit* (Prov. 16:19) that is rational, but reason is surrendered to the wisdom of God (Jer. 9:23-24). Prior to regeneration, the mind of the Christian was darkened (Rom. 1:21; 11:10; Eph. 4:18). When a person is *born again*, the knowledge and wisdom of God allows the development of rational skills. Experience is essential in the early work of regeneration.

Logical Biblical Experience

Logical biblical experience will recognize the principle of contrast.[96] The most famous example of this principle is Descartes basic statement: "I think; therefore I am." Descartes put his statement in the negative form, "I cannot think," but that only proved he possessed rationality since the same person exerts mental effort to stop thinking. By putting his statement in the negative, he used logical contrast to prove the original statement. The logical principle of contrast helps to understand the validity of a statement by thinking in the negative. Biblically, the Christian recognizes a different type of consciousness prior to regeneration, but a transformation of the same person to another type of consciousness proves the experience of regeneration.

To test the change using the principle of contrast, a Christian thinks of the past life and is conscious of a transformation. Herein is a major contrast between Eastern mysticism and occult experiences. Prior to becoming a Christian, this author would take massive doses of LSD and feel his spirit becoming one with the universe. Later, as a committed pagan, occult practices proved just as effective. The pagan experience was real, but the experience of regeneration is a complete contrast. The pagan experience resulted in the loss of consciousness in some mystical experience, and after it passed, the same person remained. However, when regenerated, a completely different experience occurred as the Holy Spirit produced a permanent intellectual, moral, and spiritual transformation. The reasons for the experience of regeneration could be described and it was possible to think about what happened as a result of the new birth.

Christian experience is possible, but it is always explained on the basis of the Word of God. For example, the transformation in the life of a believer is explained on the basis of forgiveness of sins, peace with God, and the ministry of the Holy Spirit. No longer does this Christian possess the same heart and thoughts as he did as a pagan, but the transformation can be explained whereas the former pagan experiences could not. Even though the occult experience was real, the same person always remained. As Christians contemplate the affects of regeneration, they can know they are *being led by the Spirit of God* knowing *these are sons of God* (Rom. 8:14). The intellect has been transformed and God now enables the Christian to understand *the things of the Spirit of God* (1 Cor. 2:14-16) and relate the knowledge and wisdom of God to his life and world. The Holy Spirit will continue the process of sanctification throughout the Christian's life helping him to *walk in newness of life* because of the death and resurrection of Jesus Christ (Rom. 6:1-4). True biblical experience is splendid, but the Christian is always conscious of the work of God, as Scripture always provides direction to the experience. *For WHO HAS KNOWN THE MIND OF THE LORD, THAT HE SHOULD INSTRUCT HIM? But we have the mind of Christ* (1 Cor. 2:16).

CHAPTER 18

THE MILLENNIAL RELIGION

Arnold G. Fruchtenbaum

At the time of the second coming of the Messiah, the land of Israel will undergo some tremendous geographical and topographical changes. One of the key changes in the land of Israel will be the rise of a very high mountain that will become the highest mountain of the world. On top of this mountain the millennial Temple and the millennial Jerusalem will stand.

The Millennial Mountain of Jehovah's House

There are several passages that speak of this millennial mountain of Jehovah's house. One such place is Isaiah 2:2-4.

And it shall come to pass in the latter days, that the mountain of Jehovah's house shall be established on the top of the mountains, and shall be exalted above the hills; and all nations shall flow unto it. And many peoples shall go and say, Come ye, and let us go up to the mountain of Jehovah, to the house of the God of Jacob; and he will teach us of his ways, and we will walk in his paths; for out of Zion shall go forth the law, and the word of Jehovah from Jerusalem. And he will judge between the nations, and will decide concerning many peoples; and they shall beat their swords into plowshares, and their spears into pruning-hooks; nation shall not lift up sword against nation, neither shall they learn war any more.

431

Isaiah states clearly that the mountain upon which Jehovah's House will stand will be the highest of all the mountains, and by far the most exalted (2:2a). All the nations will move toward it in pilgrimage in order to learn the ways of God because the law of the millennial kingdom will emanate from this mountain (2:2b-3). The law will result in worldwide peace because differences among the nations will be settled by the Word of the Lord coming from the mountain of Jehovah's house (2:3b-4).

Later, in Isaiah 27:13, the prophet demonstrated that the high mountain will become the center of Jewish worship. *And it shall come to pass in that day, that a great trumpet shall be blown; and they shall come that were ready to perish in the land of Assyria, and they that were outcasts in the land of Egypt; and they shall worship Jehovah in the holy mountain at Jerusalem.* However, the worship is not for the Jews only, because Isaiah 56:6-8 teaches the fact that this great mountain of Jehovah's house will become a place of prayer for all peoples, Jews and Gentiles alike.

Also the foreigners that join themselves to Jehovah, to minister unto him, and to love the name of Jehovah, to be his servants, every one that keeps the sabbath from profaning it, and holds fast my covenant; even them will I bring to my holy mountain, and make them joyful in my house of prayer: their burnt-offerings and their sacrifices shall be accepted upon my altar; for my house shall be called a house of prayer for all peoples. The Lord Jehovah, who gathers the outcasts of Israel, says, Yet will I gather *others* to him, besides his own that are gathered.

By means of the Gentile nations, the people of Israel will be brought and regathered to the mountain of Jehovah's house, according to Isaiah 66:20: *And they shall bring all your brethren out of all the nations for an oblation unto Jehovah, upon horses, and in chariots, and in litters, and upon mules, and upon dromedaries, to my holy mountain Jerusalem, says Jehovah, as the children of Israel bring their oblation in a clean vessel into the house of Jehovah.* Isaiah's contemporary, the Prophet Micah, also wrote of this great mountain (Mic. 4:1-2) with words similar to, or quoting, Isaiah.

> But in the latter days it shall come to pass, that the mountain of Jehovah's house shall be established on the top of the mountains, and it shall be exalted above the hills; and peoples shall flow unto it. And many nations shall go and say, Come ye, and let us go up to the mountain of Jehovah, and to the house of the God of Jacob; and he will teach us of his ways, and we will walk in his paths. For out of Zion shall go forth the law, and the word of Jehovah from Jerusalem;

The mountain of Jehovah's house will be exalted above every mountain and hill (4:1), and the law of God will proceed from this mountain (4:2). The prophet who received the most revelation regarding the mountain of Jehovah's house was Ezekiel, who first introduced it in Ezekiel 17:22-24, describing the mountain of the height of Israel as a place of lush greenery and vegetation.

> Thus says the Lord Jehovah: I will also take of the lofty top of the cedar, and will set it; I will crop off from the topmost of its young twigs a tender one, and I will plant it upon a high and lofty mountain: in the mountain of the height of Israel will I plant it; and it shall bring forth boughs, and bear fruit, and be a goodly cedar: and under it shall dwell all birds of every wing; in the shade of the branches thereof shall they dwell. And all the trees of the field shall know that I, Jehovah, have brought down the high tree, have exalted the low tree, have dried up the green tree, and have made the dry tree to flourish: I, Jehovah, have spoken and have done it.

Later, in Ezekiel 20:40-41, the prophet declared the mountain will serve as the center of Jewish worship in the millennial kingdom. After Israel's regeneration and regathering, she will worship the Lord in this high, lofty, and holy mountain.

For in my holy mountain, in the mountain of the height of Israel, says the Lord Jehovah, there shall all the house of Israel, all of them, serve me in the land: there will I accept them, and there will I require your offerings, and the first-fruits of your oblations, with all your holy things. As a sweet savor will I accept you, when I bring you out from the peoples, and gather you out of the countries wherein ye have been scattered; and I will be sanctified in you in the sight of the nations.

Only in the closing chapters of his book does Ezekiel give the details of what this very high mountain of Jehovah's house will be like. In three different sections he gives the details. The first is in Ezekiel 40:1-4.

In the five and twentieth year of our captivity, in the beginning of the year, in the tenth *day* of the month, in the fourteenth year after that the city was smitten, in the selfsame day, the hand of Jehovah was upon me, and he brought me thither. In the visions of God brought he me into the land of Israel, and set me down upon a very high mountain, whereon was as it were the frame of a city on the south. And he brought me thither; and, behold, there was a man, whose appearance was like the appearance of brass, with a line of flax in his hand, and a measuring reed; and he stood in the gate. And the man said unto me, Son of man, behold with your eyes, and hear with your ears, and set your heart upon all that I shall show you; for, to the intent that I may show them unto you, are you brought hither: declare all that you see to the house of Israel.

In the twenty-fifth year of the seventy years of the Babylonian Captivity, Ezekiel was given a final, special revelation of Israel's future in the messianic kingdom (40:1). As Isaiah and Micah before him, he saw a very high mountain which had the skyline of a city on its southern side (40:2). As will be seen later, this city is the millennial Jerusalem. A message is then spoken to the prophet telling him that he will soon be given certain revelations which he is to declare to the house of Israel (40:3-4).

The second passage, Ezekiel 45:1-8, describes in great detail the mountain of Jehovah's house.

> Moreover, when ye shall divide by lot the land for inheritance, ye shall offer an oblation unto Jehovah, a holy portion of the land; the length shall be the length of five and twenty thousand *reeds*, and the breadth shall be ten thousand: it shall be holy in all the border thereof round about. Of this there shall be for the holy place five hundred *in length* by five hundred *in breadth*, square round about; and fifty cubits for the suburbs thereof round about. And of this measure shall you measure a length of five and twenty thousand, and a breadth of ten thousand: and in it shall be the sanctuary, which is most holy. It is a holy portion of the land; it shall be for the priests, the ministers of the sanctuary, that come near to minister unto Jehovah; and it shall be a place for their houses, and a holy place for the sanctuary. And five and twenty thousand in length, and ten thousand in breadth, shall be unto the Levites, the ministers of the house, for a possession unto themselves, *for* twenty chambers. And ye shall appoint the possession of the city five thousand broad, and five and twenty thousand long, side by side with the oblation of the holy portion: it shall be for the whole house of Israel. And *whatsoever is* for the prince *shall be* on the one side and on the other side of the holy oblation and of the possession of the city, in front of the holy oblation and in front of the possession of the city, on the west side westward, and on the east side eastward; and in length answerable unto one of the portions, from the west border unto the east border. In the land it shall be to him for a possession in Israel: and my princes shall no more oppress my people; but they shall give the land to the house of Israel according to their tribes.

The holy mountain is denoted as the holy oblation because

this section will be for holy ritual use and somewhere on this mountain the millennial Temple is to stand, in addition to the city of Jerusalem. The very high mountain described, the highest in the world, will itself have a fifty-mile square plateau on top (45:1). The square plateau will be subdivided into three sections. The northern section (45:2-4) will be twenty miles by fifty miles, having the millennial Temple in its center, which will be approximately one mile square. The remainder of the area of the northern section will be reserved as living conditions for a certain group of priests. The central section (45:5) will also be twenty miles by fifty miles and will be reserved for the members of the tribe of Levi. The southern section (45:6-8) will be ten miles by fifty miles. In the center of the southern section will stand the millennial Jerusalem measuring ten miles by ten miles. On either side of the city will be field areas, each measuring ten by twenty miles, for growing food. The areas will be controlled by the prince, the resurrected David, who will apportion the land according to tribe.

The third section Ezekiel described the details of the mountain of Jehovah's house is in Ezekiel 48:8-20.

> And by the border of Judah, from the east side unto the west side, shall be the oblation which ye shall offer, five and twenty thousand *reeds* in breadth, and in length as one of the portions, from the east side unto the west side: and the sanctuary shall be in the midst of it. The oblation that ye shall offer unto Jehovah shall be five and twenty thousand *reeds* in length, and ten thousand in breadth. And for these, even for the priests, shall be the holy oblation; toward the north five and twenty thousand *in length*, and toward the west ten thousand in breadth, and toward the east ten thousand in breadth, and toward the south five and twenty thousand in length: and the sanctuary of Jehovah shall be in the midst thereof. *It shall be* for the priests that are sanctified of the sons of Zadok, that have kept my charge, that went not astray when the children of Israel went astray, as the Levites went astray. And it shall be unto

them an oblation from the oblation of the land, a thing most holy, by the border of the Levites. And answerable unto the border of the priests, the Levites shall have five and twenty thousand in length, and ten thousand in breadth: all the length shall be five and twenty thousand, and the breadth ten thousand. And they shall sell none of it, nor exchange it, nor shall the first-fruits of the land be alienated; for it is holy unto Jehovah. And the five thousand that are left in the breadth, in front of the five and twenty thousand, shall be for common use, for the city, for dwelling and for suburbs; and the city shall be in the midst thereof. And these shall be the measures thereof: the north side four thousand and five hundred, and the south side four thousand and five hundred, and on the east side four thousand and five hundred, and the west side four thousand and five hundred. And the city shall have suburbs: toward the north two hundred and fifty, and toward the south two hundred and fifty, and toward the east two hundred and fifty, and toward the west two hundred and fifty. And the residue in the length, answerable unto the holy oblation, shall be ten thousand eastward, and ten thousand westward; and it shall be answerable unto the holy oblation; and the increase thereof shall be for food unto them that labor in the city. And they that labor in the city, out of all the tribes of Israel, shall till it. All the oblation shall be five and twenty thousand by five and twenty thousand: ye shall offer the holy oblation four-square, with the possession of the city.

After announcing that the high mountain is to be fifty miles square (48:8), Ezekiel begins to describe the northern section (48:9-12). The northern section will be twenty miles by fifty miles (48:9) and will be inhabited by priests, for in the very center of this section, the millennial Temple is to stand (48:10). The priests who are to occupy this area, around the Temple, are the descendants of Zadok because that segment of the tribe of Levi remained faithful while the others *went astray* (48:11-12). The central section (48:13-14) will also measure twenty miles by fifty miles. The area here will be reserved for the remainder of the tribe of Levi (i.e. those Levites who did not belong to the line of Zadok). The southern section (48:15-19) is to measure ten miles by fifty miles, and in the middle the millennial Jerusalem is to be built (48:15-16). Jerusalem will be in the very center of this southern section and will measure ten miles by ten miles (48:17). The two remaining portions of the southern section, east and west of Jerusalem, will each measure ten miles by twenty miles, and will be for the purpose of growing food for the inhabitants of Jerusalem (48:18). Jerusalem will not belong to any particular tribe but will be inhabited by members of all the twelve tribes of Israel (48:19). Again, Ezekiel states the total size of this mountain of Jehovah's house is to be fifty miles square. It will be the holy oblation with both the Temple and Jerusalem built upon it (48:20).

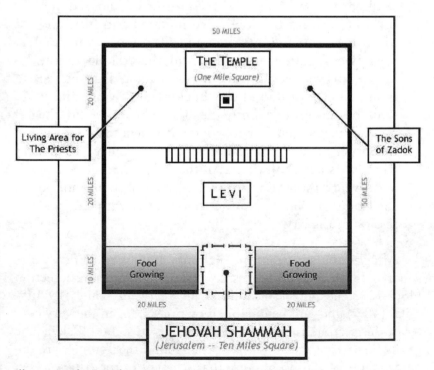

Illustration by Matthew Lipsey, © 2003 Ariel Ministries

The Millennial Temple

In Ezekiel 37:26-28, prophet predicted that God's Sanctuary will be placed in the midst of Israel.

Moreover I will make a covenant of peace with them; it shall be an everlasting covenant with them; and I will place them, and multiply them, and will set my sanctuary in the midst of them for evermore. My tabernacle also shall be with them; and I will be their God, and they shall be my people. And the nations shall know that I am Jehovah that sanctifies Israel, when my sanctuary shall be in the midst of them for evermore.

There is a great expansion and elaboration of these few verses in Ezekiel 40:5-43:27. The study of this lengthy passage will need to be limited to a survey of the material given by Ezekiel, emphasizing only a few important features. There are eight main sections which discuss the various facets of the millennial Temple.

The first section, in 40:5-27, concerns the outer court. After the measure of the outer wall (40:5), Ezekiel gives a description of the outer court (40:6-27), mentioning the eastern gate (40:6-16), the thirty chambers and the pavement around the outer court (40:17-19), the northern gate (40:20-23), and the southern gate (40:24-27).

The second section in Ezekiel 40:28-47 has a description of the inner court. There are four things which are described: the *first* item is the gates of the inner court (40:28-37), composed of the southern gate area (40:28-31), the eastern gate area (40:32-34) and the northern gate area (40:35-37); *second*, the prophet describes the table for the preparing of the sacrifices (40:38-43); *third*, the chambers for the ministering priests (40:44-46); and, *fourth*, the Altar (40:47).

The third section in Ezekiel 40:48-41:26 describes the millennial Temple itself. Included in this description are the porch (40:48-49), the posts (41:1), the Holy Place with its entrance (41:2), the Holy of Holies (41:3-4), the Temple wall and chambers

(41:5-11), the separate place (41:12-14), the interior of the Temple (41:15-20), and the exterior of the Temple (41:21-26). From all these various measurements, it is evident that this particular Temple will be larger than all previous Temples, measuring about one mile square. The area of the present Temple Compound is not large enough to hold the Temple described by Ezekiel and will require some major geographical changes which is why the new mountain of Jehovah's house will be necessary.

The fourth section in Ezekiel 42:1-14 describes the chambers of the outer court. The fifth section in Ezekiel 42:15-20 describes the outer wall. The sixth section in Ezekiel 43:1-9 records the return of the *Shechinah* Glory. Just as the *Shechinah* Glory authenticated and sanctioned the Solomonic Temple, it will also sanction this Temple by its return from the same direction that it departed (43:1-5). Once the *Shechinah* Glory returns, a message will be declared containing the promise that the *Shechinah* Glory will never depart from Israel again, but will dwell in the midst of Israel forever (43:6-9).

The seventh section, in Ezekiel 43:10-12, is a command for the prophet to identify the sinfulness of Israel. In light of the coming holy oblation, how much more should Israel be ashamed of their present sinfulness. The eighth section in Ezekiel 43:13-27 is a description of the Altar. Included in this description is the measure of the Altar (43:13-17) and the consecration of the Altar (43:18-23). The Temple is to be the center of Jewish and Gentile worship during the millennium.

The Millennial System of Priesthood and Sacrifice

Ezekiel 44:1-46:24 is concerned with the various laws regulating the millennial system of priesthood and sacrifice. While there are similarities with the commandments of the Law of Moses, there are also some discernible differences. Consequently, the millennial system of priesthood and sacrifice must not be viewed as a reinstitution of the Law of Moses, which ended permanently and forever with the death of the Messiah. During the messianic kingdom, a whole new system of law—kingdom law—will be instituted. There will be no reinstitution of any previous code of law.

Ezekiel 44:1-46:24 has seven major sections dealing with priesthood and sacrifice. The first section, in Ezekiel 44:1-3, concerns the law of the outer eastern gate. The passage states that in the beginning of the millennium, the outer eastern gate will be shut, never to be reopened again throughout the millennium (44:1). The reason for the shutting of the outer eastern gate is due to the fact that the *Shechinah* Glory returned by way of the eastern gate (43:1-9), therefore, never to leave Israel again (44:2). The closing of the outer eastern gate will symbolize the fact that the *Shechinah* Glory will never depart from Israel again. Ezekiel then describes the prince and authority and ministry he will have in relation to this outer eastern gate (44:3). The prince, as has already been shown, will be the resurrected David. He will eat before the gate (44:3a), and entrance will only be by means of the porch (44:3b). Since this gate will be permanently closed, entry and exit into and from the porch will have to be from and into the outer court.

It must be mentioned that Ezekiel 44:1-3 has no reference to the present eastern gate of Jerusalem, known today as the golden gate. The passage, in its context, is not referring to Jerusalem today, but is referring to the Temple gate in the millennium. The gate of Jesus' day was destroyed in AD 70. The present golden gate was built in the 7th century and later modified by the Crusaders. It was partially destroyed by the Ottoman Turks and rebuilt in the early 16th century. It was sealed by the Turkish governor of Jerusalem in 1530.

The second section (44:4-8) contains another message of the *Shechinah* Glory which again identifies Israel's present sins. The third section (44:9-14) describes the duties of the Levites, who will be the caretakers of the Temple. The fourth section (44:15-31) concerns the duties of the sons of Zadok, who will be in charge of the sacrifices of the Temple.[1] The fifth section (45:1-8) describes the holy oblation, or the mountain of Jehovah's house.

The sixth section (45:9-46:18) describes the duties of the prince, David. Three facts are stated concerning his duties. *First*, unlike in Israel's past history when the princes of Israel used false measures, the law of the measurements (45:9-12) will be characterized by true, faithful, and just balances. *Second*, the duties will involve the implementation of the laws of the offerings (45:13-46:16). After listing some general instructions (45:13-17), Ezekiel describes the law relating to the New Year offerings (45:18-20), the Passover offerings (45:21-24), the offerings for the Feast of Tabernacles (45:25), and the Sabbath offerings (46:1-5), which will occur at the inner eastern gate. The inner eastern gate will be shut for six days, but will always be opened on the Sabbath throughout the kingdom period. Subsequently, the New Moon offerings are described (46:6-8), in addition to the special festival offerings (46:9-12) and the daily sacrifices (46:13-15). *Third*, the prince will have some special rights because of his exalted position in relation to the Temple (46:16-18).

The seventh section (46:19-24) concerns the laws of the boiling of the sacrifices. One of the things present in the Solomonic Temple that will be absent in the millennial Temple is the Ark of the Covenant. According to Jeremiah 3:16, *And it shall come to pass, when ye are multiplied and increased in the land, in those days, says Jehovah, they shall say no more, The ark of the covenant of Jehovah; neither shall it come to mind; neither shall they remember it; neither shall they miss it; neither shall it be made any more.* Since God Himself in the Person of the Messiah will be dwelling in and reigning from Jerusalem, there will be no need for any Ark of the Covenant. Furthermore, the Ark of the Covenant contained the tablets of stone that were the embodiment of the Law of Moses. The fact that the Law of Moses is no longer in effect is another reason why the Ark of the Covenant will be missing.

To summarize, there will be a sacrificial system instituted in the millennium that will have some features similar to the Mosaic system, along with some completely new laws. Since there will be new laws, the sacrificial system of the millennium must not be viewed as a reinstitution of the Mosaic system because it is not. It will be a completely new system containing some things old and some things new, and will be instituted for an entirely different purpose.

A common argument against interpreting these verses literally is the question as to why such a system would be necessary since the Messiah has already died. If the death of the Messiah was the final sacrifice for sin, how could these animal sacrifices provide expiation for sin? Therefore, some say, these chapters of Ezekiel must not be understood literally. However if not interpreted literally, Ezekiel gives a lot of detail that would suddenly become meaningless. Furthermore, if all that detail is intended to be symbolic, the symbols are never explained. So the non-literalist is forced to be subjective in expounding them and must resort to guesswork, and for that reason have developed a large variety of contradictory views. The literal approach is the safest method to gain understanding of these passages. There are at least four reasons to interpret this whole section of Ezekiel literally.

First, interpreting literally is the normal hermeneutic used elsewhere in Scripture and all theologies use the literal approach at least in parts of the Bible. Only the dispensationalist uses the literal approach consistently. Such a consistent usage leads to the conclusion that there will be a millennial Temple and sacrifice.

Second, Ezekiel is not the only one testifying of the millennial Temple and sacrifices. Other prophets spoke of these things in a non-apocalyptic context. The millennial Temple is referenced in Isaiah 2:3; 60:13; Daniel 9:24; Joel 3:18; and Haggai 2:7, 9. The millennial sacrifices are mentioned in Isaiah 56:6-7; 60:7; 66:18-23; Jeremiah 33:18; Malachi 3:3-4; and Zechariah 14:16-21 (this last passage speaks of the observance of the Feast of Tabernacles in the messianic kingdom, but it required special sacrifices as part of its observance). Therefore, more than one passage and more than one prophet would have to be allegorized if there were no millennial Temple or millennial sacrifice.

Third, the millennial Temple is not the only Temple that Ezekiel described. In Ezekiel 8-11, he describes the departure of the *Shechinah* Glory from Israel from the first Temple. All agree his description of the Temple and the events that occurred there are quite literal. In Ezekiel 40-48, the prophet described the future return of the *Shechinah* Glory into the fourth Temple. If what he said about the first Temple was literal, then what he says about the fourth Temple should also be interpreted literally.

Fourth, Ezekiel provided a tremendous amount of detail which includes specific measurements and types of sacrifices. All accept the details of the sacrifices of the Law of Moses to be quite literal. All accept the detailed measurements of the Tabernacle and the first Temple to be quite literal. There is no good reason not to accept the details of the fourth Temple to be equally literal. If they are not and are all symbolic, then why does Ezekiel not explain the meanings of these symbols? Why have those who take these passages as allegorical and symbolic not been able to give explanations for what the symbols mean? The author is not denying that the millennial Temple and sacrifices are not symbolic of spiritual truths. Just as the Tabernacle and the Mosaic sacrifices were symbolic and typological of spiritual truths (while quite literal themselves), similarly, the millennial Temple and sacrifices can be literal while also being symbolic of spiritual truths. The very fact that Ezekiel was ordered to record all the details and declare all the facts to the house of Israel would be meaningless if such details did not mean what they said.

There are usually three main objections to interpreting these sacrifices literally. The *first objection* is thinking literal sacrifices would mean a return to the sacrificial system of the Mosaic Law which ended when Messiah died and therefore violates all that the New Testament teaches about the termination of the Law as a rule of life.

The *answer* is that while there are many similarities with the sacrifices of the Mosaic Law, as there are between the sacrifices of Noah and Moses, the differences show they are not the same. It was these very differences preventing the rabbis from accepting Ezekiel into the Hebrew Canon for some time. These differences are quite apparent. For instance, in the consecration of the altar (Mosaic: Exod. 29:1-37; millennial: Ezek. 43:18-27) there are the following differences: the Mosaic anointed the altar, while the Ezekiel had no anointing; the Mosaic offered a bullock for a sin offering for all seven days, while the Ezekiel offered a bullock on the first day only; the Mosaic offered no goat, while the Ezekiel offers goats for the last six days; the Mosaic applied blood on the horns of the altar only, while the Ezekiel applies blood on the horns, the corners, and upon the lower molding; for the burnt offering, the Mosaic offered a ram every day, while the Ezekiel offers both a bullock and a ram every day; the Mosaic offered a ram for the consecration of the priesthood, but Ezekiel has no ram for the consecration of the priesthood, only for the altar.

Furthermore, the Mosaic contained the Ark of the Covenant, but the millennial Temple will not contain the Ark of the Covenant (Jer. 3:16). Under the Mosaic Law, only the high priest could enter the Holy of Holies, but in Ezekiel 44:15-16, all priests will be able to enter. The rules of marriage found in Ezekiel 44:22 were applicable to only the high priest under the Mosaic Law, but in Ezekiel, they will be applicable to all priests. Under the Mosaic Law, the first of Nisan was not a special holy day, but will be according to the Ezekiel system (45:18). The procedure described in 45:19 differs from the Mosaic in two ways: in the animal chosen, the Mosaic had a male goat, while the Ezekiel has a bullock; in the way the animal was disposed, the Mosaic disposed of the animal outside the camp, while the Ezekiel is inside the camp.

Concerning the Passover (45:21-24) in the Mosaic, it was a family affair with the head of the household performing the ritual; while in the Ezekiel, the Prince will perform the ritual on behalf of the nation. In the Mosaic, the Passover was a one day festival; while in the Ezekiel, it will last for seven days. The Mosaic offered an unblemished lamb, while the Ezekiel offers a bullock.

There is also a difference in the number of sacrifices offered between the Mosaic (Numb. 28:16-24) and the Ezekiel. There is also a difference in the measures of the meal offering between the Mosaic and the Ezekiel. Concerning the Feast of Tabernacles (Ezek. 45:25), there is a difference in the quantity of the offerings (Numb. 29:12-34), and the Ezekiel does not have the added eighth day that the Mosaic had (29:35-38). As for the Sabbath offerings (Ezek. 46:4-5), the Ezekiel requires six lambs and a ram, which is more than the Mosaic (Numb. 28:9), which required only two lambs and a ram, and the same will be true with the meal offering. Concerning the New Moon offerings

(Ezek. 46:6-7), the Mosaic required two bulls, one ram, and seven lambs, while the Ezekiel will require one bullock, six lambs, and one ram. There is also a difference in the daily offering (Ezek. 46:13-15), since the Mosaic (Exod. 29:38-42; Num. 28:3-4) required two lambs each day, both morning and evening, while the Ezekiel will require one lamb each morning and none in the evening. There is also a difference in the daily meal offering (Exod. 29:40; Numb. 28:5). In the Mosaic Law, the observance of the Feast of Tabernacles was mandatory for Jews only, while under kingdom law, it will be mandatory for both Jews and Gentiles (Zech. 14:16-21). Under the Law of Moses, only Jews could be priests, but under kingdom law, Gentiles will also serve as priests (Isa. 66:18-21). All these differences demonstrate this is not a return to the Law of Moses, but it is a new system under kingdom law and so it does not violate what the New Testament teaches concerning the termination of the law with Messiah's death.

The *second objection* is that the measurements given by Ezekiel will not correspond to the Temple Mount and therefore cannot be literal. It is true that the size of the Ezekiel Temple will not fit the Temple Mount but it is a misconception that the Ezekiel Temple was intended to be built on that mount. The *answer* is that the details Ezekiel provided demonstrates that there will be some major geographical changes resulting from the second coming. As already demonstrated, some of these changes will create a new Temple Mount altogether.

The *third objection* is that to believe in the reinstitution of the blood sacrifices is heresy. A simple *answer* must be since when is interpreting the Bible literally and believing it literally a heresy? The burden of proof is always on the one who claims that a certain part of the Bible does not mean what it says. For the sole reason that there is no blood sacrifices for the church does not mean there cannot be such sacrifices for Israel. Similarly, even though there is no physical Temple, priesthood, and sacrifice for the church does not mean the same will be true for Israel.

What will be the purpose of these sacrifices in light of Messiah's death? Initially, it should be remembered that the sacrificial system of the Mosaic Law did not remove sins either

(Heb. 10:4), but only covered them (the meaning of "atonement" in Hebrew). The Mosaic sacrifices did not serve only one purpose but were multipurposed. One such purpose was to serve as a physical and visual picture of what the Messiah would do (Isa. 53:10-12). The kingdom sacrifices will also be multipurposed and there are at least four purposes for the sacrificial system that can be suggested.

First, the sacrifices are a memorial of the death of the Messiah. According to this view, the sacrifices will have for Israel a similar role that communion has for the church. Since the Mosaic sacrifices looked forward to the sacrifice of the Messiah, why could not the kingdom sacrifices look back and commemorate the sacrifice on the cross? The church has been asked to do something very physical, namely, to partake of the bread and the cup thereby remembering the body and the blood of the Messiah. The ceremony, however, is to be terminated with the second coming (1 Cor. 11:26). What will be used to remember the Lord's death by Israel in the messianic kingdom? The blood sacrifices of the kingdom will also be a physical ceremony to serve for Israel what communion serves for the church, that is, to remember the body and blood of the Messiah.

Second, the sacrifices are the means of restoring fellowship for the millennial saint. The Mosaic sacrifices never removed sin and were not the means of salvation for the Old Testament saint (Heb. 10:1-4). The Old Testament saint was saved by grace through faith. The blood sacrifices were the means of restoring fellowship of the Mosaic saint who sinned. In this age, fellowship for the believer is restored by confession (1 Jn.1:9). The millennial sacrifices will not remove sin either, but they will be the means of restoring fellowship for the millennial saint who sins.

Third, the sacrifices are ritual cleansing for ritual uncleanness. Since the *Shechinah* Glory will be within the Holy of Holies of the millennial Temple, it would be impossible to approach the Temple Compound in a state of ritual impurity and therefore the sacrifices will be for the cleansing of ceremonial uncleanness. Dr. Thomas Ice expressed the view as follows:

Critics of future millennial sacrifices seem to assume that

all sacrifices, past and future, always depict Christ's final sacrifice for sin. They do not! There were various purposes for sacrifices in the Bible. An overwhelming majority of sacrifices under the Mosaic system were for purification of the priests and objects used in various rites. This is why atonement can be said in the past to be effective, yet still need Christ's future sacrifice, because many of the sacrifices did atone ceremonially, cleansing participants and objects in Temple ritual. Just as we never finish the task of washing clothes, ceremonial cleansing was an ongoing need. The same is clearly the case in Ezekiel. In Ezekiel 43:20 and 26, the atonement is specifically directed at cleansing the altar in order to make it ritually fit for sacrifice. The only other uses of atonement also refer to cleansing objects so that ritual purity may be maintained for proper function of further worship (Ezekiel 45:15, 17, 20)....

Since all the sacrifices of Ezekiel relate to purification of the priests for Temple service, they do not specifically depict or represent Christ's atoning sacrifice. The presence and purpose of sacrifices neither diminishes the finished work of Christ nor violates the normal and "literal" interpretation of the prophetic passages. Nothing in Ezekiel 40-48 conflicts with the death of Christ or New Testament teaching at any point. The supposed contradictions between a literal understanding of Ezekiel and New Testament doctrine evaporate when examined specifically.[2]

Jerry Hullinger reached the same conclusion.

A solution that maintains dispensational distinctives, deals honestly with the text of Ezekiel, and in no way demeans the work Christ did on the cross. This study suggests that animal sacrifices during the Millennium will serve primarily to remove ceremonial uncleanness and prevent defilement from polluting the temple envisioned by Ezekiel. This will be necessary because the glorious presence of

Yahweh will once again be dwelling on earth in the midst of a sinful and unclean people....

Because of God's promise to dwell on earth during the Millennium (as stated in the New Covenant), it is necessary that He protect His presence through sacrifice.... It should further be added that this sacrificial system will be a temporary one in that the Millennium (with its partial population of unglorified humanity) will last only one thousand years. During the eternal state all inhabitants of the New Jerusalem will be glorified and will therefore not be a source of contagious impurities to defile the holiness of Yahweh.[3]

Fourth, the sacrifices are for the privilege of life and physical blessing in a theocratic kingdom. Dr. John C. Whitcomb, professor of theology and Old Testament at Grace Theological Seminary for 38 years, provided an additional and significant perspective on the millennial sacrifices.[4] The subscript of the article summarizes his position.

The future function of the millennial temple (Ezek. 40-48) has long been problematic for dispensationalists in view of the finished work of Christ. Light is shed on this problem by noting the original theocratic purpose of OT sacrifices. This purpose was functionally distinct from that of the redemptive work of Christ. Millennial sacrifices will not simply memorialize Christ's redemption but will primarily function in restoring theocratic harmony. The differences between the Old Covenant stipulations and those of Ezekiel 40-48 can be accounted for in terms of this solution.[5]

Whitcomb emphasized that there was a functional difference between the purpose of the animal sacrifices and the purpose of Messiah's sacrifice.[6] "What was the function of animal sacrifices in the Old Covenant?" Whitcomb answered that "animal sacrifices would never remove spiritual guilt from the offerer" (citing Heb. 10:4, 11 as evidence). Of course, this is something that has general agreement among all theologians of all schools. Nevertheless, Whitcomb also stated, "it is equally erroneous to say that the sacrifices were mere teaching symbols given by God to Israel to prepare them for Messiah and his infinite atonement." While this was certainly a purpose of animal sacrifices, "it could not have been their exclusive purpose from the perspective of Old Covenant Israelites."

Citing a number of clear statements from the Law of Moses, Whitcomb demonstrated what the animal sacrifices did with regard to forgiveness and atonement. The main issue is not whether forgiveness and atonement occurred, but the "precise nature" of this forgiveness and atonement. Whitcomb stated that whatever happened was "temporal, finite, external, and legal—not eternal, infinite, internal, and soteriological." His point is that this forgiveness and atonement was not a spiritual one because "No one was ever spiritually regenerated by works, not even by fulfilling legally prescribed sacrifices, offerings and other Mosaic requirements." The Old Testament believer received his spiritual salvation because of "a heart response to whatever special revelation of God was available at that time in history," but this saving faith did not necessarily include knowledge of a crucified Messiah, since such a view "does not do justice to the progress of revelation." While the death of the Messiah "has always been and always will be the final basis of spiritual salvation," this is not the same as saying it was the "knowledge-content" of saving faith. It was faith and not the works of animal sacrifices that saved. What the animal sacrifices of the Law of Moses did achieve was "national/theocratic forgiveness for national/theocratic transgressions." They provided for external cleansing and outward efficacy.

Under the Mosaic Law, the choice was not "either faith or sacrifices; rather, it was to be both faith and sacrifices." The former resulted in spiritual salvation and the latter was for "the cleanness of the flesh" in accordance with Hebrews 9:13. Applying these truths to the millennial sacrifices, Whitcomb affirmed, "future sacrifices will have nothing to do with eternal salvation which only comes through true faith in God." However, these future animal sacrifices will also be efficacious, but "only in terms of the strict provision for ceremonial (and thus temporal) forgiveness within the theocracy of Israel." Whitcomb concluded his point as follows:

> Thus, animal sacrifices during the coming Kingdom age will not be primarily memorial (like the eucharist in church communion services), any more than sacrifices in the age of the Old Covenant were primarily prospective or prophetic in the understanding of the offerer.[7]
>
> The distinction between ceremonial and spiritual atonement is by no means a minor one, for it is at the heart of the basic difference between the theocracy of Israel and the Church, the Body and Bride of Christ. It also provides a more consistent hermeneutical approach for dispensational Premillennialism.[8]

Whitcomb also rejected the notion that the millennial sacrifice is a reinstitution of the Mosaic Law, and noted the differences between the two systems to mean the millennial sacrificial system is a distinct system arising from the New Covenant, not the Mosaic Covenant. Whitcomb also made the following observation:

> However, such sacrifices will not be totally voluntary and purely memorial as is true of the Christian eucharist. Ezekiel says that God will "accept" people on the basis of animal sacrifices (43:27), and they are "to make atonement for the house of Israel" (45:17; cf. 45:15). In other words, just as in Old Testament times, the privilege of life and physical blessing in the theocratic kingdom will be contingent upon outward conformity to the ceremonial law. Such conformity did not bring salvation in Old Testament times, but saved Israelites willingly conformed. Only faith in God could bring salvation, and this has been God's plan in every dispensation. It is a serious mistake, therefore, to insist that these sacrifices will be expiatory. They were certainly

not expiatory in the Mosaic economy...and they will not be so in the Millennium. But their symbolic and pedagogic value, unlike the communion service, will be upheld by a legalistic system of enforced participation. For example, those who decide to neglect the annual Feast of Tabernacles will be punished by a drought or a plague.... If the true significance of the five offerings be understood, it is not difficult to see how they could serve as effective vehicles of divine instruction and discipline for Israel and the nations during the Kingdom age.[9]

The Gentiles in the Messianic Kingdom

The Gentiles who survive the judgment of the Gentiles for their treatment of Israel are the ones who will enter and populate the Gentile nations in the millennium. These are the sheep Gentiles who, because of their faith shown by their pro-Semitism, will be able to participate in and populate the kingdom.

General Characteristics

Of the Major Prophets, Isaiah is the key to learning about the role of the Gentiles in the kingdom. In Isaiah 11:10, the Messiah will be the center of Gentile attraction. *And it shall come to pass in that day, that the root of Jesse, that stands for an ensign of the peoples, unto him shall the nations seek; and his resting-place shall be glorious.* According to Isaiah 14:1-2, they will be possessed and be the servants of the people of Israel.

For Jehovah will have compassion on Jacob, and will yet choose Israel, and set them in their own land: and the sojourner shall join himself with them, and they shall cleave to the house of Jacob. And the peoples shall take them, and bring them to their place; and the house of Israel shall possess them in the land of Jehovah for servants and for handmaids: and they shall take them captive whose captives they were; and they shall rule over their oppressors.

While the Gentiles will be subject to the King Messiah,

they will also receive justice from the King, according to Isaiah 42:1. *Behold, my servant, whom I uphold; my chosen, in whom my soul delights: I have put my Spirit upon him; he will bring forth justice to the Gentiles.* At that time, in a special way, the Messiah will become the light to the Gentiles, according to Isaiah 49:5-7.

> And now says Jehovah that formed me from the womb to be his servant, to bring Jacob again to him, and that Israel be gathered unto him, (for I am honorable in the eyes of Jehovah, and my God is become my strength;) yea, he says, it is too light a thing that you should be my servant to raise up the tribes of Jacob, and to restore the preserved of Israel: I will also give you for a light to the Gentiles, that you may be my salvation unto the end of the earth. Thus says Jehovah, the Redeemer of Israel, *and* his Holy One, to him whom man despises, to him whom the nation abhors, to a servant of rulers: Kings shall see and arise; princes, and they shall worship; because of Jehovah that is faithful, *even* the Holy One of Israel, who has chosen you.

The calling of the Messiah is not only on behalf of Israel to regather the scattered nation (49:5a), but also to be the light and the salvation to the Gentiles (49:6b). So at the time of the final restoration of Israel, the Messiah will be manifested in the most complete sense as the light to the Gentiles and all the kings of the Gentiles will worship Him (49:7). A more extensive passage is Isaiah 56:1-8.

> Thus says Jehovah, Keep ye justice, and do righteousness; for my salvation is near to come, and my righteousness to be revealed. Blessed is the man that does this, and the son of man that holds it fast; that keeps the sabbath from profaning it, and keeps his hand from doing any evil. Neither let the foreigner, that has joined himself to Jehovah, speak, saying, Jehovah will surely separate me from his people; neither let the eunuch say, Behold, I

am a dry tree. For thus says Jehovah of the eunuchs that keep my sabbaths, and choose the things that please me, and hold fast my covenant: Unto them will I give in my house and within my walls a memorial and a name better than of sons and of daughters; I will give them an everlasting name, that shall not be cut off. Also the foreigners that join themselves to Jehovah, to minister unto him, and to love the name of Jehovah, to be his servants, every one that keeps the sabbath from profaning it, and holds fast my covenant; even them will I bring to my holy mountain, and make them joyful in my house of prayer: their burnt-offerings and their sacrifices shall be accepted upon my altar; for my house shall be called a house of prayer for all peoples. The Lord Jehovah, who gathers the outcasts of Israel, says, Yet will I gather *others* to him, besides his own that are gathered.

At the time of the establishment of the kingdom, there may be some feeling among the sheep Gentiles that, because of the exalted position of Israel, the Gentiles will be excluded from receiving the benefits of millennial Temple worship (56:1-3). However this will not be the case, for the Temple ministry will be open to all Gentiles who are rightly related to the King. Under no circumstances will they be excluded either because they are Gentiles or because they are mutilated (56:4-5). It is then, and only then, that the House of God will be truly called a house of prayer for all nations (56:6-7). When will that time be? At the time of Israel's final regathering (56:8). The Gentiles are to have a significant role in the millennial Temple worship, as taught in Isaiah 66:18-24.

For I *know* their works and their thoughts: *the time* comes, that I will gather all nations and tongues; and they shall come, and shall see my glory. And I will set a sign among them, and I will send such as escape of them unto the nations, to Tarshish, Pul, and Lud, that draw the bow, to Tubal and Javan, to the isles afar off, that have not heard my fame, neither have seen my glory; and they shall declare my glory among the nations. And they shall bring all your brethren out of all the nations for an oblation unto Jehovah, upon horses, and in chariots, and in litters, and upon mules, and upon dromedaries, to my holy mountain Jerusalem, says Jehovah, as the children of Israel bring their oblation in a clean vessel into the house of Jehovah. And of them also will I take for priests *and* for Levites, says Jehovah. For as the new heavens and the new earth, which I will make, shall remain before me, says Jehovah, so shall your seed and your name remain. And it shall come to pass, that from one new moon to another, and from one sabbath to another, shall all flesh come to worship before me, says Jehovah. And they shall go forth, and look upon the dead bodies of the men that have transgressed against me: for their worm shall not die, neither shall their fire be quenched; and they shall be an abhorring unto all flesh.

The *Shechinah* Glory, which will be especially manifested in the kingdom, will be seen by many of the Gentiles (66:18), and those who do see it will leave to travel among the Gentiles who have not seen it to tell them of it (66:19). At the same time, Gentiles will be used to conduct the Jews back into the land of Israel (66:20a), and they will be brought to the mountain of Jehovah's house for the purpose of worship (66:20b). Furthermore, among these Gentiles, God will choose some to serve as priests in the Temple (66:21). Not only is Israel the eternal nation, but the faithful among the Gentiles will also be eternal (66:22), and they will have a place of worship in the Temple for the Sabbath and new moon offerings (66:23). Regarding the unfaithful among the Gentiles, their dead bodies and the suffering of their souls will be visible throughout the kingdom (66:24), illustrating for one thousand years God's grace to the faithful and His severity to the lost.

The Obligation to Observe the Feast of Tabernacles
Of the various feasts and celebrations and festival offerings

of the millennium mentioned by Ezekiel, there is one feast, the
Feast of Tabernacles, that will be obligatory for all Gentile
nations. Zechariah 14:16-19 declares this truth.

> And it shall come to pass, that every one that is left of
> all the nations that came against Jerusalem shall go up
> from year to year to worship the King, Jehovah of
> hosts, and to keep the feast of tabernacles. And it shall
> be, that whoso of *all* the families of the earth goes not
> up unto Jerusalem to worship the King, Jehovah of
> hosts, upon them there shall be no rain. And if the fam-
> ily of Egypt go not up, and come not, neither *shall it be*
> upon them; there shall be the plague wherewith
> Jehovah will smite the nations that go not up to keep
> the feast of tabernacles. This shall be the punishment of
> Egypt, and the punishment of all the nations that go not
> up to keep the feast of tabernacles.

All the Gentile nations that will populate the kingdom will
be obligated to send a delegation to Jerusalem with the purpose
of worshipping the King at the time of the Feast of Tabernacles
(14:16). It may be at this time that the Gentiles will pay their
obligatory tribute to the King (Isa. 60:11). Though the Gentile
observation of the Feast of Tabernacles will be mandatory, not
every nation will necessarily be willing to obey. Therefore, if at
any time a nation should fail to send a delegation, the rains will
be withheld from them for that year (Zech. 14:17). As an example of the punishment, Zechariah mentions the example of Egypt
(14:18-19). Should Egypt fail to send a delegation, there will be
no rain for Egypt. Using Egypt as an illustration of a reluctant
nation to keep the Feast of Tabernacles is especially significant,
for originally the Feast of Tabernacles was inaugurated as part
of a memorial festival of the deliverance of Israel from the
Egyptian Bondage. Regardless of what nation may fail to obey
this mandate, the punishment will be the same for all.

CONCLUSION

Christians must be keenly aware of counterfeit spirituality. Satan is the father of lies. Jesus said of him: *He was a murderer from the beginning, and does not stand in the truth, because there is no truth in him. Whenever he speaks a lie, he speaks from his own **nature**; for he is a liar and the father of lies* (Jn. 8:44). It brings great delight to Satan to cause confusion in the church and in the world. Peter warned Christians, *Be of sober **spirit**, be on the alert. Your adversary, the devil, prowls about like a roaring lion, seeking someone to devour. But resist him, firm in **your** faith, knowing that the same experiences of suffering are being accomplished by your brethren who are in the world* (1 Pet. 5:8-9). Since the unbeliever is already living in darkness, it probably brings Satan great delight to deceive Christians with a counterfeit spirituality and will even send false teachers into the church to deceive Christians. *For such men are false apostles, deceitful workers, disguising themselves as apostles of Christ. And no wonder, for even Satan disguises himself as an angel of light. Therefore it is not surprising if his servants also disguise themselves as servants of righteousness; who end shall be according to their deeds* (1 Cor. 11:13-15).

The most basic snare for the Christian is to live a self-centered life, as opposed to living a God-centered life. Self-centeredness regarding economy, government, and religion will produce ruin. Scripture warns against counterfeit spirituality manifested in self-centeredness. Paul exhorted, *Do nothing from selfishness or empty conceit, but with humility of mind let each of you regard one another as more important than himself* (Phil. 2:3). After listing *the fruit of the Spirit*, Paul wrote, *Now those who belong to Christ Jesus have crucified the flesh with its passions and desires. If we live by the Spirit, let us also walk by the Spirit. Let us not become boastful, challenging one another,*

457

envying one another (Gal. 5:22-26).

Some of the teachings among the church have reduced the focus of Christianity to the material world thereby producing counterfeit spirituality. If the teaching of the church is limited solely to budgets, demands for the growth of Big Government, healings or miracles of the physical body, or demanding God to meet material and physical desires, then the church will have become no better than the pagans mentioned in Colossians 2:8. *See to it that no one takes you captive through philosophy and empty deception, according to the tradition of men, according to the elementary principles of the world, rather than according to Christ. For in Him all the fulness of Deity dwells in bodily form, and in Him you have been made complete, and He is the head over all rule and authority* (Col. 2:8-10). The Christian life must be God-centered and (2:16-23) self-disciplined (1 Cor. 9:24-27; Phil. 3:10-16).

What of the world? The greatest tragedy is not the bad things that occur in this earthly life, but there are many who die in their sins when they could have known Christ as their Savior. It was said of those in Noah's day: *before the Flood they were eating and drinking, marrying and giving in marriage, until the day that Noe entered into the ark and knew not* (Mt. 24:38-39a; KJV). In those days, *God saw the wickedness of man was great in the earth* (Gen. 6:5; KJV). The same can be said today. Rather than admit his accountability to the Creator, mankind continues to pursue hedonistic, materialistic, and humanistic endeavors. The world needs to hear *now is the day of salvation...as it is appointed unto men once to die, but after this the judgment* (2 Cor. 6:2; Heb. 9:27; KJV). The good news is *that Christ died for our sins according to the scriptures; and that he was buried, and that he rose again the third day according to the scriptures* (1 Cor. 15:3). To all who trust in Christ alone as Savior will there be salvation (Tit. 3:4-7).

AMERICAN GOVERNMENT AND CHRISTIANITY

Kerby Anderson

G. K. Chesterton once said, "America is the only nation in the world that is founded on a creed. That creed is set forth with dogmatic and even theological lucidity in the Declaration of Independence."[1] The founding of America, as well as the framing of the key political documents, is based upon a Christian foundation. The foundation of America does not necessarily mean the United States is a Christian nation, although some framers used that term. However, it does mean the foundations of this republic presuppose a Christian view of human nature and God's providence.

Every Christian should know "Christopher Columbus was motivated by his Christian faith to sail to the New World."[2] For example, after he discovered this new land, he wrote, "Therefore let the king and queen, the princes and their most fortunate kingdoms, and all other countries of Christendom give thanks to our Lord and Saviour Jesus Christ, who has bestowed upon us so great a victory and gift. Let religious processions be solemnized; let sacred festivals be given; let the churches be covered with festive garlands. Let Christ rejoice on earth, as he rejoices in heaven, when he foresees coming to salvation so many souls of people hitherto lost."[3]

Furthermore, "The Pilgrims clearly stated that they came to the New World to glorify God and to advance the Christian faith."[4] It could easily be said America began with the words,

459

"In the name of God. Amen." Those were the first words of America's first self-governing document: the Mayflower Compact.

The Pilgrims were Bible-believers who refused to conform to the heretical state Church of England and eventually came to America. Their leader, William Bradford, said, "A great hope and inward zeal they had of laying some good foundation, or at least to make some way thereunto, for the propagating and advancing the gospel of the kingdom of Christ in those remote parts of the world; yea, though they should be but even as stepping stones unto others for the performing of so great a work."[5] Many scholars believe the initial agreement for self-government, found in the Mayflower Compact, became the cornerstone of the U.S. Constitution. The agreement for self-government, signed on 11 November 1620, created a new government in which they agreed to "covenant and combine" themselves together into a "Body Politick." British historian Paul Johnson wrote, "It is an amazing document.... What was remarkable about this particular contract was that it was not between a servant and a master, or a people and a king, but between a group of like-minded individuals and each other, with God as a witness and symbolic co-signatory."[6]

The Puritan Influence

"The Puritans created Bible-based commonwealths in order to practice a representative government that was modeled on their church covenants."[7] Both the Pilgrims and the Puritans disagreed about many things concerning the Church of England in their day. However, the Pilgrims believed reforming the church was a hopeless endeavor; they were led to separate themselves from the official church and were often labeled "Separatists." The Puritans, on the other hand, wanted to reform the Church of England from within; they argued from within for purity of the church (hence, the name "Puritans").

During this time, there had been no written constitution in England. The British common law was a mostly oral tradition, articulated as necessary in various written court decisions. The

Puritans determined to anchor their liberties on the written page, a tradition taken from the Bible. They created the Body of Liberties which were established on the belief that Christ's rule is not only given for the church, but also for the state. It contained principles found in the Bible, specifically ninety-eight separate protections of individual rights, including due process of law, trial by a jury of peers, and prohibitions against cruel and unusual punishment.

"This nation was founded as a sanctuary for religious dissidents."[8] Roger Williams questioned many of the Puritan laws in Massachusetts, especially the right of magistrates to punish Sabbath-breakers. After he left Massachusetts and founded Rhode Island, he became the first to formulate the concept of "separation of church and state" in America. Williams said, "The civil magistrate may not intermeddle even to stop a church from apostasy and heresy."[9] In the 1643 charter for Rhode Island and in all its subsequent charters, Roger Williams established the idea that the state should not enforce religious opinion.

The Foundations of America

What was the perspective of the founders of America? Let the reader consider some famous quotes. The first example is John Adams, the second president of the United States. He saw the need for religious values to provide the moral foundation for society. In a letter to the officers of the First Brigade of the Third Division of the Militia of Massachusetts, he wrote,

> We have no government armed with power capable of contending with human passions unbridled by morality and religion. Avarice, ambition, revenge, or gallantry, would break the strongest cords of our Constitution as a whale goes through a net. Our Constitution was made only for a moral and religious people. It is wholly inadequate to the government of any other.[10]

In fact, John Adams was not the only founding father to talk about the importance of religious values. Consider the following statement from George Washington during his Farewell Address:

> And let us with caution indulge the supposition, that morality can be maintained without religion. Whatever may be conceded to the influence of refined education on minds of peculiar structure, reason and experience both forbid us to expect that national morality can prevail in exclusion of religious principle.[11]

Two hundred years after the establishment of the Plymouth colony in 1620, Americans gathered at that site to celebrate its bicentennial. Daniel Webster was the speaker at this 1820 celebration. He reminded those in attendance of this nation's origins.

> Let us not forget the religious character of our origin. Our fathers were brought hither by their high veneration for the Christian religion. They journeyed by its light, and labored in its hope. They sought to incorporate its principles with the elements of their society, and to diffuse its influence through all their institutions, civil, political, or literary.[12]

Religion, and especially the Christian religion, was an important foundation to this republic.

Christian Character

It is evident that the framers of this new government believed the people should elect and support leaders with character and integrity. George Washington expressed this in his Farewell Address: "Of all the dispositions and habits which lead to political prosperity, Religion and Morality are indispensable supports."

Benjamin Rush talked about the religious foundation of the republic that demanded virtuous leadership. He said, "the only foundation for a useful education in a republic is to be laid on the foundation of religion. Without this there can be no virtue, and without virtue there can be no liberty, and liberty is the object and life of all republican governments."[13] He also explained as follows:

A Christian cannot fail of being a republican...for every precept of the Gospel inculcates those degrees of humility, self-denial, and brotherly kindness which are directly opposed to the pride of monarchy.... A Christian cannot fail of being useful to the republic, for his religion teaches him that no man "liveth to himself." And lastly a Christian cannot fail of being wholly inoffensive, for his religion teaches him in all things to do to others what he would wish, in like circumstances, they should do to him.[14]

Daniel Webster understood the importance of religion, and especially the Christian religion, in this form of government. In his famous Plymouth Rock speech of 1820, he said,

Lastly, our ancestors established their system of government on morality and religious sentiment. Moral habits, they believed, cannot safely be trusted on any other foundation than religious principle, nor any government be secure which is not supported by moral habits.... Whatever makes men good Christians, makes them good citizens.[15]

John Jay was one of the authors of the *Federalist Papers* and became America's first Supreme Court Justice. He also served as the president of the American Bible Society. He understood the relationship between government and Christian values. He said, "Providence has given to our people the choice of their rulers, and it is the duty, as well as the privilege and interest of our Christian nation to select and prefer Christians for their rulers."[16]

Quaker William Penn, writing the *Frame of Government*, for his new colony said, "Government, like clocks, go from the motion men give them; and as governments are made and moved by men, so by them they are ruined too. Wherefore governments rather depend upon men, than men upon governments. Let men be good, and the government cannot be bad."[17] He was the main author of the founding governmental document for the land that came to be known as Pennsylvania. His document was called *The Concessions*, and not only addressed government matters but also was concerned with social, philosophical, scientific, and political matters. By 1680, *The Concessions* had 150 signers, and in the Quaker spirit, this group effort provided for far-reaching liberties never before seen in Anglo-Saxon law.

Paul Johnson demonstrated, at the time of America's founding, Philadelphia was "the cultural capital of America." He wrote, "It can be argued, indeed, that Quaker Pennsylvania was the key state in American history. It was the last great flowering of Puritan political innovation, around its great city of brotherly love."[18] Clearly, the founders believed that good character was vital to the health of the nation.

Education and Religion in America

Christian should also know "The education of the settlers and founders of America was uniquely Christian and Bible-based."[19] Education was very important to the founders of this country. One of the laws in Puritan New England was the Old Deluder Act. The name was given because it was intended to defeat Satan, the Old Deluder, who had used illiteracy in the Old World to prevent people from reading the Word of God. The New England Primer was used to teach colonial children to read and included the Lord's Prayer, the Apostle's Creed, and the text of many hymns and prayers.

One can also understand the importance of education in the rules of many of the first colleges. In 1643, the Laws and Statutes of Harvard College stated, "Let every student be plainly instructed and earnestly pressed to consider well the main end of his life and studies is *to know God and Jesus Christ which is eternal life* (John 17:3)."[20] Likewise, Yale College listed two requirements in its 1745 charter: "All scholars shall live religious, godly, and blameless lives according to the rules of God's Word, diligently reading the Holy Scriptures, the fountain of light and truth; and constantly attend upon all the duties of religion, both in public and secret."[21]

Reverend John Witherspoon was the only active minister who signed the Declaration of Independence. Constitutional scholar John Eidsmoe wrote, "John Witherspoon is best described as the man who shaped the men who shaped America. Although he did not attend the Constitutional Convention, his influence was multiplied many times over by those who spoke as well as by what was said."[22] New Jersey elected John Witherspoon to the Continental Congress which drafted the Declaration of Independence. When Congress called for a national day of fasting and prayer on 17 May 1776, John Witherspoon was asked to preach the sermon. His topic was "The Dominion of Providence over the Affairs of Men."

Gibbs and Newcombe demonstrated, "A religious revival was the key factor in uniting the separate pre- Revolutionary War colonies." Paul Johnson, author of *A History of the American People*, reports the Great Awakening may have touched as many as three out of four American colonists.[23] He also demonstrated that this Great Awakening "sounded the death-knell of British colonialism."[24] As John Adams would later state, "The Revolution was effected before the War commenced. The Revolution was in the mind and hearts of the people: and change in their religious sentiments of their duties and obligations." Johnson affirmed, "The Revolution could not have taken place without this religious background. The essential difference between the American Revolution and the French Revolution is that the American Revolution, in its origins, was a religious event, whereas the French Revolution was an anti-religious event."[25]

New Man

Historian C. Gregg Singer traced the line of influence from the seventeenth century to the eighteenth century in his book, *A Theological Interpretation of American History*. He wrote,

Whether we look at the Puritans and their fellow

colonists of the seventeenth century, or their descendants of the eighteenth century, or those who framed the Declaration of Independence and the Constitution, we see that their political programs were the rather clear reflection of a consciously held political philosophy, and that the various political philosophies which emerged among the American people were intimately related to the theological developments which were taking place.... A Christian world and life view furnished the basis for this early political thought which guided the American people for nearly two centuries and whose crowning lay in the writing of the Constitution of 1787.[26]

Actually, the line of influence extends backward even further. Historian Arnold Toynbee, for example, has written that the American Revolution was made possible by American Protestantism. Page Smith, writing in the *Religious Origins of the American Revolution*, cites the influence of the Protestant Reformation. He believes,

The Protestant Reformation produced a new kind of consciousness and a new kind of man. The English Colonies in America, in turn, produced a new unique strain of that consciousness. It thus follows that it is impossible to understand the intellectual and moral forces behind the American Revolution without understanding the role that Protestant Christianity played in shaping the ideals, principles and institutions of colonial America.[27]

Smith argued that the American Revolution "started, in a sense, when Martin Luther nailed his 95 theses to the church door at Wittenburg." It received "its theological and philosophical underpinnings from John Calvin's *Institutes of the Christian Religion* and much of its social theory from the Puritan Revolution of 1640-1660."[28]

Most people prior to the Reformation belonged to classes and social groups which set the boundaries of their worlds and established their identities. The Reformation, according to Smith, changed these perceptions. Luther and Calvin, in a sense, created a re-formed individual in a re-formed world. Central to such beliefs is the doctrine of the priesthood of the believer[29] where each person is "responsible directly to God for his or her own spiritual state.... The individuals who formed the new congregations established their own churches, chose their own ministers, and managed their own affairs without reference to an ecclesiastical hierarchy."[30] These re-formed individuals began to change their world, including their view of government and authority.

Declaration of Independence

Let the reader now consider the Christian influence on the Declaration of Independence. Historian Page Smith demonstrated that Thomas Jefferson was not only influenced by secular philosophers, but was also influenced by the Protestant Reformation. He wrote,

> Jefferson and other secular-minded Americans subscribed to certain propositions about law and authority that had their roots in the Protestant Reformation. It is a scholarly common-place to point out how much Jefferson (and his fellow delegates to the Continental Congress) were influenced by Locke. Without disputing this we would simply add that an older and deeper influence—John Calvin—was of more profound importance.[31]

Another important influence was William Blackstone. Jefferson relied heavily on the writings of this highly respected jurist. In fact, Blackstone's *Commentaries on the Laws of England* were among Jefferson's favorite books. In his section on the "Nature of Laws in General," Blackstone wrote, "as man depends absolutely upon his Maker for everything, it is necessary that he should, in all points, conform to his Maker's will. This will of his Maker is called the law of nature"

(*Commentaries* 1:2).[32]

In addition to the law of nature, the other source of law is from divine revelation. "The doctrines thus delivered we call the revealed or divine law, and they are to be found only in the Holy Scriptures." According to Blackstone, all human laws depended upon either the law of nature or the law of revelation found in the Bible: "Upon these two foundations, the law of nature and the law of revelation, depend all human laws."[33]

In his "The Rights of the Colonists," Samuel Adams[34] argued, "Among the natural Rights of the Colonists are these: First, a Right to Life; second, to Liberty; third, to Property;...and in the case of intolerable oppression, civil or religious, to leave the society they belong to, and enter into another. When men enter into society, it is by voluntary consent."[35] This concept of natural rights also found its way into the Declaration of Independence and provided the justification for the American Revolution.

The Declaration was a bold document, but not a radical one. The colonists did not separate from England for "light and transient causes." They were mindful that they should be *in subjection to the governing authorities* which *are established by God* (Rom. 13:1). Nevertheless, when they suffered from a "long train of abuses and usurpations," they believed "it is the right of the people to alter or abolish [the existing government] and to institute a new government."

The Constitution

The Christian influence on the Declaration of Independence is obvious. What about the Constitution? James Madison was the chief architect of the Constitution, as well as one of the authors of the *Federalist Papers*. It is important to note that, as a youth, he studied under a Scottish Presbyterian, Donald Robertson. Madison gave the credit to Robertson for "all that I have been in life."[36] Later he was trained in theology at Princeton under the Reverend John Witherspoon. Scholars believe that Witherspoon's Calvinism (which emphasized the fallen nature [total depravity] of man) was an important source for Madison's political ideas.[37] Eidsmoe wrote, "One thing is certain: the Christian religion, particularly Rev. Witherspoon's Calvinism, which emphasized the fallen nature of man, influenced Madison's view of law and government."[38] The Constitution was a contract between the people and had its origins in American history a century earlier.

> One of the obvious by-products [of the Reformation] was the notion of a contract entered into by two people or by the members of a community amongst themselves that needed no legal sanctions to make it binding. This concept of the Reformers made possible the formation of contractuals or, as the Puritans called them, "covenanted" groups formed by individuals who signed a covenant or agreement to found a community. The most famous of these covenants was the Mayflower Compact. In it the Pilgrims formed a "civil body politic," and promised to obey the laws their own government might pass. In short, the individual Pilgrim invented on the spot a new community, one that would be ruled by laws of its making.[39]

Historian Page Smith accepted as true, "The Federal Constitution was in this sense a monument to the reformed consciousness. This new sense of time as potentiality was a vital element in the new consciousness that was to make a revolution and, what was a good deal more difficult, form a new nation."[40] Preaching and teaching within the churches provided the justification for the revolution and the establishment of a new nation. Alice Baldwin, writing in *The New England Clergy and the American Revolution*, affirmed,

> The teachings of the New England ministers provide one line of unbroken descent. For two generations and more New Englanders had...been taught that these rights were sacred and came from God and that to preserve them they had a legal right of resistance and, if necessary a

right to…alter and abolish governments and by common consent establish new ones.[41]

Christian ideas were important in the founding of the American republic and the framing of the American governmental institutions. It is this author's assertion that they are equally important in the maintenance of that republic.

ENDNOTES

Chapter 1

[1]John Maynard Keynes, *Collected Writings of John Maynard Keynes*, 30 vols., eds. Donald Moggridge and Elizabeth Johnson (London: Macmillan, 1978), 7:383-384.

[2]For much of the information in this chapter, see John Eatwell, Murray Milgate, and Peter Newman, eds., *The New Palgrave: A Dictionary of Economics* (London: Macmillan, 1987); Robert L. Heilbroner, *The Worldly Philosophers: The Lives, Times and Ideas of The Great Economic Thinkers* (New York: Simon and Schuster, 1953); Kit Sims Taylor, "Gallery of Economists" [online] (Bellevue Community College, accessed 31 July 2004) available from http://online.bcc.ctc.edu/econ/econgallery/gallery.htm.

[3]Howard F. Vos, *Highlights of Church History* (Chicago: Moody Press, 1960), 77.

[4]Christopher Marlowe, "The Tragical History of Dr. Faustus" [online] (Universität Hannover, accessed 31 July 2004) available from http://www.fbls.uni-hannover.de/angli/Courses/WS%200304/Faustus.doc

[5]The bourgeoisie (artisans and merchants) emerged when numerous populations within villages became wealthier than those in the nearby countryside. The result of the upsurge of the bourgeoisie was comparatively more influence and strength in society, which stimulated some equality to the ruling classes and clergy, and further distinguished them from the rural classes. The classic example of the medieval bourgeoisie was the mill owner, who quickly attained great influence over the local economy to such an extent that he was able to proscribe his prince. In later centuries, the bourgeoisie were distinguished as the first bankers and those individuals who developed finance and trade.

[6]Eventually, the religious disturbances and desire for religious freedom would result in explorers seeking settlement in the New World. Protestants especially sought religious freedom in the English colonies.

[7]Josiah Child, *Circumstances on the Discourse on Trade* (1690), as quoted by Joseph A. Schumpeter, *History of Economic Analysis* (New York: Oxford University Press, 1954; revised, 1996), 347.

[8]For an excellent article on current foreign policy and favored clients similar

471

to mercantalism, see Grant M. Nülle, "The WTO's Mercantilist Flaw" [article online] (Ludwig von Mises Institute, accessed 2 July 2004) available from http://www.mises.org/fullstory.aspx?control=1380.

[9] Ludwig von Mises, *Human Action: A Treatise of Economics* (New Haven: Yale University Press, 1949; reprint, Auburn, AL: Ludwig Von Mises Institute, 1998), 67.

[10] As quoted by William Letwin, *Sir Josiah Child, Merchant Economist* (Boston: Baker Library, Harvard Graduate School of Business Administration, 1969), 28.

[11] Stanley Chodorow, MacGregor Knox, Conrad Schirokauer, Joseph R. Strayer, and Hans W. Gatzke, *The Mainstream of Civilization*, 6th ed. (New York: The Harcourt Press, 1994), 506-513.

[12] Bernard Mandeville, *The Fable of the Bees: or, Private Vices, Publick Benefits; With a Commentary, Critical, Historical, and Explanatory*, F. B. Kaye (Oxford: Clarendon Press, 1924; reprint, Indianapolis: Liberty Fund, 1988), 18-20.

[13] Ibid., 33-35.

[14] David Hume, "Of Commerce," "Of Money," "Of Interest," "Of the Jealousy of Trade," in *David Hume: Writings on Economics*, ed. Eugene Rotwein (Madison: University of Wisconsin Press, 1970), 3-18, 33-59, 78-82.

[15] Norman L. Geisler and Paul D. Feinberg, *Introduction to Philosophy: A Christian Perspective* (Grand Rapids: Baker Book House, 1980), 86.

[16] The majority of undergraduate textbooks teach neoclassical economics which focus primarily on microeconomic theory. Neoclassical economics began with the Neoclassical Revolution (sc. the emergence of marginal theory of value as the primary reason to explain the origin of value) in the late 19th century which integrated the marginal theory of value as the primary explanation for the origin of value. The majority of classical economists believed the value of a product was an indication of the labor and resources for producing it, hence the cost-of-production theory of value. Neoclassical economists acknowledged the rationale of marginal utility (sc. added utility for benefit that a consumer receives from an added unit of a product or service) for value and connected this idea with those of classical economics. The Austrian School of economics implemented marginal utility as the basis for separating from the tension that other economic schools assigned to analysis of economic data.

[17] David Hume, *Essays, Moral, Political, and Literary*, ed. Eugene F. Miller

(Indianapolis, IN: Liberty Fund, Inc., 1987) [online] (The Library of Economics and Liberty, accessed 2 July 2004) available from http://www.econlib.org/library/LFBooks/Hume/hmMPL26.html.

[18] Ibid.

[19] Ibid., http://www.econlib.org/library/LFBooks/Hume/hmMPL28.html.

[20] Rotwein, *David Hume*, lxxii-lxxxi.

[21] Hume, *Essays*, http://www.econlib.org/library/LFBooks/Hume/hmMPL24.html.

[22] Ibid., http://www.econlib.org/library/LFBooks/Hume/hmMPL29.html.

[23] "Hume, David," *Encyclopædia Britannica 2003 Deluxe Edition* [CD-ROM], 1994-2002. Encyclopædia Britannica, Inc., 2002.

[24] Regarding the Physiocracy, Schumpeter said, "Its analytical merit is negligible, but all the greater was its success." Joseph A. Schumpeter, *History of Economic Analysis* (New York: Oxford University Press, 1954), 175.

[25] *Laissez faire* (imperative) differs from *laisser faire* (infinitive). The latter refers to an injudicious approach to the function of a policy (i.e. the absence of thought is implied).

[26] Arthur Eli Monroe, ed., *Early Economic Thought: Selections from Economic Literature Prior to Adam Smith* (Cambridge: Harvard University Press, 1924; reprint, 1945), 341-348.

[27] Cantillon (1680-1734) is generally considered the precursor of the Austrian school of economic thought.

[28] Turgot (c. 1727-1781) was a French statesman and economist. He was also the administrator for Limoges under Louis XV, and Minister of Finance under Louis XVI (1774-1776). He was a friend of both Adam Smith and the Marquis de Condorcet.

[29] *Tableau* contains Quesnay's well-known zigzag diagram, which is a circular flow diagram of the economy demonstrating those responsible for production and spending. It is one of the first noteworthy economical models to relate those who produced and those who spent.

[30] Economy is analyzed in relation to its component parts (sectors): (1) the primary sector (agriculture, fishing, etc.); (2) the secondary sector (manufacturing, etc.); and, (3) the tertiary sector (commerce, etc.).

[31] Quoted by Adam Smith, *The Wealth of Nations* (1776; reprint, New York: Bantam Books, 2003), 863-864.

[32] Ibid., 572.

[33] Ibid.

[34] Ludwig von Mises, *Socialism: An Economic and Sociological Analysis*,

trans. J. Kahane (1922; reprint, New York: Yale University Press, 1951), 515.

35 Ludwig von Mises, *Omnipotent Government: The Rise of the Total State and Total War* (New Haven, CT: Yale University Press, 1944; reprint, Grove City, PA: Libertarian Press, 1985), v.

36 Mises, *Human Action*, 689.

37 Osymandias is the Greek name for Ramses II. The inscription on the pedestal of his colossus at Ramesseum reads, "King of Kings am I, Osymandias. If anyone would know how great I am and where I lie, let him surpass one of my works." Diodorus Siculus, *The Library of History*, 10 vols., trans. C. H. Oldfather (Cambridge: Harvard University Press, 1935), 1:47.

38 Isabel Quigly, *Shelley: Selected Poetry* (New York: Penguin Books, 1956), 107.

39 Ibid.

40 Mises, *Human Action*, 850.

41 R. J. Rummel, *Death by Government* (New Brunswick, NJ: Transaction Publishers, 1994).

42 Real rate is GDP growth adjusted annually for inflation and stated as a percent.

43 Inflation recognizes consumer prices which reflect an annual percent change in contrast to consumer prices of previous years.

44 Per capita demonstrates GDP on a purchasing power equivalence basis separated by population commencing 1 July for the corresponding year.

45 GDP is the value of all final goods and services produced within a nation in a particular year.

46 Central Intelligence Agency, "The World Factbook – United States" [online] (accessed 22 June 2004) available from http://www.cia.gov/cia/publications/factbook/geos/us.html.

47 Archie P. Jones, *The Influence of Historic Christianity on Early America* (Vallecito, CA: Chalcedon Foundation, 1998), 77.

48 Clarence Thomas, "Keynote Address." James Madison Day speech at James Madison University's observance of the 250th anniversary of Madison's birth, Harrisonburg, VA, 2001.

49 James Madison, "Number 47," in *Great Books of the Western World*, ed. Mortimer J. Adler (Chicago: Encyclopædia Brittannica, 1952), 40:153.

50 Ibid., 153.

51 John W. Robbins, *Civilization and the Protestant Reformation* [pamphlet] (Unicoi, TN: The Trinity Foundation, 1994), n.p.

[52] Ibid.

[53] As quoted by J. H. Merle D'Aubigne, *History of the Reformation of the Sixteenth Century*, 5 vols. (New York: Hurst & Company, 1835; reprint, Grand Rapids: Baker Book House, 1986), 3.9.8.

[54] Philip Schaff, *History of the Christian Church*, 8 vols. (New York: Charles Scribner's Sons, 1882-1910; reprint, Peabody, MA: Hendrickson Publishers, 1996), 7:388-389.

[55] Ibid., 59, 221.

[56] Ibid., 543.

[57] Robbins, *Civilization and the Reformation*.

[58] John W. Robbins, *Christ and Civilization* (Unicoi, TN: The Trinity Foundation, 2003), 41.

[59] Harold J. Berman, *The Interaction of Law and Religion* (Nashville: Abingdon Press, 1974); Harold J. Berman, *Law and Revolution: The Formation of the Western Legal Tradition* (Cambridge: Harvard University Press, 1983).

[60] Harold J. Berman, *Law and Religion*, 64-65, as quoted by Robbins, *Christ and Civilization*, 42.

[61] Robbins, *Civilization and the Reformation*.

[62] As quoted by Gary DeMar, "The Geneva Bible: The Forgotten Translation" [article online] (Center for Reformed Theology and Apologetics, accessed 24 June 2004) available from http://www.reformed.org/bible.

[63] Robbins, *Civilization and the Reformation*.

[64] Andrew Carnegie, *The Gospel of Wealth* (1889) [online] (History Department at East Tennessee State University, 2002, accessed) available from http://www.etsu.edu/cas/history/docs/gospelwealth.htm; the classic essay, *The Gospel of Wealth*, first appeared as follows: Andrew Carnegie, "Wealth," *North American Review* 148 (June 1889): 653-665.

[65] As quoted by Kiron K. Skinner, Annelise Anderson, and Martin Anderson, eds., *Stories in His Own Hand: The Everyday Wisdom of Ronald Reagan*, (New York: Free Press, 2001), 10.

Chapter 2

[1] Estimating world financial wealth is a hazardous exercise at the best of times. This author's estimate is only intended to be indicative if not approximate. The author uses world estimates of Gross Domestic Product (purchasing price equivalent, international dollars) of $48.7 trillion from the World

Bank for year-end 2002 and then multiplies by five to reach an estimate of total wealth of $240-250 trillion. While this probably is an underestimate, it is nevertheless based upon some rigor. This GDP/financial wealth ratio is actually higher for most developed nations.

2 J. Bradford Delong, "Growth in Material Wealth Across Centuries, 1000-Present" [article online] (Brad Delong's Website, accessed 2 May 2004) available from http://econ161.berkeley.edu/tech/1998_draft/World_GDP/estimating_World_gdp.htm

3 Angus Maddison, et al., World Economy: A Millennial Perspective (England: Palgrave Macmillan, 2002), 262.

4 Bank of International Settlements, Quarterly Review: International Banking and Financial Market Developments, statistical annex, various tables (Basle, March 2004).

5 Anglobalization is a term coined by Niall Ferguson, in his book Empire: The Rise and Demise of the British World Order and the Lessons for Global Power (London: Allen Lane, 2002), outlining the economic and financial impact that the spread of the British Empire had upon the entire world.

6 The terms central banking and fractional-reserve banking refer to a system and regulatory regime controlling money and credit. A powerful aspect of this system is that it can create monetary assets from nothing and can influence the allocation of these new monies.

7 US Department of Labor, Bureau of Labor Statistics, 2001 National Occupational Employment and Wage Estimates. Also, see various Organization of Economic Cooperation (OECD) reports.

8 United Nations Conference on Trade and Development, "Towards Reform of the International Financial Architecture: Which Way Forward?" Trade and Development Report (New York, 2001).

9 For brief information on this eschatological period, see Ron J. Bigalke Jr., "The Olivet Discourse: A Resolution of Time," Chafer Seminary Theological Journal 9 (Spring 2003): 108.

10 United Nations Conference on Trade and Development, World Investment Report, various annual reports (New York, 1993-2003).

11 Lowell L. Bryan, et al., Race for the World: Strategies to Build a Great Global Firm (Boston: Harvard Business School Press, 1999).

12 For more information on endtimes stage-setting, see Thomas Ice, "Stage-Setting of the Last Days," in Revelation Hoofbeats: When the Riders of Apocalypse Come Forth, gen. ed. Ron J. Bigalke Jr. (Longwood, FL: Xulon Press, 2003), 283-300.

Chapter 3

1 Charles Clough, *Dawn of the Kingdom* (Lubbock, TX: privately printed, 1974), 15.

2 Robert L. Thomas, *Revelation 8-22: An Exegetical Commentary* (Chicago: Moody Press, 1995), 179-80.

3 Ibid., 181.

4 Ibid.

5 W. M. Ramsay, *The Letters to the Seven Churches*, updated edition, ed. Mark W. Wilson (New York: A. C. Armstrong & Son, 1904; reprint, Peabody, MA: Hendrickson Publishers, 1994), 77.

6 Wes Vernon, "Cashless Society 'Inevitable;' a Boost to Globalist Taxers?" [article online] (NewsMax.com, accessed 10 August 2004) available from http://www.newsmax.com/archives/articles/2002/6/28/181711.shtml; Steve Dinnen, "Going Cashless!" [article online] (*The Christian Science Monitor*, accessed 11 August 2004) available from http://www.csmonitor.com/2004/0426/p13s01-wmgn.html; Kevin Maney, "Will That Be Cash, Fingerprint, or Cell Phone?" [article online] (*USA Today*, accessed 11 August 2004) available from http://www.usatoday.com/tech/news/techinnovations/2003-11-17-bonus-cover_x.htm; see also Apocalyptic Hope, "Cashless Society, Scanning, and Biometrics" [various news articles online] (accessed 10 August 2004) available from http://www.cybertime.net/~ajgood/chip2.html; Pay By Touch, "Press Releases" [articles online] (accessed 10 August 2004) available from http://www.paybytouch.com/press.html

7 Thomas, *Revelation*, 182.

8 For more on this subject, see William T. James, "The Mind Which Has Wisdom," in *Revelation Hoofbeats*, gen. ed. Ron J. Bigalke Jr. (Longwood, FL: Xulon Press, 2003), 119-133.

9 Thomas, *Revelation*, 185.

10 Neil Postman, *Technopoly: The Surrender of Culture to Technology* (New York: Alfred A. Knopf, 1992), 15.

11 Ibid.

12 Edward Cornish, *The Cyber Future: 92 Ways Our Lives Will Change by the Year 2025* (Bethesda, MD: World Future Society, 1996), 2.

13 Clifford Stoll, quoted in "Who's Plugged into the Future?" *Philadelphia Inquirer* (21 January 1996), H1. For an interesting comparison of views on the personal impact of computer technology on our lives, see Clifford Stoll, *Silicon Snake Oil: Second Thoughts on the Information Highway* (New

York: Anchor Books, 1995); Nicholas Negroponte, *Being Digital* (New York: Vintage Books, 1996).

14 Ibid.

15 "Visa, MasterCard Agree on Internet Security," *USA Today* (1 February 1996); IEEE Computer Society Technical Committee on Security and Privacy, "Credit Cards on the Net: MasterCard, VISA Agree; First Virtual Attacks" [article online] (accessed 14 August 2004) available from http://www.ieee-security.org/Cipher/Newsbriefs/1996/960213.cards.html; Wired News Report, "Credit Cards Hacked" [article online] (Wired News, accessed 14 August 2004) available from http://www.wired.com/news/business/0,1367,57710,00.html.

16 Marsha Walton, "New Security Device May Broaden Business of the Web," *Cable Network News Home Page* (16 January 1996).

17 Comtex Scientific Corporation, "A Cashless Society Could be in Our Future," *Knight-Ridder Wire Services* (15 December 1994).

18 eNotes.com, "Computers and Society: Introduction" [article online] (accessed 12 August 2004) available from http://www.enotes.com/computers-society.

19 Thomas McCarroll, "No Checks. No Cash. No Fuss?" [article online] (*Time*, accessed 14 August 2004), available from http://www.time.com/time/archive/preview/0,10987,1101940509-164348,00.html.

20 NTIA and the Economics and Statistics Administration, "A Nation Online: How Americans Are Expanding Their Use Of The Internet" [article online] (National Telecommunications and Information Administration, accessed 12 August 2004) available from http://www.ntia.doc.gov/ntiahome/dn/execsum.htm; Paul Eng, "A Nation of Surfers: Census Bureau Data Shows Online Population Soaring" [article online] (ABC News, accessed 12 August 2004) available from http://abcnews.go.com/sections/scitech/DailyNews/onlinenation020206.html.

21 The Media History Project, "21st Century: First Decade" [article online] (accessed 12 August 2004) available from http://www.mediahistory.umn.edu/time/2000s.html.

22 McCarroll, "No Fuss?" [online].

23 Steven Levy, "E-Money (That's What I Want)" [article online] (*Wired News*, accessed 7 June 2004) available from http://www.wired.com/wired/archive/2.12/emoney.html.

24 McCarroll, "No Fuss?" [online].

[25] David R. Warwick, "The Cash-Free Society," *The Futurist* (November-December 1992), 19.

[26] Ibid.

[27] Joel Kurtzman, *The Death of Money: How the Electronic Economy Has Destabilized the World's Markets and Created Financial Chaos* (Boston: Little, Brown & Co., 1993), 180-81.

[28] Ibid., 181.

[29] Ibid., 183.

[30] McCarroll, "No Fuss?" [online].

[31] Anne Wells Branscomb, *Who Owns Information?* (New York: Basic Books, 1994), 16.

[32] McCarroll, "No Fuss?" [article online].

[33] Amy Barrett, "Patrolling the Black Holes of Cyberspace" [article online] (*Business Week*, accessed 14 August 2004) available from http://www.businessweek.com/1995/24/b3428005.htm

[34] Levy, "E-Money," [online].

[35] Cited by Ibid.

[36] Kurtzman, *Death of Money*, 194.

[37] M. J. Zuckerman, "Terrorism on the Net," *USA Today* (5 June 1996), 1A.

[38] *Newsweek*, "Armed Forces—10 June 1996" [article online] (MSNBC, accessed 13 August 2004) available from http://msnbc.msn.com/id/3668484/site/newsweek.

[39] Stoll, *Silicon Snake Oil*, 96.

[40] Albert Borgmann, "The Meaning of Technology," *The World & I* (March 1996), 298.

[41] Bill Gates, *The Road Ahead* (New York: Penguin Books, 1995), 250.

[42] Ibid., 273.

[43] Ricardo Saludo with Assif Shameen, "Ruler of Our Lives?" [article online] (*Asiaweek*, accessed 9 August 2004), available from http://www.asiaweek.com/asiaweek/95/1103/feat6.html.

[44] Everette E. Dennis, foreword to *Who Owns Information: From Privacy to Public Access*, by Anne Wells Branscomb (New York: Basic Books, 1994), vii.

[45] Branscomb, *Information*, 8.

[46] Levy, "E-Money," [online].

[47] Quoted by Ibid.

[48] Alvin Toffler, *Powershift: Knowledge, Wealth, and Violence at the Edge of the 21st Century* (New York: Bantam Books, 1990), 20.

[49] Russell Chandler, *Racing Toward 2201: The Forces Shaping America's Religious Future* (Grand Rapids, MI: Zondervan, 1992), 46.

[50] Carl F.H. Henry, *Has Democracy Had Its Day?* (Nashville: ERLC Publications, 1996), vii.

[51] Carl F. H. Henry, *God, Revelation and Authority: God Who Stands and Stays: Part Two* (Waco, TX: Word Books, 1983), 6:297.

Chapter 4

[1] Merrill F. Unger, *The New Unger's Bible Dictionary*, ed. R. K. Harrison (Chicago: Moody Press, 1988), 537.

[2] Ibid., 441.

[3] Ibid.

[4] *Webster's Dictionary* (Springfield, MA: Merriam-Webster, Inc., 1997), 589.

[5] Wilfred J. Hahn, "Demagogues & Fables," *Eternal Value Review* 7 (February 2004): 4.

[6] "'Vintage-year' Divorces Swell in Japan," *The Kansas City Star*, 25 January 2004, A12.

[7] Central Intelligence Agency, "The World Factbook – United States," [online] (accessed 22 June 2004) available from http://www.cia.gov/cia/publications/factbook/geos/us.html.

[8] *Encyclopedia Britannica Almanac 2003* (Chicago: Encyclopedia Britannica, 2003), 307-308.

[9] The World Health Organization, "The World Health Report 2000, Health Systems: Improving Performance" [online] (accessed 22 June 2004) available from http://www.who.int/whr2001/2001/archives/2000/en/index.htm.

[10] "World Focus," *Midnight Call* (December 2001), 41.

Chapter 5

[1] Max Weber, *The Protestant Ethic and the Spirit of Capitalism*, trans. Talcott Parsons (New York: Scribner, 1958; reprint, Mineola, NY: Dover Publications, 2003).

[2] R. H. Tawney, *Religion and the Rise of Capitalism* (New York: Harcourt, Brace and Company, Inc., 1926).

[3] Peter Cornelius, ed., *The Arab World Competitiveness Report 2002-2003* (New York: World Economic Forum, 2003).

[4] There are 52 nations today considered "high-income" countries. To qualify for this category, these countries have an average income per person of greater than $9,266 as compared to an average of only $1,028 for nations

that are predominantly Muslim. See World Bank, "World Development Indicators 2001" [online] (The World Bank Group, accessed 8 May 2004) available from http://www.worldbank.org/data/wdi2001/index.htm.

[5]Ibid.

[6] For documentation, see Wilfred J. Hahn, *The Endtime Money Snare: How to Live Free* (Columbia, SC: Olive Press Publishers, 2002).

[7] Michael Novak, "How Christianity Created Capitalism," *Religion and Liberty* 10 (May-June 2000).

[8] John R. Schneider, *The Good of Affluence: Seeking God in a Culture of Wealth* (Grand Rapids: Eerdmans, 2002), 2-3.

[9] Ibid.

[10] Ibid., 26-37.

[11] Lawrence Lindsay, "The Generosity of Capitalism," *Financial Times*, 22 November 2001, 15.

[12] The objectives of the International Interfaith Investment Group (3iG) are noble: to promote socially-responsible investment policies in the world. Currently, it has the representation of 11 religious denominations. It was reported by the world's most respected financial newspaper, the Financial Times, that these 11 religious sponsors together owned $7 trillion in assets, estimating approximately half was held in financial form, and the other half in real estate accounting for 7 per cent of the habitable surface of the planet. Alan Beattie, "Religions Pray at the Altar of Pristine Profit," *Financial Times*, 19 June 2002; Alliance of Religions and Conservation, "3iG—International Interfaith Investment Group" [online] (ARC, accessed 10 May 2004) available from http://www.arcworld.org/projects.asp?projectID=48; Maggie I. Jaruzel, "Religious Alliance Seeks Ways to Use Wealth Wisely" [article online] (Charles Stewart Mott Foundation, accessed 8 May 2004) available from http://www.mott.org/publications/websites/mosaicv2n4/exploratory.asp.

[13] *Jesus answered, "If you want to be perfect, go, sell your possessions and give to the poor, and you will have treasure in heaven. Then come, follow me"* (Mt. 19:21). *But give what is inside the dish to the poor, and everything will be clean for you"* (Lk. 11:41). *Sell your possessions and give to the poor. Provide purses for yourselves that will not wear out, a treasure in heaven that will not be exhausted, where no thief comes near and no moth destroys"* (12:33).

[14] As quoted by Dinesh D'Souza, *The Virtue of Prosperity: Finding Values in an Age of Techno-Affluence* (New York: Free Press, 2000), 144.

[15] Samuel Brittan, "How Economics Can Be Seen as Religion," *Financial*

Times, 15 August 2002, 11.

16 Adam Smith, *The Wealth of Nations* (1776; reprint, New York: Bantam Books, 2003).

17 Robert H. Nelson, "Religion, Economics, and the Market Paradox," *Religion and Liberty* 12 (January-February 2002).

18 J. Bradford DeLong, "Brad DeLong's Website" (accessed 8 May 2004) available from http://www.j-bradford-delong.net.

19 Robert J. Barro and Rachel M. McCleary, "Religion and Economic Growth" (unpublished paper, Harvard University, 8 April 2003).

Chapter 6

1 Walter C. Kaiser Jr., "The Old Testament Case for Material Blessings and the Contemporary Believer," in *The Gospel and Contemporary Perspectives*, ed. Douglas Moo (Grand Rapids: Kregel, 1997), 27. Among the "more visible personalities in this broadly based group," Kaiser identifies Charles Capps, Kenneth Copeland, Kenneth Hagin, Charles and Frances Hunter, John Osteen, Jerry Savelle, and Robert Tilton.

For additional research on this apostasy in the church, see Florence Bulle, *"God Wants You Rich" and Other Enticing Doctrines* (Minneapolis: Bethany House Publishers, 1983), 23-42; Curtis I. Crenshaw, *Man as God: The Word of Faith Movement* (Memphis: Footstool Publications, 1994), 159-209; Hank Hanegraaff, *Christianity in Crisis* (Eugene, OR: Harvest House Publishers, 1993), 179-231; Dave Hunt and T. A. McMahon, *The Seduction of Christianity* (Eugene, OR: Harvest House Publishers, 1985); John F. MacArthur Jr., *Charismatic Chaos* (Grand Rapids: Zondervan, 1992), 264-290; D. R. McConnell, *A Different Gospel*, updated ed. (Peabody, MA: Hendrickson Publishers, 1995), 169-182.

2 John Calvin, *Institutes of Christian Religion*, trans. Henry Beveridge (1559; reprint, Grand Rapids: Eerdmans, 1989), 1:350-351.

3 Cf. John Locke, *Two Treatises of Government*, 3rd student ed. (1690; reprint, Cambridge, MA: Cambridge University Press, 1988), 358.

4 Ibid., 286.

5 Ibid., 289.

6 Grace Cary, "Foundations of Free Enterprise" [article online] (Texas Farm Bureau, 2002, accessed 2 September 2004) available from http://www.txfb.org/TexasAgriculture/2002/111502/111502opinions.htm.

7 Paul K. Jewett, "Justice of God," in *Wycliffe Bible Dictionary* [formerly titled *The Wycliffe Bible Encyclopedia*], eds. Charles F. Pfeiffer, Howard F.

Vos, and John Rea (Chicago: Moody Press, 1975; reprint, Peabody, MA: Hendrickson Publishers, 1998), 981.

[8] J. Ronald Blue, "Major Flaws in Liberation Theology," in *Vital Contemporary Issues*, ed. Roy B. Zuck (Grand Rapids: Kregel, 1994), 132-133.

[9] Richard N. Longenecker, *Acts* (The Expositor's Bible Commentary), ed. Frank E. Gaebelein (Grand Rapids: Zondervan, 1995), 86.

[10] Jacques Ellul, *Money and Power* (Downers Grove, IL: InterVarsity Press, 1984), 41.

[11] *Webster's Third New International Dictionary of the English Language Unabridged*, ed. Philip Babcock Gove (1961; Springfield, MA: Merriam-Webster Inc., 1993), 1458.

[12] Ibid., 1369.

[13] Ibid., 2589.

[14] Allen L. Monroe, "Money, Mammon & Wealth." Paper presented at Cedarville College Faith-Learning Institute, Cedarville, OH, 1995.

[15] Ronald Nash, *Poverty and Wealth: Why Socialism Doesn't Work* (Richardson, TX: Probe, 1992).

[16] John Thomas McNeill, *The History and Character of* Calvinism (Oxford: Oxford University Press, 1954); Max Weber, *The Protestant Ethic and the Spirit of Capitalism*, trans. Talcott Parsons (New York: Charles Scribner's Sons, 1958; reprint, Mineola, NY: Dover Publication, 2003).

[17] Loren Wilkinson, ed., *Earthkeeping: Christian Stewardship of Natural Resources* (Grand Rapids: Eerdmans, 1980).

[18] According to Genesis 1:26, the triune God stated, *"Let Us make man in Our image, according to Our likeness."* The words *image* and *likeness* seem to be virtually synonymous which means man is a representative of God (*image*) who is like God (*likeness*) in certain respects. The image of God must be a representation since God is a spirit. The *likeness* explains man's conscience and will (cf. Rom. 1-2). Man is capable of relationships because man has personality and moral consciousness. Man has dominion because he has a mind to act as master of his environment.

[19] A theological view needing a response here is that of reconstructionism, a postmillennial view teaching God created man with a mandate to subdue the earth on His behalf. The result of this mandate, which has never been revoked, would be the establishment of the kingdom of God on earth (Gen. 1:28). Both Jews and Gentiles failed to fulfill this mandate. At His first coming, Jesus established and restored the Old Testament Law (Mt. 5:17-19).

The Old Testament Law is now to be the Christian's rule of life.

All Christians would agree this mandate has not been revoked. The mandate was originally given in Genesis 1:28 but then restated as a component of the Noahic Covenant (Gen. 9:1-3). The mandate given to Adam and his entire posterity includes all humanity (saved or unsaved). Ecclesiastes 2:26 explains even rebellious unbelievers will contribute to the fulfillment of the mandate. God's sovereignty makes even the unbeliever accomplish His will. There are some aspects of the mandate that man has fulfilled; yet, there is also a complete fulfillment that man seeks even though it is *by the sweat of [his] face*; furthermore, the unbeliever will do this in a state of rebellion against God. During the millennial kingdom, Christ will create additional progress as fulfillment of the mandate.

In contrast to the above scenario, reconstructionists teach Satan was defeated and also bound through the provisions of Christ's death, resurrection, and ascension. The stronghold of Satan and his minions upon the world has been eradicated. Although satanic activity still occurs in the world, his general activity is greatly restrained.

At the end of history, reconstructionism teaches every sphere of society, including all the nations of the earth, will be subjugated to Christ's rule. When this dominion occurs, the kingdom of God will be completely established on earth which will culminate in the return of Christ to earth to receive His kingdom. The major error, regarding the dominion mandate, in reconstruction thinking is its teaching that the fulfillment of the mandate will occur, apart from Christ's physical presence, in the present age. In other words, it is not in the millennium that Christ will use to lead His people in the progress of fulfilling the mandate; rather, the church will accomplish this in the present age.

Certainly, humanity received dominion, according to Genesis 1:26-28, and it has never been revoked. However, Adam did not lose his dominion when he rebelled against his Creator; rather, he lost his relationship to his Creator. Following mankind's rebellion, man still retained the dominion that God had given since it was a stewardship responsibility. The mandate does not have to be regained. For instance, Psalm 8:6-8 clearly states man does now possess dominion over the creation.

The mandate is not to save the earth, but to be active in preaching the gospel for the salvation of souls. Christ said, "*I am not of this world*" (Jn. 8:23). In fact, the present world is *kept for the day of judgment and destruction of ungodly men* (2 Pet. 3:7). Spiritual suicide is the folly of adopting an earth-based salvation. Christians need to be active as good stewards of God's creation, but also taking every advantage to explain to a perishing world that the solution to man's dilemma is to be found in Jesus Christ.

[20] Donald Hay, *A Christian Critique of Capitalism* (Bramcote, Nottingham: Grove Books, 1975).

[21] Marjie Bloy, "Joseph Rayner Stephens on Chartism" [article online] (A Web of English History, 2003, accessed 2 September 2004) available from http://dspace.dial.pipex.com/town/terrace/adw03/peel/chartism/stephens.htm.

[22] Nash, *Poverty and Wealth*.

[23] John Stuart Mill, *Principles of Political Economy with Some of Their Applications to Social Philosophy*, ed. William James Ashley (1848; reprint, London: Longmans, Green, and Co., 1909) [online] (accessed 3 September 2004) available from http://www.econlib.org/library/Mill/mlP20.html.

[24] Ludwig von Mises, *Human Action: A Treatise of Economics* (New Haven: Yale University Press, 1949; reprint, Auburn, AL: Ludwig Von Mises Institute, 1998), 10.

[25] James M. Buchanan, *What Should Economists Do?* (Indianapolis: Liberty Fund, 1979), 20.

[26] Ibid., 39–63.

[27] John W. Robbins, "The Promise of Christian Economics," *The Trinity Review* (August-September 2000): 6.

[28] Ibid., 7.

[29] J. Vernon McGee, *Invitation into Isaiah: Part 2* (Glendale, CA: Griffin Printing & Lithograph Co., Inc., 1957), 107.

[30] Basic to this prophecy is the likely thought previously expressed in Genesis 6:3.

[31] Charles Caldwell Ryrie, *Ryrie Study Bible*, expanded ed. (1986; Chicago: Moody Press, 1995), 1144.

[32] The word "dispensation" is a compound of two Greek words *oíkos* ("house") and *nómos* ("law"). The main idea of the word is "house law," that is, "managing or administering the affairs of a household" [Charles C. Ryrie, *Dispensationalism* (Chicago: Moody Press, 1995), 25]. One can find the English word "dispensation" in the KJV four times (1 Cor. 9:17; Eph. 1:10; 3:2; Col. 1:25). In each of the four passages, the writer uses the word οἰκονομία which ordinarily indicates the management functions related to one's responsibility (cf. Lk. 16:2-4). The KJV renders οἰκονομία as "fellowship" in Ephesians 3:9 and "edifying" in 1 Timothy 1:4.

Modern translations differ in the translation of οἰκονομία. The NIV renders οἰκονομία as follows: "trust" in 1 Corinthians 9:17; "put in effect" in Ephesians 1:10; "administration" in Ephesians 3:2; and, "commission" in Colossians 1:25. The NASB renders οἰκονομία as "stewardship" in three of the passages, but renders it "administration" in Ephesians 1:10.

The word translated "dispensation" (or "economy") in English translations is derived from the Latin word *dispensation* which is a translation of οἰκονομία. Literally οἰκονομία means "house management" and describes how God manages His house (i.e. creation). Dr. Robert Lightner provided the following definition: "Dispensationalism is that system of theology which sees the Bible as the unfolding of the distinguishable economies in the out-working of God's purpose and which sees His program with Israel as distinct and separate from His program with the church" [Robert Lightner, Class Notes in *Dispensationalism & Covenants*, Ft. Worth, TX: Tyndale Theological Seminary]. Charles Ryrie quoted the summary definition of dispensationalism provided by Dallas Theological Seminary graduate Paul David Nevin as follows:

> A dispensation is God's distinctive method of governing mankind or a group of men during a period of human history, marked by a crucial event, test, failure, and judgment. From the divine standpoint, it is a stewardship, a rule of life, or a responsibility for managing God's affairs in His house. From the historical standpoint, it is a stage in the progress of revelation [Paul David Nevin, "Some Major Problems in Dispensational Interpretation" (unpublished Th.D. diss., Dallas Theological Seminary, 1963), 97, as quoted by Ryrie, *Dispensationalism*, 30].

33 McGee, *Isaiah*, 107.

34 E. Calvin Beisner, *Prosperity and Poverty: The Passionate Use of Resources in a World of Scarcity* (Westchester, IL: Crossway Books, 1988), xi-xii.

35 David W. Breese, *Seven Men Who Rule the World from the Grave* (Chicago: Moody Press, 1990), 202.

Chapter 7
1 Jean-Jacqués Rousseau, *The Social Contract*, trans. Maurice William Cranston (1762; reprint, New York: Penguin Books, 1968), 84.

Chapter 8
1 Merriam Webster, "Trap" [online] (Merriam-Webster Online, 2004,

accessed 2 July 2004) available from http://www.m-w.com/cgi-bin/diction-ary?book=Dictionary&va=trap.

2 Merriam Webster, "Snare" [online] (Merriam-Webster Online, 2004, accessed 2 July 2004) available from http://www.m-w.com/cgi-bin/diction-ary?book=Dictionary&va=snare.

3 Norman Geisler and Peter Bocchino, *Unshakable Foundations* (Minneapolis, MN: Bethany House, 2001) 215.

4 Ibid., 214.

5 Ibid., 212.

6 Ibid., 220.

7 C. S. Lewis, *Mere Christianity*, rev. ed. (New York: Macmillan, 1952), 45.

8 Robert Famighetti, *The World Almanac and Book of Facts 1998* (Mahwah, NJ: World Almanac Books, 1997), 33.

9 William J. Federer, *America's God and Country: Encyclopedia Of Quotations* (St. Louis, MO: Amerisearch, 2000), 540.

10 For remarkable evidence from linguists regarding the "mother tongue" influencing all languages, see Phillip Goodman, "The Beginning of Civilization" [CD-ROM] (Tulsa, OK: Thy Kingdom Come); Henry Morris, *The Biblical Basis for Modern Science* (Grand Rapids, MI: Baker Book House, 1984), 427-436.

11 James Rubenstein, *Human Geography* (Upper Saddle River, NJ: Prentice Hall, 1999), 290-291.

12 Phillip Goodman, "The Euphrates Connection" [article online] (Prophecy Watch, accessed 2 July 2004) available from http://www.prophecywatch.com/articles/euphrates_connection.htm; Prophecy Watch, "Articles on Prophecy" [online] (accessed 2 July 2004) available from http://www.prophecywatch.com/articles.htm.

13 At the sounding of the sixth trumpet plague, two hundred million demon-ic spirits are released to kill one-third of mankind. It is evident these are demon angels because their leaders are four fallen angels who have been bound for millennial centuries awaiting this very moment. Also, for every rider there is a *horse*. Whether this is interpreted to mean a literal horse or modern armored vehicle is insignificant. "To assemble two hundred million horses (or vehicles) would be one of the great miracles of all time. The passage clearly indicates a demonic— not human— invasion. The description of the 'horsemen' is as unearthly as the description of those demonic hordes which are released from the bottomless pit in trumpet nine. They also have a fallen angel as their leader (9:1-11)." Phillip Goodman, *The Assyrian*

Connection (Lafayette, LA: Prescott Press, 1993), 189.

Arnold Fruchtenbaum wrote the following analysis: "To summarize why these 200 million are demons and not Chinese, four things should be noted: first, they are led by four fallen angels; secondly, the location of the army is stated to be the Euphrates where Babylon is located (which in the future will be the headquarters of the counterfeit trinity); thirdly, the description given in the text rules this army out as being human; and, fourthly, the kings of the east are not connected with this at all." Arnold Fruchtenbaum, *The Footsteps of the Messiah: A Study of the Sequence of Prophetic Events* (Tustin, CA: Ariel Ministries Press, 1983), 156.

[14] This author's book, *The Assyrian Connection*, is a thorough study on the sequence of end time event. For a summarized study, see Phillip Goodman, "Sequence of End-Time Events," in *Revelation Hoofbeats*, ed. Ron J. Bigalke Jr., (Longwood, FL: Xulon Press, 2003), 301-313.

[15] For the identification of the various nations involved in the invasion, see Mark Hitchcock, *The Complete Book of Bible Prophecy* (Wheaton, IL: Tyndale House Publishers, 1999), 110-111.

[16] For details of the Russian invasion of Israel, including the identity of the nations involved and the timing of the event, see Phillip Goodman, "Jerusalem's Earthshaking Northern Threat," in *Prophecy at Ground Zero*, ed. William T. James (Lancaster, PA: Starburst Publishers, 2002), 45-61; Phillip Goodman, *The Russian Invasion of Israel—Next?* (Tulsa, OK: Prophecy Watch Books, 2004).

[17] This author's book, *The Assyrian Connection*, is also an in-depth study on the roots of the Antichrist. Since this book was first published in 1993, the author has witnessed a growing number of other publications positing the origin of the Antichrist in the ancient domain of Assyria (modern day Syria-Iraq). See Joseph Chambers, *A Palace for the Antichrist* (Green Forest, AR: New Leaf Press, 1996), 137; S. Maxwell Coder, *The Final Chapter* (Wheaton, IL: Tyndale House, 1984), 103; Zane Hodges, *Power to Make War* (Dallas, TX: Redención Viva, 1995), 3.

[18] For details on biblical and historical outline of the final Roman Empire, see Phillip Goodman, *The Identity of the Beast: The Meaning of the 7 Heads and 10 Horns* (Tulsa, OK: Prophecy Watch Books, 2004).

[19] Noted Hebrew scholar Gleason Archer wrote, "It seems much simpler and more convincing, however, to take the 'king of the North [Syria]' in this verse [Daniel 11:40] to be none other than the latter-day little horn [cf. Dan. 7:8, 24], the Antichrist." Gleason L. Archer Jr., "Daniel" in *The Expositor's Bible*

Commentary, ed. Frank E. Gaebelein (Grand Rapids, MI: Zondervan Publishing House, 1985), 7:147. Early in the twentieth century, when that possibility seemed very remote due to the geo-political alignment of nations, Clarence Larkin (1850-1924) wrote the following regarding Daniel 11:40: "This vision of the 'King of the North' (Syria), and of the 'King of the South' (Egypt), in which the 'king of the North' prevailed, revealed to Daniel that Antichrist would arise in the 'Syrian' division of Alexander's kingdom...it is clear that the Antichrist is to come from Syria...We are to understand therefore by the 'king of the North' the king of Syria, which also included Assyria. This fixes the locality from which the Antichrist shall come, [as] we read in Isa. 10:12...and 14:25...." Clarence Larkin, *Dispensational Truth* (Glenside, PA: Rev. Clarence Larkin Estate, 1918), 70, 118.

20 The Bible does not directly mention America by name, or even with a clear inference. The *young lions* reference in Ezekiel 38:13 (KJV), connecting the phrase with the Japhetic-European root city of Tarshish, could refer to the offspring colonies of Europe, which would include America. However, that is only a good possibility, and not decisive. The best reference in the Bible (by inference) to America, in this author's opinion, is found in Daniel 11:39. The Hebrew term *maoz* ("strength," "stronghold," "fortress") is translated in the KJV as follows: *Thus shall he do in the most strong holds with a strange god, whom he shall acknowledge and increase with glory: and he shall cause them to rule over many, and shall divide the land for gain.* Other translations render the Hebrew as *strongest fortresses* (cf. AB; ESV; NKJV); *strongest of fortresses* (NASB); *mightiest fortresses* (NIV); and, *strong places of refuge* (LXX).

In modern-day speech, these terms, in the vernacular, would well be rendered "super powers." The sole superpower in the world today is the United States of America. Inserting the "United States of America" into the NASB (the other versions would read essentially the same), it would read as follows: *And he will take action against the* [United States of America] *with the help of a foreign god; he will give great honor to those who acknowledge him, and he will cause them to rule over the many, and will parcel out land for a price.* In the context of Daniel 11:36-45, the action of the Antichrist will be to conquer through either diplomacy or military might (probably the latter). There are other passages which allude to the *isles of the sea*, or the coastlands (Esth. 10:1; Isa. 24:15; 42:10; Jer. 25:22; Ezek. 26:18; 27:3), implying distant continents and lands but this is the passage to examine regarding the future of America in prophecy.

[21] For a complete explanation on the meaning of the *fatal wound*, the rise of the Antichrist, and the formation of the final world empire, see Goodman, *Assyrian Connection*.

[22] See Goodman, "End-Time Events."

[23] The *many* are identified as Jews in such passages as Daniel 9:27, 11:39, 12:3.

[24] Terms such as *broken into* (Mt. 24:43), *quickly* (Rev. 22:20), *suddenly* (1 Thess. 5:3), etc., indicate a virtual explosion of long repressed divine wrath.

[25] To examine the validity of Jerusalem as the center of the world's compass from the heavenly viewpoint, see Ezekiel 5:5; 38:12, 15.

[26] BBC News UK Edition, "EU Text to be Signed in October" [article online] (accessed 12 July 2004) available from http://news.bbc.co.uk/1/hi/world/europe/3886747.stm.

[27] EU Business, "Signing of EU Constitution on November 20 in Rome" [article online] (accessed 2 July 2004) available from http://www.eubusiness.com/afp/040702130047.gvvl4tw8.

[28] Geisler and Bocchino, Unshakable Foundations, 224.

[29] Ibid., 199.

[30] Samuel P. Huntington, "Under God," *The Wall Street Journal* (16 June 2004): A14.

Chapter 9

[1] W. C. Stevens, *The Book of Daniel* (Los Angeles: Bible House of Los Angeles, 1918), 93.

[2] Ibid., 104.

[3] *Friedrich Wilhelm Nietzsche, The Will to Power*, trans. Walter Kaufmann and R. J. Hollingdale (1883-1888; New York: Random House, 1967), 531.

[4] John F. Walvoord, *Major Bible Prophecies* (Grand Rapids: Zondervan, 1991), 314-315.

[5] Ibid., 324-325.

[6] Ibid., 163-64.

[7] The book of Daniel can be roughly divided into two divisions, excluding the first chapter which is a historical introduction. Daniel 2-7 is the Aramaic division, and Daniel 8-12 is the Hebraic division. Since Daniel 2-7 is primarily concerned with the Gentile world powers, the language of the Gentiles, Aramaic, is used. These chapters communicate the prophetic history of the Gentiles. Daniel 8-12 is also concerned with the *times of the Gentiles*, but it is from a Jewish perspective, therefore, the language of the Jews, Hebrew, is

used. These chapters communicate the prophetic history of the Jews.

[8] For instance, one prominent liberal critic wrote, "...when the fourth beast was destroyed, the other beasts were spared for a time, though denied any dominion. But how can it be maintained that at any time contemplated by the various forms of this interpretation Babylon, Medo-Persia, and Greece enjoyed a measured existence that was denied to Rome?" H. H. Rowley, *Darius the Mede and the Four World Empires in the Book of Daniel* (Cardiff: University of Wales Press Board, 1935), 87.

[9] C. F. Keil noted, "The construction of the words forbids us (with Luther) to regard the first part of v. 12 as dependent on עַד דִּי of v. 11." C. F. Keil and F. Delitzsch, "Daniel," in *Commentary on the Old Testament*, trans. James Martin and M. G. Easton (Edinburgh: T. & T. Clark, 1866-1891; reprint, Peabody, MA: Hendrickson Publishers, 1996), 9:644.

[10] Ibid., 9:645.

[11] Clarence Larkin, *The Book of Daniel* (Glenside, PA: Rev. Clarence Larkin Estate, 1929), 126.

[12] William D. Mounce, *The Analytical Lexicon to the Greek New Testament* (Grand Rapids: Zondervan, 1993), 163.

[13] Paul N. Benware, "God's Judgment upon Individuals," in *Revelation Hoofbeats*, ed. Ron J. Bigalke Jr. (Longwood, FL: Xulon Press, 2003), 139.

[14] Larkin, *Daniel*, 127.

[15] Benjamin Davidson, *The Analytical Hebrew and Chaldee Lexicon* (London: Samuel Bagster & Sons, Ltd., 1848; second edition, 1850; reprint, Grand Rapids: Zondervan, 1993), 239.

[16] Ibid., 587.

[17] Karl Feyerabend, *Langenscheidt's Pocket Hebrew Dictionary*, 15th ed. (Maspeth, NY: Langenscheidt Publishers, n.d.), 240.

[18] Lewis Sperry Chafer, *Dispensationalism*, rev. ed. (1936; Dallas: Dallas Seminary Press, 1951), 20-21. Chafer also clarified the following: "This context does not bear out the interpretation that this is a description of a last and final judgment when all saved people of all the ages are ushered into heaven; for the saved, each and every one, when departing this world are immediately present with the Lord in heaven (Acts 7:55-56; 2 Cor. 5:8; Phil. 1:23); and who, according to such an interpretation, would answer to "my brethren"? The scene is at the close of the great tribulation (Matt. 24:21) after the removal of the Church from the earth, and at a time when nations will be divided over the Semitic question." Ibid., 21-22.

[19] Sir Robert Anderson, *The Coming Prince*, 10th ed. (London: Hodder and

Stoughton, 1909; reprint, Grand Rapids: Kregel, 1957), 123-127. Actually, other research has determined the actual Julian equivalents of Babylonian dates in 445 BC. This scholarship states that 1 Nisan was not 14 March, but it was 13 April. Richard A. Parker and Waldo H. Dubberstein, *Babylonian Chronology 626 BC – AD 75* (Providence: Brown University Press, 1956), 32.

[20] Anderson, *Coming Prince*, 102; Colin J. Humphreys and W. G. Waddington, "Dating the Crucifixion," *Nature* 306 (December 1983): 743-46.

[21] Harold W. Hoehner, *Chronological Aspects of the Life of Christ* (Grand Rapids: Zondervan, 1977), 127.

[22] Parker and Dubberstein, *Babylonian Chronology*, 17.

[23] Ibid., 32.

[24] Herman H. Goldstine, *New and Full Moons: 1001 BC to AD 1651* (Philadelphia: American Philosophical Society, 1973), 47; See also Jack Finegan, *Handbook of the Biblical Chronology* (Princeton, N.J.: Princeton University Press, 1954).

[25] Hoehner, *Chronological Aspects*, 138.

[26] Ibid.

[27] In other words, "away from" the "end" of the prophetic fulfillment.

[28] William F. Bauer, William F. Arndt, and F. Wilbur Gingrich, *A Greek-English Lexicon of the New Testament and Other Early Christian Literature*, 2nd ed., rev. F. Wilbur Gingrich and Frederick W. Danker (Chicago: University of Chicago Press, 1979), 810-811.

[29] J. Randall Price, "Prophetic Postponement in Daniel 9 and Other Texts," in eds. Wesley R. Willis and John R. Master, *Issues in Dispensationalism* (Chicago: Moody Press, 1994), 136.

[30] Thomas Ice and Timothy Demy, *Fast Facts on Bible Prophecy* (Eugene, OR: Harvest House, 1997), 112-113.

[31] Charles C. Ryrie, *The Basis of the Premillennial Faith* (Neptune, NJ: Loizeaux Brothers, 1953), 148-149.

[32] Arnold G. Fruchtenbaum, *Israelology: The Missing Link in Systematic Theology* (Tustin, CA: Ariel Ministries, 1989), 582.

[33] Ryrie, *Premillennial Faith*, 149.

[34] Ibid., 150.

Chapter 10

[1] The use of the Red Cross on a white background, which is actually the

Swiss flag reversed, was granted to the International Red Cross to commemorate Dunant's organization. The plenipotentiaries of 35 nations, assembled in Geneva on 6 July 1906 to revise the Geneva Convention and stated the following concerning the symbol of the International Red Cross: "To do homage to Switzerland, the heraldic arms of the Red Cross on a white field, which is formed by reversal of the Swiss Federal arms, shall be maintained as a distinctive emblem of the medical services of most armies."

2 For more details, see Ron J. Bigalke Jr., "The Implications of the Biblical Covenants" [article online] (Eternal Ministries, accessed 15 July 2004) available from http://www.eternalministries.org/articles/covenants.html.

3 Editor's note: Abraham is the father of the Jewish, the "seed of Abraham" (Ps. 105:6; Lk. 1:55; Jn. 8:33, 37; Rom. 4:13; 9:7; et al). He began his life in Ur of the Chaldees in Mesopotamia. Abram was the original name of Abraham (Gen. 11:27-17:5) when God commanded him to abandon his pagan background. The heathen meaning of Abram's name was "my (divine) father is exalted" [Robert North, "Abraham," *The Oxford Companion to the Bible*, ed. Bruce Metzger and Michael Coogan (New York: Oxford University Press, 1993), 5]. He was to travel to a land promised to him and his seed after him.

God reiterated His promise to Abram on numerous occasions (13:14-18; 15; 17; 22:15-19). Great emphasis in Scripture is given to Abram's faith in the promise of God which concerned a seed, land, and blessing to all nations. God changed the name of Abram ("exalted father") to Abraham meaning, "father of a multitude." God's promise with Abraham would be sealed by the sign of circumcision (Gal. 4:28). Abraham would also be known as *the father of all them that believe* because of his faith in God (Rom. 4:11). The change of Abraham's name indicates that the covenant God made with him is concentrated on the promise of a seed. Abraham's son, Isaac, would be the son of promise. Again, Abraham demonstrated his faith in God even in old age as he believed God's promise of a son (Gen. 15:4-6; Rom. 4:1-4; Gal. 3:6; 5:6; Jas. 2:22-23). Hebrews 11:17-19 amplifies Abraham's remarkable faith in God, who even believed if Isaac would die God would raise his son from the dead to fulfill the covenantal promise.

4 Emil Schürer, *History of the Jewish People in the Time of Jesus Christ* (Edinburgh: Clark, 1896), 2:15, as quoted in Merrill F. Unger, "Pharisees," in *The New Unger's Bible Dictionary*, rev. and updated ed., ed. R. K. Harrison (1957; Chicago: Moody Press, 1988), 998.

5 Wilfred J. Hahn, "Muslims, Money & Malice—Part I," *Eternal Value*

Review 5 (September 2002): 2-3.

[6] For a fuller treatment of this subject, see Arno Froese, *How Democracy Will Elect the Antichrist* (West Columbia, SC: The Olive Press, 1997).

[7] Chris Roberts, "S.C. Tobacco Farmers Closer to $700 Million in Payments," *The State* (18 June 2004): D1.

[8] Arno Froese, "United Europe's Power Play," in *Foreshocks of Antichrist*, ed. William T. James (Eugene, OR: Harvest House, 1997), 292.

[9] Europa, "The European Union at a Glance" [online] (accessed 14 July 2004) available from http://europa.eu.int/abc/index_en.htm.

Chapter 11

[1] For amillennial chart, see Ron J. Bigalke Jr., "A Concise History of Prophetic Interpretation: With Practical Attention to Interpretative Views of the Olivet Discourse" (unpublished Ph.D. dissertation, Tyndale Theological Seminary, 2003), 42.

[2] Augustine, "City of God" in *The Nicene and Post Nicene Fathers* (Albany: Ages Software), 2:902, as quoted in Bigalke, "Concise History," 141-142.

[3] Larry Crutchfield, "Augustine," in *Dictionary of Premillennial Theology*, ed. Mal Couch (Grand Rapids: Kregel, 1996), 58-60.

[4] Norman Cohn, *The Pursuit of the Millennium* (New York: Oxford University Press, 1970), 29.

[5] Rick Bowman and Russell L. Penney, "Amillennialism," in *Premillennial Theology*, 39.

[6] Mal Couch, "Controversy Over Prophetic Fulfillment," in *Revelation Hoofbeats*, ed. Ron J. Bigalke Jr. (Longwood, FL: Xulon Press, 2003), 315-327.

[7] For postmillennial chart, see Bigalke, "Concise History," 41.

[8] John F. Walvoord, *The Millennial Kingdom* (Findlay, OH: Dunham Publishing, 1959), 33.

[9] Arnold G. Fruchtenbaum, *Israelology: The Missing Link in Systematic Theology* (Tustin, CA: Ariel Ministries Press, 1989), 119.

[10] Paul N. Benware, *Understanding End Times Prophecy* (Chicago: Moody Press, 1995), 127.

[11] Ibid., 129.

[12] Tim LaHaye and Thomas Ice edited an excellent volume on the subject entitled *The End Times Controversy* (Eugene, OR: Harvest House, 2003). This author participated in the book project and wrote Chapter 12 entitled "The War over Words."

[13] Thomas Ice, "What is Preterism?" in *End Times Controversy*, 26.

[14] In this author's work in Chapter 12 of *End Times Controversy* (pp. 283-306), he gives an exegetical explanation as to what Christ was actually communicating.

[15] Tim LaHaye, "Introduction: Has Jesus Already Come?" in *End Times Controversy*, 11-15.

[16] Ron J. Bigalke Jr., personal correspondence to the author, 11 May 2004.

[17] For dispensationalist chart, see Bigalke, "Concise History," 39.

Chapter 12

[1] Joy Hakim, *A History of US: Sourcebook and Index*, 3rd ed. (1993; reprint, New York: Oxford University Press, 2002), 16.

[2] J. Dwight Pentecost, *Things to Come* (Findley, OH: Dunham Publishing Company, 1958; reprint, Grand Rapids: Zondervan, 1964), 473.

[3] William R. Newell, *The Book of Revelation* (Chicago: Moody Press, 1935), 318-322; quoted in Ibid., 537.

[4] George N. H. Peters, *The Theocratic Kingdom*, 3 vols. (New York: Funk & Wagnalls, 1884; Grand Rapids: Kregel, 1952), 1:224.

[5] Merrill F. Unger, *Unger's Commentary on the Old Testament* (Chicago: Moody Press, 1981; reprint, Chattanooga: AMG Publishers, 2003), 1146.

[6] Roy E. Beacham, "Kingdoms, Universal and Mediatorial," in *Dictionary of Premillennial Theology*, ed. Mal Couch (Grand Rapids: Kregel, 1996), 235.

[7] Tim LaHaye, "A Literal Millennium as Taught in Scripture: Part 4," *Pre-Trib Perspectives* (February 2004): 2.

[8] Grant Baxter, "Obediance to Authority" [article online] (University of Otago, accessed 4 June 2004) available from http://designweb.otago.ac.nz/grant/psyc/OBEDIANCE.HTML.

[9] Peters, *Theocratic Kingdom*, 1:221.

[10] John F. Walvoord, *The Revelation of Jesus Christ* (Chicago: Moody Press, 1966), 277-278.

[11] Allen P. Ross, "Psalms," in *The Bible Knowledge Commentary*, eds. John F. Walvoord and Roy B. Zuck, (Wheaton: Victor Books, 1986), 792.

[12] David Limbaugh, *Persecution: How Liberals Are Waging War Against Christianity* (Washington, DC: Regnery, 2003), 185.

[13] Ibid., 128.

[14] Arnold G. Fruchtenbaum, "The Campaign of Armageddon and the Second Coming of Jesus the Messiah," *The Conservative Theological Journal*

5 (March 2001): 16.

15 Pentecost, *Things to Come*, 500.

16 *A Dictionary of Early Christian Beliefs*, ed. David Bercot (Peabody, MA: Hendrickson Publishers, 1998), 450.

17 Jimmy Akin, "False Profit: Money, Prejudice, and Bad Theology in Tim LaHaye's *Left Behind* Series" [article online] (Catholic Answers, accessed 11 June 2004) available from http://www.catholic.com/library/false_profit.asp.

18 Ibid.

19 Tim LaHaye, "A Literal Millennium as Taught in Scripture: Part 3," *Pre-Trib Perspectives* (January 2004): 1.

20 Peters, *Theocratic Kingdom*, 1:499.

21 Ibid., 1:513.

22 George Zeller, "Do I Interpret the Bible Literally?" *The Conservative Theological Journal* 8 (March 2004): 52.

23 *Tim LaHaye Prophecy Study Bible* (Chattanooga: AMG Publishers, 2000), 1368.

Chapter 13

1 *Webster's Third New International Dictionary of the English Language Unabridged*, ed. Philip Babcock Gove (1961; Springfield, MA: Merriam-Webster Inc., 1993), 1918.

2 Allen P. Ross, *Creation and Blessing: A Guide to the Study and Exposition of Genesis* (Grand Rapids: Baker Books, 1988), 221.

3 The Hebrew word toldot is the major structural word of the Book of Genesis. It is expressed by the clause "these are the generations of" as is seen in the toldot of the heavens and the earth (2:4-4:26), the toldot of Adam (5:1-6:8), the toldot of Noah (6:9-9:29), the toldot of the sons of Noah (10:1-11:9), the toldot of Shem (11:10-26), the toldot of Terah (11:27-25:11), the toldot of Ishmael (25:12-18), the toldot of Isaac (25:19-35:29), the toldot of Esau (36:1-37:1), and the toldot of Jacob (37:2-50:26). Other usages of the word can be found in Numbers 3:1, Ruth 4:18, and 1 Chronicles 1:29.

Toldot is a feminine noun that comes from the verb דאלאי ("to give birth"). The verb form is derived from the hiphil stem (הוליד) which means "to beget" or "to bear." It is because the word is always used in the plural that toldot is commonly translated as "generations" (Ross, *Creation and Blessing*, 69-70). Traditionally, the word has been used as a heading. This would indicate that the fullest meaning of תולדות would prohibit the possibility of the word being used as an appendix to what has been previously recorded (C.F. Keil and F. Delitzsch, *Commentary on the Old Testament: The Pentateuch*, trans. James Martin [Peabody, MA: Hendrickson Publishers, 1996], 44.). E. J. Young (E. J. Young, *An Introduction to the Old Testament* [Grand Rapids: Eerdmans, 1949], 52-66) would view תולדות as a heading, whereas R. K. Harrison (R. K. Harrison, *Introduction to the Old Testament* [Grand Rapids: Eerdmans, 1969], 543-551) would take the word to be a conclusion to what has preceded.

Primarily, toldot is used to document the descendants of a man. Consequently, the etymological structure is that of a genealogical history of a man or his family (cf. Numb. 1:20-40). The basic meaning of תולדות has to do with a specific period of time, that is, from a man's birth followed by the birth of his son. The period of time differs (Gen. 15:13, 16; Deut. 1:35; 2:14; Job 42:16) at various periods of history.

4 Fred E. Young, "Babylon," in *Wycliffe Bible Dictionary*, eds. Charles F. Pfeiffer, Howard Vos, and John Rea (Peabody, MA: Hendrickson Publishers, 1998), 187.

5 Karl Feyerabend, *Langenscheidt's Pocket Hebrew Dictionary to the Old Testament* (Maspeth, NY: Langenscheidt Publishers, 1985), 195.

6 Joseph A. Seiss, *The Apocalypse: Exposition of the Book of Revelation* ([S.l.]: C. C. Cook, 1900; reprint, Grand Rapids: Kregel, 1987), 389.

7 Ross, *Creation and Blessing*, 243.

8 Alexander Hislop, *The Two Babylonians or Papal Worship Proved to be the Worship of Nimrod and His Wife* (Neptune, NJ: Loizeaux Brothers, 1916), 44.

9 Ibid., 6-7.

10 Ibid., 20.

11 Ibid.

12 Ibid., 58-59.

13 Seiss, *Apocalypse*, 388-394.

14 Richard N. Ostling, "Handmaid or Feminist?" *Time* (30 December 1991): 62.

15 Hislop, *Two Babylonians*, 284.

16 Charles Glock and Robert Bellah, eds., *The New Religious Consciousness* (Berkeley: University of California Press, 1976), 37.

17 The doctrinal statement of Eternal Ministries (Article I) reads: "The witness of Scripture is that the Holy Bible, consisting of the sixty-six books of the Old and New Testaments, is a divine revelation, the original autographs

of which were verbally inspired by the Holy Spirit. It is absolute in authority, complete in revelation, final in content, and infallible in its statements. Scripture is to be interpreted literally, as opposed to an allegorical interpretation. A consistent, literal interpretation allows for progressive revelation, which is the gradual unfolding over a period of time of certain revealed truths of God, as recorded in Scripture. Historical, grammatical, contextual, and literal hermeneutics (science of interpretation) include observation, interpretation, and application. Literal interpretation allows for figurative language, illustrations, poetry, types, and symbols in Scripture" (Lk. 1:1-4; 24:27, 44-46, 48; Jn. 5:39; Acts 1:16; 17:11; 26:6, 7, 26; Rom. 15:4; 1 Cor. 2:13; 2 Tim. 3:16; 2 Pet. 1:21).

[18] Norman Cohn, *The Pursuit of the Millennium* (New York: Oxford University Press, 1970), 108.

[19] Walter Kaufman, ed., *The Portable Nietzsche* (Princeton: Princeton University Press, 1968), 441.

[20] Richard Kyle, *The Last Days Are Here Again* (Grand Rapids: Baker Books, 1998), 22.

[21] Deepak Chopra is in wide demand as a best-selling author and spiritual guru. In 1985, Chopra visited the headquarters of Maharishi Mahesh Yogi quickly accepting the Maharishi as his spiritual guru. Later Chopra became chairman of Maharishi's Ayurvedic clinic in Lancaster, Massachusetts. He became a millionaire as a spokesman for Maharishi's movement, but when given the choice to leave or stay with Maharishi, he quickly left. Chopra is now president of the American Association of Ayurvedic Medicine. Even though Chopra broke contact with Maharishi, he still derives much of his view of holistic health from Transcendental Meditation. For instance, Chopra promoted vigorously the belief that he can control the molecules of his own body. Chopra believes his body is composed of sub-atomic elements—molecules that he has never seen—and since matter and energy is interchangeable then he can control his molecular composition. Chopra's belief is the Hindu doctrine of maya, that is, the apparent existence of the mind and the body as man experiences it.

Maharishi was the disciple of Swami Brahmananda Saraswati, the Shankaracharya of a Hindu monastery. At the monastery, he developed his monistic views of reality. Maharishi was sent to the West as a missionary for Hinduism. He brought his Science of Creative Intelligence to the United States, and recommended Transcendental Meditation to the citizenry. Maharishi desired one Transcendental Meditation instructor for every 1,000

Americans. He was an antichrist that believed his World Plan would save humanity. His "age of enlightenment" would bring about favorable conditions for everyone and the spiritual goals of mankind would be reached through him.

He was a consistent monist that identified God as part of the creation and by doing so was an idolater (Rom. 1:25). Maharishi reflects these beliefs when he wrote, "each individual is, in his true nature, the impersonal God [Maharishi Mahesh Yogi, *The Science of Being and Art of Living* (Los Angeles: International SRM Publications, 1967), 276]. His teaching is the denial of Christ as a person and Savior. In the truest sense, Maharishi was an orthodox Hindu and held the doctrines in high honor. Maharishi's plan for the world was nothing more than a substitute for the true gospel. His practices were a counterfeit form of spirituality and all who believe his lies will suffer the punishment of eternal separation from the Lord.

[22] Frank Gaynor, "Yoga," in *The Dictionary of Mysticism* (New York: Citadel Press, 1968), 206.

[23] Yogi, *Science of Being*.

[24] Colin Martindale, "What Makes People Different," *Psychology Today* (July 1975): 50.

[25] Maharishi Mahesh Yogi, *Maharishi Mahesh Yogi on the Bhagavad-Gita* (New York: Penguin Books, 1969), 257.

[26] *TM in Court* (Berkeley: Spiritual Counterfeits Project, Inc., 1978), 64.

[27] Ibid., 72.

[28] Robert H. Schuller, *Believe in the God who Believes in You* (Nashville: Thomas Nelson, 1989), 69.

[29] Compare with Norman Vincent Peale, *The Power of Positive Thinking* (Greenwich: Fawcett, 1983), 52, 146.

[30] Norman Vincent Peale, "How to Get More Power out of Your Mind" (New York: Sermon Publications, 1951), 9.

[31] Brooks Alexander, "Occult Philosophy and Mystical Experience," *SCP Journal* 6 (Winter 1984): 13-19.

[32] Jeffrey Burton Russell, *Witchcraft in the Middle Ages* (Ithaca, New York: Cornell University Press, 1972), 9.

[33] Norman L. Geisler and J. Yutaka Amano, *Religion of the Force* (Dallas: Quest Publications, 1983), 8.

[34] Bruce Handy, "The Force is Back," *Time* (10 February 1997): 74.

[35] Bill Moyers interview with George Lucas, "Of Myth and Men," *Time* (26 April 1999): 94.

36 As quoted in Tal Brooke, *When the World Will Be as One* (Eugene, OR: Harvest House, 1989), 41.

37 Shirley MacLaine, *Dancing in the Light* (New York: Bantam Books, 1985), 133.

38 William Warren Bartley, III, *Werner Erhard—The Transformation of a Man: The Founding of EST* (New York: Charles N. Potter, Inc., 1978).

39 Richard Cavendish, *Man, Myth & Magic* (New York: Marshall Cavendish Corporation, 1970), 20:2814.

40 Frank Podmore, *From Mesmer to Christian Science* (New York: University Books, 1963).

41 "Eckankar: A Hard Look at a New Religion," *SCP Journal* 3 (September 1979).

42 John Ankerberg and John Weldon, *The Facts on Hinduism in America* (Eugene, OR: Harvest House, 1991), 11; for documentation on how naturalism or secular humanism leads to nihilism, see James W. Sire, *The Universe Next Door*, 3rd ed. (Downers Grove, IL: InterVarsity Press, 1997).

43 Pico Iyer, "The God in Exile," *Time* (22 December 1997): 76.

44 Bill Higgins, "Hollywood Elite Says Hello, Dalai," *Los Angeles Times* (5 August 1996): E3.

45 MacLaine, *Dancing*, 420.

Chapter 15

1 Over the past few years, this author has written two books, which have addressed deception in the church. The first, *New Wine or Old Deception: A Biblical View of Experienced Based Christianity* (Costa Mesa, CA: The Word For Today, 1995), documented the roots of experience-based Christianity and explained how the Toronto Blessing phenomenon has swept the entire world. The second, *When New Wine Makes a Man Divine: True Revival or Last Days Deception* (Santa Ana, CA: Understand the Times, 1997), was written to warn Christians to be on the alert for the apostasy that the Bible states will happen before the revelation of the Antichrist. The most recent book, the third in the "New Wine" series, is called *New Wine and the Babylonian Vine*. This chapter will essentially draw from that research to document the direction experience-based Christianity is heading and how it is joining together with the delusion that the Bible predicts will unfold in the last days in the name of Christ.

2 *Apostasia* is "fem. of the same as 647; defection from truth (prop. the state) ['apostasy']:—falling away, forsake." James Strong, *A Concise*

Dictionary of the Words in the Greek New Testament (Madison, NJ: 1890), 15.

3 John Arnott, *The Father's Blessing* (Orlando: Creation House, 1995), 110.

4 *Charisma* (December 1999), front cover.

5 Marcia Ford, "The Blessing Spreads Worldwide," *Charisma* (July 1997): 54.

6 Ibid., 55.

7 Arnott, *Father's Blessing*, 57-58.

8 Benny Hinn, "Double Portion Anointing, Part #3," Orlando Christian Center, Orlando, FL, audiotape (A031791-3, aired on TBN 7 April 1991).

9 Arnott, *Father's Blessing*, 59.

10 Paul Carden, "Toronto Blessing Stirs Worldwide Controversy," *Christian Research Journal* (Winter 1995): 5

11 Rodney Howard-Browne, *Manifesting the Holy Ghost* (Louisville, KY: RHBEA Publications, 1992), 16.

12 Ford, "Blessing Spreads," 54-59.

13 Albert James Dagger, "Pensacola: Revival or Reveling?" *Media Spotlight* (1997): 2.

14 Ibid., 1.

15 Ford, "Blessing Spreads," 56.

16 *Charisma* (December 1996), 55.

17 Ibid., 60.

18 Arnott, *Father's Blessing*, 58.

19 Ibid [emphasis mine].

20 Richard Riss, *The Latter Rain* (Mississauga, Ontario: Honeycomb Visual Productions, 1987).

21 Twenty-Third General Council Minutes (Seattle: Assemblies of God in the U.S.A., 1949), 26-27.

22 See Oakland, *New Wine or Old Deception* and *New Wine Makes Man Divine.*

23 Bill Hamon, *Apostles, Prophets, and the Coming Moves of God: God's End-Time Plans for His Church and Planet Earth* (Shippensburg, PA: Destiny Image Publishers, Inc., 1997), v.

24 Apostle John Eckhardt, "Crusaders Church and International Ministries of Prophetic and Apostolic Churches," in *The New Apostolic Churches*, ed. C. Peter Wagner (Ventura, CA: Regal Books, 1998), 51.

25 Ibid., 47.

26 Hamon, *Apostles*, 279.

27 "Catch the Fire: The Release of the Apostolic and the Prophetic

Conference" (Pasadena: Harvest Rock Church, 1997), brochure.

28 Ibid.

29 Ibid.

30 Ibid.

31 Paul Cain, "The Latter Rain," Toronto: Toronto Airport Vineyard, 28 May 1995.

32 "From Appetizer to Main Course," *Spread the Fire* 2 (December 1996), 5.

33 Ibid.

34 Ibid.

35 Arnott, *Father's Blessing*, 61.

36 Ibid., 82.

37 Ibid.

38 Albert James Dagger, "Pensacola: Revival or Reveling," *Media Spotlight* (1997): 18.

39 Ibid.

Chapter 16

1 For more information on this subject, see David Benoit, "The Kingdom of Antichrist," in *Revelation Hoofbeats*, ed. Ron J. Bigalke Jr. (Longwood, FL: Xulon Press, 2003), 251-265.

2 C. H. Spurgeon, "Churchianity versus Christianity," *Sword and Trowel* (April 1868).

3 Terry Mattingly, "On Religion: 'Passion of Christ' Has Been Passion of Others" [article online] (*Naples Daily News*, 24 January 2004, accessed 2 October 2004) available from http://www.naplesnews.com/npdn/ne_religion/article/0,2071,NPDN_14935_2 600433,00.html.

4 The Catholic works cited bear the "Imprimatur" meaning the work "is considered to be free from doctrinal or moral error."

5 Tom Allen, "Introduction," in *A Guide to the Passion: 100 Questions about the Passion of the Christ* (West Chester, PA: Ascension Press, 2004), 2.

6 Anne Catherine Emmerich, *The Dolorous Passion of our Lord Jesus Christ* (New York: Benziger Brothers, 1904).

7 Ibid., back cover.

8 Fiscar Marison, trans., "City of God: Popular Abridgement of the Divine History and Life of the Virgin Mother of God, Manifested to Mary of Agreda for the Encouragement of Men" [online] (The Mystical City of God, accessed 2 October 2004) available from

http://www.geocities.com/Athens/Ithaca/7194/book6c2.html.

Chapter 17

[1] *Vatican Council II, Divine Revelation* III.11e. declared, "Hence the Bible is free from error *in what pertains to religious truth revealed for our salvation.* It is not necessarily free from error in other matters (e.g. natural science)" [emphasis in original].

[2] Francis A. Schaeffer, *A Christian Manifesto*, rev. ed. (1981; Wheaton: Crossway Books, 1982), 44.

[3] Dave Hunt, *Occult Invasion* (Eugene, OR: Harvest House, 1998), 53.

[4] C. S. Lewis, *The Screwtape Letters* (1941; reprint, Uhrichsville, Ohio: Barbour, 1990), 39.

[5] Hunt, *Occult Invasion*, 70.

[6] Lest the reader think the author is being unfair here, he should know that the author graduated from one of the hardest 12 step programs in the nation when he was seventeen.

[7] William C. Irvine, *Heresies Exposed* (New York: Loizeaux Brothers, 1921), 58-59.

[8] Herbert Fingarette, *Heavy Drinking: The Myth of Alcoholism as a Disease* (Berkeley: University of California Press, 1988).

[9] Ramtha is the spirit channeled through medium J. Z. Knight. Apparently, he lived over 35,000 years ago in the mythical city of Atlantis. Knight has become a multimillionaire as a result of her many books about the warrior from Atlantis whose ghost she claims to channel. He is part of the "brother-hood" to guide mankind.

The "spirit Jesus" who dictated *A Course in Miracles* to a large extent mimics the teachings of Ramtha. The rejection of man as a sinful creature, absolute truth, and belief in a personal Savior characterizes much of Ramtha's teaching. Nevertheless, the business world by the thousands has become followers of Ramtha (some paying big money to hear him chan-neled).

Whether it is Jane Roberts channeling Seth, J. Z. Knight channeling Ramtha, or Jack Pursel channeling Lazarus, each has a different voice of their own which leaves the audience enthralled. Many channelers have been given the privilege of speaking to a national audience on the Oprah Winfrey Show. These visits on television are the pulpit by which these spiritual char-latans seek to gain respectability as they spread the lies of spiritual eternality and self-deification. Popularity with channeling and the message of a New Age has grown substantially over the past several decades. The answers to the questions of life are being sought through the spirit world. Whether it is through a medium, meditation, visualization, yoga, or numerous other occult practices, there is little doubt that the New Age has gained a respectable position in today's society.

The death of materialism has resulted in fascination with the spirit world and metaphysical realities. Interaction with spirit guides and the opportunity to be "touched by an angel" are prestigious experiences being sought. The goal is open communication with the spirit world. All the above is but a counterfeit of the millennial kingdom when immortals (glorified saints) will rule with Christ on the earth interacting with the daily affairs of mortals. The counterfeiting of spiritual experiences is but a conditioning for the short reign of Antichrist and the false peace he will bring.

It is absolutely staggering to realize many Christians are not boldly resisting this delusion. The thought that Norman Vincent Peale could publicly promote blatant heresies and give support to occult practices is amazing. Perhaps more amazing is that Peale denies the Christian faith and yet is praised by Billy Graham. Graham likewise praises Peale's chief disciple, Robert Schuller. Schuller has commended all forms of Eastern meditation and hosts offices for "Christians and Muslims for Peace" in his Crystal Cathedral. Chuck Colson, Bill Bright, and Billy Graham receive the Templeton Prize for Progress in Religion for contributing toward the development of Antichrist's coming world religion. These are days when Jude's exhortation to *contend earnestly for the faith which was once for all delivered to the saints* is greatly needed.

[10] Marianne Williamson, *A Return to Love* (San Francisco: HarperCollins Publishers, 1992), 20.

[11] Susan Schindehette and Robin Micheli, *People* (9 March 1992): 39.

[12] *A Course in Miracles*, Manual for Teachers (Tiburon, CA: Foundation for Inner Peace, 1975), 445.

[13] *A Course in Miracles*, Text (Tiburon, CA: Foundation for Inner Peace, 1975), 30.

[14] Robert H. Schuller, *Self-Esteem: The New Reformation* (Dallas: Word Books, 1982), 167.

[15] Ibid., 11.

[16] Ibid., 68.

[17] Ibid., 14-15.

[18] Ibid., 75.

[19] Ibid., 47.

[20] Robert H. Schuller, *Believe in the God who Believes in You* (Nashville: Thomas Nelson, 1989), 69.

[21] Robert H. Schuller, *Peace of Mind Through Possibility Thinking* (New York: Jove, 1985), 129-132.

[22] Ernest Holmes, *The Science of Mind* (New York: Dodd Meade and Co., n.d.), 379.

[23] Fenwicke Holmes, *Ernest Holmes: His Life and Times* (New York: Dodd Meade and Co., 1970), backcover.

[24] Helen Keller, *My Religion* (New York: The Swedenborg Foundation, 1974).

[25] John Marks Templeton, *Discovering the Laws of Life* (New York: The Continuum Publishing Company, 1995).

[26] Norman Vincent Peale, Phil Donahue Show (23 October 1984), as quoted by Bob Anderson, "False Christs, False Prophets, Deceivers Arise," in *Earth's Final Days: Essays in Apocalypse III*, ed. William T. James (Green Forest, AR: New Leaf Press, 1995), 31.

[27] Norman Vincent Peale, *The Power of Positive Thinking* (Greenwich, CT: Fawcett, 1983), 52, 146.

[28] Norman Vincent Peale, "How to Get More Power Out of Your Mind," (New York: Sermon Publications, 1951), 9.

[29] Napoleon Hill, *Grow Rich With Peace of Mind* (Greenwich, CT: Fawcett Crest, 1967), 159.

[30] Napoleon Hill, *Think and Grow Rich* (Brooklyn: Fawcett Crest, 1963), 5-6.

[31] Clement Stone, *Success Through a Positive Mental Attitude* (Brooklyn: Fawcett Crest, 1960).

[32] Hill, *Grow Rich*, 218-219.

[33] Hill, *Think and Grow*, 215.

[34] Ibid., 217.

[35] Ibid., 218.

[36] Ibid., 29.

[37] Michael Ray and Rochelle Myers, *Creativity in Business* (New York: Doubleday, 1986), 36-38.

[38] Charles Capps, *The Tongue—A Creative Force* (Tulsa: Harrison House, 1976), 67.

[39] Kenneth Hagin, "Understanding the Importance of Confession," *The Word of Faith* (May 1999): 8.

[40] Benny Hinn, "Praise the Lord" program on the Trinity Broadcasting Network (1 June 1989).

[41] Paul Yonggi Cho, *The Fourth Dimension* (Plainfield, NJ: Logos International, 1979), 39-40, 66, 78, 73-74.

[42] Ibid., viii.

[43] John Ankerberg and John Weldon, *Encyclopedia of New Age Beliefs* (Eugene, OR: Harvest House, 1996), 48.

[44] Benny Hinn, "Praise the Lord" program on the Trinity Broadcasting Network (6 November 1990).

[45] Morris Cerullo, "The Endtime Manifestation of the Sons of God," (San Diego: Morris Cerullo World Evangelism), audiotape.

[46] Paul Crouch, "Praise the Lord" program on the Trinity Broadcasting Network (7 July 1986).

[47] Earl Paulk, *Satan Unmasked* (Atlanta: K Dimension Publishing, 1984), 97.

[48] Kenneth Copeland, *Believer's Voice of Victory* (March 1982): 2.

[49] D. R. McConnell, *A Different Gospel* (Peabody, MA: Hendrickson, 1995), 184-185.

[50] Harner, *Shaman*, 136.

[51] Elizabeth Turner, "Is it Therapy or Is it Prayer?" *Self* (December 1997): 166.

[52] John Leland and Carla Power, "Deepak's Instant Karma," *Newsweek* (20 October 1997): 56.

[53] Harner, *Shaman*, 136.

[54] Robert Schuller, "Possibility Thinking: Goals" (Amway Corporation), audiotape.

[55] Turner, "Is it Therapy," 166.

[56] Douglas Groothuis, "To Heaven and Back?" *Christianity Today* (3 April 1995): 42.

[57] John Kilpatrick, *Feast of Fire* (Pensacola: In Times Like These, 1995), 100.

[58] Christina Grof and Stanislav Grof, *The Stormy Search for the Self* (New York: Tarcher/Putnam, 1990), 78-79.

[59] Kilpatrick, *Feast*, 73-75.

[60] Grof, *Stormy Search*, 78-79.

[61] Bhagwan Shree Rajneesh, *Dance your Way to God* (Los Angeles: International SRM Publications, 1968), 229.

[62] Dave Hunt, *A Woman Rides the Beast* (Eugene, OR: Harvest House, 1994), 464.

[63] Timothy Kauffman, "Kauffman Response to Letters of Criticism Printed in the Last Newsletter, *SCP Newsletter* 20 (1995): 14.

[64] Jon Klimo, *Channeling* (Los Angeles: J.P. Tarcher, 1987), 345.

[65] Randall N. Baer, *Inside the New Age Nightmare* (Lafayette, LA: Huntington House, 1989), 103.

[66] Merrill F. Unger, *Biblical Demonology*, 5th ed. (Wheaton: Scripture Press, 1963; reprint, Grand Rapids: Kregel, 1994), 149.

[67] John F. Walvoord, *The Millennial Kingdom* (Findlay, OH: Dunham Publishing, 1959; reprint, Grand Rapids: Zondervan, 1995), 22-23.

[68] Ibid., 23.

[69] J. Marcellus Kik, *An Eschatology of Victory* (Phillipsburg: Presbyterian and Reformed, 1971), 4.

[70] Gary Scott Smith, "The Men and Religion Forward Movement of 1911-12: New Perspectives on Evangelical Social Concern and the Relationship Between Christianity and Progressivism," *Westminster Theological Journal* 49 (Spring 1987): 92-93.

[71] Gary North, *Unholy Spirits: Occultism and New Age Humanism* (Fort Worth: Dominion Press, 1986), 388-389, 391.

[72] Richard Kyle, *The Last Days Are Here Again* (Grand Rapids: Baker Books, 1998), 153.

[73] A term commonly used by New Ager David Spangler.

[74] Kyle, *Last Days*, 154.

[75] Al Gore, *Earth in the Balance* (New York: A Plume Book, 1993), 12.

[76] As quoted by Gore, *Earth*, 259.

[77] William Norman Grigg, "Eco-Agenda Heating Up," *The New American* (8 December 1997): 13-14.

[78] Anna Bray Duff, "More Global-Warming Hot Air," *Investor's Business Daily* (25 August 1998): A32.

[79] Gore, *Earth*, 260.

[80] Tal Brooke, "The Ecological Great Awakening—Earthcrisis and Eco-Purges," *SCP Journal* 17 (1992): 14.

[81] Peter R. Breggin, *Talking Back to Prozac: What Doctors Aren't Telling You About Today's Most Controversial Drug* (New York: St. Martin's Paperbacks, 1994), 40.

[82] Sir John Eccles and Daniel N. Robinson, *The Wonder of Being Human: Our Brain and Our Mind* (New York: The Free Press, 1984).

[83] Jonathan Henry, "Ye Shall Be As Gods," in *When Christians Roamed the Earth* (Green Forest, AR: Master Books, 2001), 170.

[84] Shirley MacLaine, *Out on a Limb* (New York: Bantam Books, 1982), 352.

[85] Whitley Strieber, *Communion: A True Story* (New York: Beech Tree Books/William Morrow, 1987), 30; Philip J. Klass, *UFO Abductions: A Dangerous Game* (Buffalo: Prometheus Books, 1989), 130.

[86] Strieber, *Communion*, 53; Whitley Strieber, *Transformation: The Breakthrough* (New York: Beech Tree Books/William Morrow, 1988), 44-45.

[87] Ruth Montgomery, *Aliens Among Us* (New York: G. P. Putnam's Sons, 1985), 51-52.

[88] Henry, "Be As Gods," 187.

[89] James Douglas Morrison, *The Lords and the New Creatures* (New York: Simon and Schuster, 1970).

[90] *Time* (16 December 1974): 39; "Joni Mitchell: Self-Portrait of a Superstar," *Macleans* (June 1974).

[91] David Henderson, *Scuse Me While I Kiss the Sky* (New York: Bantam Books, 1978).

[92] Nick Kent, *The Dark Stuff: Selected Writings on Rock Music, 1972-1995* (New York: DeCapo Press, 1995), 145.

[93] Pamela Des Barres, *Rock Bottom: Dark Moments in Music Babylon* (New York: St. Martin's Press, 1996).

[94] Edgar Young Mullins, *Why is Christianity True?* (Philadelphia: American Baptist Publication Society, 1905), 266.

[95] Ibid., 268.

[96] Ibid., 287.

Chapter 18

1 According to Isaiah 66:21, there will also be Gentile priests.

2 Thomas Ice, "Literal Sacrifices in the Millennium," *Pre-Trib Perspectives* (June 2000): 4-5.

3 Jerry M. Hullinger, "The Problem of Animal Sacrifices in Ezekiel 40-48," *Bibliotheca Sacra* 152 (July-September 1995): 281, 289.

4 John C. Whitcomb, "Christ's Atonement and Animal Sacrifices in Israel," *Grace Theological Journal* 6 (Fall 1985): 201-21.

5 Ibid., 201.

6 Ibid., 208-210.

7 Ibid., 210.

8 Ibid., 211.

10 John C. Whitcomb, "The Millennial Temple of Ezekiel 40-48," *The Diligent Workman Journal* (May 1994): 22.

Appendix

1 Gilbert K. Chesterton, *What I Saw in America* (London: Hodder and Stoughton, 1922).

2 David C. Gibbs and Jerry Newcombe, *One Nation Under God: Ten Things Every Christian Should Know About the Founding of America* (Seminole, FL: Christian Law Association, 2003).

3 Christopher Columbus, "Journal," 1492, as quoted in William J. Federer, *Library of Classics* [CD-ROM] (St. Louis: AmeriSearch).

4 Gibbs and Newcombe, *One Nation*.

5 William Bradford, *Of Plymouth Plantation*, 1620-1647, edited and updated by Samuel Eliot Morison (New York: Alfred A. Knopf, 2001), 25.

6 Paul Johnson, *A History of the American People* (New York: HarperCollins Publishers, 1997), 29-30.

7 Gibbs and Newcombe, *One Nation*.

8 Ibid.

9 As quoted in George Bancroft, *History of the United States of America, from the Discovery of the Continent*, 6 vols. (New York: D. Appleton and Company, 1890), 1:250.

10 John Adams, letter to the officers of the First Brigade of the Third Division of the Militia of Massachusetts, 11 October 1798. Charles Francis Adams, ed., *The Works of John Adams, Second President of the United States: with a Life of the Author*, 10 vols. (Boston: Little, Brown and Company, 1854), 9:228-229.

[11] George Washington, "Farewell Address," 19 September 1796.

[12] Daniel Webster, 22 December 1820. *The Works of Daniel Webster*, 6 vols. (Boston: Little, Brown and Company, 1853), 1:48.

[13] Benjamin Rush, "Thoughts upon the Mode of Education Proper in a Republic" (Early American Imprints), in *Essays, Literary, Moral & Philosophical* (Philadelphia: Thomas and Samuel F. Bradford, 1798), 8.

[14] Ibid.

[15] Webster, *Works of Webster*, 22ff.

[16] John Jay, 12 October 1816. John Jay, *The Correspondence and Public Papers of John Jay*, 4 vols., ed. Henry P. Johnston (New York: G. P. Putnam & Sons, 1893; reprint, New York: Burt Franklin, 1970), 4:393.

[17] William Penn, "Frame of Government of Pennsylvania," 25 April 1682. William Penn, *A Collection of Charters and Other Public Acts Relating to the Province of Pennsylvania* (Philadelphia: B. Franklin, 1740), 10-12.

[18] Johnson, *History*, 66.

[19] Gibbs and Newcombe, *One Nation*.

[20] "Rules for Harvard University" (1643), as quoted in "New England's First Fruits," *The Annals of America* (Boston, 1772), 1:176.

[21] "Regulations at Yale College" (1745), as quoted in Ibid., 1:464.

[22] John Eidsmoe, *Christianity and the Constitution* (Grand Rapids: Baker Books, 1987), 81.

[23] Johnson, *History*, 115.

[24] Ibid., 307.

[25] Ibid., 116-117.

[26] C. Gregg Singer, *A Theological Interpretation of American History* (Nutley, NJ: The Craig Press, 1964), 284-285.

[27] Page Smith, *Religious Origins of the American Revolution* (Missoula, MT: Scholars Press, 1976), 1.

[28] Ibid., 2.

[29] Editor's note: *Sola fide* and *sola Scriptura* are the foundation for Luther's famous doctrine of the "priesthood of all believers." In his *Address to the Christian Nobility*, he stated,

> As for the unction by a pope or a bishop, tonsure, ordination, consecration, and clothes differing from those of laymen—all this may make a hypocrite or an anointed puppet, but never a Christian or a spiritual man. Thus we are all consecrated as priests by baptism, as St. Peter says: "Ye are a royal priesthood, a holy nation" (1 Peter 2. 9); and in the book of Revelations: "and hast made us unto our

God (by Thy blood) kings and priests" (Rev. v. 10). For, if we had
not a higher consecration in us than pope or bishop can give, no
priest could ever be made by the consecration of pope or bishop,
nor could he say the mass, or preach, or absolve. Therefore the
bishop's consecration is just as if in the name of the whole congregation he took one person out of the community, each member of
which has equal power, and commanded him to exercise this power
for the rest....

A cobbler, a smith, a peasant, every man, has the office and function of his calling, and yet all alike are consecrated priests and bish-
ops, and every man should by his office or function be useful and
beneficial to the rest, so that various kinds of work may all be united for the furtherance of body and soul, just as the members of the
body all serve one another [Martin Luther, *Address to the Christian
Nobility of the German Nation Respecting the Reformation of the
Christian Estate* (The Harvard Classics), ed. Charles W. Eliot (New
York: P. F. Collier & Son, 1909–1914), 36:5, [online] (Bartleby.com,
2001, accessed 28 August 2004) available from http://www.bartle-
by.com/36/5/2.html].

Prior to the Reformation, the Roman Catholic Church had developed a
sharp distinction between clergy, "first-class" believers (those in "full-time"
ministry), and laity, "second-class" believers (those employed in "secular"
occupations). By recovering the biblical doctrine of the "priesthood of all
believers," the Reformers also clarified biblical teaching in regards to calling
and vocation. The Reformers destroyed the notion of "sacred" and "secular"
because all Christians are priests; therefore, all are ministers of God regardless of occupation (cf. 1 Cor. 10:31; Col. 3:23).

[30] Smith, *Religious Origins*, 3.

[31] Ibid., 185.

[32] William Blackstone, "Of the Nature of Laws in General," in
Commentaries on the Laws of England, 4 vols., (Philadelphia: Robert Bell,
1771).

[33] Ibid.

[34] His biographer, John C. Miller, said Samuel Adams cannot be understood
without considering the lasting impact Whitefield's preaching at Harvard
during the Great Awakening had on him [John C. Miller, *Sam Adams:
Pioneer in Propaganda* (Stanford, CA: Stanford University Press, 1936), 85,

as quoted in Eidsmoe, *Christianity and Constitution*, 248]. Adams had been telling his countrymen for years that America had to take her stand against tyranny. He regarded individual freedom as "the law of the Creator" and a Christian right documented in the New Testament [Robert Flood, *Men Who Shaped America* (Chicago: Moody Press, 1976), 35-36]. As the Declaration was being signed, Sam Adams said, "We have this day restored the Sovereign to Whom all men ought to be obedient. He reigns in heaven and from the rising to the setting of the sun, let His kingdom come."

35 Samuel Adams, "The Rights of the Colonists," as quoted in *Annals of America*, 2:217.

36 Eidsmoe, *Christianity and Constitution*, 94.

37 James H. Smylie, "Madison and Witherspoon: Theological Roots of American Political Thought," as quoted in Charles Augustus Briggs, *American Presbyterianism* (New York: Charles Scribner's Sons, 1885), 112.

38 Eidsmoe, *Christianity and Constitution*, 101.

39 Smith, *Religious Origins*, 3.

40 Ibid., 4.

41 Alice M. Baldwin, *The New England Clergy and the American Revolution* (Durham, NC: Duke University Press, 1928), 169.

Contributing Authors
Biographical Sketches

Kerby Anderson

Kerby Anderson is national director of Probe Ministries—"a non-profit ministry whose mission is to assist the church in renewing the minds of believers with a Christian worldview and to equip the church to engage the world for Christ." He is a lecturer on university campuses around the country, including Vanderbilt University, Princeton University, and Johns Hopkins University. He is visiting professor at Dallas Theological Seminary, Philadelphia College of the Bible, and Temple Baptist Seminary. He has addressed the American Scientific Affiliation, International Congress on the Bible, and the Ligonier Conference. He earned his B.S. from Oregon State University, M.F.S. from Yale University, and M.A. from Georgetown University. His articles have appeared in *Bibliotheca Sacra*, *Kindred Spirit*, and *Moody Monthly*. He has written and co-authored over 10 books. He is general editor and contributor to *Marriage, Family and Sexuality* and *Technology, Spirituality, & Social Trends* published by Kregel. He has been married to Susanne Pardey since 1974, and they have three children.

Dr. Ron J. Bigalke Jr.

Ron Bigalke Jr. is an author, lecturer, and former pastor. He graduated from Moody Bible Institute and earned his M.Apol. degree from Columbia Evangelical Seminary. He also earned a M.A. and Ph.D. from Tyndale Theological Seminary. He is currently working toward a M.Div. degree from Luther Rice Seminary. Dr. Bigalke has served as an extension studies adjunct instructor for Moody Bible Institute, a Christian school administrator and teacher, and is liaison in Florida for Tyndale Theological Seminary. He is the founder and director of Eternal Ministries—a discipleship and evangelistic ministry dedicated to teaching and proclaiming the Word of God. He and his wife, Kristin, have one child, Abigail Jane.

Dr. Mal Couch

Mal Couch is founder and president of Tyndale Theological Seminary and Biblical Institute in Ft. Worth, Texas. He earned his Th.M. from Dallas Theological Seminary, M.A. from Wheaton Graduate School, and Th.D. from Louisiana Baptist Seminary. He has taught at Dallas Theological Seminary, Moody Bible Institute, and Philadelphia College of the Bible. Dr. Couch is a prolific writer and conference speaker. His publications include *A Bible Handbook to the Acts of the Apostles*, *The Coming of the Holy Spirit*, *Dictionary of Premillennial Theology*, *The Fundamentals for the Twenty-First Century*, and *The Hope of Christ's Return*.

Arno Froese

Arno Froese is the executive director of Midnight Call Ministry and editor-in-chief of the critically acclaimed prophetic magazines *News from Israel* and *Midnight Call*, which is internationally distributed in many foreign languages. Arno has sponsored more than fifty national and international prophecy conferences, in addition to leading numerous study tours through Israel. He has authored several prophecy-oriented books including: *The Great Mystery of the Rapture*, *How Democracy Will Elect the Antichrist*, *Saddam's Mystery Babylon*, *The Coming Digital God*, and *Terror over America*.

Dr. Arnold G. Fruchtenbaum

Arnold Fruchtenbaum is one of the foremost authorities on the nation of Israel, which has made him a much in-demand speaker at Bible conferences and schools throughout the world. He was born in Siberia and his family escaped to Germany with the help of the Israeli underground. Most of his family died in the Holocaust. The Fruchtenbaums immigrated to New York, and at age 13, he became a messianic believer. He is founder and director of Ariel Ministries—a California based organization dedicated to evangelism and discipleship of Jewish people. He earned his Th.M. from Dallas Theological Seminary and Ph.D. from New York University. Dr. Fruchtenbaum also did graduate work at the Jewish Theological Seminary in New York City and

The Hebrew University of Jerusalem.

Phillip Goodman

Phillip Goodman is the founder and former president of The Spiritual Armour Project, which he directed for 10 years. In 2000, he formed a partnership with Dr. Charles Pack of Thy Kingdom Come, where he now serves as a vice president. He is a Vietnam veteran, and was the director of the award winning adult and community education program for the Tulsa Public Schools for 21 years, and has taught at Tulsa Community College. Phillip has conducted prophecy seminars in both Canada and the United States. He and his wife, Mary, a native of Bethlehem, Israel, have four sons.

Wilfred J. Hahn

Wilfred Hahn is a senior international financial executive, global portfolio strategist and manager, former mutual fund company chairman, and ranked global financial analyst. He earned his B.S. degree from the University of Waterloo, and MBA from the University of Western Ontario. He also taught graduate studies in economics at York University and holds a number of financial designations. He is the founder of Mulberry Press, publishers of *Eternal Value Review* for "thinking Christians seeking to understand the times." He has accumulated extensive and relevant experience in global financial industries during his career, allowing him to speak knowledgeably and authoritatively on global trends whether in economics, investment markets, or international social or geo-political affairs. Currently, he resides on a hobby farm near the United States-Canadian border. He is an avid canoe excursionist in the Canadian North. His wife, Joyce, is an award-winning photographer. They have three children together.

Dr. Thomas D. Ice

Thomas Ice is the executive director of The Pre-Trib Research Center in Arlington, Texas, which he founded in 1994 with Dr. Tim LaHaye to research, teach, and defend the pretribulational rapture and related Bible prophecy doctrines. He earned his Th.M in historical theology from Dallas Theological Seminary and Ph.D. in systematic theology (specializing in eschatology) from Tyndale Theological Seminary. He was the pastor of Trinity Bible Church in Fredricksburg, Virginia. Dr. Ice has co-authored over 20 books, written dozens of articles, spoken at some of the largest churches in the United States, and is a frequent conference speaker. He and his wife Janice have three boys. The Ice's oldest boy, Daniel, is recently married.

Roger Oakland

Roger Oakland is an author and lecturer who speaks internationally on Bible related topics. Roger Oakland has authored and co-authored numerous books and produced audiotapes, videos, and other publications translated into several languages worldwide. One of his books, *The Evidence for Creation*, has over 300,000 copies circulated in the former Soviet Union, where he has traveled and lectures frequently. He is founder and president of Understand the Times—an organization dedicated to equipping the body of Christ for discernment as well as reaching the lost with the Gospel of Jesus Christ. He has lectured at numerous churches, conferences, universities, and educational facilities in over 35 countries. He and his wife, Myrna, presently reside in California.

Dr. Larry Spargimino

Larry Spargimino is associate pastor and editor of Southwest Radio Church Ministries, the oldest, continuously broadcasting radio ministry in the world. He has a Ph.D. in New Testament and Greek from Southwestern Baptist Theological Seminary. His latest book, *Suddenly No More Time*, illustrates the exponential curve and its relation to Bible prophecy. He has also authored *The Anti-Prophets: The Challenge of Preterism* and is one of the contributors to *Revelation Hoofbeats* published by Eternal Ministries and *The End Times Controversy* published by the Pre-Trib Research Center. Having served as a pastor in local churches over the last twenty five years, Dr. Spargimino has also been a Christian school administrator. He currently has a ministry to Chinese students in Oklahoma City.

Dr. Andy Woods

Andy Woods has served as an interim pastor and college instructor. He earned a B.A. in Business Administration and a B.A. in Political Science from the University of Redlands, and a J.D. from Whittier Law School. He also earned a Th.M. from Dallas Theological Seminary where he is currently a Ph.D. student. His seminary thesis was adapted as a chapter in *The End Times Controversy*. He has spoken at the annual conference of the Conservative Theological Society (for whom he has also written book reviews and journal articles) and has been a co-instructor for Tyndale Theological Seminary. Andy and his wife, Anne, reside in Texas.

Eternal Ministries is a discipleship and
evangelistic ministry dedicated to
teaching and proclaiming the Word of God.
For more information on the Christian life,
or to contact Ron Bigalke Jr. please
do so through our website.
www.eternalministries.org